ARISTOTLE'S DISCOVERY OF THE HUMAN

ARISTOTLE'S DISCOVERY OF THE HUMAN

Piety and Politics in the
Nicomachean Ethics

MARY P. NICHOLS

University of Notre Dame Press
Notre Dame, Indiana

Copyright © 2023 by the University of Notre Dame

Notre Dame, Indiana 46556

undpress.nd.edu

All Rights Reserved

Published in the United States of America

Paperback edition published in 2025

Library of Congress Control Number: 2023937442

ISBN: 978-0-268-20545-4 (Hardback)
ISBN: 978-0-268-20546-1 (Paperback)
ISBN: 978-0-268-20547-8 (WebPDF)
ISBN: 978-0-268-20544-7 (Epub3)

GPSR Compliance Inquiries:
Lightning Source France,
1 Av. Johannes Gutenberg,
78310 Maurepas, France
compliance@lightningsource.fr
Phone: +33 1 30 49 23 42

For David

Reciprocity holds the city together, our reciprocating not only harm for harm, but also good for good. Shrines to the Graces are therefore placed along the roadways, to foster doing good in return, for this belongs to gratitude. One ought to help in turn someone who has been gracious, and even to initiate reciprocal giving.

—from Aristotle's *Nicomachean Ethics*, Book 5

CONTENTS

	Acknowledgments	ix
	Introduction	1
ONE	Our Unfinished Humanity: A Divine Gift (Book 1)	19
TWO	The Ethical Virtues: Nature, Character, and Choice (Books 2–3)	61
THREE	The Virtues of Living Together: Distinguishing the Human from the Divine (Book 4)	91
FOUR	A Shrine to the Graces: Justice and Tragedy (Book 5)	123
FIVE	Intellectual Virtues: Prudence, Wisdom, and Philosophy (Book 6)	155
SIX	Human Strength versus Divine Perfection: Deepening Our View of Virtue (Book 7)	197
SEVEN	Friendship: Family, Political Community, and Philosophy (Books 8–9)	231

EIGHT Divine Thoughts and Political Reform: Summing   275
       Up and Moving Forward (Book 10)

Afterthoughts: Aristotelian Piety for a Liberal Politics   317

Bibliography   327
Index   333

ACKNOWLEDGMENTS

I studied Aristotle's *Nicomachean Ethics* in the early 1970s with Joseph Cropsey at the University of Chicago. Thanks to his teaching, I have been unable to leave the book behind—I returned to it every few years in my graduate seminars, first at Northern Illinois University, then at Catholic University and Fordham University, and most recently at Baylor University until my retirement in 2018. Even after retiring, I conducted several informal seminars on the *Ethics* with Baylor students as an extension of the class that I never quite finished teaching. Aristotle's *Ethics* has been with me all my academic life. With the help of students, my thoughts have evolved, and I have seen anew, always, I believe, guided by Aristotle's text. I do not think that I ever taught the same course twice. That many of my students have written dissertations and books on Aristotle, in many ways going further than I have, witnesses the depth of Aristotle's "philosophy concerning human affairs."

Rachel Alexander, Christine Basil, Steve Block, Ronna Burger, Gerald Mara, Jeff Poelvoorde, and Denise Schaeffer have read one or more chapters. Several of them have read the entire manuscript. I am grateful for their questions and objections, and most of all for their encouragement and support. Jeff Poelvoorde's insightful comments, his Herculean efforts in compiling the index, and his apparently infinite energy and enthusiasm are to me a source of wonder. I am also grateful to friends with whom I have been close almost my entire adult life, some even longer. Without their friendship, I would not have acquired the experience to understand as much as I have of Aristotle's thought. Naming them could not approach the return for what they have given me.

Most of all, I am grateful to my family, with whom I have been blessed. My sons Keith and John tolerated my occupation with writing books and continue to share their mother with her students. I hope that they know that however much I love my work, I love them even more. Finally, without David's support and love, I would not have been able to write this book, not simply because he read revision after revision. In more ways than one, this book is his as well as mine.

Introduction

In elaborating his famous teaching that human beings are political by nature, Aristotle observes that one who is incapable of living with others or who is need of nothing and self-sufficient would be either a beast or a god (*Politics* 1253a28–29). He locates human life, even human life at its best, in a middle ground between the bestial and the divine, on which beings endowed with reason share in thoughts and actions. He gives a full and rich picture of this middle ground in his *Nicomachean Ethics*, as he explores the meaning of a good human life and how human beings can attain happiness (1097b23–26, 1098a12–18).[1] Aristotle attempts to preserve that middle ground as he encourages us to rise above the beasts by acquiring virtue and to live with a view to what is most akin to the divine in ourselves. A good human life, which reflects both the virtues and the limitations of the human, would therefore neither deny the human connection to the divine nor try to eliminate the distance between the two.[2] A good human life could, in this sense, be considered a pious one, a life

---

1. Citations in parentheses refer to Aristotle's *Nicomachean Ethics* unless I indicate otherwise. Translations of Greek texts are my own, but for the *Ethics* I have consulted the translation by Bartlett and Collins, *Aristotle's "Nicomachean Ethics."* I have often followed their felicitous choice of words to capture Aristotle's Greek. The translation by Sachs, *Aristotle: "Nicomachean Ethics,"* has also been helpful. For Greek texts, I have relied on the Loeb Classical Library editions.

2. As Salkever, "Democracy and Aristotle's Ethics of Natural Questions," 355, explains Aristotle's position, to act well we need a clear sense of who we are as human beings, and for such self-knowledge "we need to pass a moment wondering about what exists beyond ourselves." Thus Aristotle's ethical and political theory culminates in questions "about our relationship to beings superior to ourselves, that is, to Aristotle's gods."

1

cognizant both of the elevated place of human beings in the cosmos insofar as they are akin to the divine and also of a divinity beyond the human. A good political community has, in turn, the task of supporting such a life by encouraging human achievement, and we can judge it by how well it does so.

At the outset of the *Ethics*, Aristotle refers to the work of the statesman in securing the good of his community as divine (1094b7–11). He says that the individual who possesses greatness of soul is worthy of the greatest things, such as the honors we assign to the gods (1123b13–20). He encourages us to pursue happiness, the end of all our actions, and places it among the most divine things (1094a18–25, 1099b16). He contrasts reverence (*aidōs*) not only with shameless arrogance but also with cowering timidity (1108a33–b1). His references to the gods and to the divine support human activity and achievement. That we wonder at the divine, for example (1141a33–b7), elevates us above the beasts. Because we can look up, to speak metaphorically, we can look ahead. We form political communities that aim at common goods. We deliberate, make choices, and act. Like free persons rather than slaves, we rule ourselves. What we do, as Aristotle puts it, "admits of being otherwise" or is "up to us" (1140a32–36, 1113b6). This is not true of other natural beings, who develop toward their ends by nature, unless chance or human activity divert them (1140a15–16). Human beings do not receive the ethical virtues from nature; they must acquire them by their own efforts (1130a24–26). There are many virtues, intellectual and ethical, and many lives we choose in which they are manifest. We can think about who we are, we can question, and although some perplexities remain, we can resolve others (1146b6–7).

At the same time, our wonder, our awe, and even our questioning make us aware that there is something more, something higher, than human life. Piety supports the elevation of human life—for we are akin to the divine—but it also limits it. Aristotle claims that although we can become "blessed"—a state we attribute to the gods—we can do so "only as human beings" (1101a19–21). Human beings can think "divine thoughts" (1177b32–37), but thoughts about the divine that human beings think include the differences between divine and human. In spite of his admiration for greatness of soul, Aristotle warns against its assumption of divine-like perfection and attempts to turn the great-souled individual to friendship (1124b10–16, 1125a10–13, 1124b33–1125a1). Aristotle says that prudence, the virtue of the statesman who considers the good of the community, is not the highest virtue, for "the human being is not the best thing in the cosmos" (1141a19–23, 1141b24–28, 1145a6–9). And even though we can resolve some perplexities, others, such as those involving what is best in the cosmos, remain. The *Ethics* attempts no thematic discussion of the gods, as does Plato's *Republic* (379a–383c) and *Laws* (885c–907b), nor does Aristotle raise the question there of what is the pious or the holy, as does Plato's *Euthyphro*. This may be less a difference between Aristotle's political thought and Plato's than a sign that Aristotle learned from Plato the problems with such direct approaches to the divine and that a less direct and less precise approach was called for. His *Ethics* takes just such an approach. The piety that emerges in his philosophizing about human things is a source at the same time of confidence, on the one hand, and moderation, on the other. Our very activities, which we undertake in confidence and hope, manifest our incompleteness, our imperfection.

Aristotle defines the human work as the activity of soul in accord with virtue, and if there are many virtues, in accord with the "most complete" (1098a16–17). He proceeds to describe many virtues, and there does not appear to be one alone that is "most complete." Even if there were, it alone could not confer completeness or wholeness, since there are other virtues, which even "the best" does not replace (see *Politics* 1281a29–34). Aristotle speaks not only of the "best" (*to ariston*) for human beings, which is often translated as the "highest good," but also of "the complete good" (*to teleion agathon*) (cf. 1094a22 with 1097b8; see also 1098a16–18). His two formulations suggest a difference, a gap, between those goods, whether the "best" falls short of the complete or perfect, or the perfect falls short of the best. If that gap is a source of suffering and failure, it is also the condition for our attaining the blessedness that is possible for human beings (1101a21). Only incomplete beings enjoy, for example, the nurture and care of family life, the common deliberations of citizens, the loving and being loved that occur in friendships, and a wonder about the divine and our relation to it. It is in that gap that Aristotle made the discovery of the human that he contributes to philosophy.

Aristotle maintains throughout that his *Ethics* is a practical work, its goal being not simply knowledge but action (e.g., 1095a6, 1179b1–2). Such philosophizing about human things, however, and the truth that it reveals, means that the *Ethics* is both a theoretical work and a practical one.

Indeed, because the theme of the human relation to the divine is an ongoing issue in his inquiry in the *Ethics*, and at times its moving force, his philosophizing about the human things animates his philosophic enterprise more generally. At the same time that our relation to the divine both elevates human life and educates us about its limits, it also reveals the unique place of the human within the whole. No understanding of the whole could be sufficient without taking that relation into account.

When Aristotle speaks of the statesman who secures and preserves the good of the city, he says that his beneficent activity is greater and more complete than doing this for an individual alone, and more beautiful and more divine (1094b6–11). He uses the comparatives. Human activity, even that of the statesman who benefits others so much, is not simply complete or divine. When he speaks of the contemplative activity of the mind, he claims that it proceeds from "something divine" in ourselves, and that this activity is "most akin" to the activity of the gods (1177b28, 1179a27). We possess "something divine," but we are not divine. If our activity is "akin" to the god's activity, it is not the same. In these cases, human activities resemble the beneficent and knowing beings whom we might imagine the gods to be, at least if we are not the poets Aristotle criticizes for portraying the gods as jealous of human achievement (*Metaphysics* 982b34–983a5), or those whom they influence.

Aristotle indicates more about the relation between the human and the divine in his discussion of wisdom, which is one of the virtues, indeed the highest intellectual virtue. Wisdom involves "the most honorable things," "whose nature is much more divine than that of a human being" (1141a20–21, 1141b1–2). Here our relation to the divine is not one of *becoming like* the divine through our activities, but one of *knowing* the divine, however limited our knowledge may be. That the *Ethics* is a pious work in this sense does not mean that it is a work of theology, an account of the god or gods. It is not a work of theology precisely because it is a pious work. Only a god can present a theology or offer support for one through revelation. Not even the *Metaphysics* is a work of theology, although Aristotle presents there several puzzling formulations about the divine. Rather, it is a work about the human longing to know and the perplexities about being that arise from that longing (see *Metaphysics* 1028b5–6), perplexities that teach us why we alone cannot generate a theology.

When Aristotle urges us to strive to make ourselves immortal, he urges us to do so only "insofar as it is possible" (1177b34). Of course, even if divinity for us admits of degrees—as Aristotle's use of the comparative and superlative forms of the adjective suggests (e.g., 1094b11, 1141b1, 1177a17)—does "immortality," which is literally "deathless" (*athanatos*)? Human beings are subject to death. Aristotle distinguishes deliberation and choice, which involve those things within our power, from wish, which is directed to what is beyond our control. He gives the example of immortality as a possible object of wish, but not of choice (1111b20–31). Even if our souls were immortal, their being so is not "up to us," as are those things we choose. We are mixed beings, who transcend mere animal life but whose natures fall short of the perfection that we wish. Human beings, who live in time and are subject to change, cannot experience, for example, "the single simple pleasure always enjoyed by the god" (1154b26–27). Even the "wise," the "*most* self-sufficient" of human beings, are not simply self-sufficient. Although their contemplative activity proceeds from "something divine in [themselves]," it may be "better," Aristotle says, for them to have others with whom they can work (1177a28–36). That we can live "blessed" lives only as human beings does not warrant disappointment in the human condition, to say nothing of fear as a result of our limitations or anger because of them, but gratitude and joy.

Our limitations allow us to enjoy goods that are accessible to us as human beings—such as working together with others, which Aristotle mentions as "better" even for the wise. Those goods belonging to human beings that he describes in the *Ethics* include the exercise of our capacities for deliberation and choice (and hence for human freedom and self-rule), the ethical and intellectual virtues that belong to the human soul, actions in concert with others to achieve goods for ourselves, our families, our friends, and our communities, friendships in which we share thoughts and actions, exploring perplexities, and discovering how some might be resolved. Tragic attempts to become gods do not merely hold the danger of hubris and calamity but also deprive us of such human goods.

Many scholars point out that Aristotle does not include piety or holiness (*hosiotēs*) among the virtues he discusses in the *Ethics*. Some even suggest that Aristotle replaces piety simply by philosophy or wisdom. Sarah Broadie, for example, outlines the reasons that we should expect to find piety included in Aristotle's *Ethics*, and goes on to locate it in the contemplative activity Aristotle discusses in book 10, even though he does not refer to it as piety.³ Ann P. Charney gives a fuller view of Aristotle's treatment of divine activity in the *Ethics* when she contrasts the city's beneficent gods and the philosophers' contemplative god. She questions whether a piety that "manifests itself as philosophy" has any place "in the political domain."⁴ Lorraine Smith Pangle goes even further when she observes that in contrast to Plato, who ended several of his dialogues with myths, Aristotle "scarcely mentions the gods in his rich depiction of the moral life." She asks whether Aristotle had a higher estimate than Plato of the capacity of "subphilosophic individuals" to maintain a dedication to the noble without promise of rewards in the afterlife, who might, in other words, be morally decent without being either seriously pious or philosophic.⁵ She thus follows Robert C. Bartlett in understanding Aristotle's political science as a "rational science of politics" that dispenses as far as possible with piety.⁶

Such readings tend to make a radical distinction between the moral-political life and the philosophic life. This would be true whether they understand Aristotle as replacing the piety of the city with a philosophic piety (or a rational science of politics) or as exploring the tensions that will always exist between the gods of the city and the god of the philosopher (beneficent deities and a knowing one). In contrast, I attempt to show that divine knowing as well as beneficence is a model for politics, while divine beneficence as well as knowing is a model for philosophy. A "rational science of politics," as Aristotle's surely is to some extent, does not require

---

3. Broadie, "Aristotelian Piety," 54–61. See also Sparshott, *Taking Life Seriously*, 142, 146–47. Others, expecting Aristotle to discuss piety, do find it in various places in the *Ethics*. In the absence of an explicit discussion of piety in the *Ethics*, Bodeus, *Aristotle and the Theology of the Living Immortals*, 138–39, argues that it is a case of the distributive justice that Aristotle discusses in book 5. Broadie, "Aristotelian Piety," 54, 61, gives good arguments against this position. Pangle, *Reason and Character*, 31–32, argues that Aristotle comes closest to replacing piety in his treatment of munificence, but it is more of replacement than a manifestation.

4. Charney, "Spiritedness and Piety," esp. 73 and 77.

5. Pangle, *Reason and Character*, e.g., 4, 8–9, 131–32, 146, 147. Her argument seems to assume that the "seriously pious" require myths.

6. Bartlett, "Aristotle's Science of the Best Regime," 144. See also Bartlett and Collins, "Interpretive Essay," 237.

denial of the divine. Piety is not one virtue among others,[7] rather it undergirds our striving for the good, as manifest in the various virtues Aristotle discusses, and at the same time it gives us an awareness of our distance from the divine. In this way, a spirit of piety animates Aristotle's *Ethics* and the politics that his work supports.

My reading of the *Ethics* is attentive not only to what Aristotle *says* but also to what he *does* in writing the *Ethics*. The distinction between the speeches or the arguments (*logoi*) of a work and its deeds, so apparent in a drama such as a Platonic dialogue, also applies to Aristotle's work. As Leon R. Kass so well expresses it: "We must think *with* [Aristotle], from *within* the book, and allow the deed or drama of this book, no less than its speech, to work on us" (emphasis original).[8] Leo Strauss, who makes a

---

7. When Socrates asks Protagoras about the relation between virtue and the parts of virtue, he includes piety or holiness among them, along with courage, moderation, justice, and wisdom (*Protagoras* 329c–330a, 349b). We cannot conclude from this, however, that Plato thought that piety was a part of virtue along with the other parts, since the dialogue does not come to a satisfactory conclusion. Indeed, its aporetic conclusion might show the difficulty of placing piety in such a list. In the *Republic*, the interlocutors do not look for piety in the city in speech, as they do in the case of the other four virtues. No one questions why there are four and only four virtues there. The departure of Cephalus at the beginning of the *Republic* in order to participate in the religious sacrifices foreshadows the diminished role of piety in the city that Socrates describes in his absence. Plato does not, however, altogether exclude piety from the dialogue, just as he begins the dialogue with Cephalus, in whose house the conversation itself occurs. When Glaucon supposes that they have nothing left remaining for them to discuss with regard to legislation in the city, Socrates agrees, but points out that the "greatest, most beautiful, and the first of the laws that are given remain for the Apollo at Delphi [to determine]." Referring to such things as "establishing temples, sacrifices, and whatever belongs to the care of gods," Socrates claims that "we neither know such things ourselves, nor will be persuaded by another [human being]" (427a–c). Socrates, in other words, acknowledges both the need for religious worship and ceremonies in *their* city, and their need to rely on the god because of their own ignorance about what should be legislated. Socrates even describes his defense of justice as "pious" (368b–c).

8. Kass, "Professor or Friend?," 7, shows that Aristotle draws the reader into his work by its dialectical rather than demonstrative character. There are a number of good accounts and illustrations of the dialectical character of the *Ethics*, including Burger, *Aristotle's Dialogue with Socrates*; Collins, *Aristotle and the Rediscovery of Citizenship*; Mara, "Interrogating the Identities of Excellence"; Salkever,

persuasive case that one must read Plato with a view to the "deeds" of his dialogues, or to what happens, also looks to Aristotle's "deeds" in his reading of the *Politics*, as when he finds Aristotle's including "almost" a dialogue between a democrat and an oligarch "in the most fundamental discussion of the *Politics*." This is no more an "accident" than are the parts of the Platonic dialogue that all contribute to the whole.[9] Similar to the way we should read a Platonic dialogue, we must look to Aristotle's "deeds" in the *Ethics*. These include, for example, his organization, his juxtaposition of arguments and matters considered, his interruptions or digressions, his beginning again once he reaches an apparent conclusion, his returning to and revising earlier discussions, and the implicit dialogue he presents between himself and philosophers and poets of the past. Aristotle is not merely presenting conclusions he has reached about human life, but he is also showing how he reached them. He is presenting his philosophy about human affairs (see 1181b15) by demonstrating how to inquire.

THE PLAN OF THIS BOOK

In my first chapter, "Our Unfinished Humanity: A Divine Gift," I explore Aristotle's introduction of the human search for the good in book 1 of the *Ethics*, the role of politics in securing the highest good or happiness, and the difficulties that impede perfect happiness for human beings. Human beings may be political by nature, but they have ends distinct from those of their communities, as Aristotle indicates in his accounts of the arts they practice. Aristotle raises the question of the self-sufficiency of the political community when he asks whether happiness is sent to us by the gods or is in some other way "a divine lot," or comes from some "learning or care" on our part, or even comes through chance. Neither the ruling art of politics nor our belonging to a political community provides answers to such questions. Nor does Aristotle give us a conclusive answer. He nevertheless insists that if it were better for our happiness to arise from our own efforts than from chance, it would be reasonable that this is so, for something of such importance to our lives could not be "entrusted to chance." Our hap-

---

"Taking Friendship Seriously"; Smith, *Aristotle's Dialectical Pedagogy*; and Tessitore, *Reading Aristotle's "Ethics."*

9. Strauss, *City and Man*, 52–53, and esp. 21.

piness would be diminished if we merely chanced upon it, with no effort or achievement. So too, by implication, it would be diminished for us if it were simply a gift from the gods, or if it were conferred by the order a statesman gives to his city, or even if it came from Aristotle's teaching in the *Ethics*, unless we too played a part. That our happiness is at least in part "up to us," as Aristotle will insist of our virtuous deeds, means that human affairs are in a way arranged for the best, precisely because the difficulties we have in securing happiness give us an opportunity to develop and exercise our capacities for thought and action through the intellectual and ethical virtues that Aristotle will describe. This could be called our "divine lot."

Aristotle develops this understanding of our "divine lot" when he turns to the ethical or moral virtues. Human nature, he shows, has a distinctive openness that is not found in all of nature and that allows humans to acquire the virtues that might lead to their happiness, as I discuss in chapter 2, "The Ethical Virtues: Nature, Character, and Choice," which spans books 2 and 3 of the *Ethics*. Specifically, Aristotle traces the ethical virtues to habit (*ethos*) rather than to nature (*phusis*), for what is by nature cannot be changed by habit, no more than a stone that naturally falls downward can become accustomed to moving upward. The ethical virtues therefore do not arise by nature, but nature allows us to receive them (1103a18–26). Our habits give us a character, from which our choices arise and endow our actions with consistency. We thereby gain a certain independence from and power over the fluctuating world of which we are a part.

Because our parents, our teachers, and our lawmakers contribute to our upbringing (see 1103b22–25), others do share responsibility for who we are. Laws that reward and punish, for example, both presuppose and demand responsibility, while their rewards and punishments promote that responsibility. Aristotle ends his discussion of responsibility with the conclusion that we are "joint causes" of our virtues (1114b22). This is borne out by our experience of courage and moderation, the virtues of the "non-rational parts" of the soul (1117b24), which involve what we have most in common with the other animals: fear of death and desire for the bodily pleasures of food, drink, and sex. This natural inheritance alone also suggests why we are only "partly" responsible for ourselves, for we need help in acquiring the virtues that direct how we respond to our fears and desires. Since our virtues (and happiness) both come from our own efforts and find necessary aid in the human world on which we depend, Aristotle is supporting the confidence and deference appropriate to a pious relation to the divine. It is a confidence that jealous gods will not punish our achievements and a modesty that prevents us from thinking that our achievements can confer on us the status of gods. Aristotle continues to support both as he proceeds to discuss other virtues.

Whereas in books 2 and 3 he emphasizes human effort and responsibility and how ethical virtues elevate us above the desires we share with other animals, Aristotle in book 4 describes how our virtues develop through living with others, and at the same time he is educating us about the difference between the honors we assign to the gods and the goods that can become ours. My third chapter follows the ethical virtues Aristotle treats in book 4, which I argue are "Virtues of Living Together." Liberality, defined as the proper giving and taking of money, manifests our rising above material necessities, but we need others to whom to give. Aristotle describes numerous virtues that similarly involve our living together—such as the grand expenditures that serve the political community and honor the gods—and concludes with shame and reverence.

It is Aristotle's discussion of greatness of soul, however, that captures his purpose in laying out this series of virtues, for his account of this virtue describes and corrects the grand—but tragic—impulse to become the sole cause of oneself. Although the great-souled individual claims he is worthy of the greatest things (the honor we bestow on the gods) and demonstrates his freedom by initiating benefits rather than receiving them (1123b14–21, 1124b9–16), Aristotle reveals his dependence when he refers to the story of Achilles's reliance on his mother to intercede on his behalf with Zeus—and therewith his need for the gods (and his mother) to support his great deeds. Near the conclusion of his discussion of greatness of soul, Aristotle says that the great-souled individual is "unable to live in relation to another—except to a friend—since to do so is slavish" (1124b32–1125a1). Greatness of soul is completed by friendship, but in a way that seals its incompleteness, for in friendship the great of soul receive from their friends as well as give to them. The great of soul need friendship, for it teaches human beings their need for another—and of their difference from the divine—while protecting their freedom.

Aristotle goes even further in suggesting our dependence on our communities in his discussion of justice in book 5, which is the focus of my fourth chapter, "A Shrine to Graces: Justice and Tragedy." Aristotle praises justice as "the most complete virtue," for the laws, through which justice operates, "command every virtue and forbid every vice" (1129b25 and 1130b22–26). However, just as the "architectonic art" that Aristotle describes in book 1 yields to others who are capable of self-rule, so law requires human actions to supplement it and even to protect and enhance it. He discusses a reciprocity that is unmediated by law, the distinction between natural and conventional or legal justice, and equity as a correction of the law that in its universality cannot cover all cases. Consistent with the conflict that might arise for individuals from the limits of law and from the community that laws define, Aristotle makes numerous allusions to the tragic poets in book 5. He nevertheless does not draw a tragic conclusion from the tensions he discusses in book 5. Conflict is mediated by the tendency of equity to forgive or pardon, for example, by a political justice that exists among those who are free and equal, and by divine models Aristotle offers as support for human beneficence. Thus, he mentions shrines to beneficent deities—the Graces—and attributes to them the task of encouraging human beings not only to render service in turn to those who have been gracious, but also "to initiate acts of graciousness" (1133a2–6).

My fifth chapter, "Intellectual Virtues: Prudence, Wisdom, and Philosophy" discusses Aristotle's treatment of the intellectual virtues in book 6. There he contrasts prudence, which deliberates about correct actions and about what is good for human beings, with wisdom, which considers what is "eternal, ungenerated, and indestructible," the most honorable beings or being in the cosmos, whose nature is more divine than that of human beings (1139a4–9, 1141b1–5). Wisdom points human beings to what is higher than themselves. Just as medicine gives commands not to health but for the sake of health, so prudences give commands not to wisdom but for the sake of wisdom. So too does politics arranges everything in the city, as Aristotle concludes book 6, but this does not mean that politics rules the gods (1145a7–11). Aristotle does not limit virtue and happiness to the confines of the political community.

Aristotle refers us to Socrates as he draws book 6 to a close, someone who, like Aristotle, "investigates" virtue, and who was correct in linking virtue with reason (1144b19–25). Both differ from those reputed wise, such as Anaxagoras and Thales, who in looking up to the heavens do "not investigate human goods" (1141b5–8). There is a sort of intellectual virtue, in addition to those listed in book 6, that "investigates" the relation between knowledge and virtue, the eternal and the changing, the divine and the human. As Aristotle illustrates by his deeds, wisdom must seek truth by looking not simply to the eternal but to perplexities that arise when a being who lives in time and in community with others looks to the eternal. One could call this the wisdom of philosophy, which Plato illustrated in Socrates's dialogues, and which Aristotle illustrates by his inquiries throughout the *Ethics*. It might even remind us of piety.

By the end of book 6, Aristotle appears to have completed his task, for he has discussed both the ethical and intellectual virtues and offered a rich tapestry of human goods and the happiness they make possible. Aristotle nevertheless continues his inquiry in book 7 to discuss the human being who is torn between reason and desire, contrasting those who achieve self-rule (*enkrateia*) (who are, literally, "in control" or "strong" over themselves) with those who fail. Although the greater part of book 7 involves self-rule and its failure, Aristotle frames his discussion by reference to what is below (bestiality) and above humanity (a divine or heroic virtue, which is "beyond us") (1145a15–20). In chapter 6, "Human Strength versus Divine Perfection," I examine how Aristotle deepens our view of human virtue by presenting human strength in light of humanity's spirited resistance to bestiality and in light of humanity's awareness of a divinity beyond itself. Not only is human virtue a mean between contrary vices, but human life itself falls between bestiality and divine-like self-sufficiency or perfection. More than a mean between two contraries, however, human strength manifests the work of reason in ruling actions (rather than in only contemplating or studying) and in an accompanying self-awareness that is for Aristotle a distinctive mark of humanity.

Aristotle wrote two books on friendship for the *Nicomachean Ethics*, which I discuss in my seventh chapter, "Friendship: Family, Political Community, and Philosophy." Whereas book 7 lets us see the limits of the good we can achieve for ourselves (because of the imperfections of our nature), Aristotle's treatment of friendship shows us the happiness that can occur only within those limits. Specifically, in book 8, Aristotle focuses on the family, and the affection or friendship (*philia*) that develops between parents and their offspring, between husband and wife, and among siblings. The friendships that develop in the family also support political life. As Aristotle says, it is in families "that we first see the beginnings [*archai*] and springs [*pēgai*] of friendship, political governance [*politeia*], and justice" (*Eudemian Ethics* 1242b1). In book 9, in contrast, we learn that friendships within the family do not merely support and even make possible political life, but that they must also yield to friendships that go beyond the family—from the friendship of fellow citizens, or the "like-mindedness" that holds cities together, to the friends who "philosophize together" and who thereby nurture in each other "what is most divine in themselves" (1172a5).

My chapter on friendship includes a discussion of Aristotle's strange question of whether we should wish our friends to be gods, inasmuch as we wish their good. His explicit answer, that we wish their good as the human beings that they are (1159a6–12), as does his treatment of friendship more generally, teaches us the goodness of human life, which we would lose if we attained divine perfection, either for our friends or for ourselves. Human beings have goods of their own, even while they must understand themselves as part of a cosmos larger than themselves. Our awareness of the distance between the human and the divine does not merely lead us to recognize our own limits, but it also protects the goods that are ours as human beings. Whether or not anyone ever set up a shrine to the Graces to remind people to return favors and even to initiate them, Aristotle's *Ethics* serves as such a shrine.

In book 10 of the *Ethics*, which I treat in the last chapter, "Divine Thoughts and Political Reform," Aristotle "sums up" the major themes of his work and revisits them in light of the progress of his inquiry and moves forward by introducing the need for another work on politics. He examines pleasure and its relation to the good, presents happiness "in outline," and outlines a work on politics, which his *Politics* undertakes to fill in. Rather than contrasting the ephemeral and incomplete pleasures of human life with the eternal and unchanging pleasure of the god, as he did earlier, after his discussion of friendship he turns to the specifically human pleasures that belong to changing human life, including pleasures of memory and hope, and learning (1173b16–21). At the same time, when arguing that pleasure is an activity rather than a motion, he reveals a human experience of wholeness within human life itself, an experience that confirms the opinion that we have something divine in us, without collapsing the distinction between human beings and gods. Because Aristotle has taken care to preserve that distinction throughout the *Ethics*, we are entitled to refer to his work not only as one of piety but also as "a discovery of the human." Indeed, the two are connected. It is not merely that human beings occupy a space between god and beast and share something with both, but that "space" makes possible distinctive goods, such as self-awareness and friendship. It also makes possible a political life that belongs to beings who are political by nature because they have reason and speech and hence can deliberate together about what is advantageous and just. Aristotle's *Nicomachean Ethics* and his *Politics* occur within that space while at the same time they protect it.

When Aristotle has recourse to the gods as models for human happiness near the end of the *Ethics*, both in their contemplative or theoretical activity and in their serving as benefactors for human beings akin to them, he sets the stage for his recommendations of theoretical activity and political reform to his readers. The contemplative activity in which human beings engage—living in accord with what is most divine in themselves, their minds—is not merely for its own sake but also serves other ends, and is manifest in a range of human activities, such as that of the statesman who "contemplates" the soul insofar as it helps him in securing the good of the political community (1102a25), and that of Aristotle and his readers when they "contemplate" what preserves and what destroys political communities, and why some regimes are well governed and others not (1181b8–23). So too Aristotle follows the lead of the gods he describes by becoming a benefactor for those kin to himself, his good deeds extending to the majority of human beings, for whom the encouraging speeches of *Ethics* are not sufficient and who must be ruled by force as well as persuasion (1179b5–12). By the same reasoning, the *Politics*, his sequel to the *Ethics*, would not be sufficient either, for it too would suffer the limits of speech to move the many. Aristotle's work cannot replace the work of statesmen in their political communities, for the threat of punishment is necessary to effect virtuous deeds in the majority. His conclusion to the *Ethics* thus returns to its beginning, where Aristotle introduced politics as an "architectonic" art or activity. But Aristotle does not speak of anything "architectonic" in his concluding outline, and indeed he never refers to political rule or statesmanship in the *Politics* as "architectonic." Rather, Aristotle characterizes political rule as shared rule and distinguishes it from despotism. If this is "architectonic," it is a work in which many share.

Although the limits of speech to move human beings require that Aristotle write the *Politics*, at the outset of that work he explains that human beings are political by nature because they have speech or reason (*logos*). He has mentioned that human beings are political by nature in the *Ethics* (1097b7–12, 1169b16–19), but only in the *Politics* does he associate their being so with their distinctive capacity for speech. It is speech, he explains there, that reveals the beneficial and the harmful, and therefore the just and the unjust. And it is "a sharing" in the perceptions of such things that constitutes families and political communities (1253a8–19). That is why Aristotle objects at the beginning of the *Politics* to identifying "political" rule with mastery over slaves, in which there is no such sharing, or even with kingship (*Politics* 1259a39–b2). In the *Politics*, Aristotle moves political life in the direction of sharing, by his criticism of despotism, for example, by his definition of citizenship, by his arguments in favor of the rule of law, by teaching how political communities can be established and maintained by making them more inclusive, and by outlining a regime that might be prayed for.[10] With the success of Aristotle's *Politics*, speech about the beneficial and just has a greater place in political life than force or compulsion. Because "law-giving" is yet to be discovered, he observes, "we must investigate it ourselves." As he says several times in the *Ethics*, he says of his turn to politics that "the attempt must be made" (1180b24, 1181b17). His *Politics* will be such an attempt.

Since actions involve particulars, and particulars are infinite (1106a33; *Rhetoric* 1356b33–36), there can be no perfect end or completion to the human task that the *Ethics* sets forth and that we share with Aristotle. And action, inasmuch as it is a term that applies to human beings, requires choice (1139a19, 1105a32–33). Time and our own efforts therefore remain as co-workers (1098a24). This is why Aristotle's observations about happiness even in book 10 remain "in outline" (1176a30–32 and 1179a33–35). It is we who must fill in the details, by thinking and acting together (see 1155a15–16).

---

10. See Nichols, *Citizens and Statesmen*, 53–72, 86–100, 136–51; and Nichols, "How Excellence Bows to Equality," 67–88.

ARISTOTLE FOR A MODERN WORLD

My book concludes with "Afterthoughts: Aristotelian Piety for a Liberal Politics," and some of the implications of my study for liberalism and its critics. In many ways, Aristotle's political teaching is a liberal one. Human beings are the source of political authority, not a divine dispensation that orders human life or that confers authority on rulers, not a wisdom belonging to a select few that merits their ruling political communities, nor a moral righteousness that warrants an imposition of a way of life on others. Choice, defined by Aristotle as the outcome of deliberation, is the origin of action and serves as a definition of the human (1139b4–6). Politics is understood as shared rule, in contradistinction to despotism. Key elements of Aristotle's political thought are therefore consistent with our liberal institutions and practices, even if he would understand them in a different way and justify them on different grounds. Aristotle therefore has something distinctive to contribute to liberalism. For example, liberal theorists appeal to the rational choice that satisfies desires and to the industry and discipline that serve life and economic prosperity. Although Aristotle appreciates such goods, he knows that they are not the highest, even if they are its conditions. He would approve of liberal institutions and practices because of their potential to foster both deliberation about the good and virtuous actions in concert with others, that is, the capacities belonging to beings who can think divine thoughts and who can initiate acts of beneficence.

The modern separation of church and state sought to protect civil peace from sectarian conflict and to protect religious liberty and freedom of thought from political interference. If successful, a secular politics would serve both civil life and religion and philosophy. This liberal solution nevertheless left humanity's spiritual life, moral aspirations, and devotion to truth without any authoritative support, as individuals are allowed and even encouraged to pursue happiness as they see fit. Such permissiveness, which accepts no imposition of order or rank of goods, encourages a moral relativism that asserts that ways of life are equal, that the good is whatever we desire, and that moral distinctions are arbitrary. Liberalism has been criticized almost from its inception for the quality of life that emerges under its auspices, such as Rousseau's criticism of the bourgeois or Nietzsche's of the "last man." It has also come under attack more recently by theocratic regimes for its secularism and moral decadence. Aristotle offers an alternative to both liberalism and its critics, or rather support for liberal politics against the criticisms to which liberal theory leaves it open. Whether we live a good life and govern ourselves well may be "up to us," but our very freedom for Aristotle makes us responsible for living lives consistent with that freedom. We pursue happiness as we see fit, but we must see what is fit for human beings, what distinguishes us from other beings, and therewith what sort of activity will make us happy.

For Aristotle, the challenges of political life can summon the moral and intellectual excellence of which human beings are capable, without leading to the dogmatism and even fanaticism that liberal theorists sought to avert. On the one hand, a pious awareness of the distance between ourselves and the divine supports a humble toleration of different religious communities. Not the diminution of the effect and influence of religion on civil life but reverence itself begets toleration, while holding pious citizens back from any attempt to assimilate politics to religion. On the other hand, politics, including liberal politics, cannot be traced to a godless assertion of human power over nature if the achievements of our reason are made possible, as Aristotle says, by "what is most divine in us." For these reasons, liberal politics need not be understood as merely secular, but could be supported by a kind of piety, indeed one in which theocratic regimes that claim divine sanction are deficient. Politics, as Aristotle understands it, especially a politics that protects and encourages the pursuit of happiness, challenges us to develop and exercise our highest human capacities. Along these lines, liberalism has a high and demanding work to do, but also has a defense against its critics.

CHAPTER 1

Our Unfinished Humanity

A Divine Gift (Book 1)

Aristotle begins the *Nicomachean Ethics* with the observation that "every art and every inquiry, every action and every choice seem to aim at some good, and therefore it is beautifully [*kalōs*] declared that the good is that at which all things aim" (1094b1–3). He refers first to human activities, and then to our reflection on them—what we declare or say about them and what we infer from them about the world in which we live. Our reflections expressed in our speech are part of that world, and they give us a distinctive, even preeminent place in that world. We reveal our purposes not only by our deeds, but also by our words, our declarations, about what we "wish," "choose," and "long for," to which Aristotle soon refers (1094a18–21). We give an account of ourselves, to ourselves and to others. And Aristotle says that we beautifully declare that the good is that at which all things aim. The *kalon*, "the beautiful" or "the noble," which will undergo clarification and development as the *Ethics* proceeds, first appears as something that might belong to our speech about the world and our activities in it.[1]

---

1. Aristotle's first use of the "beautiful" in the *Ethics* describes something declared or said (*apophanai*). The adjective *kalos* in Greek may also be translated as "noble." Translations of Aristotle's Greek are difficult when we do not have a single English word that corresponds to the word as Aristotle uses it. *Kalos* is one

Aristotle argues further that our aiming at the good in everything we do supposes that there is a final good that satisfies our longing, for if there were no end of our actions that we wish for on account of itself, and if we merely chose one thing after another for the sake of something else "to infinity [*eis apeiron*], our longing [*orexis*] would be empty and pointless" (1094a18–26).² Aristotle formulates it thus in the *Metaphysics*: those who insist on an infinite series of goods with no limit are unaware that they undermine the pursuit of the good, for no one would attempt to do anything "if he were not going to come to a limit [*peras*]" (*Metaphysics* 994b9–17).³ Aristotle is aware of their error and will therefore avoid it, beginning with a highest good that is the end of our longing and for the sake of which we act (1094a18–22). Our very actions—and our choices, our arts, and our inquiries, which Aristotle mentions at the outset of the *Ethics*—

---

of those. I will translate the word whenever possible as "beautiful," but I will use "noble" when helpful in understanding Aristotle's meaning. Bartlett and Collins, *Aristotle's "Nicomachean Ethics,"* 1n2, in commenting on this passage, note that what is declared about the good may be "a noble sentiment," and hence "not necessarily a true one." So too Pangle, *Reason and Character*, 13, observes that "what is nobly said may be truly said or just beautifully said." Their observations nevertheless do not foreclose the possibility that our ability to experience and to declare "noble [or beautiful] sentiments" expresses truth about the human soul. See Davis, *Soul of the Greeks*, 60–61.

2. I have chosen to follow Bartlett and Collins in translating *orexis* as "longing." "Longing" captures the meaning of the common verb from which it is derived, "to reach out for" (*oregein*). It is used by Aristotle in his first words of the *Metaphysics*: "All human beings by nature long to know" (980a21). In the *De Anima*, Aristotle says that longing includes desire, spiritedness, and wish (414b2–3). The English "desire" therefore seems too narrow to capture Aristotle's *orexis*. "Longing," however, no more than "desire" fully captures the active sense of *orexis*, as Aristotle uses it. As Salkever so well puts it, *orexis* "signifies not a passive or mechanical response to external stimuli or to internal 'instincts,' but an active and focused reaching out toward something in the environment, toward something that we lack or need" (Salkever, "Democracy and Aristotle's Ethics of Natural Questions," 359). As Sachs, *Aristotle's "Metaphysics,"* 1, captures the verb in his translation of the first line of the *Metaphysics*, "All human beings by nature stretch themselves out toward knowing."

3. As Roochnik, *Retrieving Aristotle*, 152, comments: "If means and ends were infinite, then the achievement of any single item would advance the agent no closer to the end."

presuppose a good for which we act, and ultimately a highest good that is their end. In the *Metaphysics*, Aristotle designates this highest good as the divine, or god (1072b6, 1072b28–31).

Aristotle begins by locating us in a cosmos that supports our striving. Our longing is set in motion by what we long for, our thinking is set in motion by the objects of thought (*Metaphysics* 1072a24–32). The cosmos in which we live is like a divine gift that aligns with our capacities to receive it, but they require our exercising them—our longing or reaching out and our thinking. Aristotle nevertheless brings numerous perplexities about the divine to light in both the *Metaphysics* and the *Ethics*: in the former, he asks, for example, whether the highest good is something separate from the cosmos or its very order (1075a12–24); in the latter, he asks whether our happiness, or highest good, comes from divine allotment or in some other way (1099b9–12). Far from detracting from our happiness, or from calling into question the gift of a cosmos that can become a home for us, such perplexities, ever imperfectly resolved, keep our longing and thinking alive.[4] We are "blessed," as Aristotle says, "as human beings" (1101a21), and, we might add, *because* we are human beings. Such perplexities too are divine gifts, which Aristotle might help us receive.

Aristotle's inquiry in the *Ethics*—into the human good and the activities by which we can attain it—is a "political" inquiry (1094b10). It is not possible to understand our place in the cosmos without understanding our place in a political community. Human beings are political by nature (1097b8–13). We have no home in the cosmos unless we have a home in a political community, which anchoring us in time and place allows us to transcend them. We acquire the ethical virtues through habituation, as Aristotle famously teaches, and habituation comes in large part through obeying the laws of one's community. Only then can we deliberate about and choose how to act, gaining freedom from the very laws that form us. We acquire intellectual virtues through teaching or education, and then can question what we are taught, and examine the perplexities we face as citizens and human beings (1103b24–36, 1105a26–26, 1103a13–18).

---

4. Consider Leo Strauss's statement in commenting on Aristotle: "In becoming aware of the dignity of the mind, we realize the true ground of the dignity of man and therewith the goodness of the world, whether we understand it as created or uncreated, which is the home of man because it is the home of the human mind" (Strauss, "What Is Liberal Education?," 8).

Aristotle therefore begins and ends the *Ethics* with politics. He refers us at the beginning to an architectonic art of politics that orders everything in the city in light of the highest human good, or happiness. He ends the book by proposing the need for another work on politics that completes the inquiry of the *Ethics* and that investigates among other things what causes some cities to be well governed and others not (1181b20). Aristotle's *Ethics* is addressed to those who belong to political communities. He depends on their having been educated to various degrees and in various ways beforehand, in order to proceed with their education. His work begins and ends with politics, but it itself is political throughout, even if it leads beyond politics. It is a work about education, and it is a work of education.

In this chapter, I follow Aristotle's introduction of the architectonic art of the statesman, which seeks the highest good for human beings, the suppositions on which it is based, and the difficulties it encounters. Aristotle almost immediately casts doubt on any perfect or complete ordering of the community, for the arts and the human beings who practice them resist determination by the political community and its goals (as I discuss in the first section of this chapter). Indeed, Aristotle's work, his inquiry in the *Ethics*, suffers similar problems; for example, the just, the beautiful, and the good, which he studies, resist precision, and thus resist definition in the laws or customs that form any given community (second section). There are many ways of life people choose, and opinions they hold about happiness (third section). Even when Aristotle defines the human good as the activity of the soul in accordance with virtue, or at least the "most complete," he leaves open the possibility of many virtues that contribute to happiness, some only more complete than others (fourth section). When he asks whether happiness comes to us as a divine gift, or whether it comes through some learning or practice on our part or through chance, and gives no definitive answer, he lets us see that ours is an unfinished task and that it is so is indeed a divine gift. Only if our own learning and practice is necessary for acquiring the ethical and intellectual virtues can we merit the happiness that comes from them (fifth section). Hence when Aristotle returns to the statesman at the end of book 1, he argues that he must understand the human soul in order to rule well and that the human soul is capable of self-rule (sixth section). In other words, the statesman must facilitate self-rule rather than replace it. It is also a lesson that Aristotle embraces, with all its problems and challenges, in presenting his *Ethics* to us.

ARCHITECTONIC PROBLEMS

After introducing the good as the end of our arts and inquiries, our actions and choices, Aristotle presents a hierarchy of "actions, arts, and sciences," and of the goods at which they aim, culminating in politics, or statesmanship, *politikē*.[5] Politics is the most "architectonic" or ruling art (*architektonikē*) and it arranges or gives order to (*diatassein*) everything in the city, with a view to "the highest good" (*to ariston*) (1094a3–b7).[6] Aristotle's account of the architectonic role of politics nevertheless does not mean that it perfectly orders human life, or even that a perfect ordering is possible. By referring to "the single individual" whose good may not be the same as that of the political community, for example, Aristotle raises questions about the good achieved by any architectonic arrangement, including the good of the statesman himself (1094b7–11). So too in describing the arts, sciences, and actions that politics directs, he distinguishes those that have their ends in their own activities from those that have their ends in works

---

5. Aristotle avoids attaching a noun to *politikē*. The adjective implies "skilled in politics," and is modeled on the other arts, such as medicine (*iatrikē*), shipbuilding (*nauēgikē*), and bridle-making (*chalinopoiikē*) (1094a7–11). When he first uses *politikē* in the *Ethics*, as a feminine adjective it could modify science (*epistēmē*), capacity (*dunamis*), or action (*praxis*) and also art (*technē*), all of which he has used prior to his use of *politikē* (1094a1–28). With some reservations, I will render *politikē* as "political art," "politics," or "statesmanship," depending on the context. The first gives the term more precision than Aristotle does, the second loses the sense of skill or expertise implied in the Greek word, and the last loses the etymological connection between the one who practices politics and the political community (*polis*).

6. See Alexander, "Philosophical Foundations for Political Change," for an exploration of the ways in which Aristotle's *Ethics*, beginning from his description of politics as *the* architectonic art, is about foundings or beginnings, both political and philosophical. She demonstrates both the ongoing character of foundings and the ways in which they depend on and build on the past. An "architect," from which Aristotle derives the adjective "architectonic," is literally one who "rules" or "begins" a construction.

or products (*erga*) outside themselves (1094a4–7, b16–17). Just as the good of an individual may not perfectly accord with that of his city, the activity of arts that have ends in themselves may not perfectly fit into the hierarchy that serves the city's good.[7]

Aristotle argues that even if the good of the single individual (*heis monos*) (literally, "one alone") is the same as that of a political community, it is still the case that to attain and preserve that of the community would be "greater and more complete" than that of the individual. Although both should be cherished, the good of the community is nobler and more divine (1094b7–11).[8] Aristotle nevertheless leaves open whether the good of the community at which statesmanship aims is the same as the good of the individual. If it makes no difference for the statesman's work whether the good of the individual and the good of the city he serves are the same or different, Aristotle makes what seems like a gratuitous distinction. But if they were different, what difference would it make? Would attention to the good of the community require the statesman to neglect that of the individual? Aristotle's reference to the "single individual," whose good he demotes in contrast to the good of the community, moreover, reminds us of the statesman himself, a single individual inasmuch as he is distinguished by his architectonic calling. Does his good lie in the good of the community that his activity serves or in his activity itself?[9]

When Aristotle also claims that his distinction between arts that have their ends in their own activities and those that have their ends in works or products outside themselves makes no difference to the hierarchy of arts that he lays out, he seems to call attention to another gratuitous distinction.[10] He proceeds to give several examples of arts with

---

7. Several of the arguments of this book are expansions of points I made in Nichols, "Both Friends and Truth Are Dear," 70–82.

8. Aristotle refers to securing and preserving the good not only of a city but of a people (*ethnos*) (1094b10). A city differs from a people, since a city is more diverse, made up of parts differing in kind (see *Politics* 1261a23–24).

9. Aristotle's observation about the more complete and divine good could refer to either the good that is secured or the activity of securing it. For discussion, see Block, "Aristotle on Statesmanship," 97–98.

10. It seems so much beside the point to Rackham that he places Aristotle's observation about this difference in parentheses in his translation on both occasions in which Aristotle refers to it. See Rackham, *Aristotle: "Nicomachean*

products outside themselves, such as medicine, whose end is health, and shipbuilding, whose end is the ship. They can be ordered for the good of the community by a statesman. Healthy citizens can be good soldiers, for example, and ships can serve commerce or war. Aristotle, however, gives no example here of arts that have their ends in their activities rather than in a product outside their activity. Only later in book 1 does he mention a flute player, whose good resides in doing his work well, just as does a human being's (1097b26).[11]

Those whose work lies in their own activity do not fit so easily in the hierarchy Aristotle is presenting, in which activities are subordinate to the architectonic work of the statesman in ordering the political community. An activity "exercised as an end in itself," Ronna Burger observes, "would seem to resist integration into a larger hierarchy, unlike the *ergon* [the work] that is a product of an activity."[12] And Ann Ward asks, What "prevent[s] the lower or less encompassing activities from separating off and losing sight of their higher ends?"[13] The problem lies not only in the statesman's reducing human beings and their arts and activities to their place in a hierarchy that aims at an architectonic good, but the failure of human beings to recognize that their good requires their belonging to a larger community to which they are able to render service. When Aristotle later acknowledges that an activity can be both an end in itself *and* a means to higher ends (1097a33), he does not resolve the problem. He underscores the difficulty.

Ethics," 3 and 5. Curiously, Aristotle's words for the "difference" (*diaphora*) between the ends of the arts and for the lack of "difference it makes" (*diapherei*) come from the same Greek verb, *diapherein*, as if to say the difference makes no difference (cf. 1094a2 with 1094a16). If it makes no difference to an ordered or hierarchical arrangement of the arts, it would to Aristotle, who mentions the difference.

11. In the *Magna Moralia*, Aristotle does offer an example of an art whose end resides in itself, flute-playing, in contrast to the art of building, whose end is the house (1211b27). The authorship of this short work on ethics is disputed, but the author's addition nevertheless highlights Aristotle's omission when presenting an architectonic ordering at the beginning of the *Nicomachean Ethics*. Its author, in other words, makes more visible the problem that Aristotle leaves in the *Ethics*.

12. Burger, *Aristotle's Dialogue with Socrates*, 231–32n5.

13. Ward, *Contemplating Friendship*, 22, 19–23; see also Davis, *Soul of the Greeks*, 62–63; and Burger, *Aristotle's Dialogue with Socrates*, 15 and n5, 231–32.

However much the existence of arts whose ends lie in their own activity, such as flute-playing, complicates the statesman's task, and even diverts us from our pursuit of the highest good at which politics aims, it is because we choose things for their own sake, and not only as means toward something else, that we experience something as an end. We experience a longing that is not infinite or pointless. Aristotle will soon explain that the deeds of ethical virtue are chosen for their own sake, or on account of their beauty or nobility (1115b12–13, 1116b1–3, 1117b13–16; *Rhetoric* 1366a33–34) rather than as a means to some end outside themselves.[14] The beautiful, as Aristotle uses it here, is the good that is pursued and chosen apart from its serving some other good, apart from its utility. It may indeed be useful to some end outside itself, but it also possesses a beauty that is a cause of its attraction. The beautiful is not subordinate even to the political community, as Aristotle makes clear when he distinguishes courageous deeds for the sake of the beautiful or noble from the "political" courage motivated by a love of honor (1116a17–30).[15] The choices and activities that disrupt the chain of ends leading us to the highest good, at which politics aims, paradoxically, give us an experience of completion or wholeness. Although Aristotle says that securing and preserving the good of the political community is "more complete" (*teleioteron*) than doing so for only one individual (1094b8), he also maintains that those activities that have ends (*telē*) in themselves are "more complete" (*teleioteron*) than others (1097a31–33). "Complete" can be used in more than one way (see *Metaphysics* 1021b12–1022a4).

If a human action or art is undertaken for its own sake, longing finds an end or closure in the activity it prompts, even while that activity can be understood in terms of other activities on which it depends and which it might serve. Aristotle's distinction between arts that have their ends in themselves and those that have their ends in works or products outside themselves therefore is not gratuitous. It indicates that the ordered hierarchy that Aristotle presents does not merely subordinate lower to higher,

---

14. Davis, *Soul of the Greeks*, 64.

15. Collins, "Moral Virtue and the Limits of Political Community," 47–61, esp. 49, explores the status of virtue for Aristotle as "an independent end." See also Ward, *Contemplating Friendship*, 22. Both emphasize the problem that moral virtue poses as a result of its independence, whether from the hierarchy of arts, from ends outside themselves, or from the political community.

but also allows an experience of a multiplicity of goods. In this way, Aristotle's description of the hierarchy of human activities and ends at the beginning of the *Ethics* functions as a frame or outline that Aristotle fills in throughout the *Ethics*, as he refines his understanding of the good at which both politics and his own inquiry aim.

ARISTOTLE'S REFLECTIONS ON HIS OWN WORK

When Aristotle argues that it is politics that aims at the highest good, he points out that its end encompasses other goods, since it legislates what is to be done and not done in political communities, and even commands what "each person must learn and up to what point" (1094a29–b7). Aristotle soon mentions his own inquiry in the *Ethics* (1094b11–14)—something he does, in fact throughout his work (e.g., 1129a5–6, 1133b18–21, 1152b1–4, 1181b13–16). No political authority commissions the *Ethics*. He even calls his own work a *politikē*. And although the word might be an adjective that modifies his inquiry and might indicate merely that his inquiry is "about politics," it is also the word that he uses as a substantive to refer to the practice of politics itself, when he designates politics, or "statesmanship," as the "most architectonic" art of all. If he too is practicing politics in his inquiry in the *Ethics*, there would be two "most architectonic" arts: Aristotle's work in the *Ethics* and that of the statesman in his community. By calling both his work and the statesman's by the same name, Aristotle acknowledges that he sees a likeness or kinship between them, a likeness that would allow them to better understand their own work by seeing its reflection in the other's, as Aristotle later describes friends (1169b33–35).[16]

The subject matter of politics imposes limitations on both the statesman and on Aristotle himself in his inquiry about politics. The beautiful and the just, which politics involves, Aristotle points out, do not allow as much precision as does mathematics, for example. The beautiful and the just admit of so much difference and variation that they are held to exist

---

16. Bartlett, "Aristotle's Introduction to the Problem of Happiness," 679, understands Aristotle's inquiry as a competition with the efforts of the political community in identifying the human good. See also Pangle, *Reason and Character*, 17.

by law or convention, and not by nature. Even the good things, Aristotle says, vary with the harm that many suffer on account of them. Some people are destroyed on account of wealth, others on account of courage. One must therefore be content when speaking of such things that are true only "for the most part" with conclusions of the same sort (1094b12–24). It is the mark of an "educated" person, Aristotle cautions, to demand only so much precision as "the nature of the matter [*pragma*]" allows (1094b25).

Aristotle gives the examples of wealth and courage as goods that may at times be harmful. They are goods, but they cannot be simply good, for they must be judged at least in part by the consequences. Aristotle does not follow the path that Socrates took in the *Republic* (358b) to see the goodness of something stripped of its consequences, as demanded by his young interlocutors. Aristotle proceeds to further distinguish himself from Socrates when he claims that discussions of political matters are not appropriate to the young. In the first place, the young are "inexperienced [*apeiros*] in the actions [*praxeis*] of life," which politics involves (1095a3). But what do the "actions" of life teach? In the *Rhetoric*, Aristotle contrasts the young and the old: the former are hopeful, the latter are pessimistic, because the old know from their greater experience, as the young do not, the difficulties and frustrations that arise over time (1389a30–33, b25–29). Experience teaches that what is good in some cases is bad in others, that some things are true only for the most part, and that consequences must be considered in judging the good. The old know from living so long that time will not stand still. One cannot escape the consequences.

The young are not fit students of politics, in the second place, because they are guided by their passions rather than by speech or reason (1095a7). By what passions are they guided? Presumably, they too vary. The optimism that Aristotle attributes to the young in the *Rhetoric*, however, suggests that they tend to desire something perfect or complete, perhaps something simply good or beautiful that does not change with the circumstances, and for which they are willing to risk their lives. As Aristotle says in the *Rhetoric*, the young choose beautiful actions over advantageous ones (1389a34–35). His description of them suggests they are open to challenges, perhaps the challenge of an inquiry for which their author claims they are unfit. And he has just said that its subject matter involves the beautiful and the just, almost as if he were appealing especially to the young.

Moreover, given his description of the young in the *Rhetoric*, it seems that they are most in need of the lessons that Aristotle teaches in the *Ethics*. Indeed, those lessons instill the caution that in their optimism they lack. Aristotle shows, for example, how close the virtue of courage comes to the vice of recklessness (1109a6–11); he acknowledges that courage is painful (1179a34); he warns that death is the most fearful thing (1115a26). The many points that Aristotle brings up for reflection as he treats the beautiful or noble offer a kind of vicarious experience of the sort we are familiar with from the stories poets tell. He even works into his inquiry itself, as we see throughout, perplexities that are in part resolved but often in greater part remain, considerations that require weighing, twists, turns, delays, and digressions that mirror the difficulties of life itself. Such devices convey or reproduce an experience of life that his addressees, especially the young, may lack. When Kass speaks of attending to the deeds of the work and to its arguments, he says that we must do so in order to let them "work on us."[17]

Aristotle's inquiry, he says more than once, requires that "an attempt be made" to push forward or, literally, "the experience must be had" (*peirateon*) (e.g., 1094a25, 1097a25, 1098b5). The inexperienced, the *apeirioi*, are those who do not make the attempt. Experience (*empeiria*) lies "in the attempt," including the attempts the inquiry demands. Aristotle offers the experience needed by the inexperienced. He does so not only by giving them the opportunity to work their way through the *Ethics* with him. After giving the barest of outlines of the virtues and their corresponding vices, he advises his addressees to aim at the virtuous mean, even if it requires overshooting the mark (1109a31–b7). They will likely err, but they might learn from their errors. In this way, also, they must participate in their own education.

---

17. Kass, "Professor or Friend?," 7. Smith, *Revaluing Ethics*, 161–63, argues that reading the *Ethics* is "an existential exercise" because "we have to change ourselves in order to understand the text." Heyking, *Form of Politics*, 54–55, argues that Aristotle's pedagogy cultivates ethical virtues, for the *Ethics* "not only provides information on virtue and the good life; the structure of the argument dialectically brings the reader into a moral education over the course of reading the treatise." At the same time, he argues, Aristotle's "paradoxes, puzzles, and constant refinements of our common sense understanding of the world [in the *Ethics*] draw us into a process of self-reflection and philosophizing."

Aristotle observes that the young can be young in years or in character. The "deficiency does not proceed from time" (1095a7–8). If their deficiency does not proceed from time, neither does its correction. The old, as Aristotle describes them in the *Rhetoric*, are no more prepared to accept Aristotle's *Ethics* than the young. In contrast to the young, the old are concerned more with the useful than the beautiful (1389a34–b1, b34). When Aristotle describes ethical virtues in terms of the beautiful rather than the useful (e.g., 1116a12–16; see also 1094b17–19), he reminds them of what might have moved them when they were young and what they might have forgotten. Just as Aristotle offers the experience that might moderate the optimism he associates with the young, he emboldens the old, or those who possess the caution he associates with the old, when he insists that "the attempt must be made." The young are inexperienced because they have not yet made the attempt, but the old no longer make the attempt if they have had too much experience of life's hardships. Instead of acting, or thinking about the future, which of course holds the prospect of their deaths, they dwell in memory. In spite of their age, or perhaps because of it, they cling to their lives. As addressees of the *Ethics*, they too must make the attempt along with Aristotle, as they follow his lead. Experience offers not only the pain of suffering, but the pleasure of accomplishment, even of the accomplishments of those whom they love that might occur in the future. Aristotle associates virtuous deeds with pleasure (e.g., 1104b14–16), and mentions many other pleasures that human beings experience (e.g., 1118a3–8, b5–8; 1173b17), including the pleasure from hopes and memories (1173b19). The lessons he offers to both old and young are lessons they could offer to each other. The old can teach the young what they remember, while the young can teach the old to hope in the future, even to place their hopes in the young themselves. That old and young have much to give to each other is a point Aristotle makes explicit when he first introduces the benefits of friendship (1155a12–13). Connecting the beautiful with the useful might put a brake on the eagerness of the young. Connecting the useful with the beautiful might rejuvenate the old.[18]

---

18. I recognize that Aristotle writes with a view to differences among his readers, but my argument should not be confused with those of scholars who read Aristotle as if he had radically different teachings for philosophers (or potential philosophers) and for those who are incapable of accepting the harsh truths about human life, or who are simply incapable of living the best human life. There are

Of course, it is the middle-aged, whom Aristotle proceeds to discuss in the *Rhetoric*, who "have the advantages that youth and old age possess separately." They are those "in the prime of life [*akmazontes*]" who are in the middle of the extremes, neither "too confident" nor "too fearful," Aristotle explains, "neither stingy nor prodigal," neither "trusting everyone" nor "distrusting all," but "judging according to the truth." They "live with a view to neither the beautiful alone, nor the useful alone, but with a view to both" (*Rhetoric* 1390a29–b9). They do not see life as simply free, as the young who look to the future tend to do. Nor do they see life as less free than it is, like the old who focus on a past that they cannot change. If Aristotle is describing his preferred listeners for the *Ethics*, does he expect to find them often? Why does a human being reach a prime rather than

---

many weighty defenses (and variations) of this approach, for example, Tessitore, *Reading Aristotle's "Ethics,"* 17; Burger, *Aristotle's Dialogue with Socrates*, 3–4; Bartlett, "Aristotle's Introduction to the Problem of Happiness," 679–86; and Pangle, *Reason and Character*, 9–12, 23–24, 49–50. Bartlett, "Aristotle's Introduction to the Problem of Happiness," 677, 682–84, contrasts those to whom Aristotle offers a solution about happiness that satisfies their deepest hopes—that is, he offers them an "official" teaching that is "finally inadequate"—with those to whom he reveals that happiness is not possible. I argue, in contrast, that Aristotle attempts to foster the character that belongs to the prime of life, rather than offering unfounded hopes that are typical of the young or encouraging the resignation typical of the old. The word Aristotle uses for "being in the prime of life" could be translated as "flourishing" or "blooming" (*akmazein*). Similarly, Pangle, *Reason and Character*, 49–50, argues that Aristotle writes so as to speak at the same time to "the majority of people," for whom he defends "the active moral life" because it is "the best possible" for them, and to those "with a theoretical bent" who are "averse to self-deception" and whom he encourages to concentrate on the highest. In my example above, in contrast, the old and the young (whether in age or character) get the same advice, "the attempt must be made," and what they learn from following it could bring them closer together rather than keep them apart. Consider Aristotle's famous example of ethical virtue as a mean between two extremes. His description of the virtuous middle addresses both those who incline to one extreme and those who incline to the other. The mean differs from individual to individual, to be sure, but the desirability of the mean is true for all. I thus agree with Mara's suggestion that we should understand Aristotle's audience as representing continuous human possibilities rather than distinct types of human beings. Mara, "*Logos* of the Wise," 850–55, gives an incisive critique of readings of Aristotle that separate his addressees into potential philosophers and nonphilosophers.

simply become old? How long does one's prime last? Can one prolong it? For the old, Aristotle says in describing them, time is short; for the young, time is long (1389a24 and 1390a9). The former think that they have no time to act, the latter do not know that they must make the most of time. Aristotle does not mention "time" as a problem for those in their prime. It is especially for them that time is a co-worker (see 1098a24).

Aristotle says more about the addressee he is seeking in the *Ethics* when he refers to the "educated person" who seeks the precision that the subject matter warrants, someone who is neither too demanding nor too accepting of what different inquiries offer. He would neither demand demonstrations from a rhetorician nor accept probable speeches from a mathematician (1094b25–26). Aristotle is encouraging his addressees both to accept and demand, and therefore neither to trust everything nor to distrust all, but rather to judge according to the truth—that is, to acquire the good qualities he attributed to those in their prime. Learning to both demand and to accept does not come of necessity from the experience of life, but it might be facilitated by the experience of Aristotle's inquiry, which makes demands on opinions and arguments, accepting less from them when they fall short, and judging when more should be demanded and when less should be accepted.

After Aristotle concludes the "prelude" about his inquiry (its subject matter and its addressees), he turns back to the question of the highest good (1095a13, 14–27). But he immediately digresses again. His course in the *Ethics* does not run straight toward its goal. How or where should one begin an inquiry?, he now asks, even though he has already begun his inquiry. Must one have already experienced a beginning to raise the question of beginnings? In any case, Aristotle is not the first to raise the question of how to begin, he acknowledges. Plato was "well perplexed," Aristotle says. *Eu . . . ēporei* (to be "well perplexed," or to "lack resources in a good way") sounds like *euporei* (to have resources). Aristotle has a good resource in Plato himself, perhaps because Plato was "well perplexed *and investigated*" (1095a35–36).[19] The *Ethics* is a book of both perplexities and resources. Plato is a resource for both.

As to where one must begin, Aristotle claims that we should begin with what is "known to us" (1095b3–4; also *Metaphysics* 1029b5–13). By

---

19. All italics in passages quoted from Aristotle's texts (and from other Greek texts) are my emphases.

implication, we are also beginning with what is "unknown to us," since if we were content with only what we know, there would be no inquiry. We move beyond what is known to us when we inquire. To learn requires questioning the sufficiency of the beginning, or what we know, so that what is known to us might become better known, even if its becoming better known involves coming to know its insufficiency.

Because we need to begin with what is known to us, those who investigate "the beautiful [or noble] and just, and politics generally" must be "beautifully brought up in their habits," for one so brought up "has or easily obtains the principles from which one should begin [*archai*]." In such matters, the "beginning" or "principle" (*archē*) is "the that" (*to hoti*) something is and one does not need "the why" (*to dioti*) in addition (1095b4–8). Correct habits let us experience that the beautiful and the just are good. Of course, beginnings themselves are not sufficient, for they are only beginnings, however much they guide what they begin or ground. And Aristotle has much to say about the beautiful, the just, and the good as the *Ethics* proceeds. What we need "in addition to" the "habituation" that gives us the beginnings or makes it easy for us to acquire them is Aristotle's *Ethics*, which both now and in the books to come contain reflections on habituation and on much more.

Aristotle concludes his digression on the proper beginning by quoting lines from Hesiod about three sorts of human beings. In this way, he reflects further on the human beings he is addressing in the *Ethics*, and by implication where he himself must begin. Hesiod speaks of (1) the one who by himself understands all things, (2) the one who is persuaded by one who speaks well, and (3) the useless person who neither understands by himself nor takes to heart what he hears from another (1095b10–14; *Works and Days* 295–97). As he quotes Hesiod on these three types, Aristotle asks the third type, the one who neither has himself the first principles nor can easily attain them from another, to heed or listen to (*akouein*) to these lines, as if he could take them to heart. Aristotle does not heed Hesiod in dismissing this third type as someone who cannot hear another who speaks well. If the third type follows Aristotle's advice to listen to Hesiod, he would heed Aristotle himself. He would heed one who speaks well, and if he noted Aristotle's speaking to him and his listening to his advice, he would also understand that the one who speaks well in this instance could not be Hesiod.

Aristotle, as he appears in the *Ethics*, moreover, does not fit perfectly into any of the three types Hesiod mentions. We might suppose that the first of the three types describes him, but Aristotle does not claim to understand all things by himself, or even to understand all things. Hesiod's description of the second type, however, requires a fourth type: if someone is persuaded by another because he speaks well, there is someone who speaks well and persuades. This fourth type appears when one heeds or listens well to Hesiod.[20] Time and again throughout the *Ethics*, Aristotle finds in the lines of poets, in the opinions he discusses, and in what human beings say and do, truths that they themselves do not fully express or perhaps even understand. Aristotle does not understand "by himself," for he both learns from others and shares what he learns with them.

WAYS OF LIFE AND ARISTOTLE'S WAY: FRIENDSHIP, TRUTH, AND PHILOSOPHY

When Aristotle resumes his inquiry into the good that we seek, he examines different ways of life. Even though all agree that the highest good is happiness, he points out, they disagree about what happiness is, sometimes even saying one thing at one time, another at another (1095b30–1096a1). He therefore investigates not only what people say, but what they do, the different lives they choose to live. Among these, he observes, three are prominent: enjoyment or pleasure; the political life; and the theoretical or contemplative life (1095b17–19).

Many pursue a life of pleasure, but the life of pleasure with no further qualification is characteristic of cattle. The life of politics, in contrast, demands more attention. Those "active" (*praktikoi*) in their cities identify happiness with honor, for honor is "pretty much the end of the political life." Honor, however, is too superficial a good for what is being sought, Aristotle explains, since it depends on those who bestow it more than on the one on whom it is bestowed. And "we divine that the good is our own

---

20. Howland, "Aristotle's Great-Souled Man," 49n35, observes that the question of who belongs to Hesiod's first or third classes seems analogous to "the question of whether he who is without a *polis* is a beast or a god." If the analogy is intended by Hesiod, then he approaches Aristotle's view: human beings fall into two classes rather than three—those who speak well and those able to hear them.

and not easily taken away." Moreover, those who pursue honor do so in order that "they might trust their own goodness." That is why they desire to be honored by those with good sense or prudence (*phronimoi*)[21] and by those who know them (1095b20–28). That is, they themselves must trust those who honor them if they are to be satisfied by the honor they receive. Their goodness, then, could not alone constitute happiness, for they must also trust that they are good, even if their trust requires trusting others who recognize their goodness.

Moreover, since lovers of honor want to be honored for their virtue, Aristotle continues, they themselves acknowledge that there is something higher than honor, namely, virtue. Lovers of honor are therefore mistaken in viewing honor as the highest good and cause of happiness, but their own deeds—they seek to be honored *for their virtue*—serve as the evidence that refutes them and point toward what happiness itself is. Virtue alone, however, cannot be the highest good, Aristotle argues, since one could be virtuous while asleep, or while being inactive throughout life, or while suffering the greatest misfortunes. Only virtue that is active makes happiness possible (1095b33–1096a1). Of course, those who are asleep are not only inactive. They are also unaware of their virtue or goodness, and thus of their happiness.[22]

The third of the prominent ways of life is the theoretical or contemplative (*theōrētikos*), which Aristotle immediately and enigmatically defers to "an investigation that follows." Although no explicit investigation follows, at least any time soon, Aristotle does use the verb *theōrein* in what follows throughout the *Ethics* when he investigates a wide range of activities. *Theōrein* means "to see," "to behold," or "to be a spectator," and

---

21. In book 6, Aristotle identifies prudence as one of the primary intellectual virtues, a virtue concerned with human goods about which it is possible to deliberate and which are attained through action (1141b8–14). It is often translated as "practical wisdom." Here Aristotle seems to use *phronimos* broadly to mean someone whose judgment can be trusted because he is sensible or thoughtful. Wisdom (*sophia*) is the other intellectual virtue along with prudence that Aristotle discusses in book 6 (e.g., 1143b18–19). That lovers of honor look to the prudent rather than to the wise foreshadows Aristotle's later distinction between the two.

22. Block, "The Problem of Good Fortune," 10–11. For Aristotle's treatment of love of honor and virtue, see also Block and Cain, "Good, Truth, and Friendship," 13–34.

Aristotle uses it in these senses, as when he says in book 1 that the work of a statesman includes observing (*theōrein*) the soul (1102a23–24).[23] In book 4, the one who possesses the ethical virtue of munificence "contemplates" what expenditures are fitting to his virtue (1122a35–36). In book 6, Aristotle refers to the rational soul as contemplating not only eternal things but also those that admit of variation (1139a8), and hence that demand deliberation and choice. Thus prudent people are able "to see" (*theōrein*) good things for themselves and others (1140b9). Friends are better able "to contemplate" their friend's actions than their own, and the memories and hopes shared by friends give them pleasant "objects of contemplation" (1169b32–1170a1, 1166a11 and 23–26). Moreover, as Aristotle's own investigation in the *Ethics* proceeds, we too "theorize" along with Aristotle. Speaking in the first-person plural, Aristotle points out that "we contemplate" happiness and that "we" grasp prudence by "contemplating" those said to be prudent (1102a8, 1140a24). More broadly, we are theorizing about virtue itself as we make our way through the *Ethics*, even if our goal is to act virtuously, not only to contemplate or know what virtue is (1179a35–b4). By not investigating the "theoretical life" immediately or directly, Aristotle is able to show the activity of *theōrein* throughout human life.[24]

So too does the life of politics belong to all of us, insofar as we are political by nature and seek not only to be good but also to trust that we are so. And we shall see that Aristotle will attach pleasure, which he so summarily dismissed as belonging to a life fit for cattle, to myriad human ac-

---

23. No one English word corresponds to Aristotle's many uses of *theōrētikos* and *theōrein*. Their transliteration as "theoretical" and "theorize" suggests producing theories, while "contemplative" and "contemplate," as the words are traditionally translated, connote a meditative or spiritual way of life removed from the many activities with which Aristotle associates it. With these reservations, I will use one or the other as best captures in English Aristotle's meaning in the particular passage, sometimes adding the Greek word in parentheses as a reminder of the word Aristotle uses. Sherman, *The Fabric of Character*, 90, suggests the breadth of Aristotle's use of the word, with meanings ranging from "see" to "investigate" or "consider." She opts to translate it as "study." Roochnik, *Retrieving Aristotle*, 229n45, points out that a computer search will reveal that in the Aristotelian corpus "inflections of *theōrein* are ubiquitous and often mundane."

24. On the basis of similar observations, Roochnik, *Retrieving Aristotle*, 185, suggests that "human being is by nature theoretical."

tivities, such as the activity of the virtues, friendship, and indeed theorizing itself (1099a6–30, 1169b30–35, 1177a23–25). Aristotle concludes his survey of ways of life by mentioning a fourth, that of moneymaking, but is quick to dismiss any identification of wealth with happiness, for wealth "is not the good being sought, but something useful for the sake of something else" (1096a6–8). It too, by implication, could accompany many ways of life, as could theorizing or contemplating, and even to various degrees be necessary for them.

Aristotle turns next to "the universal good," which explains why other things are good, to explore whether it could be the good that is sought. He prefaces this discussion by reference to his own inquiry again, and even to his own life, which is more comprehensive than any of the lives just mentioned, if only because it involves friendship. His self-reflection comes as a digression rather than as part of his list of those lives that are "most prominent" (1095b18). And it is prompted when he turns to criticize the ideas of those whom he counts as his friends. Friendship demands he explain himself—since he is going to criticize their ideas.[25] He recognizes the obligations of friendship, but friendship does more than merely impose an obligation, it poses a dilemma, since to criticize friends "goes against the grain." The dilemma is ours too, but it belongs "*especially* to a philosopher" to reject one's "own" (*ta oikeia*), for "the preservation of the truth."[26] "Although both the truth and one's own are dear, it is pious [or holy] to honor the truth first" (1096a11–17). This is the first time that Aristotle mentions philosophy in the *Ethics*, and he appeals to it to defend why he does what he does. He does what philosophers should do. Moreover, this is the only time in the *Ethics* that Aristotle calls something "pious" or "holy." Honoring the truth before one's own is what philosophers do and what Aristotle is currently doing. He connects piety with his own philosophic activity and way of life.

Why does Aristotle speak of his honoring the truth above all as "pious"? He gives no definition. There is a striking example of Aristotle's use of this adjective in the *Politics* when he criticizes the community of women and children in Plato's *Republic* on the grounds that it would allow

---

25. See Aquinas, *Commentary on Aristotle's "Nicomachean Ethics,"* 24.
26. For further discussion of Aristotle's references here to friends and philosophy, and one's own and truth, see Block and Cain, "Good, Truth, and Friendship," 13–34.

heinous crimes (including incest) between parents and offspring, since fathers and mothers, sons and daughters would not be known to one another. Crimes in such cases would be "impious," he observes (1262a26–41). Aristotle's criticism bypasses a possible defense: if all members of the preceding generation are considered one's parents, and all members of one's own generation are considered one's siblings, refraining from crimes against family members would mean avoiding crimes against everyone. By ignoring this argument, Aristotle implicitly denies the assumption of the arrangements of the *Republic*—that "one's own" can be stretched in this manner by institutions and laws that find no limits in human nature. The attempt to do so, Aristotle suggests, both assumes a divine-like control over (human) nature and reduces human life to that of beasts. In Aristophanes's *Clouds*, Phidippides captures both the arrogance and degradation of incest when he defends father-beating (and implicitly incest) by claiming that he "was born free" and also that "the beasts do it" (1414, 1425–29). The institutions of the *Republic*'s city, from this perspective, not only destroy the city by not recognizing differences between generations, but also destroy the even more weighty differences between divine, human, and bestial. Unholy crimes come from other unholy crimes. Piety preserves those distinctions, and therefore preserves the human.[27]

Whether or not Plato and Aristotle disagree concerning incest, however, there's one way in which Aristotle acknowledges his agreement with Plato: his statement that it is pious to honor the truth before one's own echoes Socrates's claims in the *Republic* that "a man is not to be honored before the truth" (595c) and "it is not pious to betray what seems to be truth" (607c). To be deceived in one's soul about the most important things is a violation of life, a violation of *human* life or soul, with its capacity for truth and therewith its direction toward and by truth. As Aristotle says of himself and Plato, they are not only philosophers but also friends. And thus Aristotle does not merely echo his friend, but he responds to him,

---

27. Aristotle refers to "piety" a second time in the *Politics* when he claims that it is not "pious" to abort a fetus if it has "perception" and "life" (1335b25). Aristotle is obviously not providing specifics about when life occurs but revealing a principle: human life itself is holy, given to us to be protected and nurtured, not to be controlled and destroyed, a principle that presumably reflects back on other issues, such as rearing maimed children (see 1135bb20).

adding that "one's own" as well as the truth are dear (see also *Politics* 1262b22–24). When Aristotle states that one's own and the truth are both dear (*philoin*), the context suggests that they are dear to him, or friends to him who loves them, but his words could also be read as if they were friends to each other. He speaks of them in the dual. He sees them as a pair through his love of them. Contrary to the implication of Socrates's statements in the *Republic*, "honoring the truth first" is for Aristotle not at odds with loving one's own. Aristotle's specific criticisms of the ideas confirm this.

We have seen that Aristotle claims, when criticizing the lover of honor for locating his good outside himself (in what is bestowed by others), that "we divine that the good is our own [*oikeion*] and not easily taken away" (1095b24–26). It is a divination that continues to guide Aristotle's inquiry when he criticizes his friends, for they err in placing the good so far outside human life as to make it inaccessible. They too would benefit from the divination that corrects the lover of honor. After all, both the truth *and* one's own are dear.

In his reference to those who "introduce the ideas," curiously, Aristotle does not refer to Plato by name, as he does in other works, such as the *Metaphysics* where he also criticizes Plato's "ideas" (987a30–b15). We might suppose that this is a concession to friendship appropriate to an *Ethics*, for in criticizing the argument of a friend one would spare him by not mentioning his name. But Aristotle is not merely leaving the friend he criticizes anonymous, he refers to a group—"men who introduced the ideas." Perhaps his doing so suggests that his criticism bypasses Plato himself, and captures only his followers, those who have been persuaded by one whom they suppose speaks well. After all, when he does refer to Plato earlier by name, he praises him for being perplexed (1095a34)— something that does not seem to characterize the ones who introduced the ideas, as Aristotle presents them now, even if he himself will soon find many "perplexities" in what they say about the ideas (1096a12). He criticizes those who introduce the ideas, specifically, for reducing individuals to their class: the simple, universal idea of what all the members of a class have in common, and thus neglecting what distinguishes the members of a class, and hence what is their own, what is particular to each. When Aristotle refers to those who introduce the ideas, in effect forgetting about Plato, Aristotle illustrates the effect of the theory he is rejecting.

Among the perplexities that Aristotle finds is how the good as such differs from other goods insofar as they are good. And if there is no difference between the idea of the good and other goods, he asks, of what use is it in understanding the good? (1096a1–5). On the other hand, Aristotle's argument goes, if the good as such differs radically from the goodness of all other goods, how could it have anything in common with them? Would those who speak of the good as such not speak of what is "beyond themselves," like those whom the ignorant admire (see 1095a25–26)? Indeed, Aristotle asks, could all the things we consider good be truly good if being truly good characterizes only the idea itself? Would the good not end up being an empty class? From this perspective, "there would be nothing else good except the idea, with the result that the idea would be pointless" (1096b18–21). It would explain nothing but itself.

Aristotle's argument against the ideas resembles the one that Plato himself gives to his character Parmenides in the dialogue bearing his name (*Parmenides* 132d–134c). Aristotle has learned the problems with the ideas from Plato himself. He too listens to one who speaks well. His apparent "critique" implicitly acknowledges Plato's insight into the difficulty of connecting the permanent ideas or classes that make sense of our experience with the very experience of imperfect and changing goods we are trying to understand and judge.[28] We want to know that the many things we desire are good, and why they are so, so that we can choose among them, attain what is good for ourselves, and thereby become happy.[29]

So too, if all goods are identical insofar as they are good, we have no cause to single anyone out as an object of love. On the other hand, if only the idea of the good is good, we have no cause to love anyone or anything

---

28. As Aristotle observes in the *Metaphysics*, Plato claims that the many things that have the same name as the ideas exist by participation in them, but he left it open as to what this participation means (987b10–15). See Burger, *The "Phaedo,"* 150; Zuckert, "Socratic Turn," 196–98; and Zuckert, *Plato's Philosophers*, 185–89.

29. Davis, *Soul of the Greeks*, 68, asks whether Aristotle's criticisms of the idea of the good apply to his own presentation of happiness. Without denying that there may be similarities between Aristotle's account of happiness as the supreme good and the idea of the good Aristotle criticizes, Davis points out that "the good-itself" is spoken about in a way that "leaves the impression that it is altogether independent of soul," whereas happiness "makes manifest the relation between the good and the soul."

except it. But Aristotle has just said that both the truth *and friends* are dear. His statement thus anticipates his need to explain the good in a way that does not undermine our experience of what is dear, of what we love.[30] What Aristotle presents as going against the grain of friendship, his critique of the idea of the good, is also required by the truth that friendship manifests insofar as friends are loved for themselves, and not just as an expression of a universal idea in which others also share.

By implication of Aristotle's critique, Plato's "idea of the good" would deny satisfaction to the statesman whom Aristotle has just described. If only the idea of the good is good, the statesman cannot be good, or if he is good, his goodness would be identical to every other good, insofar as it is good, and hence it would not be his own. And yet we "divine that the good is our own and not easily be taken away." Aristotle's observation, which occurs just before his discussion of the idea of the good, prepares for his critique of the idea of the good. When Aristotle turns in the next section of the *Ethics* to his own definition of happiness, it is more consistent with what "we divine," even if it acknowledges the power of chance to give and take away.

Aristotle brings his discussion of the ideas to a conclusion by admitting that despite the perplexities he has pointed out, good things do not bear the same name by chance. The different things spoken of as good might all come from one good, they might all contribute to one good, or they might be spoken of as good by way of analogy: as sight is to the body, for example, so mind is to the soul (1096b27–30). He acknowledges here that there are different ways of speaking of the good, and presumably awareness (sight and mind) is not a random or chance example of an analogy (see 1170a16–18). Aristotle moves on from those who introduce the ideas to his own inquiry about the good by observing that "perhaps to be more precise about the good belongs more to another [work of] philosophy" (1096b31). The word Aristotle uses for "belong to" is *oikeioteron*, or "to be at home in." There is no transcendence of one's own (*oikeion*), not even by a philosophy that might provide greater precision about the good. Although some commentators assume that Aristotle is referring to his *Metaphysics* as the "other philosophy" that might investigate the good

---

30. Aristotle says in the *Metaphysics* that "arguments about the ideas abolish things that we wish there to be, more than we wish there to be ideas" (990b19).

more precisely,[31] in that work as in the *Ethics* Aristotle warns that the "precise speech of mathematics should not be demanded in all things" (995a15–16). Whatever precision Aristotle thought possible for his inquiry in the *Metaphysics*, his speaking there about the good would presumably seek only that precision that its subject matter warrants.

In any case, Aristotle insists, whether the idea of the good refers to what is common to all the goods or whether to "something separate and itself by itself," it would be "neither attainable by action [*prakton*] nor able to be acquired [or possessed] [*ktēton*] by a human being." But "such is the good that is being sought [*zēteitai*]" (1096b33–36). The adjective *ktētos* comes from the verb "to acquire," which means "to possess" in the perfect tense (one who has acquired something possesses it). In Greek, a "possession" is one's own that has not always been one's own, for it has been acquired. The good that is the object of "our search" might be one that we make our own by our efforts; it is in this sense "our own," and it may be so in the way that those things we acquire by our own efforts are even more "our own" than what we are simply given (see 1120b12–14). And yet at least in theory the good that has not always been our own could be lost, even if not "easily" taken away. But it is not "separate and itself by itself," a phrase that Aristotle rejects here in criticizing the good as such.[32]

---

31. Burnet, *Ethics of Aristotle*, 29, suggests that Aristotle refers to "first philosophy," or metaphysics. See also Rackham, *Aristotle: "Nicomachean Ethics,"* 22n. But we have no reason to suppose that Aristotle is referring to another work of his own by "another philosophy." A philosophy that is more precise about the good runs the risk of neglecting Aristotle's argument about precision. He might therefore mean that a philosophy that is more precise about the good that belongs to "another" philosophy is one that is "other than," i.e., "different from" his own.

32. Aristotle uses the same phrase here that he uses in the *Metaphysics* when he asks whether the whole contains the "highest good" as its order (*taxis*) or as something "separate and itself by itself." He appeals to an analogy between the whole and an army, whose good resides both in its order and in the general who effects that order. So does the highest good belong to the whole "in both ways" (*Metaphysics* 1075a11–15). The good belongs to the whole, then, not only as its order, but as its cause. Even as cause, it is not separate from the whole, "itself by itself." The activity of the general cannot be understood apart from the army that he orders. Aristotle thus uses a human, even political, example to illustrate the relation between the good and the cosmos. This is not the only time in the *Metaphysics* that Aristotle turns to a human analogy to understand the whole (consider, for example, his recourse to the household, at 1075a18–22). His recourse to such

Aristotle's investigation of what others say about happiness and the good—and the ways of life that they pursue—seems to clear the way for his own definition of happiness in the next part of book 1. That investigation, however, has taught us several things on which his discussion will build. His reservations against the statesman's pursuit of honor lead almost to the very definition of happiness that he himself soon gives, since the statesman desires to be honored for his virtuous deeds, and therefore acts as if virtuous actions were a higher good than honor. And from Aristotle's analysis of the desire for honor, we understand that human beings do not simply seek to be virtuous but also to trust that they are so, and their trust depends on their trusting others. Self-knowledge is also necessary for happiness. His prefacing his investigation of the universal good with revelations about himself puts forth another way of life for our consideration—one that combines friendship, philosophy, and honoring the truth. These reflections on what he holds dear or loves, and therefore on what is known to himself (see 1095b3–4), support his criticisms of the universal good. Those criticisms set the stage for his seeking a good that (unlike the universal good he criticized) might be acquired by human beings and attained through action.

HAPPINESS AND THE HUMAN WORK

Aristotle proceeds to establish that happiness is the best and complete good that we seek. Goods that are chosen as means to something else are incomplete, for they would be completed by their end, whereas we choose

---

analogies raises the question of the relation between his philosophizing about the human things and his more theoretical inquiries, and even suggests the dependence of the latter on the former. Winthrop, *Democracy and Political Science*, 7, 18, finds that the questions Aristotle discusses in the *Metaphysics*—for example, What is being? Is there a whole or a cosmos? What are the first principles or causes?—are at work in his political works. She makes her case primarily with reference to the *Politics*, through a commentary on book 3 of that work. She argues that "the philosopher learn[s] about wholes and being only from taking the political seriously." By implication, Aristotle's own *Metaphysics* would be informed, even guided, by his political thought. For my reflections on her book, see my review in Nichols, review of *Aristotle: Democracy and Political Science*, 107–18.

happiness "on account of itself and never on account of anything else." To be sure, "we choose honor, pleasure, [the activity of] intellect or mind [*nous*], and every virtue on their own account," but "we choose them also for the sake of happiness, for we suppose that through them we will be happy" (1097a26–b7). Happiness completes the other goods we seek. It is those goods, in fact, that we choose, not happiness itself, as Aristotle later clarifies (1111b28–30). When Aristotle says that we choose them "for the sake of happiness" (1097b5–7), he uses *charin* rather than other prepositions often translated "on account of" or "for the sake of" (e.g., *dia* or *heneka*). Etymologically related to *chara* ("joy") and *charein* ("to delight in" or "to take joy in"), *charis* means "grace" or "graciousness," almost as if we choose goods that grace us with happiness, as if happiness were a sort of grace that accompanies good choices.[33] We may merit it, to be sure, if we make good choices, but we experience it less as a product of our activity than as a gift that comes along with it. "All is arranged for the best" not simply because we are able to choose goods and act to bring them about, but also because happiness graces them, because they bring us "joy."

So too Aristotle is now able to bring back honor and pleasure, which he dismissed earlier in discussing what people believe to be happiness, as goods that might contribute to happiness, including them along with "mind" or "intellect" and "every virtue" that are chosen "for the joy of" happiness. After all, there are pleasures that human beings experience that are unavailable to cattle, such as those that accompany noble actions (1099a11–17). That the pursuit of honor makes the statesman dependent on those who confer it—and hence qualifies his self-sufficiency—does

---

33. For discussion of the evolution of *charin* from a noun in the accusative case to a preposition, see MacLachlan, *The Age of Grace*, appendix 2, "The Prepositional Use of *Charin*," 161–64. Thus *charis* in the accusative case followed by a genitive would mean "in regard to the grace of happiness." MacLachlan points out that its use as a preposition "retains little of the semantic color of the word," and that nothing of its original meaning of "grace" was left, but only a "dead metaphor" (ibid., 161, 164). She is looking at early Greek poetry, however, not writing about Aristotle, who is capable of reviving dead metaphors. In his translation of *Aristotle's "Metaphysics,"* at 1050a9–10, Sachs recognizes this meaning of *charin* used as a preposition, when he renders the passage "the being-at-work is an end, and it is for the enjoyment of [*charin*] this that potency is taken on" (178).

not preclude honor's contribution to happiness. Indeed, if he were self-sufficient, he would not pursue honor, and therefore not experience the happiness that it brings.

Aristotle turns directly to what self-sufficiency means for human beings: it does not mean "what suffices for someone by himself, living a solitary life, but with respect to parents, children, a wife, and, in general, friends and fellow-citizens, since by nature a human being is political" (1097b8–12). In explaining just how many goods are required for human self-sufficiency, Aristotle also indicates how great human insufficiency is, and on how many others our happiness depends, just as happiness can grace the goods we choose only if we attain them. Since self-sufficiency "extends to ancestors and descendants, and friends of friends, it will go to infinity" and so "a boundary [*horos*] must be drawn [*lēpteos*]" (or "a limit must be grasped") (1097b12–15). Aristotle does not address where that boundary lies. Presumably it varies according to particular cases.[34]

Aristotle next attempts to clarify how we become happy by examining "the work [*to ergon*] of a human being." Aristotle thus implies that one is happy when one does one's work well, "just as a flute player, a sculptor, and every artisan has a work, and his good lies in doing his work well" (1097b28). Happiness for Aristotle, it almost goes without saying, is not a subjective feeling, as is assumed by surveys that ask individuals whether they are happy. Happiness is possible only for one who does well the work or task that belongs to a human being qua human.[35] What, then,

---

34. Bartlett, "Aristotle's Introduction to the Problem of Happiness," 680, 684, argues that Aristotle begins with what we seek in happiness—completeness and self-sufficiency—in order to reveal hopes that can only be disappointed. He concludes that the teaching of book 1 is "at once most fundamental and least obvious"—that "'the human good' is not indeed happiness." Beings who are subject to death cannot be happy. See also Pangle, *Reason and Character*, 30–37: in this section of the *Ethics* on happiness, Aristotle "invites his most philosophic students to ponder how much of what we want is neither coherent nor possible." My emphasis, in contrast, is less on how Aristotle is disappointing hopes than on how he is teaching ways in which they can be satisfied. Contrary to readings that suggest that Aristotle's philosophy despairs of happiness, I find in book 1 a call to search for happiness that requires hope tempered by experience and reflection.

35. Many scholars have in recent times translated *eudaimonia* as "flourishing" rather than as "happiness." Roochnik, *Retrieving Aristotle*, 157, points out a

is the human work? Aristotle looks to what belongs to human beings, as distinct from other animals, ruling out nutrition, growth, and sense perception, which other animals share, and arriving at reason. From here, he concludes that the work of a human being is the activity of soul in conformity with (*kata*) reason, and that human beings do this work well when they do it with the virtues proper to the work. In this way, he arrives at a definition of the human good (and therewith happiness): "an activity [*energeia*; or "being-at-work"] of the soul in accord with virtue, and if there are several virtues, then in accord with the best and most complete" (1097b33–1098a18).[36]

If this is a definition, it nevertheless begs for further definition, as Aristotle makes explicit when he leaves open whether virtue is one or many, and what makes a virtue best and whether that also makes a virtue more complete. In this sense, Aristotle's definition thus contains questions that prompt the rest of the *Ethics*. Aristotle's use of *energeia* for activity is also striking. Although the adjective *energos* occurs in Greek literature, meaning "to be in working (condition)" or to be "at work" (*en* + *ergon*), Aristotle seems to be the first to use the noun. He uses it in a special way, to capture an activity distinct from a movement or a motion, as he makes clear later in the *Ethics*. A motion occurs over time and is not complete until it has reached its end, as when we walk to a destination, or build a house, or learn, whereas an activity is whole or complete at any moment it occurs, as in seeing, or understanding, to use Aristotle's examples. It occurs in time, to be sure, but it does not become more complete over time, he explains. Thus we might come to see or understand slowly or quickly, but once we have done so there is no quickness or slowness in the activity of seeing or understanding. Quickness and slowness belong to motion (1174a15–74b14; *Metaphysics* 1048b28–40; *De Anima* 431a7–8).

---

good reason for doing so, since Aristotle uses it to refer to "an objective condition." For a thoughtful discussion, see Clark, *Aristotle's Man*, 145–63. As Kass, "Professor or Friend?," 11, formulates it, Aristotle "grounds our happiness . . . in our own peculiar activity: happiness is 'humaning' well. If only we could discover what 'humaning well' means."

36. The preposition *kata* I translate here as "in accord with" is as vague in Greek as it is in English. It could also be translated as "in conformity with" or "in accordance with."

When Aristotle introduces *energeia* into his definition of the human work, using a word not found in common parlance, he implies that we have not understood our own work as human beings. We at least have had hitherto no word that identifies it and thereby helps us to understand it. His calling the human work an *energeia* locates it in something that does not depend on time for its completion, as building a house would do. What is characteristically human, the human work, involves touching the timeless from a standpoint in time, as would an act for the sake of the beautiful or for its own sake, rather than for any consequences that come from it (1105a33, 1116a12). *Energeia* nevertheless requires an explanation, which Aristotle delays until he discusses pleasure in book 7, and more fully in book 10 (e.g., 1153a9–14, 1173a28–b8, 1174a13–b13), and thus after he has discussed the virtues. His introduction of *energeia* as the human work and his later explanation occur in the course of his own work, the *Ethics*, which is more like a motion than an activity, since its author like a housebuilder moves step by step toward its completion.

Aristotle, it seems, is attempting to understand human life in terms of both the eternal and the temporal, looking for ways so to speak of bringing us into contact with the eternal without severing us from our temporal lives, for human beings have access to the eternal only through their experiences in time, even though their temporal lives make them aware of the limits of their experience of the eternal. Oedipus's tragedy can be understood as arising from his blindness to those limits. When he answers the riddle of the Sphinx, for example, he sees the human being who abides throughout the temporal changes of human life—first crawling on all fours, then walking upright, and later using a cane as he ages. His answer suffices to destroy the Sphinx, but it is not sufficient to understand himself, or even to preserve Thebes, as he learns in time. His answer to the Sphinx reflects his crimes of patricide and incest—which deny the need to regularize the succession of generations over time and therewith human mortality. Aristotle's definition of the human work, in contrast, does not require collapsing our manifold appearances in time to understand the human. Nature is growth, with multiple causes, and human nature must be completed in more than one way by human beings themselves. There are many virtuous actions that aim at the beautiful and many ways of attaining the truth, as Aristotle will recount in book 6, all of which bear on self-knowledge. The incompleteness of Aristotle's statement about the human good is its saving grace. As we have seen from his description of the young, old, and those in their prime in the *Rhetoric*, young and old are not the same. That is why they can learn from each other. Aristotle is more like the Sphinx, who asks the question, than like Oedipus, who gives a one-word answer. Aristotle understands even the prime of life only by examining the experiences of the young and old.

Aristotle brings incompleteness to his definition of the human in another sense: he reminds us of time. Happiness is the activity of soul in accord with virtue over a "complete" life. Happiness may not become more complete over time, but it must last a lifetime. One swallow, he observes, does not make a spring, nor does one day, and a short time does not make one blessed or happy. But what makes a life complete? Does death "complete" life? Does chance draw a boundary around one's life, with one's birth and death? With Aristotle's reference to "a complete life" as a requirement for happiness, death enters into his treatment of happiness.[37] At this point, Aristotle digresses, and reflects once more on his own inquiry in the *Ethics*, but now on the way in which his own work is itself limited by time and death.

Aristotle now acknowledges the incompleteness of his account of the good and its need for further elaboration. "Let the good be sketched in this way," he says of his discussion, "for perhaps one must outline it first, and fill it in later" (1098a21–22). The verb he uses for "sketch," *perigraphein*, implies that he has drawn a line "around" the subject, showing its "out" lines or boundaries, marking a shape that must then be filled in. Although Aristotle fills in his "definition" as he discusses the virtues in

---

37. In the *Metaphysics*, when Aristotle discusses different meanings of "complete" (*teleion*), he refers to one of them as an end (*telos*), that for the sake of which other things are means. "Metaphorically" (*kata metaphoran*) death is called an end because it too is an "ultimate" or "last" (*eschaton*) (1021b28–30). He appears to mean that just as the end for which other things are means is the last of a series, death is the last in a series of moments of a life. There, of course, he is not discussing happiness, as he is in the *Ethics*. By raising the question of whether the fortunes of the living can make the dead unhappy, as we shall see, he suggests that death may not be simply the "last" or "the end." On the other hand, from the perspective of a human life, calling death an end may not be simply "a metaphor." Aristotle does not use this expression in the *Ethics* when he refers to death as an "end" of life.

subsequent books of the *Ethics*, he indicates here that this work is not his alone, and that it will not be completed within the confines of the *Ethics* itself, and perhaps not even within the confines of his own lifetime. "It would seem to belong to everyone to carry forward and articulate [the project] if the sketch is well done," he admits, "and time is a good discoverer of such things and a co-worker [*sunergos*]" (1098a21–25). Like the human work itself, as he defines it, Aristotle's own work in the *Ethics* is a work of his soul accompanied by reason. It is one that he offers to share with others, who will in time be his co-workers. If time is a "co-worker," it does not merely cut short one's work by death (cf. *Physics* 221a31–b2). Rather, time allows one's work to be continued by others beyond one's death. Time lets one extend one's life. Even though he speaks of drawing a boundary or limit, Aristotle's sketch is one that opens his work to a future that he does not control. Even near the end of book 10, Aristotle refers to his work as a sketch or outline (1176a30–31 and 1179a34–35). Outlining for others to fill in is Aristotle's way of following his advice "to make oneself as immortal *as possible.*" He earlier used immortality as an example of something we can only wish for but not choose since it is not within our power (cf. 1177b34 with 111b21–23). His work is thus characterized more by the hopefulness of youth than the pessimism of age, even if that hopefulness is tempered by such difficulties he mentions throughout, from the limits of persuasion to the power of chance.

In the context of this digression on his own work, Aristotle reiterates that one must accept and demand the precision appropriate to the inquiry. This time he illustrates his point not with the difference between a rhetorician and a mathematician, but with that between a carpenter and a geometer. His earlier example turned on a difference of the subject matter, whereas this one turns on the purpose of the inquiry. The former investigates the right angle "to the extent that it is useful to his work," the latter investigates "what or what sort a thing it is," for he is a spectator (*theatēs*) of the truth (1098a27–33). Aristotle uses a word applied to the spectator at a theater, as if the geometer were satisfied by seeing rather than acting, staying on the sidelines rather than playing a part. As Aristotle soon observes, only those who compete are crowned at the Olympic Games, for "those acting obtain the beautiful and good things in life" (1098b30–1099a6). In his contrast between the carpenter and geometer, it is to the former Aristotle attributes a "work." Both seek to understand the right angle, but it is only the carpenter who understands from his work the use to which it can be put. The carpenter's knowledge may be less precise than the geometer's knowledge, but the carpenter knows what the geometer does not—what the right angle is good for, or why it is good.[38] The carpenter's work comes closer to Aristotle's, for without reflection on the good, one could not judge between ways of life (the geometer's or the carpenter's, for example), or whether Aristotle's philosophy or some other is worthy of pursuit.

In summary, Aristotle has defined the human work, clearly linking it to the human capacity for reason or speech, and to virtue, regardless how many virtues there are and how they are ordered or ranked. He will have more to say in the next books of the *Ethics* about particular virtues. He mentions, almost in passing, his own work, specifically, his own work in the *Ethics*, which he must leave in outline for others to fill in over time. That is, he moves from the human work, with all its ambiguities, to his own work, which is "known to him" and will become "known to us," as we follow along and in various ways make it our own. Whether the virtuous are happy, he also claims, depends on "a complete life," and more must be said on this. After defining the human work and digressing about his own, Aristotle looks at the effect of chance on human life, which can bring those prospering to misery and even their lives to an end.

---

38. Some scholars understand Aristotle's contrast between two ways of knowing the right angle to support the view that Aristotle thought that there was a second, more precise way of knowing political matters, and that the imprecision of the *Ethics* turns less on its subject matter than on the limitations of his primary audience and his purpose in speaking to them (see Bartlett, "Aristotle's Introduction to the Problem of Happiness," 678–79). Pangle, *Reason and Character*, 18, 46–47, 125, asks whether Aristotle's reference to the imprecision of his inquiry "signals" that he will proceed "not as a careful investigator of one part of nature—human nature—but only as a kind of craftsman or rhetorician," all the while "in some way conveying his deepest reflections on human nature." She finds that Aristotle's imprecision "reproduces the gentleman's imprecision." The attempt to give a mathematical or scientific account of human nature, however, loses the richness and complexity of Aristotle's understanding of human beings, and seems more characteristic of modern political science than of Aristotle's political thought.

LOOKING TO THE END: DIVINE GIVING AND THE POWER OF CHANCE

Having acknowledged the incompleteness of his work and his dependence on others, Aristotle turns to how his definition of the good "harmonizes" with the things that are said about happiness (1098b9–12). His view is consistent with those who say that happiness is virtue, for example, if one adds that happiness resides not in the possession of virtue but in the activity. Aristotle also concedes something to the opinion that identifies happiness with pleasure, since virtuous actions are themselves pleasant for lovers of the beautiful (1099a7–17).

Moreover, although Aristotle continues to deny that happiness lies in external goods, as some assert, he concedes that some external goods are necessary for noble actions, for example, "friends, wealth, and political power." He even admits that happiness could be marred by an unshapely appearance, low birth, childlessness, or unworthy children or friends, or good ones who are lost to death (1099a31–b7). Aristotle's concession to the need for external goods, which alerts us to the diversity of goods that contribute to happiness, at the same time indicates the influence chance has on our lives. Our happiness once again faces a need for a myriad of goods over which we have no control. Aristotle uses tragic language when he refers to the goods of which fortune can make us "bereft" and to the evils that "maim" or "disfigure" our lives (1099b3).[39]

The power of fortune or chance leads to the question "whether happiness comes through learning or habituation or some other practice, or whether it comes as a sort of divine lot [*moira*],[40] or through chance" (1099b9–11). Gods, of course, might protect virtuous human beings from

---

39. As pointed out by Bartlett and Collins, *Aristotle's "Nicomachean Ethics,"* 27n25.

40. Among the meanings of *moira* are "part," "portion," "share," "lot," or "fate." My choice of "lot," which suggests "what is allotted," accords with Aristotle's immediately referring to this option as "a gift of the gods" (*theosdotos*) and "god-sent" (*theopemptos*) (1099b12–15). In Greek mythology, the *Moirai*, the Fates, were three sisters who weaved patterns of lives. In telling the myth of Er in Plato's *Republic*, Socrates refers to them as "daughters of Necessity," to whom souls come to choose their lives before they are born. In spite of the parentage of

the power of chance (ensuring that the just prosper, for example, and the unjust are punished). Aristotle is silent about any divine care that relieves human beings of the burden of chance, but he concedes that "if there were a gift of the gods to human beings, it would be reasonable that it would be [happiness], especially since this is the best of all human things." He goes further: Even if happiness "comes on account of virtue and a certain learning or practice, it appears to be among the most divine things," since "the prize [*to athlon*] of virtue or its end" appears to be "something divine and blessed" (1099b14–18). That is, we have a "divine" lot, even if it is not given to us by the gods and cannot in any way be taken for granted.

Although Aristotle defers the question as to whether happiness is "divinely sent" as "appropriate to another investigation" (1099b14),[41] he explicitly rejects the view that leaves our happiness utterly dependent on the vicissitudes of chance. He appeals, instead, to nature. Since "what accords with nature is in the most beautiful possible state," if it is better for us to be happy "through some learning or practice" than through chance, it is therefore reasonable that this is how our happiness comes to be: "To entrust the greatest and most beautiful thing to chance would be extremely discordant" (1099b24).[42] But if it is better for us to be happy through some learning or practice, would it not also be discordant if our happiness were a gift from the gods? Human beings desire to be happy, but their happiness requires that they also trust their own goodness, as Aristotle's discussion of the love of honor indicates, and therefore they desire to be worthy of their happiness.[43] Aristotle reminds us of this here, when after referring to our happiness as a possible "gift," he calls it the "prize" of virtue. Prizes

---

the Fates, he emphasizes the choice that each soul makes: "the blame belongs to him who chooses; god is blameless" (617c–e).

41. Rackham, *Aristotle: "Nicomachean Ethics,"* 44nb, notes that he does not "reopen the question in the *Metaphysics* or elsewhere."

42. Aristotle makes a similar point in the *Metaphysics*, concerning the cause that some beings are or come to be well and beautifully disposed: "It is not likely that the cause could be fire, or earth, or any such thing, nor that [thinkers] could believe this, nor would it be beautiful to entrust so great a matter [*pragma*] to chance" (984b11–15).

43. Block's analysis ("The Problem of Good Fortune," 1) of Aristotle's view of happiness in the *Ethics* focuses on the human "resistance to providence" that comes from our desire to merit our happiness, or "our desire to be self-sufficient." His reading is consistent with mine, but I emphasize how Aristotle might recon-

are earned for a virtuous life, even if they come as a sort of grace belonging to the life we live. Like the lover of honor Aristotle described, we want our goodness to be our own. It cannot be simply bestowed on us. We must make it our own. What is better accords with nature, but that does not mean that nature arranges all things for the best, securing the good for human beings, but that it is the lot of human beings to do so.[44] If we were so self-sufficient that our virtue—and happiness—were not in question, choices and actions would not be required for our happiness. Our very lack of self-sufficiency allows us to make our goodness our own, even if it leaves us vulnerable to chance. Our happiness cannot come by chance, but chance can take it away. At the end of this discussion, Aristotle refers to Priam, who in the tales about Troy suffered great misfortune as his life neared its end (1100a8–9; Homer, *Iliad* 24.493–501).

The fall of Troy and the miserable end of Priam remind Aristotle of Solon's advice to "look to the end" before you call anyone happy, since anyone living is subject to suffering and disaster. Solon's advice is echoed in the last lines of Sophocles's *Oedipus Tyrannus*, when the chorus concludes from Oedipus's life that "no mortal should be counted happy until he has passed through the end without grief" (1528–30, 1186–88). But waiting until death to call someone happy would be a "altogether strange," Aristotle admits, for someone like himself who claims that happiness is a certain activity (1100a13–14). His bringing up this strange position allows him to distinguish it from his own, which can acknowledge the happiness of those living, at least those living well, and which refuses to concede such an overpowering sway to chance. Although Aristotle himself refers to Priam's misfortune and admits that "the future is not clear" (1101a15), he reminds us of the distinction between the virtuous activity that is authoritative for happiness and the conditions for virtuous activity that can be affected by chance (1100b7–11). He also distinguishes small instances of good and bad fortune, which do not tip the scale of life, from great ones. He claims that when misfortunes are great and deprive one of happiness, the virtuous person bears them more calmly and his nobility or beauty

---

cile us to our lack of self-sufficiency, since that lack is necessary for the happiness that is possible for us.

44. Pangle, *Reason and Character*, 44–45, 57, makes a similar observation, but instead of concluding that nature in this way makes virtue possible, she observes that "nature may not in fact equip us well for virtue."

shines through. He even imagines the person with a great soul who endures immense suffering and eventually regains his happiness after accomplishing great and noble things (1100b8–1101a8). Perhaps most important of all, if our futures were manifest, we would have no choices to make, our virtue would not be up to us, nor would our happiness be our own. Given these various considerations, Aristotle concludes, nothing prevents us from calling those happy who are active in accord with complete virtue in their lifetimes and adequately equipped with external goods. But given that we cannot see their future, we must say not that they are "blessed," but that they are "blessed as human beings" (1101a15–21).

Aristotle nevertheless proceeds to discuss another problem for human happiness that arises from human mortality. Some refuse to call even the dead happy, since their friends, children, and descendants might suffer misfortune, "even if [the deceased] are not aware of it." They say that even those who have died "share in reversals, and become now happy, now wretched again," as the wheel of fortune turns for countless descendants. Others say that "nothing of the affairs of their descendants reach the ancestors," not even for a limited time. Aristotle acknowledges that both positions are "strange." The first implicitly denies that happiness is "something lasting," and "not easily subject to reversals," as he has just argued. Moreover, for Aristotle one's happiness involves one's own virtuous activity and one's awareness of it. The second is too "unfriendly" (*aphilon*) a view, for it discounts the ties that human beings form by their affection or love. Aristotle proposes a middle ground: How those who were dear fare does affect the deceased, but not "in such a way or to such degree" to make the "happy unhappy or those happy who are not" (1100a10–b12, 23–28; 1100a36–1101b9).

Aristotle's speculations about the happiness of the deceased, surprisingly, turns not on whether a human being survives death, which he neither affirms nor denies, or on whether survival entails rewards and punishments for one's deeds, as is the issue in myths typically recounted by Socrates (*Republic* 614c–d; *Gorgias* 523e–524a; *Phaedrus* 256d–257a). By focusing instead on how the fortunes of the living affect the dead, Aristotle turns attention to this life, and the weighty import of our deeds. After all, "faring well" (literally, "doing well"), which Aristotle uses throughout this section (1100b8–12, 1101b6–9), has two meanings, "prospering" and "doing good deeds" (see 1095a19–20 and 1098b22–23). What we do—not merely what happens to us—affects our ancestors, because we are their progeny, they have given us birth, and they have served as models for us. We speak of honoring (or dishonoring) our forebears by the lives we lead. We want to be worthy of them. By the same token, we want to live lives that our own progeny can live up to, both because we have good will for them and because their lives will reflect on our own. We try to be worthy of them, so that they can be worthy of us. The world does not belong only to the living, for the living belong in part to those who have come before, just as those who come later will belong in part to them. What we owe our parents and friends is not wiped away by their deaths. Aristotle's reflections on these "strange" questions leave us with our responsibility to the past and to the future, at least to those who are dear to us. His reflections on the state of our souls after death, paradoxically, urge us to reflect on our present lifetimes, in which our good deeds manifest gratitude to the past and care for the future. His rather imprecise answer that the dead are affected to some extent by the lives of those dear to them encourages the virtuous deeds of the living, and at the same time it acknowledges connections between human beings that not even death can sever.

After lending support to the connections between the living and the dead, the past and the future, Aristotle raises a new question: Is happiness something to be praised or honored? He points out that we praise those who are virtuous and the virtues themselves "in relation to" or "relative to" something. Specifically, we praise virtues because of the actions or works that come from them. In contrast, we do not praise happiness, for it is something "greater and more divine," just as we regard the gods as blessed and happy. We therefore honor happiness, as we do the gods (1101b10–20). By implication, the statesman who pursues honor must settle for praise. Or, rather, the honor that humans receive is analogous to praise. Their goodness is not good simply, but good for something, for others and not least for themselves. When we distinguish honor from praise, reserving the former not only for the gods but also for happiness, we recognize that there is something higher than the praise we merit for our deeds, and yet something that might grace our good deeds. Aristotle is further elaborating his statement that we can be blessed only as human beings.

Aristotle concludes book 1 by returning to politics, with which he began the *Ethics*. He concedes to the statesman's love of honor that his work is an honorable one because he must know about the soul, more specifically, that his work is more honorable than other works, such as medicine, that have to know only about the body (1102a20–21). The statesman's work deserves honor, but only in relation to other things, only as a matter of comparison. This is the way we honor human beings.

THE STATESMAN AND THE SOUL

Having begun with politics as the architectonic art that orders everything in the city, even ordaining who is to learn what and up to what point, Aristotle now turns to the statesman himself, to discuss what he should know and up to what point. This is the next step of his argument, he explains, because the one "truly" a statesman, who wishes to make the citizens good and obedient to the laws, "must somehow know about the soul" since happiness is an activity of the soul in accordance with complete virtue. "We have a model in the lawgivers of the Cretans and Spartans and any others of that sort there might be" (1102a6–18), Aristotle says, but he does not hold up any of their practices for imitation. He appears to be offering a new model.[45]

When investigating what the statesman must learn about the soul, Aristotle begins with a distinction found in "the exoteric speeches [*logoi*]" between the rational (*logon*) and nonrational (*alogon*) parts of the soul. "Exoteric speeches" are literally those that exist "outside," and are thought to refer to arguments that are commonly accepted or circulated outside the schools of learning (1102a26–27, 1096a3–4). Whether the division of the soul found in the exoteric speeches exists only "in speech [*logōi*]," like the convex and concave in the circumference of a circle, but not in nature," Aristotle claims, "makes no difference for the present [argument]" (1102a29–31). And yet Aristotle calls attention to this possible distinction between speech about the soul and the soul itself. He offers the

---

45. Only in book 10 does he allude again to either of these lawgivers, and as here he does not mention their famous names (1180a25–27). In his discussions in the *Politics*, we see that they are not model lawgivers for Aristotle (1270a6–8; 1271b1–2, 16–17, 32–33; 1324b8; and 1338b12–32).

statesman not only the exoteric distinction between the rational and nonrational parts of the soul, but also the analogy between those parts and the convex and concave sides of a circle. In nature, these sides of a circle cannot exist apart from the other, as they can in speech. In this way, he urges the statesman to look beyond the exoteric speeches.

The division between rational and nonrational parts of the soul bypasses (or misunderstands) any part that does not fall readily on either side of the division. In addition to the part of the nonrational soul that causes nutrition and growth (the vegetative part), Aristotle points out, there is "a certain other nature of the soul that is nonrational, although it does share in reason in a way," and is characterized by "desiring," and by "longing, in general" (1102b29–32). It "battles with and strains against reason," but it can also obey or be persuaded by reason, as it does when someone rules himself (1102b13–19, 36). The exoteric speeches view the soul "from outside," as their name suggests. Aristotle's speech, in contrast, also points out what occurs within a soul, a struggle that is not necessarily manifest outwardly (1102b23). If he looked at the soul only from the outside, that is, as it is manifest in a human being's actions, a statesman might see only human beings who need to be ruled and those who do not, whereas if he could look at the soul from within, he would see human beings who are capable of ruling themselves but who at times fail to do so. He would see, in other words, someone capable of self-rule.

Moreover, the exoteric speeches, by dividing the soul into rational and nonrational parts, leave no place for the distinctively human, as they split the human into what has reason "in the authoritative sense," as "in mathematics," and the nonrational soul that oversees nutrition and growth, which belongs to all animate beings and whose work occurs even during sleep. But "the good and the bad," Aristotle says, "are least distinct during sleep" (1102b5–6). In the human soul Aristotle describes, in contrast to the exoteric speeches, there is a longing that might be persuaded by reason, and a reason that might persuade it. Such a soul longs for the good (see 1094a21). Its struggle against itself makes it aware of itself (see 1150b37–1151a1).

The statesman who "somehow knows the soul" as Aristotle describes it, sees the possibility of self-rule, which exists for others and for himself. His rule of the city, at least if he is "truly a statesman," leaves room for the work of the citizens, who desire not only to possess happiness or to be happy, but also to be a cause of their happiness.[46] Their happiness cannot be something that they are given, but something that they must earn. As Aristotle concludes book 1 with discussion of the statesman's contemplation of the soul, he reminds us that the investigation of politics is "the choice we made at the beginning" (1102a11–12). We have begun the *Ethics* by choosing; the habits in which we have been brought up do not preclude choice. Choice is the last of the four human activities that aim at some good that Aristotle mentions in the first sentence of the *Ethics*. We do not simply possess the good. We aim at it. Indeed, Aristotle's choice of the verb "to aim at," which he uses for his own inquiry in the *Ethics* (1094b12) and also for the arts, inquiries, actions, and choices of human beings that "aim at" some good, suggests self-direction toward the end.[47] So too we make something our own by choosing, but it is not simply our own if we must choose it. We can be blessed, but only as human beings. Our being blessed in this way keeps our longing alive. This may be what it means to be blessed as human beings.

Aristotle concludes book 1 by connecting two different sets of virtues to these differences within the soul. The next books of his *Ethics* will fill in what these virtues are and what they mean for human happiness. Aristotle associates the intellectual virtues (he names wisdom, comprehension, and prudence) with what is rational in the authoritative or sovereign sense (*kuriōs*) sense, while the ethical or moral virtues (he names liberality and moderation) belong to that in the soul that is able to listen to reason as to a father. These are the virtues relating to "character" (*ēthos*) (1102b29–1103a1–8). When citizens obey the laws of lawgivers, there is an element of self-rule insofar as they are persuaded, as the twofold meaning of

---

46. Block, "Aristotle on Statesmanship," 104, points out the difficult task of the statesman who "must choose for the ruled and leave his subjects free like himself to choose."

47. "Aiming at" (*ephiesthai*) comes from *hienai*, "to throw" or "to hurl." When it occurs in the middle voice, as it does here, it means literally "aiming oneself at," "throwing oneself at," or "hurling oneself toward." It suggests the human effort involved. Aristotle uses the verb approximately forty-three times in the *Ethics*, but it does not occur in the *Metaphysics*.

peithesthai, "to obey" and "to be persuaded," suggests (1102b34–35).[48] Aristotle adds that this persuasion by reason resembles listening to or heeding (*akouein*) not only a father but also a friend, who "admonish" and "exhort" (1103a1–3). Aristotle uses the same verb (*akouein*) here, "listening" or "hearing," that he quotes Hesiod using in his verse for one unable to "listen" to the words of another and to take them to heart (1095b13). It is also the verb that he uses to refer to the activity of his addressees—those who listen to his inquiry in the *Ethics* (1095a3–5, 1095b6). Aristotle's work will constitute the model for a politics that fosters self-rule and supports happiness in a way that the lawgivers of Crete and Sparta were unable to do. We must, as Aristotle advised of Hesiod's verse, listen carefully to Aristotle's words and take them to heart.

---

48. Frank, "On Logos and Politics," 13–14, 17–19, esp. 24, points out the difference between the two meanings of *peithesthai*, both a passive obedience and an obedience only insofar as one has been persuaded. She makes a persuasive case that the desiring or longing part of the soul that Aristotle describes as listening to or heeding speech manifests a kind of self-rule and thus mirrors the self-rule of citizens.

CHAPTER 2

The Ethical Virtues

Nature, Character, and Choice (Books 2–3)

In books 2 to 5 of the *Ethics*, Aristotle treats the ethical virtues, beginning with their origin in both habit and choice, and their character as a mean between extremes, and then moves to a detailed examination of each of the ethical virtues. He thus executes with great care the task of examining the virtues that he set for himself in book 1 when he defined happiness as "the activity of the soul in accord with virtue, and if there are several virtues, then in accord with the best and most complete" (1098a16–18). In this chapter, I follow Aristotle's introduction of the ethical virtues in books 2 and 3, including the role that habit, nature, and choice play in their development, and how courage and moderation, which Aristotle discusses at the end of book 3, dispose the passions that we share with beasts (fear for our lives and desires for food and sex) toward human virtue. This chapter, which emphasizes human achievement by rising above the bestial, thus prepares for my chapter 3 on book 4, in which Aristotle emphasizes the virtues of human life in community with others and the distinction between human and divine.

It is by repeating certain acts that we acquire the virtues: we become moderate by performing moderate acts, and courageous by doing courageous ones. Habit (*ethos*) thus produces character (*ēthos*), which Aristotle refers to as "a steady and unwavering [state]." It is then that our actions become our own, proceeding from our characters and the choices we make. And we act with awareness that they do so (1103a17, a32–b2; 1105a31–35). If we heed the laws of our communities or the dictates of our parents, we might act virtuously, but we are not virtuous unless our actions originate in ourselves. Aristotle is concerned not only with acts of virtue but the state of the person who performs them (1105a29–34). But when do habits coalesce in character, so that our actions proceed from our characters and choices rather than merely from the habits we acquire as members of a community? Aristotle's discovery that character differs from the habits that engender it lies at the heart of his *Ethics*, whose title means literally "those things that involve character." In the first section of this chapter, I explore Aristotle's treatment of the ethical virtues and the dilemmas posed by their origin in habituation.

In the last half of book 2, to which I turn in the second section of this chapter, Aristotle gives a brief outline of the virtues and the vices that he will discuss, presenting each as a mean between two extremes—for example, courage as a mean between cowardice and recklessness. He appeals to common opinions about virtue and vice, but he revises them in the process. He builds on common opinion, while attempting to instruct and educate it. After outlining the virtues and their extremes, he advises us to begin to practice the virtues by aiming away from the extreme to which we are inclined. We learn more about the virtues as we proceed through the *Ethics*, but there need be no delay in attempting to acquire them. We must begin with ourselves. By his advice, Aristotle acknowledges that we too are causes of our habits, and therewith of our characters, from which our virtuous actions proceed. The difficulty in locating the point between actions on their way to virtue and those coming from virtue renders the identification and attainment of virtue more uncertain. At the same time, it also makes space for our owning our actions and for sharing responsibility for our becoming good (1179b4).

In book 3, Aristotle confronts the difficulties with his argument for virtue by asking when actions can be considered voluntary and involuntary. If all actions are involuntary, as some argue, or even if many are "mixed," as Aristotle admits, what becomes of free actions, and therewith of virtue? If we were good by nature (1103b13–15), or if laws or parents compelled virtuous deeds, we would be good "by necessity." No choice would be involved. All praise would be unmerited, and all punishment (though necessary to prevent crime) would be undeserved by the one punished. Aristotle raises these questions about the possibility of virtue at the beginning of book 3, only after urging us at the end of book 2 to begin to practice the virtues he has outlined, or to make the attempt. The proof lies in experience, in our attempting to act virtuously, or in testing Aristotle's advice by our deeds. Courage and moderation, which Aristotle associates with the nonrational part of the soul (1117b24), are most of all test cases, for they involve the passions that might enslave us to our bodies—our fear for our lives and our desires for food and sex, which we possess "not insofar as we are human, but insofar as we are animals" (1115b13, 1118b1–4, 1119a16–20).

In the last two sections of this chapter, I discuss book 3 of the *Ethics*, beginning with the distinction between voluntary and involuntary actions, and the human potential for choice. My last section looks at Aristotle's treatment of courage and moderation, with which he concludes book 3. By acquiring these virtues, we are no longer determined by physical necessity. Books 2 and 3 thus prepare for a new set of virtues, which Aristotle details in book 4, beginning with liberality (which is etymologically related to freedom), and he proceeds to virtues involved in our living together (1126b12–12), and then to justice in book 5. Aristotle's first two books on the ethical virtues, books 2 and 3, I argue, prepare us for the subsequent books that show how our freedom acquires greater scope and realization in living with others, to whose lives we contribute, just as they do to our own.

ETHICAL VIRTUES, HABITS, AND CHARACTER

Aristotle begins his discussion of virtue by asking about its origin, or how it comes into being (1103a14–16). By beginning with the question of how virtue comes to be, Aristotle raises the question Meno asks Socrates at the beginning of the Platonic dialogue bearing his name. There Socrates reproaches Meno for asking the wrong question: we should not pursue how virtue is acquired before we know what virtue is. After all, we would not know that we acquired virtue if we do not know what it is (*Meno* 70a, 71a–b). Aristotle, in contrast, does not focus the attention of his addressees on what they do not know, but simply observes how virtue is acquired, even pointing out that different virtues are acquired in different ways: whereas intellectual virtue comes mostly from teaching, ethical virtue is the result of habit (1103a14–16). He not only begins with Meno's question, one that is more practical than theoretical (the "what is" question on which Socrates insists), but he has a ready at hand answer, almost as if it were not a question that required discussion, or one for which discussion would be useful. Aristotle soon criticizes those who "take refuge in words," using a phrase Socrates applies in the *Phaedo* to explain his own way of seeking truth (99e). Those who do so, Aristotle says, suppose that by speaking of virtue they are philosophizing. But the end in asking about virtue is not to know what virtue is, but to become good, and that requires doing virtuous deeds (1105b10–14).

In asking Meno's question and criticizing those who take refuge in words, however, Aristotle is not following the demands of a simply practical work, in distinction from a theoretical one, or pursuing a path that is more political than philosophical. He denies that those who take refuge in words are philosophizing, as they suppose of their activity. And he claims that his approach yields "greater truth" (1107a28–34) about virtue, and about the beautiful, the just, and the good. His approach therefore has a better claim to "philosophizing" (1152b1–2, 1181b15; see also *Politics* 1282b23). Answering the question of the origin of virtue, it turns out, is of the greatest theoretical import, for it bears on what virtue is. There may be virtuous actions, but there is no virtue unless those actions come from ourselves. The more critical question, therefore, is what it means to understand virtue and character as a human being's own when their origin and so much of their development depend on external factors.

In tracing ethical virtue to habituation, Aristotle explains that we do not possess the ethical virtues by nature, "for nothing that is by nature can be habituated to be otherwise." A stone could not be habituated to move upward, just as a flame could not be habituated to burn downward. Nor are the virtues potentials or capacities. Because we have sight, we can use it, for example. Because we "use" the virtues, in contrast, we acquire or "have" them (1103a14–31). With the virtues, the activities come first. We come to have ethical virtue only because we have done virtuous deeds. This does not mean that the ethical virtues are contrary to nature, for we are "such by nature as to receive them, and we become completed through habit" (1103a15–26, b13–14). Nature does not bestow the virtues, as it does the capacity for sight, but it allows human beings to acquire them. Even with regard to our natural capacities or potentials, nature has left it to us to use them well or badly: we have the potential to contemplate, as we do to see, and no amount of contemplating can give us the potential if nature had not. And yet we must practice contemplating (*Metaphysics* 1050a10–16).

When Aristotle says that how we are habituated makes "the whole difference" as to whether we become good (1103b25–26), he reminds us of the statesman, who wishes to make citizens good. He now explains that the statesman does so by "by habituating [through laws that command virtuous deeds]" (1103b4–5). He also mentions teachers (1103b13), and these include parents, whom he later credits with both nurturing and educating their children (e.g., 1162a5–8). Legislators, even with their authoritative work in their communities, are not the only ones who make human beings good. Even if habituation makes "the whole difference," their architectonic art does not. Moreover, Aristotle indicates that our habits also depend on ourselves, not merely on other human beings, whether they be legislators, parents, or other teachers. "We must make our activities be of a certain sort," Aristotle says, for our virtues proceed from our activities (1103b21–23).

When Aristotle says that we "become completed" by habit, he uses a form of the verb that in Greek can mean either that we "become completed [or perfected] through habit" or that we complete or perfect ourselves through habit.[1] Aristotle allows the ambiguity in the Greek to reflect the truth of human life, which involves both self-rule and dependence on others. When he refers to our "becoming habituated" from our youth, it could be read as "habituating ourselves," and when he refers to "our being correctly led in our habits" so as to become fit students of politics, his words also mean "our correctly leading ourselves" (1103b17, 23; 1095b6; 1140b12). Like Aristotle himself, statesmen need "co-workers," and the success of their work requires the work of citizens.

Once our habits take hold and impart character, moreover, we can take hold of ourselves. Just as virtues are not capacities that belong to us

---

1. Bartlett and Collins, *Aristotle's "Nicomachean Ethics,"* 26n1. In other words, Aristotle exploits the Greek "middle" voice, which indicates that the subject acts upon itself, which in many cases is identical in form with the passive.

by nature with no effort of our own, virtues are not passions (*pathē*) or "affections," such as desire, anger, fear, or joy, which are ways in which we are "affected" or "moved" by the external world. Rather, the virtues are *hexeis*, or "dispositions," a word formed from the common Greek verb "to have" (*echein*) (1105b19–1106a12). Our "dispositions," the virtues acquired from habits that form character, dispose us to act in a certain way when our passions are aroused. An enemy, for example, might arouse fear, or a fancy dessert might arouse a desire to eat it. But we are not praised or blamed for being moved by such objects, but for how we respond when this happens. Do we run away from the object we fear? Do we indulge our desire for sweets?

When Bartlett and Collins translate *hexeis* as "characteristics," they capture in English the connection between virtue and character. Our "characteristics" display our character, and once acquired through habituation constitute a certain way of "holding [ourselves] toward the world."[2] We are given capacities by nature, and our passions are aroused by the external world, but we acquire characters through habituation, and because we have characters we can choose to act in accordance with who we are. That the actions of virtue proceed from a steady and unwavering state (*ametakinētōs*) (1105a31–b35) means that we have a character. We are not just the sum of the forces that come from without. Our character prompts us to receive what affects us in a certain way. However much we are affected by the world outside ourselves, that world does not determine our actions. Neither do our actions flow inexorably from our characters. Choice is involved. We may act in character or not. Even the education of the laws that attempts to make us good citizens by inculcating virtuous habits paradoxically fosters independence. Without the move from habit (*ethos*) to character (*ēthos*), there would be no *Ethics*.

The laws might command virtuous actions and forbid their opposites, but virtues and their opposites differ from individual to individual. As a disposition toward the passions, Aristotle explains, virtue falls in the

---

2. Bartlett and Collins, *Aristotle's "Nicomachean Ethics,"* 306, defend their translation and explain this meaning of Aristotle's use of this word in their glossary. For a useful account of the difficulties in finding an English word that captures what Aristotle means by *hexis* and also a compelling account of how Aristotle uses the word, see Salkever, *Finding the Mean*, 79–81, 94–95.

middle between excess and deficiency. Courage, for example, a disposition toward the passions of fear and confidence, falls between cowardice and recklessness. But exactly where the mean lies for any individual varies, just as the appropriate amount of food or exercise for a wrestler differs from what is appropriate for any one of us, but excess and deficiency is possible in every case. Virtue is "a mean relative to us" rather than an arithmetical mean in the sense that six is the mean between two and ten (1106a26–b4). Hitting the mean relative to us requires being affected and experiencing passions "when we ought, at the things we ought, in relation to those whom we ought, for the sake of what we ought, and in the way we ought" (1106b17–24). Thus Aristotle says that virtue is a characteristic "defined by reason" and "as the prudent person would define it" (1107a1–2). Although Aristotle associates the virtue of prudence with the statesman (1141b24–28; see also *Politics* 1277b26), no one can possess ethical virtue without also possessing prudence (e.g., 1107a1–2, 1145a4–6). Only then are our virtues, and whatever happiness they provide for us, our own. Thus, in the same complex way that our actions both shape and are shaped by our character, ethical virtue both precedes and follows from intellectual virtue.

BEGINNING TO ACT

After this introduction to ethical virtue, Aristotle gives a brief outline of the virtues that he plans to discuss. He "must speak not only in universal [*katholou*] terms," for what he says "must conform to particulars," claiming as it were to follow the advice he gave to those who introduced the ideas (see 1096a17–29, 109711–13). In speeches about actions, moreover, those pertaining to particulars "have more truth," for "actions concern particulars" (1107a28–34). Aristotle's "outline" prepares for his discussing these virtues in greater detail in subsequent books of the *Ethics*. After laying out his outline for what follows, however, he does not proceed immediately to elaborate each of the virtues in his list. Rather, he advises his addressees to begin practicing the virtues. His outline apparently provides sufficient understanding for addressees to begin to act. Acting itself, or as Aristotle says elsewhere, "making the attempt" (or "gaining the experience"), helps us to see the truth in the speeches about acting that Aristotle proceeds to give. When Aristotle earlier claimed that the student of politics needs experience of the actions of life, he explained that "the speeches come from these and are about these" (1095a3–5).

The speeches of the *Ethics* not only "come from" from the actions of life or build on our experience. They also affect our actions. When we are persuaded by Aristotle and aim at the virtuous mean, or when we weigh options and make choices, we come to know from experience that speech or reason can influence our actions, that the world is one in which we can act. Aristotle claims that the end of his inquiry about virtue is acting rather than knowing, but it is by acting that we come to know the world. If the end of knowing is acting (that is, we know what to do), it is also true that the end of acting is knowing—knowing what sort of beings we are and what sort of world we live in. It is a world that imposes limits on our actions but also one that our actions affect. We learn from our failures and our successes. Those who take refuge in words should not suppose they are philosophizing, as Aristotle says. They miss the truth one learns from acting.

Aristotle distinguishes himself from Plato/Socrates, not only because he refuses "to take refuge in words" as if that were sufficient to understand the truth, but also by the list of the virtues in his outline. In Plato's *Republic*, the four virtues that Socrates locates in the city, and then in the soul, are courage, moderation, justice, and wisdom/prudence (e.g., 435b). Aristotle starts along Socrates's path, beginning his list with courage and moderation, but he delays his inclusion of justice and wisdom (which he discusses in books 5 and 6, respectively) to offer a host of other virtues and means, which he discusses in book 4, including liberality and munificence (which involve means concerning giving and spending money), and greatness of soul, love of honor, and gentleness, and then means expressed in living together and sharing in speeches and actions, both "in play and in everything concerning life" (1108a14). Whether or not Aristotle's list of virtues is more comprehensive than Socrates's in the *Republic*, it is certainly more crowded. Human life teems with more possibilities and goods than the *Republic* presents. There are many means at which we can aim, and therefore many goods that we can achieve. Only at the end of the outline does Aristotle's return to the virtues in the *Republic*, saying of justice only that it is spoken of in more than one way—presumably in more ways than Plato does. Finally, after justice will come the "rational" virtues (or, more precisely, those that involve "speech"), as he now refers to the intellectual virtues (1108b8–10). When Aristotle later fills in the details of this part of the outline, he speaks of the intellectual virtues too in more than one way, distinguishing two intellectual virtues, prudence and wisdom, the former directed to human and political life, the latter to the highest things in the cosmos. Whereas in the *Republic* Socrates uses the two words apparently interchangeably, assigning wisdom the task of ruling the city (e.g., 429a, 433b), Aristotle's distinction elevates politics by attributing to it an intellectual virtue of its own, while leaving wisdom a greater independence for its own activity.

The first virtues in the outline, courage and moderation, are commonly understood as virtues, as we see when Aristotle appeals to them to illustrate his points, as when he mentioned courage as a good that might nevertheless cost one's life (1094b17–19). What is less commonly understood, Aristotle shows in his outline, is that the virtues are means between excess and deficiency. The middle in the case of both these virtues is so little visible that it often appears simply as the opposite of the more common extreme. Courage, for example, appears to resemble recklessness more than cowardice, rather than as a mean between them (1108b31, 1109a1–4). Hence we confuse recklessness with courage. Moderation appears as the opposite of licentiousness rather than as a mean enjoying pleasure neither more nor less that one ought. The extreme on the side of the deficiency in the latter case is so little known in common discourse that it is not even identified with a name (1107b8, 1119a8). By giving the deficiency a name, "insensibility" (*anaisthēsia*; literally, "lack of perception or sensing") (1107b8, 1119a8), Aristotle makes room for speaking of moderation as a mean in enjoying pleasure rather than merely as a resistance to it. So little is common opinion aware that virtue is a mean between extremes that when Aristotle describes what rhetoricians praise and blame in the *Rhetoric*, he lists only one vice for each of the virtues (1366b13–20). Virtue and vice are typically understood as opposites, as extremes.[3] Aristotle's introduction of virtue as a mean may be the most obvious way in which he revises—and both moderates and elevates—common parlance about the virtues.[4]

---

3. For an account of Aristotle's treatment of the virtues in the *Rhetoric* and of how that treatment complements that in his *Ethics*, see Colmo, "The Virtues and the Audience in Aristotle's *Rhetoric*," 439–56.

4. In Plato's *Statesman*, the Eleatic Stranger also has recourse to the mean and distinguishes as Aristotle does between a mathematical mean between more

Liberality (*eleutheriotēs*), which is derived from freedom (*eleutheria*), is commonly used as a term of praise, as characteristic of a free (*eleutherios*) person rather than a slave (e.g., *Politics* 1254a14–18; *Metaphysics* 982b26–28; and even *NE* 1118b5; 1128a19–20, a26; 1179b8). It is Aristotle who defines it as the proper disposition toward giving and taking of money (1107b9–14).[5] So important for Aristotle is the proper disposition toward money to a good human life that he gives it the very name of freedom (also *Politics* 1263b12). The liberal person is not simply free—for he needs resources to give to others—but he is free enough from the necessities of life to do so.

So too does Aristotle's use of "munificence" (*megaloprepeia*) to refer to spending money on a grand scale (1107b12–20) originate with him. *Megaloprepeia*, literally, "fitting greatness," is often translated as "magnificence," and at times included by Plato among the virtues (e.g., *Meno* 74a, 88a; *Republic* 402c), but it is Aristotle who associates it with money. In the *Republic*, Socrates attributes magnificence to the philosophic nature when he observes that "to an understanding endowed with magnificence and contemplation of all time and all being" human life "would not seem anything great" (486a; see also 490b, 494b). Instead of such contemplative pursuits, the munificent individual serves his city by his munificent works, such as building temples for worship or outfitting triremes (1122b19–24). Far from supposing that "nothing is great," he produces

---

and less and a mean that falls between the excess and deficiency as appropriate to the case at hand. The Stranger's discussion, however, arises in defense of the length of his speech about weaving, which might be considered "rather long," but should be judged according to whether its length is fitting or needful (283b–284b). The Stranger does not associate the mean with the virtues, as does Aristotle. Although several commentators find Aristotle's teaching about the mean foreshadowed by the Stranger's, Cherry, *Plato, Aristotle, and the Purposes of Politics*, 118–25, offers a persuasive discussion of the ways in which Aristotle's recourse to the mean differs from the Stranger's. This is not to deny, of course, that Aristotle's discussion is indebted to the Stranger's, even as it uses its insights in a different way.

5. This usage is suggested by Theodorus's praise of the young mathematician Theaetetus as "liberal with the regard to his money" in one of Plato's dialogues (*Theaetetus* 144d), but his language implies that actions in regard to money are only one way in which a free person might express his freedom.

wondrous works for his city. Aristotle redefines the virtue so that it has a place in the city.

Most interesting is Aristotle's invention or discovery of greatness of soul (*megalopsuchia*), which seems to embody greatness itself, and which is concerned "with great honor," as munificence is concerned with great expenditures (1107b22–26). Before Aristotle, at least in extant Greek literature, there are few uses of "greatness of soul," and often the term is used in a derogatory way. In Xenophon's *Hellenica*, for example, it refers to being stubborn or refusing to heed another (6.1.9), presumably because the great-souled is too proud to do so. Today we might say that such a person has a big head. In the *Alcibiades II*, Socrates tells Alcibiades that the name is applied to those characterized by folly (*aphrosunē*), when people wish to speak in euphemistic terms of foolish people (140c; also 150c). Aristotle thus appropriates a word that has somewhat negative connotations to refer to human greatness. He says little about this virtue in his outline, although he later gives it extensive treatment (in book 4), except to say that it is a "mean concerning honor and dishonor" (1170b23). As a mean with respect to honor, this virtue too, like that of the liberal and munificent persons who precede him in the outline, would be manifest in a community with others.

So too is the love of honor that Aristotle includes next in his outline, which is concerned with smaller honors in comparison to greatness of soul, which is concerned with great ones. The lover of honor also longs for honor neither more nor less than he ought. In this case, common opinion vacillates about whether love of honor or ambition (*philotimia*) is a virtue or a vice, for sometimes we praise the one who has it and criticize the one who lacks it, while at other times, we do the reverse. In either case, we leave the mean "nameless," and by praising and blaming the extremes we allow those who manifest the extremes to claim to possess the virtue (1107b27–1108a3). By arguing that there is a mean with respect to love of honor, Aristotle relegates the extremes to their places as excess and deficiency, again refining, even correcting common opinion.

There is also a mean with respect to anger (*orgē*), but both the extremes and the mean are "almost nameless," Aristotle points out. He asks that names be given to the extremes, one moved by anger (*orgilotēs*) and one lacking it (*aorgesia*), and that their mean be called gentleness (1108a4–9). Gentleness, like anger, comes into play in our relations to others (e.g., 1126a1–3, 18–19, and 26).

In other cases when the means and extremes that Aristotle proposes are without names, he claims that "the attempt must be made to fashion a name" (*onomatopoiein*) for what is "nameless" (1108a19; also *Categories* 7b10–13), even "fashioning a name" for his own act of fashioning names, or, as we might say, "coining words" when the words we need to express our thoughts do not exist. In these ways and in his connecting virtue with a mean between two vices, Aristotle's outline indicates his fashioning what we might call a moral language for understanding and speaking about what makes human beings good. He thus indicates how far his understanding of the virtues and vices is from the opinions held about them, not only from Plato's account of them in the *Republic*, but also the common opinions as they are expressed in the names we have and do not have for them. And yet Aristotle's learns from and builds on common opinions. He does not merely invent new words, he "coins" them from previously existing words, as he does with fashioning (*poiein*) names (*onomata*). He is not an advocate of the altogether new, as he indicates in the *Politics* when he speaks against the radical political reforms of his predecessors, but he does allow that one might "bring [previously existing] things together," and puts other things that are known "to use" (*Politics* 1264a4–5). He fashions new words out of previously existing ones and puts words to new uses to reveal there is more in what is known to us than of which we are aware.[6]

Aristotle uses the common word for "truth" (*alētheia*) to identify a way of speaking about oneself that falls between boasting and irony. He uses a version of "versatility" (*eutrapelia*) to mean wit, falling between buffoonery and boorishness. These are often called "the social virtues" by commentators, since Aristotle says that they involve "sharing in words and actions" (1108a12). A third, which Aristotle calls "friendship," but later reveals he does so because, even though it is "like" friendship, it has no

---

6. Aristotle's putting things previously known to new uses is illustrated in the *Politics* by his using "polity" (*politeia*), the generic word for "regime," to apply to one of the six forms of regimes, the correct form of the rule by the many (1279a27–b10), and then expanding the term to refer to a "mixed regime," in which the rule of the many is expanded and moderated by participation of the few (1293a35–b21, 1293b34–1294b40). See my discussion of Aristotle's use of polity in his classification of regimes in Nichols, *Citizens and Statesmen*, 61–65, 95–100.

name (1126b19–21), involves giving others pleasure through one's words and deeds, of course in the proper way. Such a "friendly" person falls between the obsequious and the surly (1108a19–31). By emphasizing how many of these means and extremes are "nameless," Aristotle underscores his expansion of common parlance in light of his vision of human goodness. He does so also by including yet two more means in his list, shame and righteous indignation (or *nemesis*), even though they are passions rather than virtues (1108a33–b8).

Aristotle's exposition of the virtues moves in the direction of inclusiveness not only in his increasing the number of the virtues he discusses. His treatment of the relation between virtue and passion renders the virtues accessible to a greater number of human beings. Virtues are rooted in passions that most of us experience, and they consist in our becoming properly disposed toward them rather than in rejecting them altogether. The courageous "fear" neither too much nor too little, while those without fear may be reckless rather than courageous. There are some things that are fearful to anyone with sense, Aristotle points out in his discussion of courage, and the courageous person is as "undaunted" only insofar "as a human being can be" (1115b8–12). Similarly, those who pursue bodily pleasures as they ought are moderate, not those who experience no such desires for pleasure, who have the rare condition without any name, which Aristotle calls "far from human" (1119a10). Because virtue guides, rather than denies, the passions, it is not beyond our reach. To be sure, Aristotle later attributes an exalted character to the one possessing greatness of soul, but he also criticizes him as haughty (1124b20, 22–23). Initially, in his outline, Aristotle mentions only the great-souled individual's concern with great honors, while saving until later his reservations about him. When greatness of soul looks out of the reach of most human beings, it also looks less like virtue.

After presenting the virtues in outline, in each case as a mean between extremes, Aristotle urges his addressees to practice them, even before his more detailed treatment of them. Our experience of them comes first and will help us to understand them. His brief outline is sufficient for beginning. Each of us must consider toward what he naturally inclines, Aristotle observes, "for some of us incline to some things, others to others." We will know ourselves from the pleasures and the pains that we experience. Once we know to what we incline, we "should drag ourselves away from it toward the opposite, for by leading ourselves far from error, we will arrive at a middle, just as those do who straighten warped timber [by bending it in the opposite direction]" (1109b5–9). Or, if we do not attain the middle, we will arrive closer to it than we otherwise would. Aristotle describes overshooting to arrive at the middle as "a second sailing" (1109a35), using a euphemism for taking to the oars when the wind fails. There is no sailing, but hard work can get us where we are trying to go, or at least near to it. Curiously, Aristotle speaks of virtue both as something we "grasp" (*lambanein*) or "take hold of" and as something we "take aim at" (*stochastikē*), using a word for aiming at a target rather than hitting it (1109a20–26). He also observes that "the one who deviates [only] a little" from correct action is not blamed (1109b18–19). At least he is not blamed by Aristotle and by those who are taught by him.

Aristotle finds support in Homer for overshooting the target to better arrive at the mean. Odysseus's voyage home required him to pass through a strait with the monsters Charybdis and Scylla waiting on either side for oncoming ships. Since Charybdis holds the greater danger, Odysseus must steer closer to Scylla (1109a31–32; *Odyssey* 12.219). There is more detail in Homer's text: better for Odysseus to steer toward Scylla, whose many arms will capture only a few of his men, than toward Charybdis, who will swallow the entire ship and all the men on it. For Odysseus, there is no safe passage between the monsters, at least according to the nymph who tells Odysseus what he will encounter and advises him how he should proceed (*Odyssey* 12.73–100). There is no mean that protects him and his men. There is nothing he can do to bring *all* his men home, even if saving some, or even most, falls between saving all and none. Taking to the oars will not suffice. For him, there can be no "second sailing." Aristotle's gloss on Homer's text, "of the extremes one is more in error, the other less," and "to hit the mean is extremely difficult" (1109a33–35; see also 1109b26–27), is therefore somewhat of an understatement. Odysseus laments that watching Scylla devour his companions was "the most pitiable thing my eyes ever saw" (*Odyssey* 12.258–59). Aristotle may find support in Homer for steering one's ship away from one side and toward the other, or "grasping the lesser evil" (1109a35), but not for safe passage or for a satisfactory middle. Despite the nymph's advice, Odysseus arms himself for battle with Scylla in an attempt to pass by without loss of men, but he fails in his attempt (*Odyssey* 12.225–50). By advising us to veer to one side rather than another, Aristotle offers us a way to hit the mean. It is he who is offering us a second sailing. His model is Odysseus, in his attempt although not in his failure.

Aristotle concludes book 2 with a second reference to Homer, quoting what the "town elders" of Troy say to one another as they watch Helen move along the city walls: "Let her go away, for she will be a calamity for us and for our children" (*Iliad* 3.154–60). Aristotle advises that we utter their words to Pleasure itself, commanding it to go away, so powerful is it a force that impedes virtue. In this way, we would come closer to the mean by overshooting it and thereby "err less" than if we aimed at the mean directly (1109b8–13; see also 1105a2–6). Once again, Aristotle offers the possibility of a mean that Homer does not. The elders at Troy recognize the disaster that Helen's presence in their city entails, but they do not send her away. They speak in the imperative, "Let [Helen] go away," only among themselves, never to Helen herself, or to their ruler, Priam. "She looks like an immortal goddess," they admit in Homer's epic (*Iliad* 3.158). They also claim that they are without indignation (*nemesis*) at the Trojans and the Achaeans who have fought and suffered so long on her account (*Iliad* 3.156). The elders cannot blame others for doing what they themselves would do. They seem resigned to the inevitable suffering that follows from human desire. Nor does Paris resist his desire when he steals Helen away from her husband and brings her to Troy. Attraction to beauty in this instance lies in tragic conflict with the preservation of the city, for it leads to the city's destruction. By repeating the elders' words about Helen to Pleasure itself, as Aristotle says we should, we would "err less" than the elders at Troy. Aristotle therefore does not expect that pleasure will "go away," or that we will avoid error. But perhaps we will err less, and our lives will admit of a mean that the elders' appreciation of beauty did not.

Aristotle uses the verb for err (*harmartein*) that he uses in his *Poetics* to refer to the "error" (*hamartia*) that the tragic protagonist makes from which his tragedy unfolds (*Poetics* 1453a10 and 17). This is not the only time that we will see Aristotle refer to tragic error and attempt to diminish its scope in human life. Priam did not send Helen away. The disaster that he suffered at the end of his life, we now see, was not as much a work of chance as Aristotle's earlier discussion supposed. Paris had insufficient moderation, and Priam did nothing to correct him, either as his father or as his ruler, either in raising his son or in his correcting his crime by returning Helen to her husband. If virtuous actions can avert disaster, if injustice could be checked or punished, there would be a stronger ground for diminishing indignation than the elders' resignation to an inevitable suffering belonging to the human lot.

By concluding book 2 with elders who feel "no indignation," Aristotle prepares us for the place of "pardon" or "forgiveness" in his discussion of voluntary and involuntary actions at the beginning of book 3. But though some actions should be pardoned, others should be blamed. To understand all is not to pardon all, as the proverb has it. Rather, the task is to distinguish between actions that are "up to [the one who does them]" (1113b5–14) and those that are not, that is, to distinguish between what should be blamed—and praised—and what forgiven.

PRAISE, BLAME, AND FORGIVENESS

Advising us in book 2 to aim at the mean in our actions by examining ourselves and by compensating for our own proclivities, Aristotle lets us imagine ourselves making the attempt to act virtuously. Even imagining ourselves doing so is a first step, and whether we take other steps is up to us. Only then, as he begins book 3, does Aristotle explicitly raise the question of when our actions are voluntary, and when not, and therefore when they deserve praise or blame, and when they deserve forgiveness, and even pity. Our experience of attempting to hit the mean will help us understand what to demand of others and what to excuse. Defining the voluntary and the involuntary is necessary for those examining virtue, Aristotle says. Indeed, "doing so is useful also to lawgivers in assigning both honors and punishments" (1109b30–35). What lawgivers do—judging the actions of others—we too do.

The voluntary, *ekousion*, is literally what comes "out of (*ek*)" or "from" someone, while something is involuntary, *akousion*, if its origin lies outside of us. If we are forced or compelled to do something, we are not acting voluntarily, as would be the case if we are carried off by the wind, or by someone who kidnaps us (1109b30–1110a4, 1110a13–18). One of the clearest illustrations of a voluntary act, in contrast, occurs when we deliberate about what we should do and then act after we make a choice between options. Then the cause, or the origin of the action, lies in us (1112a14–15). Aristotle derived the word for "choice" (*prohairesis*) from *hairesis*, "taking," and *pro*, "before." In choosing, we "take" something or undertake an action "before" or "rather than" another (1112a17; *Eudemian Ethics* 1226b8). That is why for Aristotle choice occurs only after deliberation, which weighs alternatives.[7] By weighing alternatives, human beings gain a distance from what they desire or fear. Their motion toward desired or feared objects, if it is chosen, comes from themselves. Although choice is not an uncaused cause—it follows deliberation, and as Aristotle states at the outset of the *Ethics*, all human activities aim at the good—by choosing we become agents, or the causes of our actions, not merely passive objects affected by the external world (1112b31–32).[8]

In between these clear cases of compulsion and choice, matters are more ambiguous. It "admits of dispute," for example, whether someone acts voluntarily when he obeys a tyrant who threatens to kill his parents and children unless he does his bidding (1110a7–8). Aristotle gives another example: when someone throws his cargo overboard during a storm at sea in order to preserve his life and those of others, his action is "mixed"—involuntary in itself, for no one would voluntarily throw away his belongings apart from the circumstances, but voluntary in the circumstances, and it is in the circumstances that we judge an act (1110a9–10, b3–9). Aristotle poses a dilemma that seems easy to resolve, but it would not be so easy if sacrificing both passengers and cargo were necessary to save the ship and the majority of the passengers. This dilemma resembles the one faced by Odysseus when he decides to incline his ship toward Scylla, sacrificing several of his men rather than his whole crew, himself included.[9] Aristotle

---

7. Salkever, "Democracy and Aristotle's Ethics of Natural Questions," 354, 359, who notes that *prohairesis* is among Aristotle's "significant coinages or near-coinages," explains that the word Aristotle uses for "choice" is "hard to translate and to understand because it joins together two qualities, independence and reflectiveness," in a way that is unfamiliar both to us and to Aristotle's contemporaries. Translations such as "deliberative choice" or "thoughtful choice" attempt to capture both meanings. For further discussion of this key Aristotelean term, see Salkever, *Finding the Mean*, 69–71.

8. See also discussion by Pangle, *Reason and Character*, 76, 77, 82.

9. I am grateful to Rachel Alexander for pointing out the connection between Odysseus's dilemma and Aristotle's example of the one who must sacrifice his belongings to save the ship and those on it. See Alexander, "Philosophical Foundations," 97–98.

does not say what either the individual whose relatives are held by a tyrant or the one whose survival depends on throwing away cargo should do. Aristotle's judgment does not replace that of the individual who must consider what is appropriate in the circumstances. As Aristotle says, "it is not easy to explain what is to be chosen in return for what, for there are many distinctions involved in the particulars" (1110b8–9). Rather, Aristotle gives us things to think about when we make decisions and judge those of others. But in both cases that Aristotle presents, the demand of the tyrant and the storm at sea, the choice of one good entails the loss of another. Disaster may follow from such choices, but those making them know the consequences—the doom of relatives or the loss of cargo. The circumstances they face produce conflicting goods, but those circumstances are not inevitable. Sea voyages run the risk of perilous storms, but not all voyages encounter them. All political communities run the risk of tyranny, but some more than others. Those who face such conflicts because of the circumstances and have to make difficult decisions are not tragic figures who assume more responsibility than is warranted for their situation, or who relegate responsibility to what is beyond their control, such as fate or the gods. They learn from choosing both that their options are limited and that they have options.

Moreover, when "the matters involved surpass human nature and can be endured by no one," Aristotle says, "forgiveness arises" (1110a24–26). Aristotle does not give an example of what so surpasses human endurance that we should forgive actions in such situations. There are nevertheless certain deeds that compulsion cannot excuse, cases in which one should die, "even suffering the most terrible things," rather than do such deeds. But even when Aristotle appears to give an example of such a deed that cannot be excused—at least he observes that Alcmaeon's claim that he was compelled to murder his mother is laughable—he immediately proceeds to say that "it is difficult to decide what *to choose* in return for what and what ought to be endured in return for what" (1110a24–31). Alcmaeon, it seems, had options if he made a choice. It is those who act in the circumstances who must choose, just as we too must choose whether to blame or forgive them.

It is also, Aristotle claims, "ridiculous" or "laughable" for someone to blame his shameful or base deeds on the compulsions of pleasure, while attributing his beautiful or noble deeds to himself and taking credit for them (1110b9–15). Our experience of desert tells us that our good deeds come at least in part from ourselves, even if we are grateful that we have been given the opportunity to do them. Moreover, why do we deny our responsibility for our base deeds by insisting that their cause lies elsewhere? We are ashamed of them. We would experience no shame if we did not hold ourselves responsible. Our experience of our beautiful or noble deeds and hence of our responsibility for them should make us ashamed of trying to avoid blame for our base ones. Aristotle makes us ashamed of ourselves when he points out that our inconsistency deserves laughter (also 1111a28–31).

Aristotle extends responsibility to acts originating in spiritedness or desire, for not only reason but "also spiritedness and desire belong to a human being" (1111b3–4). Of course, our passions are provoked by external events, as when someone arouses our anger by insulting us, or a threatening object moves us to fear. But as Aristotle made clear in defining the virtues as dispositions rather than as passions, we are neither blamed nor praised because of our passions, but for the way in which we are disposed toward them. We are not simply moved; rather, we are moved in a certain way depending on our dispositions. We are not blamed because we become angry, to use Aristotle's example, but because we become angry in a certain way (1105b25–1106a7). Because of our dispositions (our virtues and vices), our passions belong to us, not only to the objects that arouse them. From Aristotle's argument, we may infer that someone like Sophocles's Oedipus, who strikes out in anger at someone who impedes his travels, and kills him and almost all his retinue, is the cause of his evil deeds. So too when we act "in ignorance" of what we are doing because we are drunk or angry, rather than with deliberation and choice, our deeds are nevertheless voluntary, for they come from ourselves. We may act "in ignorance" in such cases, but not "on account of ignorance" (1110b25–28). We act on account of our failing in virtue, such as moderation or gentleness. Blame in such cases would be just.

There are other sorts of ignorance, however, for which one is not responsible, such as ignorance of the circumstances surrounding one's act. In such a case of ignorance, one acts involuntarily, and "there is both pity and forgiveness." Among Aristotle's examples is Merope, who supposes that "her own son is an enemy" (1110b21–1111a18), but she discovers his identity just in time to prevent her from killing him (*Poetics* 1454a5–6). Had she killed her son, her act would have been involuntary, because she was ignorant of who her victim was. Horrific as her act would have been, however, it does not occur. An involuntary act that does occur is the "crime" of Oedipus, since he kills a man without knowing that the man is his father, and even marries his mother, not knowing that she is his mother. Given Aristotle's argument, Oedipus deserves forgiveness for these terrible deeds rather than punishment. He knew what was evil—killing his father and marrying his mother—and he strove to avoid both by exiling himself from the parents and the city he believed to be his own. That was in fact why he left Corinth when it was foretold that he would commit such crimes. When he committed patricide and incest, he did not know the particulars of his action—that he was the son of Laius and Jocasta. Just as Aristotle's treatment of the passions implies that Oedipus is responsible for the murders he committed out of anger, his treatment of ignorance implies that Oedipus was not responsible for his patricide (and incest), and therefore wrong to blame and punish himself for the latter and not the former (see Sophocles, *Oedipus Tyrannus* 1397). To be sure, Aristotle considers Oedipus's crimes against his parents impious, as is implied in his criticism of the *Republic*'s violations of the family, but when we look to the circumstances of Oedipus's case, we see a man who did not know what he was doing. Aristotle seems ready to pardon, for the patricide but not the murder, so difficult are particular cases to resolve. His discussion of the voluntary and the involuntary here prepares for his introduction of equity in book 5 (which weighs circumstances) as a superior kind of justice (1137b24).

In contrast to ignorance of the particulars, ignorance of what is good and bad cannot serve as an excuse for unjust deeds (1110b29–32, 1113b15–21). In this case, ignorance does not merit either pity or forgiveness. Here Aristotle addresses those who say that "no one does evil voluntarily," for if one knew the good, one would do it. The position to which he objects resembles one that he later attributes to Socrates (1145b25–28). In the *Apology*, for example, Socrates applies a version of this argument to his own case: if he corrupted the young, he did so involuntarily, and he should be taken aside and instructed, not punished as if he were to blame (*Apology* 25c–26a). Having implicitly blamed Oedipus for punishing himself for crimes whose extenuating circumstances allowed forgiveness, Aristotle in like manner blames Socrates for a position that does not allow the laws to punish. Socrates is too forgiving, if he excuses bad deeds on the grounds of ignorance and calls for teaching rather than punishment. Aristotle refuses to collapse the political community into a classroom (or at least a Socratic dialogue), just as he refuses to replace it with the tragic stage.

Even if someone who did wrong could be made to see the error of his ways by being taught rather than punished, however, would such knowledge be sufficient for his becoming good? Some may be so corrupted by their bad habits and vices, that even when they are persuaded and wish to stop being unjust, Aristotle observes, it is not possible for them, just as a sick person's wish to be healthy does not make him so. One cannot retrieve a stone one has thrown away after one has done so. One cannot erase the past. Where, then, is human responsibility?

Aristotle responds that it is impossible for someone who tosses a stone away to retrieve it, but it was "up to him" to toss or not to toss it "at the beginning." Just as an unjust or intemperate person may be unable to change, it was possible "at the beginning" for such a person to have become otherwise (1114a13–22). But is there a "beginning" of our acquiring habits that is "up to us"? By attributing to human beings such an unqualified authority over their habits "at the beginning," Aristotle's argument seems to forget that we are children before we are adults. This argument is as problematic as its counterpart that Aristotle put forth in book 2: "How we are habituated from childhood makes no small difference [for our acquiring virtue], indeed, the whole difference" (1103b23–25). The one attributes to us inordinate control over the "beginnings" of our habits and virtues and vices, the other hardly any control at all. Aristotle's connecting ethical virtues with both habit and choice offers a middle ground between tracing one's character to one's community and tracing it to one's own choices and actions. We do not control the beginning as much as we might like, but we do control what comes after the beginning more than it might seem. If the changes or development that come over time may escape our notice, like an illness, there are changes or development that can come after the beginning (1114b31–1115a2). What pertains to human beings admits of being otherwise. Aristotle's case relies on experience, such as the experience we have of legislators, who punish wrongdoers and honor those who do beautiful or noble things. By doing so, they encourage beautiful deeds and discourage shameful ones, whereas no one would try to persuade (*peithein*) someone not to feel heat or pain or hunger (1113b20–29). Although there are such things to which no persuasion can reach, persuasion proves that human beings can be the causes of their actions, both those who persuade and those who are persuaded. Persuasion is not force.

Aristotle does not articulate his middle position, however, until he considers another extreme view, one that traces what we become neither to our communities nor to ourselves, but to nature. In this case, he does not present the argument himself, but invents an interlocutor who engages him in argument: he refers to what "someone might say" (1141a31).

Someone might say, Aristotle reports, that those who are truly good are so by nature. They have an inborn "vision" or sight (*opsis*) "by which they judge nobly and take hold of the true good." This is not something that they can obtain or learn from another, or something that they can acquire by their own efforts, rather, they have it by birth. As a result, according to Aristotle's interlocutor, no one could be "the cause of one's own bad actions" (1114a32–b12). It also means, Aristotle responds, that no one could be the cause of one's own good ones (1114b13). This position squeezes out Hesiod's middle group of human beings, who, although they cannot by themselves understand all things, can be persuaded by another who speaks well (1096b10–13). If followed consistently, the position also deprives Aristotle of any reason for writing the *Ethics*.

Aristotle responds with more gentleness than anger, even conceding to his opponent that we owe something to our natural endowment. However, he insists, even if this were true, the actions we take come from ourselves (1114b20–23). Aristotle's interlocutor looks simply to the beginning for his understanding of human life—inasmuch as he thinks that all is determined at birth, by a "vision" or "sight" with which one is born. He overlooks the difference between ethical virtue and vision or sight that Aristotle pointed out: because we have sight we see, whereas because we perform virtuous deeds we acquire and then have virtue (1103a26–32). Aristotle's interlocutor does not go beyond vision or perception to the human mind that is capable of deliberating about the good and choosing it. If everyone were determined by what he is given at birth, there could be neither blame nor teaching. Aristotle's more complex position, in contrast to that of his imagined interlocutor, has greater affinity with both Oedipus, even if Oedipus too quickly jumps to blame, and Socrates, even if he too quickly jumps to teaching as an alternative to blame.

Aristotle imagines his interlocutor as speaking to him. His interlocutor states a position and addresses Aristotle's. He tries to persuade Aristotle, just as Aristotle tries to persuade us throughout the *Ethics*. If his position were correct, he would not be engaging Aristotle in argument, for Aristotle would be either born with a vision of the good or not. There could be neither persuasion nor education nor even improvement. Speech—and politics—would be nothing more than force or manipulation. His engaging Aristotle in argument implies otherwise. He is as inconsistent as the one who took credit for his good actions but not his bad. Speeches and arguments inform actions, as Aristotle claims in his reference to "mind and all that comes about through a human being" as possible "causes" (1112a31–32). Aristotle does not defeat his interlocutor in argument but allows him to defeat himself by engaging Aristotle in debate. His deeds speak more truly than his words.[10]

Aristotle mentions not only "mind and all that comes about through a human being" as "causes" but also "nature, necessity, and chance" (1112a31–32). To the extent that nature, necessity, and chance contribute to misdeeds, we should forgive, but to the extent that mind and all that comes through a human being does so, we should blame. The difficulty is understanding causes, specifically, that "we are somehow co-causes [*sunaitioi*] of our dispositions" (1114b24). Aristotle's "somehow" leaves the matter indefinite, or perhaps he leaves the matter "up to us."[11] By acting we become co-causes of ourselves. Our acting bears on our sight or vision of things. When we act, we experience ourselves as causes, but only co-causes. We experience the limits of our actions, both from ourselves and from the world in which we act. Aristotle thus ends his discussion by referring to a human being as a "co-cause," just as he earlier referred to actions as "mixed," in part voluntary, in part involuntary. But he has let us see why the goal of his *Ethics* is not to know what virtue is but to act

---

10. Like the one who argues that something can both be and not be at the same time, Aristotle's determinist refutes himself by attempting to make his case (*Metaphysics*, 1006a12–28).

11. Soon before addressing the determinist and reaching this conclusion, Aristotle repeats the phrase "up to us" no fewer than eight times in the lines 1113b8–14, almost as a counter to the laments of a tragic chorus that denies human responsibility.

virtuously. We could not do the former without doing the latter, for we would not know that anything could be up to us or that everything was not up to us. Our choices and our actions make a difference. The encouragement that Aristotle proceeds to offer by discussing the virtues on his list, and our acceptance or rejection of them, offer further proof for us that we can be the beginnings or causes of our actions, at least up to a point (see 1113b18–19).

COURAGE AND MODERATION

The first two virtues that Aristotle discusses, courage and moderation, which he pairs by associating them with the nonrational parts of the soul, are crucial for our living a *human* life, which, unlike the life of beasts, is free rather than slavish. Without courage we are moved by our fear of death and focus on preserving our lives rather than living well. Without moderation, we succumb to the bodily pleasures that we share with beasts.

Courage is a disposition toward the passions of fear and confidence, Aristotle says, especially toward fear. Although Aristotle at first refers to the one possessing courage as "fearless," he soon corrects this: the one who "fears what he ought, for the sake of what he ought, and in the way he ought" is courageous (1115a18, b18–20). Virtue, after all, is a mean between experiencing a passion too little and too much. For virtue to demand fearlessness would be to demand too much; virtue demands instead that we endure, and even recognizes that there are some things that are too frightening for anyone to bear (1115b8–11, 1110a24–26). Moreover, there are many things we fear—disrepute, poverty, sickness, lacking friends—but courage is manifest with respect to the most frightening thing, which is death (1115a13, 27). This does not mean that death is the greatest evil and hence that we should do everything we can to escape it. If so, courage would not be superior to cowardice. Rather, death is what we most fear. It is in the face of death that we require courage.

Moreover, courage occurs not with respect to every death, such as death at sea, or from disease, but with respect to the most beautiful or noblest death. That death is death in war, "which happens amid the greatest and noblest danger," at least according to the honors bestowed by cities and by monarchs (1115a25–b6). Whatever honors they may or may not receive, however, it is not for them that courageous persons risk their lives. They do so for the sake of the beautiful or noble. Their "end" is the beautiful (1115b13, 21–24; 1116a10–13, 16; 1116b1–3, 31–32; 1117b8). It is in reference to courage that Aristotle introduces the beautiful as the end of virtue. To act for the sake of the beautiful is to do the virtuous deed for its own sake, because it is beautiful to do so, and not for its consequences. The courageous person resembles those whose end lies in their own activity rather any further end that the activity serves or to which it is subordinate. So understood, the act of courage is the paradigm of a free act.[12] It is complete in itself, not moved by nor subordinated to anything outside itself. Thus Aristotle distinguishes courage from what he calls "political" or civic courage, which is based on a love of honor or shame, passions that tie one to a political community (1116a17–30). If one acted for the sake of gaining honor or out of a fear of a commander, one would be moved primarily by passions; a love of honor would overcome fear, or a greater fear would overcome one's fear of facing the enemy. So too would one moved by spiritedness, who acts "not for the sake of the beautiful" but "out of pain, as a result of being struck or afraid" (1116a32–33).

Someone who acts based on knowledge, or on ignorance, or on good hope (for the outcome) might also perform the same deed as would a courageous person, but that individual would not be courageous. If soldiers fought because they possessed a skill superior to the enemy, for example, or knew their side held the advantage in battle, they would fight because they believed in their safety, as would those ignorant of their enemy's strength or who had hope of victory. In these situations, considerations of the beautiful or the noble do not arise for those who do not perceive the danger to their lives. Soldiers who fight with knowledge of their superiority would turn and run, Aristotle points out, if the advantage changed to the other side, as would ignorant soldiers, if they came to know their situation, or those of good hope if their hopes were shattered (1116b16–23; 1117b15–17, 24–25).

Although Aristotle makes a strong appeal to lovers of the beautiful—and hence to the young (see *Rhetoric* 1389a36)—he qualifies that appeal

---

12. In the *Metaphysics*, Aristotle explains that a human being is free "whose being is for his own sake and not for the sake of someone else" (982b26–28; see also *Politics* 1254a14–18 and *Rhetoric* 1367a32).

in several ways.[13] He maintains that courage is action for the sake of the beautiful, and not for the honors that may be conferred on it, but he concedes that honor is a beautiful thing (1116a28). Moreover, if courage lies most of all in facing death in war, it is one's political community that offers the occasion for courage. When Aristotle argues that those who fight with skill or knowledge of their situation will flee when they lose the advantage, he contrasts them not with those who act for the sake of the beautiful but with "citizen soldiers" (literally, "those [fighting] for the political things"), who stand their ground and die, for it is shameful to flee, and death is preferable to safety in such a situation (1116b18–21). They act from passion, the passion of shame. When Aristotle turns to his account of political courage, and courage based on knowing, spiritedness, good hope, and ignorance, he calls them "other [courages]," leaving their status ambiguous (1116a17).[14] He thus isolates the beauty of courage from all the other factors involved in courageous actions, so that it can shine forth in purity. Although such isolation preserves beauty as an end for those whose circumstances require risking all other goods for its sake, what Aristotle said earlier of his division of the soul may apply—that what can be separated by speech may not be separable in nature (1102a29–30). Aristotle gives no exemplar of courage simply, as he does of political courage, when he refers to the Homeric heroes, whose inner motivations we know because the poet tells us about them. They desire honor, for example, or they are moved by spiritedness (1116a22–26, b27–30). And yet the courageous person is also spirited. Indeed, if the courage arising from spiritedness includes choice and acts for the sake of the beautiful, Aristotle says, it is courage (1116b26, 1117a4–6). Courageous acts can have mixed causes and

---

13. See Ward, "Nobility and Necessity," 71–83; Pangle, *Reason and Character*, 104–22.

14. Bartlett and Collins, *Aristotle's "Nicomachean Ethics,"* 56, translate "there are other kinds of courage, spoken of in five ways." Other translators, taking their bearings from Aristotle's distinguishing them from "true courage," find ways of avoiding the problem. Sachs, *Aristotle: "Nicomachean Ethics,"* 50, translates, for example, there are "other things called courage in five ways." Rackham, *Aristotle: "Nicomachean Ethics,"* 163, refers to them as "divergent types of character." He seems to understand Aristotle's "other" or different "courages" to mean "things other than courage."

purposes without depriving them of their beauty or nobility. Their pleasure is also mixed with pain.

Although Aristotle insists that the beautiful is pleasant to lovers of the beautiful (1099a13–14), he acknowledges that "courage is a painful thing" (1117a34). Indeed, that is why courageous acts are justly praised. Its end is nevertheless pleasant, he continues, comparing the courageous person to a boxer in a gymnastic contest. The latter's end—the crown and honors—is pleasant, while being struck is painful, for boxers are made of flesh and blood (1117b5). Aristotle's analogy to the boxer, who suffers for the sake of the pleasant consequences of boxing, implies that the end of courage lies outside the courageous act itself, which after all may bring wounds and even death (1117a34–b8). Aristotle earlier referred to "the honors bestowed by cities and by monarchs" to confirm the view that the noblest death occurs in war, as we saw (1115a25–b6). Their honors confirm the nobility of death in war only by affirming that such deaths should be honored by the community they serve.[15]

The courageous act is beautiful or noble, but is it good for the person who performs it? Only as he concludes his discussion of courage does Aristotle mention its relation to "happiness" and "complete virtue," using the terms that set off his inquiry into the virtues: "The more one possesses complete virtue and the happier one is, the more one will be pained at the prospect of death. To this sort of person living is especially worthwhile, and to knowingly be deprived of the greatest goods is a painful thing" (1117b10–15). When Aristotle argued earlier that the beautiful, the just, and the good admit of variation, he gave the example of courage along with wealth as goods that may bring a person to ruin (1094b15–19). His observation continues to resonate in his discussion of courage. The one to whom living is especially worthwhile is courageous in war despite being

---

15. Pangle, *Reason and Character*, 107, 121–22, offers an insightful and sensitive analysis of two strands she finds in Aristotle's treatment of courage—that courage is both intrinsically good and good for something—and shows how they are exemplified in Lincoln's Gettysburg Address and Churchill's "finest hour" speech. She raises the question whether "untangling this knot" would "cut the nerve" and destroy "the noble essence of courage." In the end, however, she comes close to doing this very thing when she argues that "the citizen's [tangled] intuition" of these two strands can find clarification on the level of the philosophic life, and that courage serves philosophy.

aware of what might be lost (1117b15). Such a one is a lover of beauty, but one who knows that beauty is not the only good. To those eager for beautiful deeds, Aristotle delivers a word of caution; to those timid from experience of life's sufferings, Aristotle insists on the beauty of even the greatest sacrifice. Neither a spiritedness with no thought of death nor a fear that seeks to preserve life at any cost can define a human life.[16]

When Aristotle turns to moderation and its extremes, he continues to acknowledge our attraction to pleasure and aversion to pain, and to educate both in light of the difference between a human life and a beastly one. Moderation and its extremes concern the bodily pleasures of touch and taste, that is, the pleasures of food, drink, and sex. The moderate person experiences such pleasures as he ought, when he ought, and from what he ought (1119a11–20, b16–18). The licentious person desires in excess the pleasures in which other animals share, pleasures that are "slavish and bestial." Licentiousness "belongs to us not as human beings but as animals" (1118a24–b4). Aristotle mentions gluttons, who "gorge themselves" and are "extremely slavish" (1118b20–21). In a way, gluttons sink even below the beasts. In the *Politics*, Aristotle alludes to cannibalism and incest as bestial acts involving eating and sex, observing that a human being is "the worst of all without law and justice" (1253a31–35). In his analysis in the *Politics*, however, law and justice do not merely hold the bestial in check, they also offer goods and their accompanying pleasures, by giving us opportunities to exercise our capacity for speech, for example, and for deliberation about the advantageous and the just (1253a15).

Similarly, in his discussion of moderation, Aristotle defines the virtue as experiencing the pleasures of food, drink, and sex, as one ought, as a human being rather than as a beast. So far is Aristotle from engaging in a

---

16. Commenting on Aristotle's statement that some fearful things are "beyond a human being [to bear]," and therefore frightening to everyone, at least to those with any sense (*nous*) (1115b7–9), Charney, "Spiritedness and Piety," 73, beautifully articulates the extremes involved in fear of the gods: "Fearing the divine too much results in paralysis because of the vastness of the unknown. The belief that they are loved by the gods causes the rash spiritedness of the Homeric heroes: they feared such things too little." I find in her observation an excellent insight into how the impiety implied in either of these extremes makes a good human life impossible. Atheism, paradoxically, might have a similar effect as the belief in the gods' unbounded care.

diatribe against pleasure that he attaches to moderation a vice of the deficiency and the excess. The vice of the deficiency belongs to those who experience the pleasures in which moderation is involved, food, drink, and sex, less than they ought. The vice is so rare that speech does not accord it a name, but Aristotle does: "insensibility." In designating this extreme as "not characteristically human" (1119a6–8), Aristotle indicates that there are experiences of the pleasures of food, drink, and sex that are characteristically human.

In the *Politics*, Aristotle quotes Homer's Odysseus to describe the pleasures that belong to the pastime of free persons (*eleutheroi*): there is no better way to spend our time, Odysseus tells his host, than what occurs when human beings "enjoy good cheer" and "the banqueters seated throughout the hall listen to a singer" (1338a24–30). Odysseus continues in Homer's text: "Near them tables are filled with bread and meat, and the cup-bearer draws wine from the bowl, carrying it around and pouring it into goblets. For me this is the most beautiful thing" (*Odyssey* 9.5–11). For him, the most beautiful thing is not as it was for Achilles—facing death in war—but belongs to peace. Moreover, the pleasures of food and wine can belong to free persons, not merely to slavish ones, pleasures Aristotle (and Homer) connect with music. So too in discussing moderation in the *Ethics*, Aristotle refers favorably to a passage in Homer's *Iliad* in which Thetis tries to distract her noble son from his grief and anger. She reminds him of the pleasures of sex, for "it is a good to lie in love-making with a woman" (1118b9–12; *Iliad*, 24.130). Animals experience the pleasures of sex; human beings can recognize them as good.

Beyond those pleasures of food, drink, and sex, to which moderation is directed and whose experience Aristotle acknowledges is good for a human being, lie a range of pleasures, moreover, that a *human* life also holds. There is "the most liberal of the pleasures involving touch," such as "those in the gymnasia connected with massage or heat" (1118b5–8). Many of the pleasures from the senses that human beings enjoy are unavailable to beasts, Aristotle explains further, referring to the pleasures of sight, hearing, and smell. Human beings enjoy seeing colors, shapes, and drawings, hearing melodies and dramatic oratory, or smelling roses or incense: "In the case of the other animals, there is no pleasure associated with these perceptions, except incidentally, for it is not the smell of hares that hounds enjoy but the meat." It is not the sound of the cow's lowing that pleases the lion, but the meal his hearing anticipates (1118a14–23).

Human pleasure in the senses therefore differs from that of beasts, and from that of the licentious who enjoys the smell of perfumes and foods in the way a hound enjoys the smell of a hare (1118a12–13). So too are there pleasures that Aristotle explicitly attributes to the human soul, including the pleasure of learning and the pleasure of honor (1117b28–29).

Aristotle's references to the "liberal" or "free" pleasures of the gymnasia, to say nothing to his mentioning the range of pleasures that belong to human beings as distinct from other animals, speak to lovers of the beautiful, offering them pleasures for times of peace rather than war. Aristotle may follow Thetis in advising her noble son to enjoy pleasure, but he goes further than she does. Although Aristotle began his discussion of moderation by calling attention to "the nonrational parts" of the soul to which courage and moderation belong, his conclusion emphasizes reason's work. "Just as a child ought to live under the guidance of his teacher," so ought the desiring part of the soul be guided by reason (1119b13–14). With this observation, Aristotle concludes book 3 by reminding us that human life extends beyond our bodily existence, for we are rational beings whose desires can be guided by reason. In book 4, he continues to explicate the virtues he has listed in outline. Those virtues both expand the scope of the human freedom that is manifest in courageous and moderate acts and occur more directly in our relations with others. As long as humans live the life of beasts, slaves to necessity and therefore lacking in freedom, the virtues that involve their living together cannot flourish. Courage and moderation, proper dispositions toward fear and bodily pleasures, support our experiencing even more distinctly human pleasures and pains, and our extending the human work required for happiness to our lives in community with others.

CHAPTER 3

The Virtues of Living Together

Distinguishing the Human from the Divine (Book 4)

In book 4, Aristotle places even greater emphasis on ways in which the ethical virtues manifest the freedom possible for human beings that we saw in his accounts of courage and moderation. Although "human nature is enslaved in many ways," as he observes in the *Metaphysics* (982b31), Aristotle discovers in the ethical virtues a route to freedom. A courageous person acts for the sake of the beautiful rather than out of fear, and the moderate person seeks bodily pleasures only as appropriate. More generally, through habituation we acquire a character from which our choices and actions proceed. Aristotle pursues the many ways in which freedom is achieved through the virtues in book 4—the first that he discusses there, liberality (*eleutheriotēs*), is even related to the word for freedom (*eleutheria*)—and at the same time he shows that freedom finds expression through our relations with others, in the way that liberality involves spending our resources on others. The emphasis in book 4 on community prepares for his discussion in book 5 of justice, which is "complete virtue" because the just person acts not only "with regard to himself but also in relation to another" (1129b30–34).

Liberality involves the proper giving and spending of money (1120a3). Rather than cling to the goods necessary for life, the liberal share their goods with others. Their focus is not on mere life, but on virtuous action.

The person characterized by munificence is liberal on a grand scale, as the name of his defining virtue (*megaloprepeia*) (literally, "fitting greatness") suggests. Aristotle defines the person with greatness of soul as worthy of the greatest things, and honor is the greatest of the external goods, but in his greatness he considers even honor "a small thing" (1123b18–24, 1124a19). The great-souled individual Aristotle describes most manifests the freedom and independence of which humanity is capable, a freedom and independence implicit in all the virtues.

At the same time that ethical virtues elevate human beings over the beasts, the question of presumption and hubris arises. Could the individual who occupies the peak of virtue come to believe that he is divine? Aristotle cautions against such presumption when he points out that "the greatest things" that the great-souled individual claims to merit are honors, but honors are what "we assign to gods" (1123b19). His wry comment serves as a reminder of the distance between gods and human beings. Aristotle's treatment of courage and moderation in book 3, which involve passions we share with beasts, distinguished the human from the bestial, but in book 4, throughout his exposition of the virtues that culminate in greatness of soul, Aristotle cautions against impiety, encouraging deference to the divine at the same time he shows how the virtues manifest freedom. In the first section of this chapter, I discuss liberality and munificence, which Aristotle pairs, inasmuch as both involve giving, albeit on different scales (1122a18–22).[1] In the second section, I discuss greatness of soul, its grandeur along with its need.

Following greatness of soul, Aristotle places even greater emphasis on human community, first presenting a longing for honor, neither too much

---

1. Collins, "Moral Virtue and the Limits of the Political Community," 47–48, argues that "in the movement of the first five virtues from courage to magnanimity [greatness of soul]," Aristotle "presents the elevation of virtue to its fullest expression and natural peak as an independent end," while his turn to justice looks at the virtue in light of law and the common good. My analysis finds support in hers, but I argue too that Aristotle's very presentation of these virtues that culminate in greatness of soul shows that even they properly belong to human actions in community with others. I also emphasize the educative effect of Aristotle's account on those who pursue these virtues, and I find the ongoing theme of piety in Aristotle's discussion of these virtues in book 4.

nor too little, as a virtuous mean. Whereas a great-souled person does not long for honor from others and accepts it because they have nothing else to give him (1124a5–9, a29), Aristotle proceeds to describe a proper longing for honor that occupies a virtuous mean and therewith requires dependence on those who assign honors (1125b7). The lover of honor who seeks a mean does not suppose that he is worthy of the honors we assign to gods. Gentleness, the proper disposition toward anger, belongs to the one who defends himself and his relatives from harm and insult, while avoiding the extremes of anger that make a person "hard to live with" (1126a31). Both in defense of his own and his forgiveness for wrongs inflicted on him, the one attaining the gentle mean recognizes his common humanity in a way that rules out a transcendence of the human in the direction of divine sufficiency. Aristotle's treatment of the love of honor and anger and their virtuous dispositions, I argue in the third section of this chapter, revises our view of the peak of virtue and further demonstrates how freedom is manifest in the goods that living with others makes possible. This is true also of the three means that arise in our "living together" and in our "sharing in speeches and deeds": giving pleasures to others as is fitting, telling them the truth about oneself, and engaging them in times of play and amusement (1126b28–31, 1127a20–22, 1128a19–22). These virtues that belong to our living together are expressions of our freedom, as I argue in the next three sections (fourth, fifth, and sixth sections) of this chapter, each dealing with one of these "social virtues."

In discussing the virtue associated with play, Aristotle recurs to the liberal person, who reveals what is and is not fitting to say and to hear in play. Although Aristotle admits that what is fitting may escape definition, he speaks of the "shameful language" employed in comedies, and he insists that "slandering and mocking some things" are impermissible (1128a23–32). His observations lead him to his final topic of book 4, which I discuss in the last section of this chapter, the question of shame. To refer to shame, Aristotle uses a word, *aidōs*, whose meanings range from "fear of disrepute" to "reverence or awe" before the divine. Shame or reverence checks shameful deeds, and it teaches us that we are worthy of higher ones. In book 4, Aristotle moves from the self-direction and freedom manifest in virtuous action, without losing sight of our limits, to our dependence on the direction of others, and even on reverence, without losing sight of our achievements.

LIBERALITY AND MUNIFICENCE

Aristotle defines liberality as both the proper giving (and spending) of money and the proper taking of money, but especially giving (1119b25–27).[2] Liberal human beings rise above necessity in that they direct "the resources necessary for life" to virtuous actions. They are characterized by correct giving—to those whom they ought, as much as and when they ought, for the sake of the beautiful or the noble (1120a24–27). The very name of the virtue is related to freedom. They do not cling tightly to life's necessities, as do the stingy, who are more concerned with living than with living well. As Aristotle says, the stingy are "more serious" about money than they ought to be (1119b29–30). Nor does the liberal person suffer the vice of the prodigal, who dissipates "the resources through which [a human being] is able to live," for he gives so much away that he "destroys his resources" (1120a1–4). The word translated as "resources," *ousia*, is the Greek word for "being." In destroying his own substance, the prodigal expends himself. He is, literally, "unsaving" or "unpreserving" (*asōtos*), and since many adjectives in Greek can have both passive and active senses, Aristotle is able to play on this ambiguity in saying that the "unsaving" prodigal is "unsaved," or "destroyed" (1120a1).[3] Like the reckless person, his excess may take his life, in that it consumes his livelihood. And like the reckless person who may become a coward and run when the going gets tough, his excess in giving may lead the prodigal to become stingy: "Resources quickly run out for those who give their own things to others" (1121a18).

This description of the prodigal serves as a warning to the liberal person. When Aristotle explains how the liberal person must not only give to those whom he ought but also take from those he ought, he gives the example of his taking from his own possessions "because it is necessary so that he be able to give" (1120a35–b2). The liberal person even hesitates to receive from others: "He is uninclined to ask [anyone for anything], for

---

2. For thoughtful discussion of Aristotle's treatment of liberality and the place it occupies among the other ethical virtues, see Mathie, "Aristotle's Liberality," esp. 78–137.

3. See, for example, Aeschylus, *Agamemnon* 1598, and Sophocles, *Ajax* 190.

one who is a benefactor is not readily the recipient of a benefit" (1120a32–35). As a result, he will have "little left for himself" (1120b4–6) or for others to whom he might give. In distinguishing prodigality from liberality, Aristotle shows how preserving one's own is not at odds with virtuous action, and how it is in this case its precondition. His argument here foreshadows his understanding of friendship—that loving oneself is the condition for loving another, even while friendship strengthens one's self-love (e.g., 1170b14–17; 1166a6–33; 1166b10–18).

Of the two extremes, "stinginess is said to be the contrary of liberality," Aristotle observes, "for it is the greater evil than prodigality, and [people] err on its side more often than on the side of prodigality" (1122a13–17). Our ties to necessity have a greater pull on us than the freedom achieved by giving. We speak of "illiberality" (*aneleutheria*) as only one of the extremes, stinginess, whereas literally the word could also refer to prodigality. Neither extreme is liberality. Common speech tends to blur prodigality and liberality when it identifies its contrary as stinginess. Aristotle observes that the liberal person because he is a benefactor is "the most loved" of those who act from virtue (1120a22). The praise of those who desire to receive encourages giving without limit. Aristotle's account of liberality buttresses liberality from the praise that would lead it to prodigality.

It is a tyrant who has resources so great that he can give without limit, or at least it seems so. On this account, we "do not speak of tyrants as prodigal," Aristotle observes, for it is difficult for a tyrant's spending to "exceed his great wealth." No one is prodigal unless he "spends more than [his] resources allow" (1120b24–27). But although the tyrant is no prodigal, in that he can be "unsaving" (*asōtos*) without being ruined (*asōtos*) as a result, even he cannot be free from taking, Aristotle soon points out.[4] The tyrant's great resources come from great injustice: that he takes from improper sources ("plundering cities and pillaging temples") shows that he is "wicked, impious, and unjust." Impiety is at the center or core of the tyrant's vice. His wickedness extends to pillaging temples as well as plundering cities. His unlimited giving, as it were, requires even divine resources, which he steals from the gods. The liberal person, in contrast, who gives only "to whom he ought and as much as and when he ought"

---

4. Mathie, "Aristotle's Liberality," 131. Also *Rhetoric* 1366a7.

(1120a26), does not require the unlimited resources of a god. Just when Aristotle emphasizes the exalted humanity the virtues make possible, he also reminds us of piety—and its violation by the tyrant. Human beings must protect the temples in which they worship along with civilized life against those who would destroy both.

Aristotle connects the virtue of liberality with that of munificence (*megaloprepeia*), which also involves spending and giving, but on a grand scale (1122a18–23). Not only is munificence concerned with grander objects than liberality, but Aristotle does not include taking along with giving in his definition of the virtue. He nevertheless explicitly raises the question of where the resources that support munificence come from. Those who are munificent, Aristotle observes, must have resources "to begin with" (*proüparchein*), whether on account of themselves or on account of their ancestors or connections (1122b30–33). In this way, Aristotle reminds munificent spenders of their dependence on what came before (*pro*), the acquisition or taking on which giving and spending depend, specifically, on the efforts of progenitors who might have bequeathed wealth. If one must have resources to begin with, one is not, strictly speaking, beginning (just as the virtuous person who chooses to do the beautiful deed has habits to begin with). When Aristotle observes that "the poor person cannot be munificent" (1122b28), he is not—as he is sometimes understood to be doing—restricting virtue to the wealthy classes. Rather, he is underscoring the problem of virtuous action, especially for the wealthy: the "greater" the virtuous action and hence freedom, the greater one's dependence on others, in this case on one's ancestors or other connections from whom one's wealth came. Those who are causes of their actions might forget what they owe to others, to the past, and to the circumstances that make their acting possible, and therefore forget that their noble giving required their having received. Aristotle reminds those who desire freedom of what they are inclined to forget. If the munificent spenders have "resources to begin with," they are the cause of their actions, but only the co-causes.[5]

---

5. Mathie further emphasizes the problems that Aristotle reveals in his account of the virtue, including its tendency to the vice of vulgarity (Mathie, "Aristotle's Liberality," 148–63). She argues that Aristotle's insistence that the munificent person is liberal "if taken seriously, [is] a demand for liberality to im-

Distinguishing the Human from the Divine (Book 4)   97

For munificence, "the expenditure will be great and fitting to the work" (1122b2–3). A munificent work produces wonder, Aristotle says (1122b17–18). Since munificence produces a work outside its own activity, the one who possesses the virtue and the others in the community can share in wonder at the work. As is fitting to his discussion of giving on such a grand scale, many of Aristotle's examples of munificent acts involve the gods, such as gifts for votive offerings, sacred buildings, and sacrifices. Aristotle even generalizes his list of munificent deeds to those that concern the entire "daimonic" realm (1122b19–23). He uses a word that Socrates uses in the *Symposium* for what exists between divine and human and connects the two (202e).[6]

Aristotle extends his examples of munificent works to include endowing splendid choruses in the dramatic festivals, providing public feasts, and outfitting triremes (1122b19–24). Aristotle gives an example of even a private work of munificence, "furnishing one's house [*oikos*] in a way appropriate to one's wealth, for it too is a sort of cosmos," or an ordered or beautiful whole. Like the god Aristotle refers to in the *Metaphysics* who imparts order (*taxis*) on the cosmos (1075a11–15), munificent persons give order to their home, to that small part of the world that is their own. Their homes, however much ordered wholes, do not replace the whole, no more than human beings can replace the gods: "The same things are not fitting for gods and human beings," nor are the same expenditures appropriate to temples and tombs (1123a5–11). Gods have temples, but human beings have tombs.[7]

---

pose its limits upon magnificence [munificence], too." If munificent persons are really liberal, "in order to spend nobly or fittingly, they will have to recognize and act in a way that befits their true limitations as well as their greatness" (ibid., 164).

6. Observing that Aristotle includes in munificence honoring the gods with festivals and temples, Pangle, *Reason and Character*, 131–32, suggests that it "comes the closest of Aristotle's virtues to replacing piety, which he has omitted from the ranks of the moral virtues." It is a "replacement" because instead of "fearful obedience" or "reverent devotion," it involves "contemplation and celebration of all that is best in the cosmos and in humanity itself." But if contemplation and celebration of the good is at odds with fearful obedience, is it also at odds with reverent devotion?

7. I agree with Collins, *Aristotle and the Rediscovery of Citizenship*, 159, that "a magnificent [munificent] work that pertains to the divine must take into

Given the "greatness" that defines munificence, it is difficult to explain the virtue as a mean. The "vulgar" person, as Aristotle characterizes the vice of the excess, spends great sums on small objects, while "shining with lustre [*lamprunetai*]," as when he endows a comic chorus more lavishly than he should and leads it onto the stage. He acts not for the sake of the beautiful, or for the sake of the virtuous act itself, but in order "to display his wealth, believing that he will be wondered at" (1123b20–26). In contrast to the one who possesses the virtue of munificence, who produces a work to be wondered at, the vulgar seeks to be the object of wonder, as he makes himself shine in public. The word we translate as "vulgarity" is literally a "lack of experience of the beautiful" (1122a31). Whereas endowing splendid (or lustrous) choruses is an example of munificence, Aristotle mentions only in the case of the vulgar that he leads the choruses he sponsors onto the stage. His display is not only ostentatious; he makes a display of himself. And yet Aristotle says that vulgarity does not bring reproach if it does not harm others and is not too unseemly (1123a34). He treats the vulgar as a comic figure, a boaster who pretends to virtues he does not possess. Aristotle even singles out comedies as the dramas for which the vulgar provide choruses and then lead their choruses onto the stage.

Aristotle's reference to the ostentatious display of the vulgar echoes Thucydides's description of Alcibiades. In Thucydides's work, Alcibiades claims before the Athenian assembly that he "shines with luster" (*lamprunomai*) by means of his public expenditures that bring renown to his city, and even boasts of the choruses he sponsored in the dramatic festivals (Thucydides, *Peloponnesian War* [*PW*] 6.16.3, 5), using the very verb that Aristotle then uses in the *Ethics* to describe the vulgar. Like those of vulgar excess in Aristotle's account, Alcibiades makes a display of himself, but unlike them he causes great harm to his city: suspected of plotting tyranny and accused of impiety, Alcibiades escaped to Sparta and offered

---

account the distance between gods and men, and not least the fact of [human] mortality." However, I have reservations about her interpretation that a munificent work overcomes that distance by endowing the munificent spender "with a kind of immortality" that challenges "conventionally pious views." The munificent person builds a tomb for himself, not a temple, while it is the one whom Aristotle criticizes as excessive whose lavish display reveals a desire to become an object of wonder (1123b20–26).

advice to his city's enemy (*PW* 6.27–28, 88–93). By distinguishing munificence from vulgarity, Aristotle offers something of greater beauty to those like Alcibiades who are tempted by tyranny. Those with the virtue of munificence, after all, give munificent works to the public that are objects of wonder. They do not attempt to make themselves objects of wonder (see *PW* 6.5–6). And unlike the vulgar, they do not belong on the comic stage. By conforming their deeds to the fitting, they also save themselves from tragedy.

Although Aristotle does not mention him by name in the *Ethics*, Alcibiades makes a brief appearance in the *Posterior Analytics*, when Aristotle includes him among those who might possess one form of "greatness of soul," the very virtue to which he turns next in the *Ethics*. In the *Analytics* he associates Alcibiades with an inability to endure being wronged (97b18–19),[8] but in the *Ethics* he characterizes greatness of soul as forgetting wrongs received (1125a3–6). In his discussion of liberality, he has already warned against tyranny, another vice to which Alcibiades was prone. Only a reformed Alcibiades would have a place in the *Ethics*.

GREATNESS OF SOUL

"Greatness of soul," which Aristotle describes next, appears to bring "munificence" and all the other ethical virtues to their highest point. The one "who is truly great-souled must be good and what is great in each of the virtues would seem to belong to [him]" (1123b28–30). It is "the crown [*cosmos*] of the virtues, for it makes them great, and it cannot come to be without them." Aristotle's treatment of this peak of virtue reveals what is

---

8. In the *Posterior Analytics*, Aristotle looks for what great-souled individuals have in common that defines them. Alcibiades, Achilles, and Ajax were unable to endure insult. On the other hand, there were Lysander and Socrates, who were indifferent to good and bad fortune. He thus places Alcibiades in the class of the more dependent types of greatness of soul, "*if* they are great souled" (97b16–26). In the *Rhetoric*, Aristotle finds it characteristic of the young to be unable to endure slight, and to become indignant when they believe they have been wronged (1389a18–19). In Thucydides, the elderly Nicias reproaches Alcibiades for his youth when the latter urges his city to undertake an expedition against Sicily, while Alcibiades brags of his youth (*PW* 6.12.2, 6.17.1).

at stake in virtue itself. As we have seen, Aristotle understands virtue as a disposition toward the passions rather than a passion, and acting virtuously as requiring that we do so with "awareness" and "choice" (1105a32–33). Virtue is possible when we step back, so to speak, from the impulsion of our bodies, through which we experience the passions, and of the external world that arouses them, so that we can deliberate about the best course of action and make choices. Only then are we the cause of our actions. The great-souled individual manifests this human potential for freedom and the virtuous activity it makes possible, stepping back even from acting until he finds action worthy of his greatness (1124b23–26). When he acts, he therefore does so from choice and with awareness of himself and his action. We look up to the great of soul, for they demonstrate what human beings can achieve. They help us to trust, in other words, that virtuous activity is possible.

Although Aristotle admires greatness of soul, he is aware that the great-souled individual tends to forget his limits, and that he is not as independent and self-sufficient as he tends to assume. The great-souled individual may attempt to be simply what he is, without bending to accommodate the world, but Aristotle's account of him is not simple. In showing that he forgets his own limits, Aristotle attempts to educate him, to remind him of his humanity while preserving the greatness that manifests humanity's achievement. By bringing him into the human fold, Aristotle saves him from the tragedy to which a lack of self-knowledge might lead, and the comedy to which boasting makes one prone. There is no doubt, however, that Aristotle thinks that erring on the side of the excess is preferable to erring on the side of the deficiency. He calls the former "vanity," but it is the latter to which he gives the name "smallness of soul" (1124b8–13).

Aristotle begins his exposition by defining the great-souled individual by a correspondence between his worth and his claims about himself. The great-souled person "deems [or claims] that he is worthy of the greatest things, while being worthy of them" (1123b2). Aristotle admits that it is difficult to explain how greatness of soul is a mean between two vices, since it is "an extreme" (*akros*) with regard to greatness (1123b13–15). He nevertheless understands the great-souled as a mean between the vain person, who deems that he is worthy of more than he is worthy, and the small-souled one, who deems he is worthy of less than he is (1123b8–13). The great-souled both *is* great and deems himself to be so.

Of what is the great-souled person worthy and of what does he deem himself worthy? Worth is a term of relation, Aristotle says, and therefore if one is "worthy," one is worthy of something. The great-souled person is worthy of honor, Aristotle explains, for "honor is the greatest of external goods"; it is "what we assign to the gods" (1123b14–24). In book 1, Aristotle distinguishes praise from honor, the former being a term of relation, for we praise something as good for something else, whereas we honor what is divine and complete. We therefore praise virtue and virtuous individuals on account of their activities and works, whereas honor is reserved for the gods (1101b12–27).[9] The goodness that is worthy of honor, in contrast to that worthy of praise, comes not from benefiting others, or from good and beautiful deeds in which goodness is manifest. Whatever good deeds they perform, the deeds of those worthy of honor are not a measure of their goodness, for honor, Aristotle says, is not a term of relation. They are not good because they do good deeds; they do good deeds because they are good. Unlike the lovers of honor who devote themselves to politics, they need no confirmation from others to trust their own goodness (1095b28). They trust their own goodness. Otherwise they would not deem themselves worthy of the greatest things. Their opinion of themselves is not mediated by others, for they assign honor to themselves. Aristotle says that the great-souled themselves are "beautiful and

---

9. Howland, "Aristotle's Great-Souled Man," 41–42, also has recourse to Aristotle's earlier distinction between praise and honor in his discussion of greatness of soul. That the great-souled individual deems himself worthy of honor, which we assign to the gods, he argues, illustrates his acceptance of the standards of the community about the gods and about the highest virtue—that the gods are benefactors of human beings and that the most divine virtue human beings can possess lies in doing great deeds for the city, especially saving the city when it is threatened. From this perspective, the city fails to understand the distinction between praise and honor when it understands the gods as benefactors, as does the great-souled when he wants to be honored for his deeds. They both reduce honor to praise. By implication, the advantageous is more important to the city than the beautiful. I suspect, however, that this distinguishes the city from the great-souled individual. That is, precisely because he understands the distinction between honor and praise, he claims he is worthy of honor. He does not want to be honored for his deeds. He does not want to be honored for anything he does, but for what he is.

good."[10] They experience completeness or wholeness in themselves. Only then can beauty and goodness become one.

The great-souled person accepts honors only from "serious human beings on the ground that he obtains what is proper to him or even less—for there could be no honor worthy of complete virtue, but he will nevertheless accept it since they have nothing greater to give him" (1124a5–9). For him, "honor is a small thing" (1124a19). Although greatness of soul concerns honor (*peri timēm*) (1123b23), he would not pursue it as a good that he needs for himself. His taking from others, the honor they bestow on him, is indistinguishable from his giving to them, inasmuch as he allows himself to be honored. He takes no great pleasure in it (1124a6–7); he receives only out of a noblesse oblige. Aristotle never calls him "a lover of honor."

Aristotle indicates problems with greatness of soul in a number of ways. Unlike the case with the other virtues, greatness of soul has no characteristic deeds. The courageous individual risks his life in battle, for example, and the liberal one gives to others as is fitting. When Aristotle says that the great-souled possess (*kektēsthai*) beautiful but fruitless things, for this is the mark of a self-sufficient person, he indicates that they make no use of their possessions, unlike those who do liberal and munificent deeds. Aristotle does not say that they "acquire" beautiful things, but that they "possess" them, that is, he uses the perfect form of "acquire." For the great of soul, the "acquiring" in the past is lost in the perfect present, just as one who practices munificence has possessions "to begin with." Even more important than Aristotle's silence about how the great of soul has acquired beautiful possessions is his silence about the genesis of the virtue itself. As Jacob Howland notes, this silence "creates a misleading impression of his self-sufficiency."[11]

The great-souled person possesses what is beautiful and fruitless, but fruitless suggests sterility. Aristotle also describes him as "idle" (*argos*) and a procrastinator (*mellētēs*) and "disposed to act" (*praktikos*) in few things,

---

10. Or as Aristotle says more cautiously, they are "not without *kalokagathias*" (1124a4). Burger, *Aristotle's Dialogue*, 83, observes that "perhaps [the great-souled individual] cannot be said to act for the sake of the beautiful, since that would mean aiming at a *telos* outside himself." See also Kass, "Professor or Friend?," 27n3.

11. Howland, "Aristotle's Great-Souled Man," 53n44.

and "only where a great honor or deed is at stake" (1124b23–26). In effect, he acts only if he deems an honor and deed worthy of him. "Idle" means literally "without a deed" or "without a work" (*a* + *ergon*), but human beings have work(s) to do. When Aristotle sought to define happiness in book 1, he sought the human work (*ergon*). There he questioned whether all the artisans could have works while the human being could have none and be idle (*argos*) (1097b28–30; see *Politics* 1265a15). The word translated as "procrastinator" means literally "one who is about to." But one who is about to do something is not doing it. He seems to hover outside of time, outside the act that can occur only in time.

Although Aristotle names this virtue from greatness of *soul*, he describes the *bodily* characteristics of the one who possesses it. Nothing about him is left to chance. His movement (*kinesis*, "gait") is slow, his manner of speaking steady (*lexis stasimos*), and he "hastens about" few things (1125a13–14). *Stasimos* means "stationary" or "standing," as well as "steady."[12] It also refers to the song that the chorus sings in tragedies once it has taken its stand in the orchestra, rather than as it enters or departs. Aristotle gives us the impression that the great-souled individual hardly moves at all, as would be the case for someone who is self-sufficient, for he would have no need that would prompt his moving toward satisfying it. We might say that presenting greatness of soul so understood as the peak of virtue would be "altogether strange" for someone like Aristotle who claims that "happiness is an activity" (see 1100a13–14).

Aristotle expresses his clearest reservations about the great-souled individual in observing that he is "not given to wonder" (*thaumastikos*) (1125a3–4). Yet wonder, Aristotle says in the *Metaphysics*, is the beginning of philosophy (982b12–13). He is not given to wonder, Aristotle says, because "nothing is great to him"—a phrase that Aristotle repeats several times in describing the great-souled person, almost as if it were a refrain of a tragic chorus (1123b32, 1125a16, and 1125a3–4). He does not even think his living is worthwhile (*axion*), for he throws his life away by facing great dangers (1124b7–9).[13] Far from suggesting that he is a model for

---

12. Ibid., 54.

13. See Collins, "Moral Virtue and the Limits of the Political Community," 52n12, for discussion of the alternate translation, "for him living at any cost is not worthwhile," and her preference for the one I have used.

humanity, Aristotle has offered another model, if not of "complete virtue," of someone who approaches it, as we have seen at the end of his examination of courage: one who "is more pained at the prospect of death *the more he possesses complete virtue* and the happier he is." "For him, living is especially worthwhile [*axion*], and as a consequence he would be aware that [death] would deprive him of the greatest goods" (1179b10–13). It could not be said of him, as Aristotle says of the great-souled individual, that "nothing is great to him." He nevertheless chooses what is noble at the risk to his life. No disdain for life makes his choice easier.

Aristotle described the liberal person as uninclined to ask others for help, for "a benefactor is not readily the recipient of a benefit" (1120a32–35), but he goes further in describing the great-souled person, who benefits others but "is ashamed [*aischunetai*] to be benefited by them." Although he claims at the end of book 4 that shame is not a virtue, since a good person would not do anything that brings shame (1128b21–23), Aristotle reveals what brings shame to the great-souled person. Perhaps even more shameful, the great-souled person remembers benefits he has bestowed but forgets benefits bestowed on him (1124b10–15, 1125a4–5).[14] If he were sufficiently shamed, he would accept a benefit from Aristotle, and shame would be instrumental in his correction.

Aristotle further shames the great-souled with his reference to how Thetis, the mother of Achilles, asked Zeus for a favor. In Aristotle's account, Thetis reminds Zeus not of the benefits she conferred on him in the past, but of the favors he had previously conferred on her (1124b16–17). She knows that the great of soul like to regard themselves as benefactors rather than as beneficiaries. As a result of her understanding of greatness of soul, Aristotle implies, she can manipulate the great-souled

---

14. Aristotle's observation that the great of soul forgets benefits received echoes Tecmessa's reproach to Ajax in Sophocles's play: "The one from whom the memory of benefits received flows away is not a noble man [*eugenēs*]" (523–24). Tecmessa—the same woman whose advice Ajax attempts to silence ("For a woman silence is a [fitting] adornment" [*Ajax* 293; *Politics* 1260a30])—formulated Aristotle's implicit point. That is, Aristotle's understanding of the noble comes closer to hers than to her husband's. To forget benefits received is ignoble and ugly.

Zeus. She does so by confirming his understanding of his own greatness.[15] Aristotle, in contrast, shows the great-souled that they have in fact received benefits, when he describes them as forgetting the benefits they receive. He reminds them of what they forget. In the *Posterior Analytics*, Aristotle includes Achilles among those thought to be great-souled, but his mother's asking Zeus for a favor was on her son's behalf and at his urging. Achilles requires a favor from Zeus, and he asks his mother to obtain it for him. He needs the gods, including his semidivine mother. And this is not the first time that Aristotle mentions an incident from the *Iliad* in which Achilles needs his mother's help, but there too he does not refer to Achilles by name (1118b10–11). Just as Aristotle does not mention Alcibiades by name in the *Ethics*, he never names Achilles. If his mother has a place in Aristotle's work, Achilles, like the "great-souled" Alcibiades, does not.[16]

If the great-souled individual is "inclined to the truth" (*alētheutikos*) as Aristotle says (1124b30), his forgetting of benefits received shows that his inclination to truth does not always win out. Aristotle nevertheless attempts to appeal to it in his description of greatness of soul. Aristotle's telling him the truth in this case coincides with his helping him, for he not only causes the great-souled the pain of shame, but also offers him the pleasure of friendship when he proceeds to observe that the great-souled is "unable to live in relation to another, unless to a friend, since to do so is slavish" (1124b35–1125a1; *Rhetoric* 1367a32). Aristotle, in effect, attempts to move the great-souled individual from his "steady stance" on stage into

---

15. Aristotle revises Homer's account when he puts it to use in the *Ethics*. In the *Iliad*, Thetis does remind Zeus that she has benefited him in the past (*Iliad* 1.503). Homer's Thetis does not understand greatness of soul, as Aristotle implies that she does. Or perhaps Thetis does not attribute greatness of soul to Zeus. She does persuade Zeus to grant her request (*Iliad* 1.510–29).

16. Nor does Aristotle mention Ajax in the *Ethics*, his third example of an individual who cannot endure insult when he discusses possible definitions of greatness of soul in the *Posterior Analytics*. Nor does he mention any of the three by name in the *Politics*. When in the *Politics* he quotes Ajax's dismissive words to his wife from Sophocles's *Ajax*, for a woman, "silence is a [fitting] adornment," he avoids naming him by referring to them only as the words of the poet (*Politics* 1260a30; Sophocles, *Ajax* 293). Aristotle's own silence (even though it speaks volumes) about these seemingly heroic figures is "a fitting adornment."

the audience with others or, less metaphorically, into the human community.[17] After all, he is "eager to be of service," Aristotle says, even though he has difficulty in finding deeds worthy of his performance (1124b18–19, 23–26). Should he see himself in Aristotle's description, he might accept his work as a human being and no longer be an idler or a procrastinator. Only then could he experience happiness—a word that does not appear in Aristotle's description of greatness of soul, but it does appear in that of his courageous counterpart, who knows what goods he would lose by dying (1179b10–13). And should he understand the benefits of friendship, he would see how dependence on another does not deprive him of freedom. Since friendship is reciprocal, and friends help each other (1155b28–56a5), friendship links the receiving of goods to the giving of them. One can live "in relation to" a friend, without being slavish. To trust his own goodness, a friend looks to another, as does the lover of honor, but he trusts not simply one who knows him and has good judgment (*phronimos*) (1095b29), but also one who loves him. And he could not be so "unsparing of his life" as one who had no friend and who considered nothing great (1124b9).[18]

In one of the few times "greatness of soul" is found in the Platonic corpus, in the *Alcibiades II*, Socrates calls it is "the most beautiful of the names for folly," belonging to someone who has not yet learned "how to be disposed toward gods and human beings" (150c). Aristotle, almost as if in response, brings greatness of soul into the *Ethics* as a virtue, indeed a peak of virtue, and attempts to teach the great-souled individual how to be disposed toward gods and human beings without diminishing his greatness but even enhancing it.

---

17. For further discussion of greatness of soul and friendship, including Homer's depiction of the friendship between Achilles and Patroclus and of Achilles's reconciliation with Priam after Hector's death, see Cain and Nichols, "Aristotle's Nod to Homer," 60–66.

18. Burger, *Aristotle's Dialogue*, 84–85, argues that "the great-souled individual, who should be complete in himself, aims however unwittingly at something whose fulfillment necessarily lies beyond himself." Although she refers to his desire for self-sufficiency and the greater claim that theoretical activity can make to satisfy that desire, friendship in a sense also lies "beyond oneself," since it requires another. The fulfillment of the great-souled individual could lie in friendship, however at odds with self-sufficiency it may be.

LOVE OF HONOR AND GENTLENESS

Aristotle moves from the "grand" scale of munificence and greatness of soul back to a virtue that more obviously occupies a mean, when he argues that there is a mean and extremes with regard to the longing for honor. The mean with respect to honor, he argues, is not commonly understood: "We praise the lover of honor [*philotimon*] for being manly, but also blame him for aiming at honor more than he ought." So too do we praise the one who does not love honor (*aphilotimon*) as measured and moderate, but also blame him for not choosing to be honored, not even for noble things (1125b8–14). Common opinion, like greatness of soul, is riddled by contradictions when it comes to honor, both admiring it and disparaging it. Neither common opinion nor greatness of soul understands that love of honor admits of a praiseworthy mean. Common opinion is nevertheless right in one way, for however torn it may be with regard to love of honor and its lack, it confers honors and dishonors by means of praise and blame. Our common way of speaking, at least as reflected in Aristotle's report of it, gives the love of honor the praise it deserves, not the honor that belongs to the gods.

Although there is also a proper disposition toward anger (for one can become angry at what and with whom one ought, and how and for how long one ought), it has no name. Aristotle calls it "gentleness." Almost as if recognizing the anomaly in calling the virtuous experience of anger gentleness, he points out that the virtue falls closer to the deficiency than to the excess. Since human beings are inclined to anger (as Aristotle's says, "to seek revenge is more human [than not to do so]" [1126a30–31]), Aristotle is undershooting the target in the very name he gives to the virtue. Those who do not get angry when they ought are nevertheless considered foolish, for they do seem uninclined to defend themselves when attacked. Moreover, to hold back when one is treated insolently and to overlook insolent treatment of one's relatives (*oikeioi*) is held to be slavish (1126a8–9). Freedom (vs. slavishness) still belongs to virtuous actions, and it is manifest in defending one's kin (1126b4).

Aristotle's treatment of anger, like his discussion of love of honor, bears on greatness of soul. One to whom nothing is great would not be quick to anger. But Aristotle now indicates that being angry in the proper circumstances is a virtue, as in the defense of one's relatives. Moreover, the gentle, like the great of soul, are not inclined to revenge wrongs, but there is a telling difference. Whereas the great of soul do not remember wrongs done to them (1125a4–5), the gentle are inclined to forgive rather to seek revenge (1126a1–2). Forgiveness (*suggnōmē*) replaces forgetting, and "knowing from the perspective of others" (literally, "knowing with" another) therewith replaces the sense of one's worth or superiority to others.

In support of gentleness, Aristotle concludes that the one who "deviates only a little from the mean" with regard to anger "is not blamed." As he explains, "it is not easy to put into speech how far deviating from the mean is to be blamed, for this depends on circumstances, and judgment lies in perception" (1126a36–b6). Once again, the guidance of speech, even Aristotle's speech, however helpful in identifying virtue as a mean, cannot replace the judgments that must be made in each case and the perceptions on which they are based. When these limitations come to the forefront of the discussion, so too does "forgiveness." Gentleness, which is inclined to forgiveness, is not only the proper disposition to those who wrong us, but toward those who deviate from virtue more generally, at least if only "a little" (see also 1109b14–20). Gentleness is a virtue conducive to our living with others, Aristotle points out. The angry who err on the side of the excess "are difficult to live with," just as those bitter in their anger are "troublesome to themselves and above all to their friends" (1126a31, 25–26).

FRIENDLINESS

Aristotle next speaks of three means that can be found in "our associations with one another, both in living together and in sharing in words and actions" (1126b13–14). All three, he says, are nameless. Commentators refer to them as "social virtues" and typically translate them as "friendship," "truthfulness," and "wit" (or "wittiness") on the basis of Aristotle's descriptions, but he clearly says that the first differs from friendship (1126b23), narrows the meaning of the second to speech about oneself (1127a2426), and appropriates a word for the third that means literally "making good turns" or "versatile" and associates it with play (1128a8–11). These "means" as Aristotle describes them do not appear in common discourse about the virtues. No one would notice if Aristotle left them out.

Distinguishing the Human from the Divine (Book 4) 109

What place do they have in his search for the virtue or virtues that make happiness possible?

Aristotle acknowledges that his speaking of these means having to do with our living together requires explanation. In the course of discussing them, he mentions two purposes: "seeing more about character" and "trusting that virtues are means" by seeing that even in these cases there are means and extremes (1127a15–18). No matter how many praiseworthy means we learn about, our accepting that the virtues are means, it seems, requires trust. That Aristotle examines each one of the means relating to character for the sake of learning about it seems obvious from his doing so. That he is doing so also for a more general purpose, to foster trust that virtue is a mean, is something we know from his telling. His deeds speak for themselves only in part. "Seeing" Aristotle's purposes requires trusting his words, precisely because our trusting him proceeds from our having come to know him, through hearing his words, observing his deeds, and judging both, as he gives us the opportunity to do throughout the *Ethics*.[19]

In speaking of his purpose in treating these means, Aristotle interjects himself into the discussion more clearly than he has done since he prefaced his criticism of the ideas with observations about himself. Aristotle tells us there that he holds both friends and truth dear, but as a philosopher he honors truth before all, even while suggesting that friendship and truth accompany each other (1096a12–16). Since the means to which he now directs attention involve friendship and truthfulness, his examination of them serves further reflection on himself. With wit as the third, they include a sort of verbal playfulness. They occur in a movement Aristotle makes in the latter part of book 4 to "re-vise" greatness of soul, to look at it anew, as it were, so that the great-souled person might live in relation to others, beginning with a friend (1125a1). That re-vision involves not only the proper love of honor and a gentleness conducive to

---

19. Consider Aristotle's discussion in the *Rhetoric* of the character of the speaker as a cause for trust or means of persuasion (*pistis*), indeed the most authoritative cause of persuasion. Trust of the speaker should come from his speech, Aristotle says, not from his prior reputation (1356a1–15). He reveals his character from his speech, when it demonstrates his prudence, virtue, and good will (1378a8–19).

living with others, but also truthfulness about oneself, and movements of character that Aristotle locates in play. These various means represent a revised understanding of greatness of soul, or what the great-souled individual might become, if he sought honor and friendship, if he directed his truthfulness to himself, and if he appreciated that both play and seriousness belonged to life (see 1124a8, 1125a10).

The first mean relating to our living together resembles friendship, Aristotle says, for it pertains to one who approves and disapproves as he ought, who praises and opposes as is fitting, giving pleasure for the right things and in the right way, and even pain when doing so serves what is noble and beneficial (1126b29 and 1127a6). Aristotle's treatment of the great-souled individual might serve as an example of what Aristotle describes here—paining him by shaming him and pleasing him with the prospect of friendship. At any rate, the mean falls between obsequiousness, which praises everyone on every occasion, and surliness, which never gives pleasure. Unlike the extremes, the mean requires judgment. Aristotle uses similar words to describe this mean that he applies to distributive justice, which he later treats, and which involves "distributing the fitting" (1127a2; e.g., 1131a25).

This mean resembling friendship differs from friendship, as Aristotle explains, in that the person who possesses it acts in regard to those with whom he is acquainted and to those with whom he is not, and to those with whom he is close and to those with whom he is not. Furthermore, he acts not from the affection that friends have for each other, but because he is the sort of person he is (1126b20–25). Aristotle's description of this person who is like a friend fits Aristotle himself as author of the *Ethics*. He may or may not be acquainted with his addressees, and in many cases he would not, and he may or not be close to them, and in most cases he would not, but he praises and blames (both what we say and what we do), and approves and opposes as is fitting. As he says of the person he now describes, he chooses to give pleasure, and is cautious about giving pain, as he considers the consequences with regard to both the beautiful and beneficial (1127a2–6).

To trust the mean, we must understand that it is at work in Aristotle's own deeds. He is not simply setting a standard for the virtuous activity of others, but he is also describing one by which he himself can be judged.

He is aiming at this standard in his deeds. He is doing for his addressees what friends do for each other, approving and disapproving as is fitting, giving pleasure and not pain as far as he can. Aristotle's own work in the *Ethics* is nevertheless incomplete, not only because time is his co-worker, and not only because others will fill in and even modify his outline, but because it lacks the reciprocity of friendship, which requires friends' awareness of each other's good will (1155b33–37), and without friendship no one would choose to live (1155a5–6). His discussion of this resemblance to friendship prepares for his fuller examination of friendship in later books of the *Ethics*. Not only is his treatment of this resemblance to friendship incomplete—since it is only a resemblance—so too is his speech in the *Ethics*, which must be completed by the deeds of life. After all, Aristotle has pointed us beyond the *Ethics* to his own life when he told us that those who introduced the ideas are his friends. Similarly, his praising and blaming in the *Ethics* can be completed only outside the *Ethics*, in the praise and blame that citizens render to one another, and in the pleasures and pains that friends share with each other.

TRUTHFULNESS

The next mean that Aristotle describes is "truthfulness" in words and deeds, which belongs to the one "who admits that he is neither more nor less than he is." Aristotle contrasts him with the boaster, who pretends to qualities he does not have or who pretends to possess them to a greater extent than he does, and the ironist, who pretends not to have qualities he does have or to have them to a lesser extent than he does. Unlike these extremes, the truthful person neither exaggerates nor diminishes himself (1127a19–27). Why would the boaster and ironist choose to exaggerate or minimize themselves? Aristotle gives greater attention to the boaster than to the ironist. He explains that someone might pretend to be more than he is "for the sake of something," such as gain or reputation. In such cases he might be acting unjustly, for example, seeking to gain more than he merits. Or he might seek honor in excess. Such a person boasts, but he is not a boaster. He is an unjust man or a lover of honor more than he ought to be. The boaster does not boast "for the sake of anything," but simply because he is the sort of person he is (1127a27–b18). He has no ulterior motive, as Rackham translates it.[20]

Rackham's translation captures in English the dilemma Aristotle is presenting. English usage implies that one with an ulterior motive deceives others, as would the unjust person who acts "for the sake of gain," but "ulterior" literally suggests "more final" or "more complete." Aristotle's reference to those who act "for the sake of something" recalls his statement at the beginning of the *Ethics* that human beings act for the sake of some good. We all have ulterior ends (and purposes) when we pursue a good that contributes to another. The hierarchy of our ends with which Aristotle introduced the *Ethics* militates against any understanding of words and deeds as simply what they appear to be. We have multiple ends, some immediate, others less so: we make a bridle for the sake of riding, to use Aristotle's example, and ride for the sake of war, and go to war for the sake of protecting the city (1094a10–17, b2–4). And yet, a bridle-maker might take pride in his craftsmanship, a rider might take pleasure in riding, to say nothing of a soldier who is courageous for the sake of the noble rather than for his city. What we need is a vision of a whole to which our activities belong that does not minimize the goods that our various activities provide as merely instrumental. Even so, how our ends fit together or how they are ranked in any hierarchy is only more or less visible from our activities.

What looks like an end may in fact be a by-product. What looks like a means may be one's end. The difficulty in drawing precise distinctions does not necessarily mean that we deceive others and even ourselves about why we do what we do, but that we pursue many goods. Imprecision saves the phenomena and preserves the truth. Aristotle has been doing this throughout the *Ethics*, as when he began with an architectonic capacity or art and left it open whether the more complete good lies in its practice or in the good it secures because of its activity, the order it provides for a political community. So too when Aristotle comes to "truthfulness" about oneself, as we have seen, he finally makes explicit that he has more than one purpose in investigating the ethical virtues: "seeing [or knowing]" the mean under consideration and "trusting" the mean by seeing the extent of its being at work in human affairs. His inquiry goes beyond the specific

---

20. Rackham, *Aristotle: "Nicomachean Ethics,"* 241.

mean or virtue at issue, for it also serves a more general purpose. His two purposes are nevertheless inseparable, neither serving as a means or end of the other, but co-workers. To be sure, Aristotle's truth-telling about himself runs the risk that he will not be trusted, since his several purposes allow that he might have an ulterior one. But Aristotle takes that risk. That is the sort of person he is (1127a14–18). He has an ulterior motive.

Aristotle coins the word *authekastos* to describe the truthful person (1127a23), literally, one who "[speaks] each thing as it is." As we might say today, the truthful person "tells it like it is." Those who do so would be truthful about themselves, for they would have no ulterior motive for saying something, only its truth. In the *Eudemian Ethics*, Aristotle calls the one who is *authekastos* "simple" (*haplous*) (1233b36), which can mean "without duplicity" (or "honest"), as well as "lacking complexity." But the truth itself is not simple, especially in regard to human affairs, which admit of variation and where actions have more than one purpose. One whose speech spoke "each thing itself" would act as if he could speak with more truth or precision than his subject matter warrants. One who tells it like it is speaks precisely, but he does not tell us everything we might want to know about something, such as the purposes it might serve. The one who attempts to speak so precisely about human things boasts that his speech says more than it does. He is a boaster.

Aristotle claims that whereas "in itself, falsehood is base and blameworthy, and truth beautiful and praiseworthy," boasting is more blameworthy than irony (1127a28–33). If falsehood were the reason for blaming the extremes that verge from the truth, and if one of them (boasting) could be less true than the other (irony), then the truth itself would not be simple. In any case, saying less rather than more leaves to one's addressees to fill in or interpret in different ways. The one who guards against the false, Aristotle says, "inclines [in his words and deeds] toward what is less than the truth rather than toward what is more" (1127b5–9).

Aristotle therefore expresses his preference for irony over boasting: "Those who show irony in a measured way" can be "gracious in their irony" (1127b23–33). They are unlike the great-souled person who "speaks and acts openly," who is "given to saying everything [*parrhēsiastēs*] on account of contempt for others," and who "is truthful, except when being ironic before the many" (1124b29–32). Aristotle's gracious ironist, in contrast, is not frank out of contempt for others nor ironic out of consideration for them, nor does his irony arise from distinguishing the few from the many.[21] Perhaps he is ironic in his speeches and deeds because he knows the difficulty of "saying everything," because, in words that Aristotle uses to speak about the boaster, the truth is "the sort of thing it is." It is the sort of thing that leads Aristotle to a third mean appropriate to our living together, one that belongs to play, and one that involves perceiving double meanings in words.

WIT

Relaxation or rest (*anapausis*) "also belongs to life," Aristotle points out, and relaxation involves play (*paidia*). In the activities of play, as Aristotle describes them, reciprocity is more at work than in other means hitherto discussed. Even liberality, which involves both giving and taking, has more to do with the former than the latter. As to the other of the means that arise in "living together" and "sharing in words and deeds," "friendliness" lacks the affection and reciprocity of friendship, and truthfulness and its extremes involve how one presents oneself to others. The mean involved in play, as Aristotle presents it, concerns both speaking to others and listening to them, both giving and receiving.[22]

The mean in speaking and listening to others in play is nameless, but Aristotle names it "good turning" (*eutrapelia*), or "facility in turning." The word is used elsewhere in extant Greek literature to mean "versatile."[23] Based on Aristotle's application of the word to speech, scholars

---

21. For other treatments of Aristotle's sympathetic presentation of irony, see Collins, *Aristotle and the Rediscovery of Citizenship*, 152–54, and Smith, *Revaluing Ethics*, 112.

22. Aristotle even mentions what is fitting to say and hear "in turn [*en merei*] at play" (1128a20), using the same expression he uses elsewhere for ruling and being ruled in turn (*en merei*) (e.g., 1161a25; *Politics* 1261b1, 1279a10, 1371b1). In their insightful examination of Aristotle's treatment of wit, Craig and MacDonald, "Wit's Justice," 47–70, argue that wit's freedom and concern with others serve as a preparation for "a just life in a free and equal community."

23. *Eutrapelia* (good turning) and *eutrapelos* (the person of good turns) are found infrequently in Attic Greek. Pericles, in his funeral oration in Thucydides's *Peloponnesian War*, praises the "versatility" of the Athenians (2.41.1), while Pindar uses the term in a negative sense, in reference to "versatile profit-seekers"

typically translate it as "wit" or "wittiness." By the same token, we might also call it "wordplay." In its literal sense, however, it could apply to what Aristotle has been doing throughout the *Ethics*, making "good turns" as he turns from one virtue to another, even turning to a variety of perspectives in order to see them in light of both the beneficial and the beautiful. In any case, Aristotle is versatile enough now to apply the word to what can occur during play, and to use it to refer to speaking and listening to others. The versatility at issue involves "the movements of character," he observes, rather than those of body, even though we judge bodies also by their motions (1128a10–13).[24] Once again, he juxtaposes the person he describes with the great-souled one he portrayed earlier. The latter's movement (*kinesis*) is slow, and his manner of speaking steady (*lexis stasimos*) (1125a13–14). He lacks ease in turning. His movements, moreover, are bodily ones, and they reflect the lack of motion and of "versatility" that follows from his character, that is, from his presumption of self-sufficiency.[25] He does not hurry. In contrast, a witty person could be described as "*quick*-witted." Just as the great-souled individual must learn to act, and even interact, so the virtuous one, defined as he is by his activity, must learn to rest ("relaxation belongs to life"), and the serious must learn to play.

The one with facility in wordplay would be able to see more than one meaning in words, and to turn from one to the other in speech. He might present new possibilities by combining words, or by using them in different ways. He is free from conventional usages that limit seeing by limiting speech, and he can therefore find more in ordinary speech than usage captures. He exploits conventions to reveal the unconventional in conventions through his "turns" of phrase. Aristotle gives no explicit examples now of wordplay, but he illustrates how he uses words in new ways

---

(Pythian 1.92). Neither occurrence is explicitly in reference to speech, as Aristotle uses the word.

24. Aristotle says also that the witty person possesses "dexterity" (*epidexiotēs*) (1128a18). To give meaning to Aristotle's use of the word in this context commentators typically translate it as "tact."

25. For a helpful discussion of Aristotle's implicit juxtaposition of greatness of soul and "wit," see Block, "Aristophanic Comedy and Aristotelian Wit," 8. Block contrasts the great-souled person as a tragic figure and the witty person, who is the comedian of the *Ethics*.

in the case of *eutrapelia* itself. In fact, we have seen throughout book 4 how he uses the words that name the virtues in new ways, such as munificence and greatness of soul. Other instances of his wordplay involve dubious etymological connections that make use of chance to reveal truth. The very title of his work derives *ēthos*, "character," from *ethos*, "habituation," which helps us to understand how who we are (our characters) is dependent on but not reducible to habits that we have acquired. His dubious derivation brings two things together while keeping them apart. In other cases, Aristotle exploits the active and passive sense of adjectives, as when he calls the prodigal person *asōtos*, both "unsaving"/"wasteful" and "unsaved"/"ruined," and thereby lets us see the potential tragic character of nobility that he attempts to avert by his teaching about ethical virtue as a mean. He coins the word *authekastos* to describe the truthful person, a word that suggests someone who says what each thing is in itself, or (as I argued above when discussing *authekastos*) whose speech misses the complexity of things. In either case he would not be given to wordplay. Aristotle's wordplay, inasmuch as it discovers and reveals truths not apparent in the conventional use of words, does not belong merely to times of relaxation as opposed to work. It does the human work of truth-telling. The play Aristotle describes belongs to a truthful person who knows one cannot say each thing precisely as it is, and play serves as a means of his truth-telling. So does Aristotle's many coinages of words, such as *energeia* (activity) and *prohairesis* (choice) combine ordinary words to reveal truths that he has discovered.

When Aristotle coins a word for coining words in cases of nameless means and extremes (*onomatapoiein*), he also coins a word for his purpose in doing so, "for the sake of clarity and ease in following along [*euparakolouthētou*]" (1108a17–19). At the same time that Aristotle fashions a name for his "coining names," he fashions one for our activity in response to his: because he fashions names, we can follow (*akolouthein*) by his side (*para*) and might do so well or with ease (*eu*). Aristotle's word has so many components that we must "follow along" simply to grasp its meaning. Aristotle thus remembers his addressees and includes them in his work, and in his play. His purpose is their following along with him. His wordplay is for them as well as for himself. He does not play alone.

In the matter of play, the extremes are the buffoons, who aim at laughter in every situation no matter how unseemly or painful to the one mocked, and the boors who never say anything funny and are annoyed with those who do (1128a4–10). Neither buffoon nor boor need exercise judgment, for they are always the same, resembling the extremes in relation to friendliness: the obsequious who try to please everyone and the surly who please no one (1126b13–16). They are no more versatile than either the buffoon or the boor. "Good turning" or "wit" thus resembles friendliness, which gives pleasure and pain as are appropriate. Aristotle also connects wit with freedom, for the witty person says and listens to the sorts of things appropriate to a liberal or free person (*ho eleutherios*). There are certain things that are fitting "with regard to what one should say and how one should say it, and what one should listen to" and "to what sort of people one should speak and to what sort one should listen" (1127b33–1128a2). It is the free person who serves as a standard, because different things are pleasant for different people, such as the "shameful speaking" (*aischrologia*) of old comedy and the "innuendo" (*huponoia*) of more recent comedy (1128a23–25).

Previously, Aristotle held up the "serious" person (*spoudaios*) as a standard for others. What the serious person wishes, for example, is truly good, whereas a base person wishes for whatever chances to appear good to him, just as healthy things appear so to the healthy person, but not to the sick one (1113a20–33). Accordingly, scholars sometimes render the *spoudaios* as "morally serious" to capture his goodness, but Aristotle introduces the term in the *Ethics* before making the distinction between ethical and intellectual virtues.[26] *Spoudaios* is related to a verb "to hasten," "to hurry," or

---

26. When defining human work as the activity of the soul accompanied by reason in book 1, Aristotle observes that the serious human being does this work well, just as the serious cithara player plays the cithara well (1098a7–17). Here *spoudaios* refers to the good or exemplary member of a class. Mara, "Interrogating the Identities of Excellence," 311, 316, 319, examines several conceptions of the *spoudaios* that Aristotle brings forward for interrogation in the course of the *Ethics*—"the spectacular daring associated with the noble," "the broad decency exhibited by the just," "the deliberative excellence characteristic of the prudent," and even "the contemplative engagement with the highest things." Mara shows persuasively that Aristotle's dialogic treatment of the *spoudaios* presents complications that lead to further refinement (e.g., ibid., 305, 307, 310, 313, 316, 317). I would add that Aristotle's reference to the liberal or free person (rather than the *spoudaios*) as a standard for what is appropriate in times of play and, indeed, his

"to be serious about" (*spoudazein*), which is also the opposite of the verb "to play" (e.g., 1157b2–4; Plato, *Gorgias* 481b–c; *Republic* 452d, 535c). Relaxation (*anapausis*) is "ceasing" (*pauein*) from work, a sort of "letting up" or "letting go," and the serious person by definition rushes. The *spoudaios* is good without being playful. When Aristotle comes to seemly and unseemly play, he therefore defers not to the serious person but to the free or liberal one, and also to the "gracious" one, using the same word he applied to the ironist (1128a33). The liberal and gracious person, he says, is "a law for himself" (1128a33). He is therefore not lawless. He ought not do everything (1128b30). Neither ought his playmates, insofar as they too are liberal and gracious.[27]

In this way, Aristotle avoids saying that play participates in lawlessness, for the person of good turns is "a law" for himself. It is a law that Aristotle takes it upon himself to declare: it is lawful for a liberal person "not to cause pain to his listener and even to delight him," Aristotle says, using a standard reminiscent of the mean that resembles friendship (1128a26–27; cf. 1127a3–5). Aristotle here defers to the "equitable person" along with the free one in matters of play (1128a19), foreshadowing his discussion on law and equity in the next book of the *Ethics*. Equity too is

---

very choice of a word (*spoudaios*) that serves as the antonym for playful also offer complications.

27. Collins, *Aristotle and the Rediscovery of Citizenship*, 158, 162, also emphasizes the connection between wit and freedom, pointing out the power of comedy to "liberate a person from the conventions laid down by the lawgiver." To laugh at a convention, she observes, is to free oneself from it. Aristotle praises the witty person as "a law unto himself," inasmuch as "the liberation this apparently minor virtue makes possible—liberation from convention and our primary attachment to a regime—is preparatory to philosophy." My analysis, which also highlights this apparently minor virtue and its importance for understanding human freedom, focuses on Aristotle's choice of *eutrapelia* to name "wit." The "turns" we make with commonly used words indicate not only freedom from convention but also dependence on conventions and the ways in which we speak about things for understanding and revealing truth. So understood, "witty" activity is not only "preparatory" for philosophizing but a reflection of its activity. The witty person's "tact" leads him "to acknowledge the prohibitions of the lawmaker," as Collins speculates (158), but it is also the case that his wit teaches him to respect the conventions from which truth emerges, albeit with the assistance of his facile wit.

versatile when it judges extenuating circumstances that fall outside and qualify the law. But equity is nevertheless a kind of justice (1137b24–27), just as the free person is "lawful." In another sense, by referring to the law of the free person as one of delighting others, and also by connecting play with reciprocity, Aristotle foreshadows his discussion of friends in later books of the *Ethics*, for friends delight in each other's virtues (1162a28, 1157b2–4).

Aristotle speaks not only of the one who is a law for himself but also of the lawgiver, who forbids slander or abuse. Since "a joke is a kind of slander," Aristotle observes, "perhaps lawgivers should prohibit joking about some things" (1127a30–31). Aristotle does not elaborate, nor say "what kind" of slander a joke might be, or what things should not be the butt of jokes, or whether lawgivers should in fact forbid such jokes. Although he says nothing more definite about curtailing speech, he nevertheless implies that there are some things that should not be laughed at. If "good" turning is praiseworthy, there are some turns that are not. Aristotle speaks of wit as "good" turns, not the "many turns" that Homer associated with the wily (*polutropos*) Odysseus, who sacked the "sacred" citadel of Troy (*Odyssey* 1.1–2). If there are some things that should not be laughed at, those things would restrain or even direct wit in its enjoyment of freedom. Before moving to justice, laws, and legislators, Aristotle turns to the next mean in his outline, "shame" or "reverence." It is a fitting move, since there are some things that should not be laughed at.

SHAME OR REVERENCE

Shame is not a specific virtue, Aristotle begins, because it "is more like" a passion than a disposition or virtue (1158b10). It is therefore not simply one thing or the other—a passion or a disposition—and requires more ambiguous speech than the wont of someone who tries to tell everything like it is. As "a fear of disrepute" (*adoxia*), Aristotle points out, it "comes near" to the fear of terrible things, as we see from its effects. The person who is ashamed blushes, just as the one who fears death turns pale (1128b11–16). Aristotle began book 4 with the virtue of "liberality" and moved to the "free person" as a standard for what should be said and heard, but he ends by reminding us of our body, our lack of control over what affects us, the influence of common opinion (the fear of disrepute), and our mortality (fear of death). It is an appropriate conclusion to a movement that educates one who possesses greatness of soul, who is defined by his soul in abstraction from his body. His soul is so all encompassing that it even determines his bodily movements, such as his deep voice, his steady speech, and his slow gait (1125a14–15). If Aristotle succeeds in shaming him by describing his shame at being benefited, the great-souled person would come to blush—a quite different sort of revelation of his inner state.

A good person would not do anything for which he would be ashamed. We suppose, however, that shame is appropriate to the young, Aristotle observes further, "who often err because they live by passion," and that shame checks them (1128b16–24). Shame is therefore not only something one feels after acting basely. It is also something that checks one from doing something base. Shame supports the courageous acts even of the Homeric heroes, as Aristotle showed when quoting Homer in his account of their courage (1116a20–29). Moreover, all who do not possess virtue live by their passions, confidence or fear, for example, or desire for those pleasures with which moderation is concerned. And how many possess virtue so strong that their passions never threaten to lead them astray? Shame would be appropriate to anyone else, as it is to the young. Through fear of disrepute, shame checks vice and leads to virtuous actions, even when one does not possess virtue. Shame is a support for virtuous activities and a check on vicious ones. Law, to which Aristotle will turn in his discussion of justice in book 5, is another.

When referring to "shame," Aristotle uses both the word *aidōs* and the more common *aischunē*. As Bartlett and Collins point out, the former can "refer to 'awe' or 'reverence' due to the gods and divine things."[28] The

---

28. Bartlett and Collins, *Aristotle's "Nicomachean Ethics,"* 38n24. Aristotle could have given his account of this mean with reference only to "shame" (*aischunē*) and with no mention of *aidōs*. This is what in fact he does when discussing shame in the *Rhetoric* (1383b14–1384a34). In that discussion, he uses *aidōs* only when quoting a poet (1384a30). In the *Ethics*, where he refers to "reverence" in addition to "shame," he uses *aidōs* frequently in his own name. In his outline of the means in book 2, he uses *aidōs* or its derivatives four times, and alludes to *aischunē* only once in his reference to someone who is shameless (*anaischuntos*) (1108a32–

shameful can be laughed at or ridiculed, as Aristotle's reference to the shameful speech (*aischrologia*) of comedy attests, but we do not mock or laugh at what we revere.

Shame is a mean, Aristotle says, between being ashamed at nothing (or shamelessness) and being ashamed at everything, for which Aristotle offers the Greek *kataplēx*, which means literally "struck down [by the world]," and is usually translated as "timid" (1107a31–1108b1). Lacking *aidōs*, the shameless would be godless, while the "timid" is cowed or overcome, perhaps discouraged by poetic tales that the gods are jealous of human beings who prosper. But poets lie when they say that the gods are jealous, Aristotle says in the *Metaphysics* (983a2–4). The one with *aidōs*, who is neither cowed (perhaps by the fear of jealous gods) nor shameless, is sufficiently confident of himself to pursue the good, and not so confident that he is unchecked by shame. Such *aidōs* belongs to the virtuous individual who aims at the mean, avoiding both excess and deficiency. Whereas Aristotle said unambiguously in his outline of the means in book 2 that *aidōs* is not a virtue, he now speaks more ambiguously that it is not "a particular virtue" (*tis aretē*) (cf. 1128b10 with 1108a32). His language allows it to belong to all of them.

A great-souled individual who deems himself worthy of what is assigned to gods would not possess *aidōs*, while the "small-souled" who deems himself worthy of less than he is worthy and who "refrains from beautiful actions and pursuits" (1125a25–26) would be timid. In his account of the extremes attached to *aidōs*, Aristotle implicitly criticizes the shamelessness of the former, and the timidity of the latter. *Aidōs* supports both confidence and deference, protecting our humanity against succumbing to the slavishness of beasts and against presuming the status of gods. As such, *aidōs* is a fitting conclusion for Aristotle's survey of the virtues that manifest our resources for acting and our involvement with others when we do so. Aristotle's criticism of poetry's hubristic and jealous gods, whether models of hubris or sources of fear, is therefore at one with

---

b1). So too in his discussion of courage in book 3, he divides political or civic courage into a lower and higher form: that coming from fear of one's commander is inferior to that arising from shame or reverence. Here he uses *aidōs* rather than *aischunē*. His brief treatment there foreshadows his treatment of *aidōs* at the end of the book 4.

his political reform. The virtues Aristotle offers to potential tyrants, such as Alcibiades, might turn them from a godlike and godless tyranny to gratifications in serving the community, from a tyrant's pillaging temples, for example, to a munificent erection of them. Similarly, Aristotle's shaming the great of soul who forget the goods they have received from others, as when he alludes to Achilles's dependence on a favor from Zeus, holds the potential of expanding shame into reverence, *aischunē* into *aidōs*. It is fitting that Aristotle deliberately blurs the two in his last discussion in book 4. When Aristotle describes human beings as political by nature in his *Politics*, he claims that "a human being is the best of animals when perfected [in political communities]." So too is he "the most *unholy* and savage without virtue," "the worst of all without law and justice" (1253a31–35). As is also fitting, Aristotle concludes book 4 with a mean that produces a blush and with the exhortation: "Now let us speak of justice" (1128b36).

CHAPTER 4

A Shrine to the Graces

Justice and Tragedy (Book 5)

In his outline of the virtues in book 2, Aristotle treated justice as an anomaly, claiming that is not spoken of in "a simple way" and that he will go through each of the ways of speaking about it (1108b9–10). His reference to justice in his outline is brief, as is his treatment of it lengthy, for he accords to it alone of the virtues he discusses a book of its own.[1] He repeats his statement about the complexity of justice near the beginning of book 5, explaining that the various ways of speaking about justice "escape notice" because they all use the same name (*homōnumia*) (1129a24–32). Aristotle's observations about justice echo his criticisms of those who introduce the ideas in book 2: they too pay insufficient attention to the various ways in which we speak about the good, for good belongs to numerous categories, such as quantity, quality, relation, time, and place (1096a17–29). As a result, they propose that there is a "universal" (*katholou*) good, literally, "a good that pertains to the whole," to "all" those things we call good, to which we give "the same name" (*homōnumois*) (1096b27). If there is an idea of the just (and the beautiful), justice can be spoken of in only one way, for only the idea is simply just (or simply beautiful). But justice "is not spoken of simply" (1108b8). Wit, which Aristotle recently

---

1. This chapter adapts and expands Nichols, "A Shrine to Graces," 121–43.

discussed near the end of book 4, made us aware of how words can have more than one meaning, for wit brings out their multiple meanings, as it turns one way and then another, and serves truth-telling as well as play. Now, Aristotle argues, if we paid sufficient attention to speech, we would see that justice, like the good, is spoken of in more than one way. Indeed, justice is one of the ways we speak of the good; the beautiful is another way.

In the *Republic*, to be sure, Socrates appears to speak of justice in more than one way, not only of the idea of justice but also of justice in the city he describes and in the soul that resembles it. In that city, however, philosophic rulers use the ideas as patterns that they embody "in the city and the dispositions of human beings" (501a–c). For many reasons, Aristotle argues in the *Politics*, this political project is misconceived: if justice is one idea, the just city that tries to use it as a model will destroy itself, for an idea in Plato's sense is simple, or without parts, whereas a city is made of dissimilar parts. To speak like Aristotle, the city will be reduced to a family, from a family to an individual, and from an individual to an idea (*Politics* 1261a19–25). Socrates even describes the attempt to found a just city as a tragic enterprise. Their "beautiful city" (*kallipolis*) (527c) falls to faction when its citizens are no longer willing to do what is best for the city, but instead compete for honors and wealth. The city degenerates into a series of inferior regimes culminating in tyranny (547b–c). Socrates calls upon the Muses to assist his account of its decline in "high tragic talk" (*Republic* 545e).[2]

Following his tragic presentation of political life, Socrates asks his interlocutors to look for justice in the proper ordering of the soul rather than in the affairs of a political community. Justice, Socrates says, is "not with respect to someone's minding his external business, but with respect to what is within, ... giving order [*kosmēsanta*] to himself, becoming his own friend, and harmonizing [the parts] of his soul" (443d). The individual who harmonizes his own soul becomes, as it were, a cosmos, sufficient unto himself. He is as self-sufficient as an idea. From Aristotle's perspective, although Socrates is now looking to the soul rather than to the city to see justice, he is still speaking of justice in only one way. The

---

2. So too in the *Laws* an Athenian Stranger founds a regime that he insists is "the truest tragedy" and understands the tragic poets as his rivals (817b).

individual who orders his soul may imitate the cosmos and its order but he is no part of a cosmos, just as he is no part of a city.

Aristotle, in contrast, insists that justice is "complete virtue" because it is practiced "not only in relation to oneself but in relation to others," even mentioning that "justice alone of the virtues is held to be another's good" (1129b28–33, 1130a4; cf. *Republic* 343c). His emphasis throughout is on the many ways that justice becomes manifest in relation to others. His treatment of justice continues the movement in his account of the ethical virtues toward "living with others and sharing in speeches and actions" (1126b11–12).[3]

Aristotle nevertheless argues that there is a sense in which justice is "virtue as a whole" (*holē aretē*) (1130a10, b7), using an expression reminiscent of the universal or the whole (*katholou*) good or "idea" he criticized earlier. As he explains, justice is virtue as a whole in the sense of the lawful, for laws command the deeds of *all* the virtues and forbid those of *all* the vices (1129b19–26, 1130b23–25). Its wholeness resides in its comprehensiveness. It is not so much that the law fits all the virtues together into a whole, with an identity or purpose, but that it leaves no virtue outside the law. There is also justice in the particular sense, "a part" of the "whole virtue," which secures and maintains what is fair or equal (*isos*). The one who obeys the law is considered just, but so is the one who grasps for no more than his fair share (1129a32–b2). Aristotle then divides even this "partial" justice into parts: distributive justice distributes the goods of the community; corrective justice restores that distribution when it is violated (1129b32–1131a2).

In the first section of this chapter, I explore these two meanings of justice that Aristotle identifies at the outset: justice as the whole and justice as a part; the lawful, on the one hand, and the equal or fair, on the other, both manifest in different ways in the laws of a political community. Aristotle gives the law an elevated role in the community, since it commands all the virtues, and since it is able to take on the task that Aristotle

---

3. Kraut, *Aristotle: Political Philosophy*, 100, 121–22, 135, 169–74, argues that Aristotle's analysis of justice in book 5 is an implicit criticism of Plato's approach in the *Republic*, especially its definition of justice as the proper order in the soul, and the "idealistic aloofness" from political life that this understanding of justice permits.

originally described as architectonic; the law secures and preserves the community (1094b6–11) by implementing a just and fair distribution of goods and by providing remedies against crimes. Aristotle nevertheless indicates that the law is not sufficient for avoiding conflict. A range of difficulties appear, including potential controversy over the ways in which goods are distributed and the inadequate compensation awarded to the injured. Moreover, the law, in its very universality, can fail to provide justice in particular cases. But Aristotle does not emphasize the tragic character of politics or suggest turning from our relations with others to cultivating order within our souls. The very incompleteness of law and justice opens up other ways in which Aristotle is able to speak about justice. Reciprocity, natural justice, and equity, I argue, complement, direct, and even correct the justice of the law. I treat these in the next three sections of this chapter.

Aristotle's last topic in book 5 involves the injustice of suicide, which I discuss in the final section of this chapter. I argue that the law against suicide that Aristotle attributes to all cities affirms the goodness of life that his politics supports and that suicide denies. I conclude this section with reflections on Aristotle's omission of *nemesis* ("righteous indignation") from his discussion of the ethical virtues and justice, after including it in his outline in book 2. Aristotle's presentation of the potentials of political life in his discussion of justice make it more difficult to justify indignation at the human lot.

JUSTICE AND THE LAW

Aristotle begins book 5 by reminding his addressee of the method and the goal of the inquiry—to examine justice and injustice, what sort of actions they happen to involve and what sort of mean this virtue is, and between what extremes it is a mean. Although he claims that he will use the "same method of inquiry" that he has been following (1129a5–6), his treatment of justice does not follow this pattern. Unlike the extremes of the other virtues, those of justice share the same name, injustice. The virtue is not easily located as a mean between extremes when its extremes have the same name and when that name is simply its negation. Anomalies abound. By reminding us of the general rule he has been following in defining each of the virtues, and by then deviating from it, Aristotle prepares us for his discussion of justice understood as lawfulness, and the limits of that understanding. In this way, his own treatment of justice resembles the justice he later calls "equity," which deviates from the law when required by particular cases (1138a24). Both in Aristotle's own treatment of justice and in equity as he describes it, justice requires looking beyond the rule. So too in the case of his definition of ethical virtue as a mean between excess and deficiency, not in a mathematical sense but in relation to us, virtue is "not one and the same for all" (1106a26–b4). This includes justice.

Justice is first and foremost "the lawful," for law commands the deeds of every virtue and forbids those of every vice (1129a32–b1, 1130b20–24). Aristotle of course does not infer that the just person is obedient to the law neither more nor less than he should be, and only when he should be, as prudence or right reason dictates (see 1106b21–24, 1107a1). He never explicitly applies the mean to a citizen's obeying the law. Nevertheless, he observes, almost in passing, that a good man and a good citizen may not always be the same (1130b29). At the end of the first book of the *Ethics*, Aristotle claims that the statesman must contemplate the soul, for he "wishes" (*boulesthai*) to make the citizens good and obedient to the laws (1102a9–10). He wishes for two things. Making citizens obedient to the laws—and hence good citizens—is not the same as making citizens good, no more than obeying a law, however reasonable the law may be, is the same as obeying the rational part of one's soul (1102b26). In the latter case, obeying and commanding belong to the same soul.[4] The statesman who

---

4. In explaining that there is something in the soul that resists reason, Aristotle gives the example of paralyzed limbs of the body that move in their own way. He says that "perhaps it must be held [*nomisteon*] that there is something in the soul that resists reason no less [than does a paralyzed limb]" (1102b). That is, we must "hold it as a law" (*nomos*). As is often the case, Aristotle's precise use of words captures a range of meanings, and hence the imprecision of words. *Nomizein*, "to suppose" or "to hold," means literally "to hold" or "to enact as law or convention" for ourselves. Just when Aristotle's comparison suggests the difficulty of ruling ourselves, if not the impossibility (we have no control over a paralyzed limb), he also appeals to our resources that support self-rule, our ability "to hold as a law." Statesmen, in other words, should understand the citizen's capacity for self-legislation.

contemplates the soul and its parts as Aristotle presents them at the end of book 1 would see this. His wish to make the citizens both good and obedient to the laws is a wish that his work involved both. Perhaps it is even a wish that the distinction could be overcome, and hence that his own work would be unnecessary. If citizens were good men, they could act as laws for themselves. In book 3, Aristotle distinguishes wish from deliberation and choice: we deliberate about and make choices about what is in our power, but we might wish for the impossible (1111b20–26). Aristotle uses the same language of "wish" in book 10, in the course of turning from the *Ethics* to the *Politics*: "Perhaps it is necessary for someone who wishes through his care to make others good, whether few or many, to attempt to acquire the legislative art, if it should be through laws that we become good" (1180b23–25). Aristotle is not suggesting that it is impossible to make others good, for "the attempt must be made," but he is still leaving open the extent to which this can happen through laws.

Justice is also part of virtue, a part of what the law commands, when it aims at the "equal" or the "fair," the distribution of what is due. In this sense of justice also, the mean does not easily apply.[5] The unjust person "grasps for more" (*pleonektēs*) (1129a33), and the just one seeks what is his due, but Aristotle does not present taking less than one is due as a vice on the side of the deficiency. By the time that he brings the discussion around to equity, near the end of book 5, Aristotle claims the "equitable" person "is inclined to take less for himself even though he has the law on his side." Such is characteristic of equity, which is "a certain sort of justice" (1137b36–1138b2). Justice, again, seems to look to the "the good of others."

Aristotle brings up another question about justice at the outset, one that arises also in the *Republic*: If a just person is good at guarding or keeping safe, as Polemarchus says, does it not follow that he is also good at stealing, just as a doctor who is good at guarding against a disease is also best able to produce it (333e–334b)? Aristotle immediately insists that the just person is not like a doctor, but rather like a healthy person. "What holds for sciences and capacities does not hold for dispositions": the former involves opposites; the latter does not. As a consequence of health,

---

5. Burger, *Aristotle's Dialogue with Socrates*, 92, 253n46. Kraut, *Aristotle: Political Philosophy*, 98–99, acknowledges that justice in Aristotle's account does not conform like other virtues to his teaching about the mean. He observes that Aristotle is not "troubled by this."

one does only healthy things (1129a12–16). So too the just person does just deeds; he is not a "clever thief" (*Republic* 334a).

Aristotle's clear answer to this discussion in the *Republic*, however, leaves open several questions applicable to his own discussion. The just person is "lawful," while the unjust is a lawbreaker (1129b11). But who lays down the law (see *Apology* 24e)? Aristotle insists that justice is a disposition and not a science or capacity, but he immediately refers to "lawgiving" (*nomothetikē*), which "defines the lawful" (1129b13), using a word for "lawgiving" whose ending (like that of medicine in Greek, *iatrikē*, for example) suggests expertise or skill. Even if justice is a disposition belonging to the good citizen, does the lawgiver have a skill that is analogous to the doctor's? Could he be a good lawgiver without such skill? If he does have the skill that would seem necessary for his being good at his task, can we trust him? Aristotle underlines these difficulties when he proceeds to point out that laws aim at the common advantage "either for all persons, or for the best, or for those who have authority, whether on the basis of their virtue or on the basis of some other such thing" (1129b14–17). Laws command virtuous actions and forbid vicious ones, "correctly when correctly laid down, but worse when laid down haphazardly" (1129b25–26). Laws are good, but by implication only more or less good, depending on the lawgiver. That the just coincides with the lawful is therefore only Aristotle's first word in his discussion.[6] Justice and injustice, after all, "are spoken of in more than one way" (1128b8, 1129a33).

Turning to the particular virtue of justice that the law commands, Aristotle observes that the law pursues the equal (*ison*) or the fair through a distribution of goods, such as honors and wealth, or "any of those things divisible among those who share in the regime"—in proportion to the worth of the individuals to whom they are distributed (1130b30–35). This is a formula for equality, in the sense that what each receives is equal to what he deserves. As Aristotle explains, the proportion in distributive justice involves a ratio between the persons and things involved (1131a30–b15). Distributive justice is proportional rather than arithmetical.

---

6. Burger, *Aristotle's Dialogue with Socrates*, 96, argues that "the movement of the argument in the course of book V can be understood precisely as an effort to put into question" the claim "that obedience to the laws of one's community, whatever they are, is sufficient to make one just." See also Winthrop, "Aristotle and Theories of Justice," 1201–16; and Tessitore, *Reading Aristotle's "Ethics,"* 38.

Corrective justice, which is arithmetical, restores the balance when the proportion established by the law is violated. In such a case, corrective justice takes from the one who has taken from another and returns it to the one from whom he took it (1132a9–19).

Like justice understood as the lawful, distributive and corrective justice depend on the regime and its laws. Because the equality involved in distributive justice is proportionate to worth, "fights and denunciations arise," as when those who are equal are distributed unequal things, or those who are unequal are distributed equal ones. Disagreements arise because all do not mean the same thing by "worth." Indeed, such disagreements, Aristotle warns, account for the differences in regimes: democrats say that all who are free and not slaves are equally worthy; oligarchs would measure worth by wealth, others by good birth, and aristocrats by virtue (1131a23–29).[7]

Just as we can ask whether justice as the "lawful" means that the just person is the one who makes the laws or the one who obeys them, we can ask in the case of distributive justice whether the just person is the one who makes the distribution or the one who receives his just portion. Whereas justice as the lawful seems to reside in the law-abiding person, who by obeying the law does virtuous deeds and refrains from vicious ones and whom Aristotle contrasts with the "lawbreaker," distributive justice seems to reside in the one who makes the distribution. He is the one who dispenses what is merited to himself and others. Aristotle nevertheless is

---

7. Mathie, "Political and Distributive Justice," 64–66, points out that the distributive justice that Aristotle describes is "neutral" toward "the criteria of merit belonging to the various regimes" and that its operation presupposes that the question of who should rule has already been settled. As Winthrop, "Aristotle and Theories of Justice," 1204, observes, "no significant political controversy would be resolved by the application of the principle of distributive justice as stated. It is too general, and it abstracts from the hardest political problem." She argues that the difficulties with justice that Aristotle presents point to the need to move beyond theories of justice to friendship, as he explores it later in the *Ethics* (ibid., 1201–2, 1212–15). I agree with her that "the problems that arise in politics can be solved only in the spirit of friendship, trust, and goodwill, not in the spirit of punitive justice or even impartiality" (ibid., 1212), but I try to show in my analysis of reciprocity, political justice, and equity that friendship, trust, and goodwill can arise in political life itself.

strangely silent about the agent in discussing distributive justice by referring to the distribution in the passive voice (1131a24; see also 1131b5). If the just person practices distributive justice, distributing the goods of the community in accordance with worth, the question of his possessing a skill or knowledge—and if so why he should be trusted—also arises here. If he distributes to himself as well as to others, he acts as judge in his own case. When Aristotle later suggests that the just person includes himself in his distributions (1134a3–6), he also indicates the danger of tyranny that arises from someone's distributing to himself (1134a30–b1; see also *Politics* 1280a15–16). Moreover, if distributive justice resides in the ruler, the one to whom he accords honors or wealth according to his deserts is the recipient of the justice of another. He possesses not justice, only its consequences.

Sliding over these difficulties, Aristotle turns to a second form of justice as the equal or fair, which comes into play when laws are violated. Then the judge, Aristotle says, takes from the perpetrator what he gains from his crime and returns it to the victim from whom he has taken it (1132a9–19). Aristotle suggests the inadequacy of corrective justice by his deceptively simple mathematical language, as if subtracting and adding could restore what existed before the "exchange." His examples of gains and losses, however, include not only cheating in business deals, but also theft, adultery, poisoning, pandering, stealing slaves, abduction or rape, assault, maiming, and murder (1113a1–9). Aristotle's list of possible injustices makes it difficult to understand how every loss will be restored or every gain returned. In the case of murder, would even the execution of the murderer restore the balance? A life for a life, to be sure, might be just, but it could hardly be said (as Aristotle does) that corrective justice deprives the unjust of gain and restores the loss so that one who has suffered injustice "has [no] less than he had from the beginning" (1132b13–15; see also 1132b19–20). In removing the perpetrator's gain and restoring the victim's loss, Aristotle says, corrective justice "makes equal the before and the after," as if what was done could be undone, as if the crime had never been committed. In his account of corrective justice, Aristotle speaks of "correcting" exchanges of gains and losses that violate what the law has established, never of "punishing." "Corrective" (*diorthotikos*) (1131a) is literally making "correct" or "right" (*orthos*). And what is right is what has been determined by the law. Corrective justice restores. If punishment were needed, in addition to correction, crimes would add something that justice must address, and restoring would not be enough. Underlying corrective justice appears to be the wish that justice were unnecessary. Aristotle's list of crimes, especially those that involve violence, suggests that such a wish cannot be fulfilled.

So too an abstraction from punishment manifests a wish that laws could operate without the judgments of rulers about guilt and innocence, for as Aristotle says in the *Politics*, desire and spiritedness pervert rulers and even the best human beings, whereas law is "mind without longing" (1287a29–32). His locution alone is sufficient to indicate that his argument will not rest here, since mind without longing is without a longing for justice. And mind without longing "moves nothing" (1139a31–b7). Justice as the lawful, including the corrective justice that restores the distribution determined by the law, becomes even more static and idle than greatness of soul. The judge who restores losses and deprives of gains, Aristotle says, "wishes to be, as it were, the just ensouled" (1132a21). In his wish to be impartial, he appears to forget that his justice requires wishing, which is one of the forms that longing takes, along with spiritedness and desire (*De Anima* 414b2–3).

Although the lawful and distributive and corrective justice may be adequate in most cases, they are therefore not adequate in all cases for securing an end of violent conflict, to say nothing of cultivating good human beings. The distributions of the community's goods can be—and are—contested, and Aristotle's list of crimes, some of them violent, indicate the limits of the law in controlling crime and in providing satisfactory corrections. If Aristotle's account of justice stopped here, he would have an insufficient answer to tragic conflict, and like Plato would teach that political life is tragic. But Aristotle does not stop here. In the remaining parts of book 5, Aristotle proposes three things that might diminish the tragic character of human and political life: reciprocity, natural justice, and equity. I discuss each in turn.

RECIPROCITY

"Reciprocity" (*antipeponthos*) means literally "suffering in turn." It occurs when one suffers what he has inflicted on another. As Aristotle says, "people seek to reciprocate harm for harm—if they do not, that is held to be slavish" (1132b34–1133a1). Unlike the case with corrective justice, there is no judge to "correct" the injustice; the one wronged takes it upon himself to do so. If leaving a crime against oneself unanswered is slavish, however, would it not also be slavish to leave its correction up to the law, or up to the judge, however fair he might be? Aristotle soon mentions rulers in his discussion of reciprocity: if a ruler strikes another, he ought not be struck in turn, or if someone strikes a ruler, he should not only be struck but punished (*kolasthēnai*) (1132b28–30). Reciprocity appears to take into account the particulars (for example, who strikes and who is struck), and to provide the punishment as well as the restoration of loss in which corrective justice seemed deficient.[8] Responding in kind will not always be sufficient for justice. Aristotle's example of someone striking a ruler is strange, if only because striking and being struck are not the most obvious interactions we wish to see between ruler and ruled. On the other hand, Aristotle's example may be the most appropriate for indicating the problem to which he is calling attention, for those who inflict harm in return because not doing so is slavish are likely also to resist being ruled by another. Homer's Achilles serves as a famous example: He inflicted harm in return on Agamemnon and did not think his commander worthy of ruling over him (*Iliad* 1.89–90, 149–51, 223–25).

Aristotle observes that people wish justice as reciprocity to mean "the justice of Rhadamanthus" (1132b24–27). Rhadamanthus was a mythical judge in the underworld, one of the judges whom Socrates claims to look forward to meeting after his death, one who is "truly a judge" rather than those who merely claim to be judges in this life (*Apology* 41a). In Plato's *Gorgias*, Socrates's myth about the afterlife indicates what people might wish from the justice of Rhadamanthus, who sees within the souls of those he judges, assigning some to Tartarus for punishment and others to the Isles of the Blest, where they will possess "every happiness." Before the reign of Zeus, as Socrates tells the tale, human judges made such determinations, judging the living on the day they were to die. Their judging

---

8. The common verb for "punishment," tellingly, does not occur until now in book 5, only after Aristotle has apparently completed his discussion of justice as the lawful and of corrective justice. Political life cannot dispense with punishment, however much it may wish to do so.

was done badly. They were hindered from seeing clearly, since their own bodies obstructed their souls' visions, while the souls of those whom they judged were hidden by beautiful bodies, ancestry, and wealth. For the sake of justice, Socrates recounts, Zeus changed the practice, appointing three of his sons, one of whom was Rhadamanthus, to judge souls when they arrive in Hades, visible because stripped of their bodies (*Gorgias* 523a–524a). Needless to say, their unobstructed insight into souls is shared neither by the judge who restores losses in Aristotle's account of corrective justice (who would not need it) nor by the one who inflicts suffering in turn on the one who harmed him (who seeks only retaliation). It is only the god who can claim to be "the just ensouled," but human beings "wish" their justice were that of Rhadamanthus.[9] They wish not only for perfect insight but also that justice not come too late to correct the errors of this life.

Instead of dwelling on the ways in which harm for harm falls short of the justice we might wish, and its correction after death, Aristotle turns to the workings of reciprocity in exchanging goods for goods (1132a1–2). He gives the example of the exchange of goods and services between those who possess different arts or skills, such as doctors and farmers, housebuilders and shoemakers. Exchange makes it possible to acquire the diversity of goods necessary for life and even an abundance beyond what is necessary. Aristotle gives the example of a shoemaker who makes so many shoes he can exchange them for a house (1133a7–25). His example also makes clear the need for a medium of exchange, or "money," that makes the exchange of products of different worth possible. Aristotle emphasizes that money (*nomisma*) exists by convention or law (*nomos*) rather than by nature and is therefore "up to us" to establish (1133a28–31), using the same expression that he uses for voluntary actions. When he observes that "all things ought to have a value assigned to them," he does not say who assigns the value (he speaks in the passive voice) or how far we can expect the value to remain constant. He suggests that even the value of money

---

9. Socrates's tale casts doubt even on the justice of Rhadamanthus, when he explains that when two of the judges, Rhadamanthus and Aeacus, disagree, they can be overruled by the third judge, Minos (*Gorgias* 523a–524a). Thus when he mentions Rhadamanthus in the *Apology*, he imagines meeting him along with others, and "examining and investigating those there, as [he] did here, to find out who among them is wise, and who believes he is when he is not" (41a–b).

changes over time, when he observes that its value "tends to stay more constant" than that of particular commodities (1133b13–16). Money exists by convention, but different communities have different conventions. Nevertheless, the exchange that money makes possible within cities is essential to the variety and bounty conducive to both living and living well. The need for a variety of goods that different human beings share and to which they contribute in different ways, Aristotle says, leads to the mutual giving (*metadosis*) that "holds the city together" (1132b33–34).

Aristotle speaks more broadly, albeit more briefly, of the mutual exchange of goods that holds the city together when he mentions the Graces, the daughters of Zeus, as Hesiod describes them in the *Theogony*, who dwell with the Muses in "delight" or "good cheer" (*thalia*) (*Theogony* 64).[10] Because communities remain together through mutual exchange, Aristotle observes, "[people] place a shrine to the Graces [*Charites*] in the roadway, to foster reciprocal giving, for this belongs to gratitude" (*charis*) (1133a3–5). The Graces encourage us to render service in turn to those who have been gracious to us. The Greek word *charis* refers both to the "graciousness" (often translated as "kindness" or "benevolence") of one who "acts graciously" toward another (or "does a favor" for another) and to the recipient's response to the favor, gratitude or appreciation. The one word, *charis*, captures a reciprocal relation—an act of grace and the gratitude it prompts.[11]

When Aristotle says that shrines to the Graces have been placed "in the roadway" so that they act as reminders, the word he uses (*empodōn*) is literally "in [the way of] one's feet" (*podes*), or "as an impediment." It serves as a "stumbling block." By reminding us of the Graces, Aristotle's

---

10. Pangle, *Reason and Character*, 158, argues that by "distancing himself from the viewpoint associated with Rhadamanthus while praising the Graces, Aristotle nudges traditional piety in a direction both gentler and more rational."

11. In her discussion of Aristotle's treatment of the passions in the *Rhetoric*, Sokolon, *Political Emotions*, 140, points out that although a gracious act prompts gratitude, the gracious person does not act for the sake of any return or gain for his favor that might stem from gratitude. Indeed, *charis* is "the least self-interested or self-centered of all of Aristotle's political emotions" because it "motivates voluntary acts of kindness and assistance without any regard for merit or reward." MacLachlan, *The Age of Grace*, gives a helpful background of the way the word was used in early Greek poetry.

Ethics, metaphorically speaking, serves as a stumbling block to those who desire to return harm for harm rather than good for good.[12]

Rhadamanthus, the punitive judge whom souls encounter on their way to the underworld, is supplemented by these feminine deities. Their emphasis is on "service in turn" (*anthupēretēsai*) rather than on "suffering in turn" (*antipeponthos*), the term Aristotle used when he introduced reciprocal justice and spoke about reciprocating harm for harm. The Graces, as Aristotle presents them, encourage us not only to serve in turn, but also to "initiate [*arxai*] acts of graciousness" (1133a4–5). Human beings can be the "beginning" (*archē*) of their actions, as Aristotle earlier taught (1113b18), but he now solicits the help of the Graces for his lessons. Aristotle's Graces are a stumbling block not only to those who insist on returning harm for harm, but also to great-souled individuals who insist on being the sole benefactors in that the Graces remind them that their good deeds, even when they initiate them, are fostered by the Graces, and therefore that they must share responsibility for them. Moreover, those encouraged by the Graces do not insist on giving *rather than receiving*, for they give in return for what they have received; they therefore do not forget the benefits they receive (1124b11–15). The gracious render service not merely by conferring benefits on others, but also by prompting others to serve *in turn*. They are not the only givers. Their benefiting others is not an act of self-sufficiency (see 1125a8–13), but of grace, and makes them part of a community of reciprocal giving. In the *Politics*, Aristotle associates "serving" with the virtue of women (1260a21–25), but serving does not exclu-

---

12. According to Winthrop, both the exchange of harm for harm and the need that gives rise to the exchange of goods indicate for Aristotle "nature's imperfection." Aristotle "characteristically obscures the harshness of nature and human nature," she argues, "by emphasizing economics, speaking *as if* the exchange necessary for survival were an exchange not of harms but of goods like beds and shoes" (emphasis added). Winthrop mentions Aristotle's reference to the Graces in this context, which she understands in the same light—as a way of obscuring the harshness of nature implied in justice's requiring "reciprocal harms." See Winthrop, "Aristotle and Theories of Justice," 1205, 1205n8. Frank, *A Democracy of Distinction*, 100, understands the reference to the Graces as crucial to Aristotelian reciprocity, including the importance of the initiation of benefits that the Graces encourage. "Most commentators," as Frank points out, "treat [Aristotle's references to the Graces] as not germane to his account."

sively belong to women, for in "serving" and "serving in turn" lies the reciprocity that holds the city together. Even the great-souled individual is "eager to serve," even though he finds few services worthy of him, Aristotle says (1124b18). Serving "in turn" never arises in Aristotle's description of him, nor does grace or gratitude.

In his *Oresteia*, Aeschylus dramatized the efforts of the goddess Athena to stem the cycle of crime and vengeance by converting the avenging Furies into "Eumenides," "kindly" goddesses who support the city, on which they confer their grace or favor (*charis*), and who wish that the people "give joys [*charmata*] to one another in friendship" (*Eumenides* 865–69, 881–926, 937, 984–85). In his own way, Aristotle takes his turn at rendering service by furthering Aeschylus's attempt to make political life less brutal and more humane. Aristotle's Graces, also "well-intentioned" or "kindly" goddesses, as is the meaning of the new name Athena gives the Furies, remind human beings to initiate and return acts of graciousness. They hold out the prospect that human life involves an exchange of goods that goes beyond that exchange measured by money, even if the latter exchange teaches us both our common needs and our ability to meet them, and thereby prepares us to worship at the shrine of the Graces.

As he moves away from his discussion of reciprocity, Aristotle reminds us that human beings cannot attain the insight of Rhadamanthus into souls, when he again points out the discrepancy between a person's actions and the disposition of his soul. "Since someone who does an injustice may not yet be an unjust person," Aristotle asks, how do we identify someone who in fact is unjust if we look only to his deeds? (1134a17–23). But it is the deeds that the law commands or forbids. The law can forbid a soldier to throw down his weapons or flee the battle, or it can forbid adultery, to use Aristotle's examples, and these are the acts of a cowardly and immoderate person (1129b19–25). But the law cannot command courage or moderation, however helpful the law may be in fostering these virtues by forbidding cowardly and licentious acts. Law remains incomplete. In various ways in the rest of the *Ethics*, Aristotle seeks ways to address its incompleteness. It is possible for natural justice to inform the laws, conventions, and political structures of a community, as he discusses next, especially in cases of reciprocal ruling and being ruled. The difficulty of seeing within souls, and with it the imperfect justice in punishing, moreover, points to Aristotle's discussion of equity later in book 5, and the "equitable" person who gives beyond what is due, at least in the sense of the lawful. The Graces, who encourage reciprocal good deeds, point even further in the *Ethics*—to Aristotle's discussion of friendship in books 8 and 9. Aristotle begins those books by observing that "lawgivers appear to be more serious about friendship than justice," for "it appears to be what holds the city together" (1155a23–27). The Graces, metaphorically speaking, remain at work when Aristotle takes his turn in serving, most immediately in book 5, by his discussions of natural justice and equity, and finally in his recognition of a law against suicide.

NATURAL JUSTICE

Aristotle prefaces his discussion of "natural justice" with an account of "the just in the political sense," of which natural justice is a part (1134a26, b19). Natural justice is not an alternative to political justice, but belongs to it. Although the senses in which Aristotle has discussed justice thus far might be called "political" (justice as the lawful, justice as distributing goods in the community and correcting violations of the law, and reciprocal justice that holds political communities together), he now brings his discussion of political justice to the fundamental character of a just human association: "The just in the political sense ... exists among those who share a life in common," "who are free and equal," and it exists for those for whom law is natural, namely, those for whom there is "equality in ruling and being ruled" (1134a26–31, b14–15). "Equality in ruling and being ruled" does not imply a simple democracy. As in the distribution of goods such as property and honors, so in the distribution of ruling offices the "equal" means the portion equal to one's merits in relation to others. The just ruler, Aristotle tells us, derives nothing more from his ruling than his just portion in proportion to those of the ruled. Whatever inequality may exist between himself and others, he is part of the community, subject to the same measure of worth as its other members. That is why, Aristotle observes, he must receive some wage or payment for his ruling, such as honor or privilege. Those for whom this is not sufficient become tyrants (1134b1–8). The just ruler, in contrast, receives a wage in addition, honor or privilege, but he receives it from those who confer it, who are also judges of worth, and he would be a beneficiary as well as a benefactor.

The ruler about whom Aristotle is speaking here is one who is ruled by the law that structures his sharing rule with others. Whatever proportionate equality exists for those "for whom the law is natural," no one is so different from others as to be "a law unto himself" (*Politics* 1283a3–14). The law (*nomos*) that establishes and maintains institutions that structure shared governance, as Aristotle said of money (*nomisma*), facilitates the mutual exchange of goods that holds the city together (132b34).[13] There is a reciprocity between rulers and ruled, and it does not consist in striking and being struck, but in shared governance, in which ruler and ruled fulfill their potential as political and rational beings. Where there is "equality of ruling and being ruled," to be sure, the ruled cannot rely simply on the knowledge or skill of a ruler that militates against error. But there is greater opportunity for citizens to develop their capacity for deliberation and to make more considered choices.

Since "justice in the political sense" pertains among the "free and equal" who share in ruling and being ruled, Aristotle does not find political justice in the family. The justice belonging to "a master [of slaves] or to a father" is just only in a qualified sense. One's property (including slaves) and one's offspring (until they attain a certain age and become independent) are part of oneself. One cannot, strictly speaking, do injustice to oneself (1134␤8–14). Justice, once again, must be understood as virtue in relation to another. Aristotle therefore refers to the just in the political sense—and not justice within the family—as the just simply. There is insufficient distance in the family for there to be the equality between ruler and ruled that defines justice, but Aristotle does admit that for the head of the family "the just exists more in relation to his wife than to his offspring and possessions" (1134b8–17; see also *Politics* 1259a40–b11).

After elaborating this understanding of political justice, Aristotle divides political justice into natural justice and conventional or legal justice. The naturally just, he says, "has the same potential everywhere"

---

13. In the *Politics*, Aristotle says that "reciprocal equality preserves cities" in the context of discussing ruling among the free and equal, and he refers his addressee there to his discussion of reciprocal equality in the *Ethics* (*Politics* 1261a30–35; see also 1277b8–13). See also Yack, *The Problems of a Political Animal*, 136; Frank, *A Democracy of Distinction*, 101; and Nichols, *Citizens and Statesmen*, 88.

regardless of opinion (1134b19). Thus whereas fire burns the same here and in Persia, for us what is just by nature is "altogether changeable," since regimes differ from one another. And yet, "there is only one regime everywhere that is according to nature, the best regime" (1134b24–1135a5).

Aristotle notoriously says very little here about this best regime, which alone exists according to nature, but he has laid out its foundations and limits by including natural justice within political justice. As Aristotle has just suggested, human beings have the potential to share in ruling and being ruled, at least those who are neither slaves nor masters by nature (should there be any), and who are no longer children. The best regime is one in which this human potential is realized, but it varies according to human deliberation and choice, the very capacities on which shared rule depends. According to Leo Strauss, "what Aristotle suggests is that the most fully developed form of natural right is that which obtains among fellow-citizens; only among fellow-citizens do the relations which are the subject matter of right or justice reach their greatest density, and indeed, their full growth."[14]

At the same time, Aristotle recognizes the compromises with necessity that belong to all human affairs. In describing "the regime that we would pray for" in the last books of the *Politics*, Aristotle describes what the best regime would look like, making clear the many compromises that any regime entails, even the best. We should not pray for the impossible, even if we wish for it (1325b36–40; cf. *Republic* 456b, 450d). The best regime is not in a class of its own, even if it is an exemplary member of its class. There are many regimes that are not tyrannical, all based on some degree of equality among their members.[15] The human potential to share in ruling and being ruled therefore finds expression in various ways, but Aristotle would not have seen it among the Persians (see 1160b27–32).[16]

---

14. Strauss, *Natural Right and History*, 157.

15. For discussion of Aristotle's "regime according to prayer" in the *Politics*, see Nichols, *Citizens and Statesmen*, 125–76, esp. 126, 130, 146, and 154. For elaboration of the many forms of democracy and oligarchy, and how the more moderate of each tend toward greater inclusiveness or shared rule, see ibid., 85–100.

16. But even in Persia, the benefits of a democracy can be articulated, even though they are rejected (see Herodotus, *Histories* 3.80–83). In commenting on Aristotle's description of the naturally just, Winthrop, "Aristotle and Theories of Justice," 1208n13, points out that that the Persians worshipped fire as a god (Hero-

After discussing the naturally just, Aristotle turns to the conventionally or legally just, the other manifestation of political justice. Here, Aristotle explains, things that make no difference in the beginning do make a difference once they have been set down: decrees that determine the sum of money to offer for ransom, whether to offer a sacrifice of a goat or two sheep, whether or not to sacrifice to Brasidas, or other such things (1134b20–24). Aristotle's examples show that the naturally just—and the human potential on which it is based—is relevant to the legal or conventional form of political justice. Aristotle says it is conventional or "up to us" to determine how much we should offer for a ransom, but he does not say the same about whether or not we should offer a ransom if circumstances permit. Conventions are just when they favor the freedom of human beings.[17] So too it is a matter of indifference whether a goat or two sheep are originally designated for sacrifice, but Aristotle makes no similar observation about human sacrifice. The latter is never a matter of indifference (see also *Politics* 1324b40–41). Nor is it a matter of indifference whether there is to be sacrifice or, more generally, some way in which human beings worship the divine.

Aristotle's third example of a law or convention that may be a matter of indifference until it is decided is that of sacrificing to the Spartan general Brasidas, a custom adopted by the Greek city of Amphipolis after he sacrificed his life for that city's freedom (Thucydides, *PW* 5.11.1, 5.9.9). In this last example, a city must decide not the amount to be spent in an activity (a ransom) or the kind of sacrifice to be made (a goat or sheep), but whether it should engage in the activity itself. Should there be sacrifices to Brasidas? When the people of Amphipolis celebrate Brasidas's heroism by worshipping him as a god, their honors suggest that achievements such as

---

dotus, *Historíes* 1.131). Even fire does not burn the same for Persians, for they have not adequately understood the differences between the natural and the divine.

17. In the *Rhetoric*, Aristotle speaks of "common law that exists by nature," which "all [human beings] divine as naturally just and unjust" (1373b5–8). Among his illustrations is a reference to a play by Alcidamus, the *Messeniacus*, now lost, presumably to the line we have as a fragment: "The god has left everyone free, nature has made no one a slave" (1373b17–18). Aristotle's denial of natural slavery here, however inconclusive, supports my reading of his criticism of slavery in Nichols, *Citizens and Statesmen*, 19–24.

his are beyond what human beings can ask of themselves. But they must ask such deeds of themselves in order to preserve their freedom. By sacrificing to Brasidas, and thereby treating him as divine, the Amphipolitans give more to Brasidas than his due and less to themselves. If honoring a human being as a god implies or presages their own loss of freedom, Brasidas's noble sacrifice for their freedom fails to achieve its purpose. The loss of freedom is not a matter of indifference (see Thucydides, *PW* 8.68.4).

Although conventions or laws set down "at the beginning" might be decided one way or another, once they are set down they become binding. But what cannot be binding are those that undermine the equality and freedom that makes possible the shared governance appropriate to human beings. Laws or conventions such as human sacrifice treat human beings like beasts. Those such as worshipping Brasidas treat humans as gods. Because they undermine human equality and freedom they are not a matter of indifference, and therefore cannot be decided one way or another at the outset. Laws or conventions concerning worship must be consistent with human freedom. Once again, Aristotle is teaching legislators and statesmen, who may be in error, for they are not divine nor the conduits of divine revelation.[18] He teaches them that justice cannot consist simply in abiding by law or convention; rather, it requires preserving the natural equality and freedom that serve as the indispensable support for the laws' justice. Aristotle's understanding of the human and its relation to piety and politics is at work in his discussion of natural justice, inasmuch as piety preserves the distinction between human and beast, on the one hand, and human and divine, on the other. By treating natural justice as a form of political justice, Aristotle teaches that there should be limits to laws and conventions and calls upon political communities to support them. To echo Aristotle's statements about incest and abortion (*Politics* 1262a26–41, 1335b25), sacrificing human beings is impious or unholy. So is worshipping them as gods.

---

18. The laws that Minos gave to Crete and Lycurgus to Sparta were thought to have come from Zeus and Apollo, respectively. See *Laws* 624a. Aristotle does not mention any divine source when he discusses these regimes in the *Politics*. Indeed, he is critical of their legislators (1269b18–24; 1270b1–6; 1271b1–11, b20–32; 1272b20–22).

TRAGEDY AND EQUITY

Aristotle's next way of speaking about justice in book 5, the justice of equity, is embedded in references to tragedies and allusions to problems that appear in tragedies that equity, as he soon describes it, attempts to address. Reminding us of the distinction between voluntary and involuntary actions, he points out that "one acts unjustly or performs a just act [only] when one does so voluntarily." Voluntary acts are those that are up to the one acting, and the one who acts must do so knowing (*eidōs*) who the person is who is affected by the action, the means being used, and the end in acting. Aristotle illustrates his point: If one strikes one's father not knowing that it is one's father whom one is striking, the act is involuntary (1135a17–30). His example obviously applies to Oedipus. As in his earlier discussion of voluntary actions in book 3, he expresses his reservations about tragedy, or at least about those who in ignorance commit horrific acts such as patricide or incest, and are held responsible, or who hold themselves responsible. They are pitiable, to be sure, but forgiveness, not blame, is appropriate (see 1111a1–2).

Even when one harms another while knowing what one is doing, Aristotle observes, one's act is not necessarily unjust. One might have acted from spiritedness or other natural passions. Although such deeds come from ourselves, and hence are not involuntary (see 1111a22–b4), the harm we do is nevertheless not intended (*ouk ek pronoia*), since it proceeds from passion rather than vice or wickedness. It would not be noble or beautiful (*kalon*) to judge it as intended and hence its perpetrator as wicked (1135b25–26). Aristotle's observation supports pardon or forgiveness. It is noble, in other words, to take the circumstances of the action into account (someone may have acted from anger at injustice), and therefore the inner state of the agent. Aristotle is preparing for his treatment of equity as a kind of justice. Although earlier he suggested that "the origin" of actions stemming from spiritedness or desire lies in the person acting, he now says that one who has made someone angry is the origin of his spirited response (cf. 1111a22–b3 with 1135b26–30). Perhaps there are co-causes. In any case, there are two sides to be considered. This is one of the few times that Aristotle refers to the "noble" or "beautiful" in book 5. He applies it not to the act of a spirited or angry person (one might think of the wrath of Achilles), but to the one who is open to forgiveness. Beauty still involves a vision of completeness or wholeness, but it involves looking beyond a timeless present, to the origin of an act and the intention or purpose of the actor.

Aristotle's usage is in accord with his calling the mean with respect to anger "gentleness" in book 4, and in explaining that "the gentle person inclines to forgiveness rather to revenge" (1126a1–3). It is also anticipated by his quick move in his discussion of reciprocity from returning harm for harm to initiating and returning good, even though those who do not exact the former are held to be slavish (1132b25–1133a5). Aristotle does not deny this, but his move from the justice of Rhadamanthus to the graciousness of the Graces responds in effect that the greater freedom lies in an act of grace.

Aristotle gives further examples that point us in this direction of generosity. In arguing that we cannot wrong or harm ourselves voluntarily, he gives the example of Glaucus, who gave more to Diomedes than he received from him: "gold for bronze, the worth of a hundred cattle for nine." Glaucus is someone who takes less for himself in an exchange but nevertheless does not suffer injustice voluntarily, Aristotle explains, or do injustice to himself, for his "giving is up to himself" (1136b1–14). Homer's story about Glaucus, from which Aristotle quotes (*Iliad* 6.236), however, is not about liberality, or voluntary giving. Rather, Glaucus gives away his own resources because "Zeus stole his wits" (*Iliad* 6.234). He does not suffer injustice voluntarily, to be sure, but it is not because his act is "up to him"—Zeus is responsible. Aristotle transforms Homer's account, for he does not mention Zeus, and makes Glaucus responsible for his act. Aristotle's Glaucus is a liberal man. His reference to Glaucus delivers another strike against the poets and their presentation of the divine. Just as Homer's Glaucus expends his resources when deprived of his wits, protagonists in tragedies may seem deprived of their wits, metaphorically if not literally (as in case of Ajax), as they move toward self-destruction.

Aristotle also quotes lines from one of Euripides's tragedies, when the play's title character Alcmaeon admits that he killed his mother. Alcmaeon supposes that his admission of the deed is sufficient, for he can reduce his tale to "a brief speech," as he says in the line that Aristotle quotes. But Aristotle also quotes a question asked by a character in the play, "Did you [kill her] voluntarily, and [was she killed] voluntarily, or was she killed involuntarily, and did you do so involuntarily?" (1136a10–14). Even within tragedy, at least in this play, someone asks about the circumstances of the actions and the internal states of the doer and sufferer of the deed. Because Euripides's play has been lost, we do not know how or if Alcmaeon responded to the question, nor do we know who asked it or why. But by quoting the question, Aristotle indicates that more should be understood about Alcmaeon's deed in order to judge it properly, and even that understanding the circumstances might cause us to judge it less harshly (see also Aeschylus, *Eumenides* 425–27).

One might ask, for example, whether Alcmaeon killed his mother voluntarily, since his dying father commanded him to do so on account of his wife's treachery (cf. 1110a28–29). Earlier, Aristotle insisted that some deeds were "mixed," voluntary only in the circumstances, but in themselves involuntary, as when someone obeyed a base command of a tyrant who threatened his closest relatives. But such judgments, Aristotle admitted then, "are open to dispute" (1110a4–13, 29). Claims of justice "are disputed" by both sides in a conflict, Aristotle again observes shortly before turning to equity (1135b30–1136a1). Aeschylus dramatized this point in the *Oresteia*, which involves another man, Orestes, who like Alcmaeon kills his mother to avenge the death his father suffered because of his wife. He too acted in extenuating circumstances. Both Orestes and his avengers appeal to justice (e.g., *Libation Bearers* 269–77, 1026–32; *Eumenides* 135–36, 163, 269–75).

In Aeschylus's trilogy, the goddess Athena sets up a jury of Athenian citizens to try Orestes for murder. After hearing "evidence and proofs" from both the prosecution (the Furies) and the defense (Apollo), the jury delivers a tie vote (*Eumenides* 458–67). The just remains in dispute until Athena resolves the deadlock in favor of pardon, proclaiming that she gives her vote to Orestes, since she is born solely of Zeus and "favors the male in all things," even if she wouldn't marry one (*Eumenides* 734–35). Like Aeschylus, Aristotle seeks a politics that stems cycles of violence and vengeance such as plagued Orestes's family, but he does not rely on stories of divine intervention for establishing institutions and securing their operation. Aristotle finds a less arbitrary reason for pardon than did Athena's preference for the male when he discusses a more human expedient, equity, which examines extenuating circumstances and modifies the law as circumstances demand, both holding responsible and pardoning.

However much Aeschylus's *Eumenides* remind us of Aristotle's Graces once they are transformed into kindly goddesses by Athena, the goddess lodges them under the earth, from which their favors and graces will proceed (1003–6). Aristotle goes further, in effect, by placing shrines to the Graces "in the roadways" or public places, where human beings can stumble upon them, and be reminded that they should confer favors and grace. His divinities allow and even encourage reciprocity among human beings. Aristotle thus builds on and refines Aeschylus's portrayal of the gods in the *Oresteia*, even if the "Eumenides" of the tragedian are a step toward Aristotle.

Because law necessarily speaks in universal terms, it holds only "for the most part," while "*not being ignorant* of its error in doing so" (1137b15–16). Like a tragic protagonist, the law errs, but unlike the tragic protagonist it knows that it is doing so—that it must speak in universal terms, and that it cannot know the circumstances that will occur over time. The lawgiver who understands this also understands that he can rule only in part, even if it is for the most part, and that there will be limits to the extent that he can legislate about everything in the city (see 1094b1–2). The lawgiver who recognizes the problem with the law has learned what Aristotle has been trying to teach from the beginning of the *Ethics*, namely, in political matters, where the just, the noble, and the good are involved, matters hold only "for the most part" (1094b12–22).

When extenuating circumstances occur, then equity should come into play. Although common usage refers almost interchangeably to the equitable and the good, as Aristotle points out, he gives it a specific meaning (1137a34–b2).[19] Equity is a kind of justice that corrects the defect of the

---

19. Although Aristotle has used "equitable" on many occasions throughout the *Ethics*, he does not clearly indicate whether he means anything other than the good (e.g., 1113b14, 1132a2). Translators use a variety of terms to translate *epieikēs*, including "decent," "virtuous," and "good." Whether Aristotle's many usages of the term are relevant to the specific definition he gives it, as he elaborates it in the book on justice, depends on the context. See Burger's discussion of his use of this word in the context of shame at 1128b27 (Burger, *Aristotle's Dialogue with Socrates*, 90), and my discussion of his use at 1128a18, in my section on "wit" in chapter 3. Among other uses of equity that have overtones of its specific meaning, see 1162a26, 1163b17–18, 1167b5, 1172a11–12, 1180a24.

law stemming from its universality (1137b11–14).[20] Whereas the just person first appeared in book 5 as "the lawful" (*nomimos*) and the unjust as the lawbreaker (*paranomos*) (1129a32–b2), equity looks at and gives justice to what falls "outside" (*para*) the law (1137b20) because of the circumstances that arise. Aristotle's speaking of equity's "correction" of the law is reminiscent of "corrective" justice,[21] which equity complements. Whereas corrective justice restores the universal in response to violations, equity bends the universal to the particular case in rendering judgment. It is therefore not arbitrary. Equity applies the universal rule, as it were, neither more nor less than it ought, when it ought, toward whom it ought, and for the sake of what it ought, presumably according to correct (*orthos*) reason, as Aristotle's formula for acting according to the mean requires (1106b21–24, 1115b11–21, 1103b31–34).

Because the universal terms of the law capture only what holds "for the most part," law is necessarily partial. So too is the justice of equity,

---

20. According to Hamburger, *Morals and Law*, 90, "the concept of *epieikeia* [equity] as defined by Aristotle has no antecedent in the whole of pre-Aristotelian literature." The usages prior to Aristotle that Hamburger cites (with meanings ranging from "clemency," "leniency," "indulgence," "forgiveness," and "moderation") confirm Aristotle's observation that the word is used interchangeably with the good (ibid., 91). In Plato's *Statesman*, the Eleatic Stranger recognizes the deficiency of a law that is promulgated "about all things and for all time," when "human things are never at rest." The lawmaker who makes law for all collectively will therefore fail to provide what is proper for each individual (*Statesman* 294b and 294e–295a). But there is no occurrence of equity there, either the word or the meaning that Aristotle gives it as a response to this problem. The Stranger criticizes the law to establish that the best rule is that "without laws" by "the wise [or prudent] [*meta phronēseōs*] king," who will be able to deal with whatever circumstances arise. In his absence, the rule of laws must allow no deviation or questioning and can be only a "second" best (297d–e). The wise ruler does not err (297a–b), and the erring laws allow no correction. Once again, Aristotle's treatment of justice is an implicit response to Plato. For a rich treatment of Aristotle's differences with Plato's Eleatic Stranger, see Cherry, *Plato, Aristotle, and the Purposes of Politics*, esp. 99.

21. For example, in the discussion of equity, Aristotle uses *epanorthōma* (correction) and *epanorthoun* (to correct) (1137b13, b23). He earlier used *diorthōtikon*, and even *epanorthōtikon*, to refer to corrective justice (1131b25 and 1132a19). All are based on *orthos*, "right" or "correct."

which applies only in the case at hand and does not become a law for others. Equity does not replace the law; nor does the person who corrects the law in the particular case replace the lawgiver, for he decides cases "as if" the lawgiver were present (1137b11–24). His judgment must nevertheless supplement that of the lawgiver, for he looks not merely to the law that has been violated, as Aristotle elaborates in the *Rhetoric*, but to the sort of person the wrongdoer is or has been "always or for the most part," rather than "in the moment" he acts. Equity looks not to the deed of the wrongdoer but tries to see the "choice" (*prohairesis*) behind it. In the *Rhetoric*, moreover, Aristotle connects equity to pardon or forgiveness: "Equity pardons what is human" (*Rhetoric* 1374b3–16; see also *NE* 1143a19–24).[22] In considering how the lawgiver would have judged had he been present, the equitable person also looks to the intent or the choice of the lawgiver, who errs "knowingly" in prescribing something to apply to everyone. Equity would also be able to pardon the lawgiver.

The questions that equity considers address the conflicts that might lead to tragedy. Matricide is against the law, but should Orestes be pardoned for his matricide? Or, to use another example familiar to us from tragedy, burying the city's enemy may be forbidden by the ruler, but should one bury the city's enemy if he is one's brother? Is Antigone's intention to violate Creon's decree, or to obey a divine one? And what sort of person has Antigone been always or for the most part, rather than in the moment of her act? Equity, as Aristotle describes it, would consider all these things in judging Antigone's act. There is much that equity should consider, even if its task is more difficult and less certain than simply seeing into souls, in the manner of Rhadamanthus.

Aristotle concludes his discussion of equity by describing the equitable person himself: he is inclined to take less for himself, "even though he has the law on his side" (1137a1–2). The one who tends to forgiveness in his judgment of others, and thereby grants them more leniency than the law requires, also takes less than the law grants in cases when he himself is

---

22. Hamburger, *Morals and Law*, 99, compares Aristotle's treatment of equity in the *Magna Moralia*, the *Nicomachean Ethics*, and the *Rhetoric* and finds the most developed form of Aristotle's theory of equity in the *Rhetoric*. Aristotle does add helpful remarks in the *Rhetoric* about the character of the equitable person. The *Rhetoric*, like the *Politics*, in many ways builds on the *Ethics*.

involved. He is not "exacting about justice," Aristotle says (1137b33–a2).[23] In taking less for himself, Aristotle makes clear, he does not do injustice to himself, or wish his own harm, for he "grasps more of another good, such as reputation or what is simply noble [or beautiful]" (1136b20–23). Like Glaucus, he exchanges good for good, and takes less than he is entitled for himself. He is in fact a more apt illustration than is Homer's Glaucus of someone who does not do injustice to himself by taking less for himself. Zeus has not deprived him of his wits. The equitable person has his wits about him, for he understands the beauty that is manifest in taking less.[24] For him, the beautiful is less in tension with the good than it is for the courageous who risk their lives for its sake and than it is for the great of soul who possess *kalokagathia* ("beauty and goodness") only as long as they do not choose to act.

Aristotle's description of the equitable person here offers a model for the noble or beautiful that contrasts with the characteristic tragic figure, who chooses the beautiful or noble over his own good.[25] Aristotle in the *Rhetoric* gives the example of Achilles as someone we praise for doing what is noble, disregarding his own benefit, for whom death was nobler than living, even though living was advantageous (1359a5–8). Death for Achilles was noble but not simply good (see also *NE* 1094b17–19). He grasped the noble, like the equitable person, but only at the cost of his life.

---

23. Aristotle apparently coined *akribodikaios*. It is found only here in extant Greek literature. Someone not "exacting" about justice would demand only that amount of precision (*akribeia*) that justice allows. He would thus qualify as Aristotle's preferred addressee of his political inquiry, who expects only the exactitude or precision (*to akribes*) about the just and the beautiful that his subject matter warrants (*NE* 1094b13 and 24). Someone accurate "to a fault" (*eis to cheiron*), unlike the equitable person (1137b36), would demand more precision than is warranted.

24. Compare Portia's advice to Shylock in Shakespeare's *Merchant of Venice* that "earthly power doth then show likest God's / When mercy seasons justice" (4.1.202–3). "It blesseth him that gives and him that takes. / 'Tis mightiest in the mightiest" (4.1.193–94).

25. See Smith, *Revaluing Ethics*, 186, 228–29, who argues that the "drama" of the *Ethics* includes a "transformation of the meaning of *to kalon*," whereby Aristotle "devalues the ethos of honor" and redirects ambition to the practice of "fairness and reasonableness," away from "virtue-as-virility" to "virtue as equity."

When Aristotle describes the equitable person as taking more of the simply noble by taking less for himself, he severs the connection between nobility and death, just as he recently connected nobility with forgiveness rather than with spiritedness or anger. The equitable person does what is noble, without the sacrifice of his life that Achilles's nobility required.[26] Resembling the one encouraged by the Graces, and unlike the great-souled individual described in book 4, the equitable person, Aristotle says, "remembers the benefits he received rather than the ones he conferred" (*Rhetoric* 1374b18–19; cf. *NE* 1124b12–13). To lovers of the beautiful, who are ready to sacrifice themselves, Aristotle will offer friendship, a different way to take both less and more, in the later books of the *Ethics*. Here in his discussion of equity he offers them the "superior" justice he calls equity and assigns to the equitable the beautiful work in the political community that those who take less for themselves might accomplish with less ostentation than Achilles's sacrifice.

THE LAW AGAINST SUICIDE

After his discussion of equity, Aristotle returns to the question of whether it is possible to do injustice to oneself, and this time he mentions suicide. Suicide seems to call into question Aristotle's view that one cannot do injustice to oneself, along with its underlying assumption that no one wishes to harm himself (1134b11–12, 1136a34–b9). Is Aristotle ending his discussion of book 5 with an exception to his general rule? Doesn't one who commits suicide wish to harm himself? When Oedipus blinds himself, he understands his self-mutilation as worse than death, lamenting that he is evil and born from evil. Jocasta's silence when she leaves the stage is still more ominous (*Oedipus Tyrannus* 1397, 1366–67, 1073–75). These characters doubt their own goodness. Oedipus asks that he be sent away from Thebes, for he is hated by the gods (1518–19). Such characters are harsher

---

26. Salkever, "Taking Friendship Seriously," 55, makes a parallel point when he argues that Aristotle in both his *Ethics* and his *Politics* "wishes to open to critique" the typical Greek admiration for the friendships of male warriors and political heroes, and "the staunch preference for death over dishonor."

on themselves than Aristotle teaches they should be, and they have a harsher view of the gods than any Aristotle countenances.

Aristotle nevertheless maintains that one cannot do injustice to oneself, even when one commits suicide; rather, one does injustice to the city, for the city forbids suicide and imposes penalties and dishonors on those who kill themselves (1138a9–14). He thus revisits at the end of book 5 his initial presentation of justice as the lawful. One might understand Aristotle here to confirm the all-embracing character of the city and its laws that order everything in it, if the laws treat even the life of the individual as not his own to take. The way that Aristotle infers the existence of a law against suicide even implies the all-embracing character of the law: "The law does not command suicide, and what the law does not command it forbids" (1138a6–7). However, Aristotle has pointed out throughout book 5 the limits of the law. He continues doing so here, for a law against suicide indicates not the city's power, but its weakness, for it imposes penalties only after it fails to protect life from a self-inflicted death. The law goes into effect only when the city has failed. The community can neither prevent suicide, nor can it bring the one who commits suicide back to life; it cannot restore the loss to the city inflicted by the one who deprives the city of his life. There is no corrective justice here, no restoring what has been lost. In imposing dishonor and penalties on those who take their lives, it punishes those whom it is too late to save from death, almost like a tragic protagonist whose actions come "too late" to prevent death (see *Antigone* 1270).

Aristotle is not merely criticizing the city for its failure or calling attention to its limits in providing good lives for its citizens. Rather, by the dishonor and penalties it imposes, the city honors life, and the good for which life is the condition. It thereby asserts the goodness of life, even of the one who disavows it by committing suicide. In denying life, and the goodness of the life that has been given, his crime is not only unjust, but it is also impious. Oedipus presumes that he is hated by the gods. It may be too late for punishing one who commits suicide, but it is not too late for teaching others. This is the work of a good city. Aristotle does not accept the tragic lament, "too late."

The law that Aristotle presents, indeed, transforms, in the course of his discussion of justice is not one that asserts its all-embracing authority over human beings, but one that supports human choice and action, as we have seen in so many ways. There are laws or conventions (*nomisma*) that facilitate the exchange of goods, for example; there is ruling and being ruled that is just for those for whom "law is natural"; there is law that knows it errs and therefore that it must be supplemented by equity; and now, in response to the poets whose tragedies are replete with suicides, there is law that dishonors suicide and thereby insists on the goodness of life.

So too do laws that command the deeds of virtue and forbid those of vice, regardless of their success, affirm which deeds are worthy and which not. If the law succeeded in guaranteeing that the deeds of citizens were always virtuous, citizens could not satisfy their desire to trust their own goodness, for their goodness would come not from themselves but from the law. Trusting one's own goodness nevertheless does not belong to a self-contained soul, whose virtue lies in the proper relation between its parts, as Aristotle affirms in his concluding allusion to the *Republic* (1138b5–14). Trusting our goodness requires confirmation from our deeds—seeing their effect in the world in which we act or imagining their effect in the future. Such deeds would involve others, such as those that Aristotle's treatment of justice in book 5 brings to light—that of pardoning when appropriate, for example, or of sharing in ruling and being ruled, or of erecting shrines to divinities who encourage our initiating acts of goodness and benefiting others in turn. Aristotle's elaborations of such experiences offer us models for directing or perhaps reforming the political communities in which we live.

In the light of this understanding of Aristotle's political teaching, one curious feature of the *Ethics* may fall into place: after including righteous indignation (*nemesis*) in his outline in book 2 of the means that he will be discussing, Aristotle drops *nemesis* from his exposition. *Nemesis*, the indignation or pain felt when others fare well without deserving to do so, that is, when the unjust prosper (1108b1–7), is experienced by Socrates's young interlocutors in the *Republic* (e.g., 360a–361e). Socrates addresses their indignation by defining justice as the proper order of the soul, which implies that justice is its own reward. By the same token, injustice is the disorder in the soul, and its own punishment (444c–445b). From this perspective, whatever suffering befalls the just and whatever benefits the unjust reap from their injustice, the former always "prosper," the latter never do. If there are rewards and punishments, the *Republic* suggests, they come in the afterlife, and we know of them only through myth.

Aristotle, however, does not take this path away from political life. By showing that we can be blessed as human beings, that virtuous actions are within our reach when we aim at the mean, and even that our virtues become more complete by serving others' good as well as our own, Aristotle diminishes our susceptibility to *nemesis*, at the same time he responds to tragedy.[27] There is less cause for indignation, for example, if politics can improve upon chance in doling out just rewards and punishments, or in structuring political activity so that citizens share rule, if it recognizes natural justice as part of political justice, and if the laws allow their correction by equity.[28] And perhaps the law against suicide could have better effect, if political communities that announce such a law also improve the prospects for justice among their citizens. Had Aristotle followed his outline of the means in book 2, he would have discussed *nemesis* just before his treatment of justice in book 5. He omits *nemesis* but concludes his examination of justice with reference to a law against suicide. Once again, he in effect offers those like Glaucon and Adeimantus a better political life than they could imagine from watching the unjust prosper, or even from watching Socrates found a city that will remain only in speech while advising them to cultivate justice within themselves (see *Republic* 472d–73a, 592a–b). Aristotle can therefore turn the young toward political life, not away from it. By the same token, he does not exclude the poets, not even the tragedians, from the city, as Socrates does in the *Republic* (607b). His *Ethics* serves as an invitation to a reformed poetry, such as he encouraged in his *Poetics*, one, for example, in which human beings commit the

---

27. Aristotle gives a fuller treatment of *nemesis* in the *Rhetoric*, where he teaches the rhetorician how to direct the passions of his addressees—and thus also his own. See Basil, "Justice Speaks," 174–95, for a discussion of *nemesis* and forensic rhetoric.

28. Burger points out that one would be less vulnerable to indignation at underserved good fortune if one did not expect or even hope that just gods guarantee justice; see Burger, *Aristotle's Dialogue with Socrates*, 91–92, and Burger, "Ethical Reflection and Righteous Indignation, 127–39. Pangle, *Reason and Character*, 146–47, traces indignation to a failure to understand the ignorance underlying injustice. Both suggest that Aristotle tries to temper or correct indignation by lowering expectations of what can be demanded of the world. I agree that this is to some extent true of Aristotle's project, but it is also the case that if political life were reformed and thereby provided greater satisfaction for the human longing for justice, there would be less cause for indignation.

errors that lead to tragedy and hence bear at least some responsibility for the consequences. Indignation at the gods, or the fates, would be misconceived to the extent that we bring our suffering upon ourselves.

Insofar as conceiving justice as internal to a soul in which its parts do their own work, including ruling and being ruled, serves as Socrates's response to indignation or *nemesis*, it is appropriate that Aristotle ends book 5 by taking issue with this very view of justice. According to this view, justice—and injustice—lies in a relation between parts of the soul (1138b6–18). This view of justice that finds the same idea of justice in both city and soul (see *Republic* 435b), Aristotle points out, is only "metaphorical" (1138b6–7). He in effect warns us against identifying justice in the city with justice in the soul, and even against seeing one and the same idea in all the appearances of justice. Far from advocating a philosopher-king's rule of citizens, Aristotle teaches the statesman that his ruling in the city must take into account the capacity of citizens for self-rule. Moreover, even if the relations between the parts of the soul could be said to involve justice, it would not be "all [*pan*] justice," but the justice of a master (*despotikon*) or household manager (1138b8–10). Socrates's city in speech lacks what Aristotle calls "political justice," which exists among those "for whom law is natural, that is, those for whom there is equality in ruling and being ruled" (1134b7–17).

Aristotle's conclusion to book 5 thus reinforces his earlier discussion, reminding us that complete virtue involves the good of others as well as of oneself, and highlighting a political justice that belongs to those who rule and are ruled in turn, his answer to those who deny anything just by nature. He has now concluded his investigation of the ethical virtues, and what remains are the intellectual ones, according to the plan he proposed at the end of book 1 and the outline he gave of his work in book 2 (1103a4–10, 1108b8–10). To those virtues he now turns.

CHAPTER 5

Intellectual Virtues

Prudence, Wisdom, and Philosophy (Book 6)

At the end of book 1, Aristotle distinguished a rational part of the soul and a part able to hear and obey reason, associating the ethical virtues with the latter, and the intellectual virtues with the former. Now that Aristotle has described each of the ethical virtues (books 3–5), it remains for him to consider the intellectual ones. We are prepared to understand his examination of the intellectual virtues as another step, presumably the last step, in his inquiry into the virtues that constitute the "human work," with a view to finding "the most complete" (1098a17). Prudence and wisdom are the two intellectual virtues prominent in book 6, the first involving human affairs and things that admit of change and variation, the second concerned with the most divine things in the cosmos (1141a19–21, b1–2). Wisdom would therefore appear to be "the most complete" of the virtues, if not simply complete because there are other virtues, including prudence.

Although Aristotle soon mentions this rationale for discussing the intellectual virtues (1139a1–3), he also reminds us that when he previously discussed the mean in the context of the ethical virtues, he left his presentation incomplete, insisting that we must choose the mean as determined by reason, "as the prudent person would define it" (1106b36–1107a3, 1115b2). Someone knowing only that virtue is a mean defined by correct reason resembles one who knows only that he should follow the advice of medicine, or that he should do what the doctor commands. But to choose the mean, and thus to act virtuously, one needs more than the knowledge that one should act according to reason. One needs to know what is reasonable. The "correct reason" that determines the mean must now be defined (1138b18–1139a3). Aristotle is both moving on to the intellectual virtues and taking a further step in exploring ethical virtue itself.

These two strands of inquiry are both present throughout book 6: one highlights wisdom as the goal or end of the inquiry into happiness, the second highlights the centrality of prudence for the discussion of book 6. Aristotle appears to be weaving these two possibilities together, as if they were distinct but inseparable. In book 6, the ethical and intellectual virtues meet in Aristotle's inquiry into the human good, at times side by side, at times directly involved in the other. The "correct reason" needed for following the ethical mean requires prudence's deliberation about the human good, while wisdom about the whole cannot be complete without considering the good that belongs to the one who seeks it.

When Aristotle designates five ways in which we can attain truth: art (*technē*), science (*epistēmē*), prudence (*phronēsis*), wisdom (*sophia*), and mind (*nous*) (1139b14–18), prudence is at the center; wisdom and mind occupy the final place in the discussion. But what is central to all five is attaining truth. This list of truth-attaining qualities is unique to Aristotle, and unique to his *Ethics*. Although all five terms occur in common discourse and also have a rich resonance with discussions and occurrences in Plato's dialogues, their meanings are somewhat vague and open-ended. Socrates raises the question "What is science?" in the *Theaetetus*, for example, but every attempt that his interlocutor makes to answer proves inadequate (210a–b). In the Platonic corpus, "mind" or "intellect" (*nous*) is used to refer to our highest cognitive faculty and appears in a range of idioms that show the pervasiveness of mind in ordinary human life.[1] Both "prudence" and "wisdom" are at times used interchangeably in the *Republic* to refer to the virtue of the rulers (e.g., 429a, 433b). Previous usage gives

---

1. In the account of the divided line in the *Republic*, for example, *nous* is the capacity or faculty for grasping the objects on the highest segment of the line (511c–d). As to its idiomatic usages, they include "intending" or "having a mind to" (*exein noun*) (*Symposium* 189c), "paying attention to" or "holding in mind" (*prosexein noun*) (*Symposium* 191e, 192b), and "according to one's preference"

Aristotle leeway for his own clarification and refinement, as was the case with the ethical virtues. And just as Aristotle expanded the number of the ethical virtues that human beings can attain, his account of five distinct ways in which human beings can attain truth reinforces the breadth and variety in which our cognitive capacities give us access to the world. After exploring Aristotle's presentation of the soul at the beginning of book 6, I discuss in the next three sections of this chapter the five truth-attaining faculties he designates, first science, then art and prudence, and then mind and wisdom.

Whereas science contemplates what is necessary or eternal, subject to neither generation nor decay, art and prudence involve what is subject to variation and change. Art and prudence reveal truths about the latter, while also serving as testaments to human action and achievement. They originate in human beings, in the maker in the case of art, and in deliberation and choice in the case of prudence (1140a11–14, 1140a31–1140b7; *Metaphysics* 1025b20–24). Finally, like science, mind and wisdom give us contact with what is necessary or eternal. Aristotle uses "mind" here to refer to a grasping of the first principles or beginnings from which science proceeds (1140b31–1141a8). Wisdom, bringing together the work of science and that of our mind's grasping first principles, is itself "a science of the most honorable matters," indeed of "the best of things in the cosmos," whose nature is "much more divine than that of human beings" (1141a18–22).

In addition to his survey of the five ways in which we attain truth, Aristotle points to the sort of wisdom that moves his own inquiry. He implicitly distinguishes himself, for example, from "Thales and Anaxagoras and the wise of that sort," for in their study of the eternal and the unchanging they do not seek the good for human beings (1141b6–8). Aristotle does seek that good, which is the end of his inquiry in the *Ethics* (e.g., 1094b8). When he examines the human soul, he speaks of theorizing about what admits of change and variation as well as what is eternal and unchanging. He does not focus on only one or the other, but on our theorizing about both, just as he himself offers two rationales for his own move to book 6, one serving our making good choices, the other our gaining a

---

(*kata noun*) (*Symposium* 193c–d). I have taken these examples from Aristophanes's speech in Plato's *Symposium*. Plato gives his comic poet only idiomatic uses of *nous*.

more complete view of the virtues. Underlining the differences between his own philosophizing and that of the wise, such as Thales and Anaxagoras, Aristotle returns to politics in the last half of book 6, in the context of further thoughts about prudence and its place in human life. In the final three sections of this chapter, I discuss Aristotle's simultaneous return to politics and his reflections on his own way of philosophizing.

First, Aristotle revisits the architectonic character of politics by expanding the reach of prudence throughout the members of the political community. Here Aristotle's emphasis is less on the hierarchical character of ruling, with which he began the *Ethics*, than on the ways in which others in the community—those occupying ruling offices, those with authority in the family, and individuals more generally—exercise prudence in their work. In all these ways, prudence, like ruling, is shared. Aristotle then elaborates the work of prudence in ways that reflect on his own work, as he discusses "investigating" or "searching," exploring "perplexity," and "knowing together" with other human beings (1142a33–1143a35), faculties, I argue, that also characterize Aristotle's own inquiry in the *Ethics*. Finally, Aristotle himself puts forward a "perplexity" as he concludes book 6: How are wisdom and prudence useful? (1143b18–19). By exploring a "perplexity," he shows us in his own actions the intellectual activity he has just described. Aristotle's "wisdom," which does not eliminate all perplexity, culminates in book 6 in directing political life to what transcends politics. Politics arranges everything in the political community, Aristotle says, without ruling over the gods (1145a11–12). Once again, the architectonic art is less than architectonic. Aristotle's exploration of our cognitive capacities in book 6 does not merely fill in one of the items in his outline ("the rational virtues") (1108b10), it enriches our understanding of the ethical virtues, which require the intellectual virtue of prudence, while it connects our rational capacities with our longing for the good.

LOOKING AGAIN AT THE SOUL

Aristotle gives the name "scientific" (*to epistēmonikon*) to that part of the rational soul that "contemplates" the eternal and unchanging things, or, more specifically, "those things whose principles cannot be otherwise." With this part, he associates science, wisdom, and mind. The other part of the rational soul "contemplates" what admits of being otherwise, the "reasoning" (to *logisitkon*), to which art and prudence belong (1139a4–9, b23–24). Although he gives no examples of sciences here, they presumably include such disciplines as physics, which studies natural beings that change but whose principles do not admit of change, mathematics, and the science of being that he pursues in the *Metaphysics*.[2] As to what "admits of being otherwise," he earlier described the subject matter of politics, the just, the noble or beautiful, and the good, as admitting of change and variation (1094b14–28). His division of the rational soul follows from the differences in what the soul contemplates, for there must be a likeness (*kata homoiotēta*) or kinship (*kata oikeiotēta*) between what knows and what is known if knowledge (*gnōsis*) is to be possible (1139a5–12).[3] Inasmuch as the whole is composed of things that change or perish and those that are "eternal, ungenerated, and indestructible" (1139b24–27), the human soul that knows them must be akin to both. The world is one that we can understand, for it is "like" us and is "our own," or "akin" to us. It is our home. Our "divination," to which Aristotle referred us in book 1—that the good is "our own" (*oikeion*) (1095b25–26)—remains with him as the *Ethics* proceeds.

---

2. In the *Metaphysics*, Aristotle mentions "three theoretical philosophies": physics, mathematics, and theology, associating the last with "theorizing about being as being" (*Metaphysics* 1025b19–21; 1026a19–20, a30–34; 1064b2–3). Sachs, *Aristotle's "Metaphysics,"* 111n5, connects theology with ontology because "being as being" is "the highest, divine, kind of being, universal because everything else depends on it for its being."

3. There are several Greek words for "knowing" and "knowledge" that Aristotle uses. *Gignōskein* (and related words, e.g., *gnōrizein*, *gnōrimos*, and *gnōsis*) has the broadest range of meanings, including "to recognize," or "to be acquainted or familiar with." It is the verb found in the expression on the temple at Delphi, "Know yourself." Since both parts of the rational soul have *gnosis* of objects akin to them, there is a knowing common to both parts. The word that Aristotle uses for science (*epistēmē*) and its verb (*episthamasthai*) are also used in a broad sense (e.g., 1094a27–b4, where Aristotle seems to use science and art interchangeably), but Aristotle narrows its meaning to scientific knowledge in book 6. A third verb to know, *eidenai*, is related for the verb "to see," and appears in Aristotle's opening of the *Metaphysics* with "all human beings long to know."

Our world, however, is not an open book, from which truth can be read as easily as words on a page. The difficulty is implied even in our divination that the good is our own. We do not *know* this. We *divine* it. Aristotle says that we know not only what is kin (*oikeion*), but also what is like (*homoion*). But what is "like" is not "the same." To know something as "like" ourselves is also to know it as other, as different. Even the household (*oikos*) is composed of those who are dissimilar—man and woman, parents and children (1160b23–1161a6; *Politics* 1254a28–32). Aristotle's recourse to the assumption that "like is known by like" in order to divide the knowing soul is rife with difficulties.

Since the parts of the soul are like the objects they know, Pangle is able to ask, "Would what grasps unchanging truths have to be itself unchanging?" And would this rule out "learning" and hence "teaching," whereby someone comes to know, and hence changes?[4] One could also ask, What part of the soul knows the soul? One might suppose that the soul as a whole knows the soul as a whole, if Aristotle had not located our cognitive capacities in discrete parts as a result of his division. If either part were to know the soul as a whole or even the different parts of the soul, it would have to stretch its capacity to know to what is both like and unlike itself. Of course, if knowing something as like implies knowing it as other, knowing likeness holds the potential for knowing unlikeness.

Moreover, which part of the soul, as Aristotle has divided them, knows the world and the soul as wholes that can be divided?[5] Does any capacity of soul that Aristotle discusses in book 6 have the capacity to make such a division? More generally, where in the divided soul is the capacity for undertaking the inquiry of the *Ethics* concerning the virtues that connect us to both the eternal and the changing?[6] Aristotle's division

---

4. Pangle, *Reason and Character*, 186.

5. Among those who give accounts of soul whom Aristotle criticizes in the *De Anima* are those who say that like must be known by like. "Since the soul knows all things," they "construct the soul" from the elements of the cosmos, such as fire or air. But even if the soul so understood were able to know the elements out of which things are composed, Aristotle asks, how will the soul know anything "as a whole" (*sunolon*), such as "what a god or human being" is? (405b13–18, 409b23–410a3).

6. Kass, "Professor or Friend?," 6–7, asks to which of the five truth-attaining qualities Aristotle discusses does Aristotle's *Ethics* belong? "Careful examination," Kass notes, "will show that it belongs to none."

of the soul in terms of what it knows, strangely, leaves out the one who knows. In particular, it leaves out the one who makes the division. What is required for the inquiry is presupposed by the inquiry: there would be no inquiry without the one who inquires. If no "part" of the soul could know the soul, if the soul cannot become an object for itself, does Aristotle's division of the soul preclude self-knowledge? At the outset of *De Anima* (*On the Soul*), Aristotle warns us that "to attain any trust about [the soul] belongs to the most difficult of things in every way" (402a12). Is this because knowing the soul is possible only indirectly, by observing, to use Socrates's words in the *Phaedrus*, "how it is acted upon and how it acts," literally, its "sufferings" or "passions" and its "deeds" (245c)? This would involve the passions and deeds connected not only to the ethical virtues but also to the intellectual ones, what the soul does in their exercise and what it suffers when it encounters limits.

In all these ways, Aristotle's division of the rational soul implicitly raises the question of self-knowledge, as we might expect when Aristotle turns to the intellectual virtues, our diverse faculties for attaining knowledge or truth. The world of changing and unchanging objects about which we theorize is one in which we must find a place for ourselves. That place is not simply given to us, as Aristotle has been showing from the outset. By becoming habituated in respect to the ethical virtues, for example, we come to have a character, a "steady and unwavering state" from which our choices and actions proceed (1105a31–34). Our actions are then our own, since they originate in ourselves, and they connect us to the world, as we become a cause in the world that allows us to take part. So too when the perplexities of the world engage us, our questions and inquiries let us make our thoughts our own, whether by resolving perplexities or by understanding the difficulties in doing so. Throughout Aristotle's discussion of the ways in which we attain truth, we see how each in a different way gives us access to the world while remaining partial. We become aware that we long to know as we encounter obstacles in our search and aware that knowing is possible for us as we make progress in our search (see *Metaphysics* 980a21). Through intellectual and ethical virtue, and not least through knowing ourselves through our deeds and sufferings and through dealing with the perplexities we encounter, the world becomes a home for us. This truth is reflected in Aristotle's turn in his introduction to book 6 from his division of the rational soul, which seems to leave no space for self-knowledge, to his definition of choice as "either longing mind or intellectual longing." A "principle [or starting point] [*archē*] of this sort is a human being" (1139b5–7). This "unitary principle of the human," as Burger refers to it,[7] is more fundamental than and underlies the division of the soul that he makes at the outset of book 6, for our attempt to grasp either the changing or the unchanging leads us back to ourselves, who are like and akin to both. After all, action comes from choice only when it comes from "a steady and unwavering [*ametakinētōs*] state" (1105a33), while the unchanging and eternal cannot be something "separate and itself by itself" (see 1096b33) if it comes to light only to a mind that longs for it.

So does Aristotle's statement of the principle of the human revisit the division of the soul he made at the end of book 1, where he described the nonrational part of the soul as "characterized by desire, and by longing in general." Even then, he claimed that this part of the soul "somehow has reason" since it can obey or be persuaded by it (1102b30–1103a2). His definition of the human at the beginning of book 6 brings the longing part of the soul even closer to reason, at the same time it indicates that the rational part of the soul is characterized by longing. Longing does not belong to only one part of the soul that must be ruled. It belongs to the highest, the mind, what Aristotle later in the *Ethics* calls the most sovereign part of ourselves (1178a1–9). Aristotle hinted at this development in passing, and almost gratuitously, when he insisted at the end of book 5 that justice does not lie in the proper ordering of the soul, even though its parts

---

7. Burger, *Aristotle's Dialogue with Socrates*, 115, observes that the discussion of choice concludes with "a formula that cannot be understood as a hybrid of two independent subjects," longing and mind, "but only as an inseparable unity in which each is indeterminately substance or modifier." This "unitary principle of the human," as longing mind or intellectual longing, is "the condition ethical virtue aims to produce, by habituating desire in accordance with correct opinion," and this unitary principle is "the natural condition of the philosopher moved by erotic rationality." By implication, if what comes naturally to the philosopher comes by habituation to the ethically virtuous, "what is exhibited paradigmatically by the soul of the philosopher" (ibid.) becomes for Aristotle the model for the human soul as such and in particular for the ethically virtuous. See also Salkever, "Democracy and Aristotle's Ethics of Natural Questions," 359.

might "suffer something contrary to their respective longings [*orexeis*]" (1138b6–18). "Longing" can be found throughout the soul.[8]

Aristotle has prepared us for the centrality of longing in the human soul from the very outset when he argued that there is a highest good at which we aim, which is the object of our "longing" (1094a18–22; see also 1095a14–15). Longing connects human beings with the highest good while it indicates their incompleteness. Mind is inseparable from longing, at least the human mind, and at the same time longing is elevated (along with the ethical virtues) by this connection. The first formulation ("longing mind") indicates our capacity to pursue truth; the second ("intellectual longing") indicates our capacity to engage in a political life as rational beings who share in thinking and acting with others. Without the conjunction there would be no *Ethics*, which searches for the highest good and never leaves behind politics, which was its starting point, and to which Aristotle explicitly returns at the end of book 6, and at the end of the *Ethics* as a whole.

SCIENCE (*EPISTĒMĒ*)

Of the ways in which we attain truth, Aristotle begins with science. In the background of his effort lies the *Theaetetus*, Plato's dialogue on science, in which Socrates asks the young mathematician Theaetetus, "What is science?" The youth gives examples, including geometry and shoemaking and other such things (146c–d). From the perspective of book 6 of the *Ethics*, he fails to distinguish science from art, a faculty oriented toward eternal and unchanging things rather than toward production, almost as if his mathematical approach were a source of power over the world of change rather than a way of attaining truth. Socrates, for his part, reproaches his interlocutor for giving examples when asked for a definition, for "counting" (*arithmein*) the sciences rather than saying what science itself is (145e–147c). The particular examples that Theaetetus knows, or thinks he knows, do not add up to a definition. The dialogue's ultimate

---

8. Aristotle is more explicit in the *De Anima*, but he consistently raises a doubt about whether the soul can be said to have parts: "*if the soul* [*has parts*], there will be longing in each part" (432b8).

failure to define science (210a–b) leaves Aristotle a challenge that he takes up in his exposition of the intellectual virtues. His "list" of truth-attaining qualities, "five in number [*arithmos*]," as he says (1139b16), reenacts Theaetetus's counting, presumably in order to reach a more satisfactory result, and science itself becomes only one in the list, differentiated from art and the others Aristotle mentions. He finds a use for counting, in other words, that serves the search for science. Or, rather, he draws a broader picture of the ways in which human beings can attain truth, so that we can see the place of science in a larger whole.

At the same time, counting is insufficient, and even misleading. We count discrete units, for example, but it turns out that there are numerous overlaps and similarities and differences among the components in the list. Prudence and art could be paired, for example, but it is only by seeing the difference between them can one understand what each is. Science and mind (grasping first principles of science) may be discreet, but they are necessary to each other and only when conjoined is there wisdom. And if prudence has a central place in book 6, we cannot understand it as a member of a list of truth-attaining capacities coequal with the others, no more than an architectonic art can be considered a coequal member of the class of arts. Counting collects all the members of a class in its count, as Theaetetus counted the sciences and the arts without distinguishing better and worse, or higher and lower, members. Aristotle's beginning with an architectonic art, whatever its difficulties, recognizes that the study of politics cannot be a mathematical discipline.

Although Aristotle distinguishes the five ways of attaining truth from "supposition" (*hupolēpsis*) and "opinion" (*doxa*), which are "susceptible of error," he proceeds to appeal to what "we all *suppose* about science—that its objects do not admit of being otherwise." He even says that every science "is *opined*" [or "seems"] to be teachable" (1139b18–22, 24). He admits at the outset of his treatment of science that it might be liable to error, but he's apparently willing to accept common opinion among his starting points. He also spends less time on what science is than on how it comes to be, as if to say that we must consider not only the objects science seeks to know but how we *come to know* them. If science is acquired through teaching, we depend on teachers, who themselves learned from their teachers, just as our acquiring ethical virtues required the guidance of others (parents and lawgivers), who had acquired them previously. "All teaching," Aristotle says now, "comes from things previously known [*pro-*

gignōskein]," whether teaching involves demonstrations from universals (as in syllogisms) or the use of induction (*epagōgē*), which is the starting point (*archē*) of the universals, from which the demonstrations of science proceed. Science is "demonstrative" science (1139b24–33). But what capacity enables us to grasp the starting points of universals? And how do the universals come from the starting points? Aristotle acknowledges that his highly compressed account of science requires more, when he twice mentions the *Analytics*, where he also discusses these things (1139b27–28, 1139b33).

In the first instance, Aristotle refers to a discussion found in the *Posterior Analytics* (Aristotle's *Analytics* was later divided into the *Prior* and the *Posterior Analytics*) concerning how "teaching and learning proceed from what is known previously," a discussion that would be known previously by those familiar with that work. There too Aristotle refers to the previous knowledge from which all teaching and learning proceed, as in the mathematical sciences and all the arts, and also in arguments using syllogisms and induction (*Posterior Analytics* 71a1–6). Induction, Aristotle also observes there, "shows" or "reveals" (*deiknunai*) the universal from the "clarity" of a particular, but he admits that all things are not equally clear (71a8, 17). Moreover, in what way can a particular "show" a universal? When something "is known" to us from the clarity of particulars, do we know only "that" it is? Must we also know "what" it is, if the particular is to be sufficiently clear, and even "why" it exists (cf. *NE* 1095b7)?

In his account in the *Posterior Analytics* to which he refers us in the *Ethics*, Aristotle presents syllogisms as equally puzzling, for they begin with universals that can be acknowledged by "those with comprehension" (*sunientes*) (71a6–9).[9] Such comprehending human beings seem to intervene between the inductions leading to universals and the universals from which demonstrations proceed. Who are those who comprehend and how do we identify them? The *Analytics* thus gives us further questions about the principles from which science, and indeed all knowing, proceed. When in the *Ethics* Aristotle refers to the *Posterior Analytics*, he does not say that the work resolves the issue of "knowing previously," but only that "we speak" of it there.

---

9. Tredennick, *Aristotle: "Posterior Analytics,"* 25, plausibly translates Aristotle's phrase as "making assumptions as though granted by an intelligent audience."

In the *Posterior Analytics*, Aristotle states explicitly what he implies in the *Ethics*, that the need to "know previously" questions the very possibility of knowledge or science. Would knowing previously, as required by science, also require knowing previously, leading to an infinite regress? This perplexity, Aristotle says, leads some to deny that science or knowledge is possible, for "it is impossible to traverse an infinite series." Even if we came to a stop, and discovered "beginnings" or "first principles," there would be no way to demonstrate them, for a beginning could not be derived from anything prior to itself. This perplexity too persuades some either that science is not possible or that it must proceed merely from hypotheses rather than from knowledge. Some who do not give up on science, on the other hand, insist that "all things are demonstrable," and they attempt to demonstrate the first principles, but their circular reasoning (for example, the conclusions or results prove the principles) inevitably fail. They demand too much, for the "immediate" cannot be demonstrated. By doing so, they only arrive at another beginning, which they would then have to demonstrate. They would never reach an end, or a beginning (72b1–35).

Both to those who suppose that because beginnings cannot be demonstrated there is no way to know them and to those who suppose that they can know beginnings by demonstrating them, Aristotle responds that there is a way of knowing other than "demonstrative science" by which we can know the very principles on which science is based. He refers us to the necessity for trust in order to know: "To possess demonstrative science" one must "trust [*pisteuein*] the beginnings, all or some of them, more than the conclusion," and "not only know [*gnorizein*] the beginnings but also know and trust them more than what is demonstrated" (*Posterior Analytics* 72a35–b1). Similarly, he appeals to trust in his section on science in book 6 of the *Ethics*: When "someone trusts [*pisteuei*] in something in a certain way and the beginnings are known [*gnōrimoi*] to him," he "acquires science [*epistamai*]," for "if someone does not know the beginnings to a greater degree than he knows the conclusion, he will possess science only accidently [*kata sumbebēkos*]" (1139b33–35). The discussion in the *Posterior Analytics* to which he refers in the *Ethics* thus elaborates how those who require too much certainty (demonstrable first principles) threaten science itself, and it confirms the place of trust in science that he alludes to in the *Ethics*. When in the *Ethics* Aristotle refers us to the *Posterior Analytics* a second time—for "what we must add to the definition of science" (*prosdiorizimetha*) (1139b33), we expect that it is "trust" that must be added.

Bartlett and Collins explain the meaning of the Greek word for "trust": it "means in the first place to trust or have faith in something, and then, following from this, the sense of confidence or certainty one may feel as a result of such trust or faith."[10] But even though confidence follows from trusting, why do we trust? Do we trust the beginnings because they are known to us? Then the difficulty of knowing beginnings remains. Or are the beginnings known to us when we "somehow" (*pōs*) trust in them, as Aristotle's language suggests?[11] "Somehow" we trust, and what we trust becomes known or familiar to us (*gnōrimoi*), because we trust it. But can nothing more be said about the "somehow"? How do we come to trust?

In the *Posterior Analytics*, Aristotle discusses how we should go about defining, and throws some light on what must be "added to a definition," or on how a definition is incomplete. He uses the example of deriving a

---

10. Bartlett and Collins, *Aristotle's "Nicomachean Ethics,"* 119n22. We have taken note of several occasions in which Aristotle mentions the need for "trust," as when he describes love of honor as a desire to trust one's own goodness (1095b28) and when he examines the "social virtues" in part so that we will "trust" that virtues are means (1127a16). These virtues are nameless and hence unknown or unfamiliar, but they will become better known and more familiar as a result of Aristotle's invention of names for them and his discussion of them as means between extremes. Apart from Aristotle's use of "trust" in relation to what we know (e.g., 1142a30, 1146b31, 1154a25), trust also plays an important role in friendship, which requires knowing and trusting one's friend (e.g., 1156b29, 1157a23).

11. Pangle, *Reason and Character*, 192–93, 200, also observes Aristotle's reference to trust in his discussion of science, but she understands the need for trust to call knowledge into question rather than to support it. As she asks, "Does science not involve trust in the general reliability of perception, the real existence of the things we perceive, and the assumption that the patterns and regularities we perceive in things rest on underlying necessities? Without such necessities we could scarcely speak of the nature of anything. But it is not clear that science itself is ever able to prove that these necessities exist." She finds that Aristotle "casts [a dark] shadow over science." In the passage from the *Analytics* that I discuss above, however, Aristotle explicitly attributes casting such a dark shadow to others, those who despair of science, to whom he responds.

definition from particulars in the case of greatness of soul, and hence speaking further about what must be known beforehand in order to define. To define greatness of soul, he says, we must consider what all the great-souled individuals whom we know (*eidenai*) have in common. He mentions five great-souled individuals either from history or poetry, and he notes that some of them were unable to endure insult (Alcibiades, Achilles, and Ajax), and others were indifferent to fortune (Lysander and Socrates). Greatness of soul itself divides into those who are moved by the external world (in reacting to insult) and those who are not (in not reacting to what chances to happen). But how do we "know" that this is the appropriate way to divide greatness of soul, especially since making this distinction seems to leave nothing in common to those we know as great-souled? If the two things characterizing each group of individuals have nothing in common, Aristotle admits, then there are "two forms of greatness of soul" (*Posterior Analytics* 97b16–26). By concluding that "the definition [*horos*] is always universal" (97b26), however, he questions whether those we "know" as great-souled are correctly known, or at the very least why we can attribute to both groups he mentions greatness of soul.

This example of defining in the *Analytics* does not arrive at a definition. Rather, this exposition leaves perplexity about what greatness of soul is. How do we know that these individuals are great-souled unless we already know what greatness of soul is? Only then could we know why either an inability to endure insult or an indifference to chance, which can be seen in the actions and lives of Aristotle's examples, would belong to a great-souled individual. It is the sort of explication of greatness of soul that Aristotle gives in the *Ethics* that helps us make such a judgment. His description of greatness of soul there does not rest with knowing "that" a host of propensities and deeds manifest greatness of soul, but "why" they proceed from such a character. As a result, we can understand why Alcibiades, Achilles, and Ajax fall short of the greatness Aristotle describes, even while they come closer to beings such as we are, who react against unjust treatment. And we can understand why those who are indifferent to fortune possess something that belongs to greatness of soul, even while they are further from beings such as ourselves who are moved by good and bad fortune.

Greatness of soul, because of the fullness of Aristotle's description of its deeds and its sufferings, serves as an especially good example of his treatments of the virtues. Aristotle begins with a definition but then supplements it with what we might call his "psychology," showing us by his deeds what must be added to a definition, just as the many deeds he attributes to the virtues he describes allow universals (definitions, standards that guide judgment) to emerge (see *NE* 1107a30–33). In doing this, Aristotle puts to work his insight about poetry at its best that lies at the heart of his *Poetics*: poetry is philosophic to the extent that that it reveals the universal in the particular (1451b6–11). We need additions to the definition, as Aristotle says when he points us to the *Analytics*, which that work confirms by its failure to *define* greatness of soul. Aristotle's descriptions of the various virtues in the *Ethics* offer additions to their definitions. The descriptions help us to trust the definitions, or to judge the universal with the help of Aristotle's descriptions.

It is in his *Rhetoric*, however, that Aristotle most clearly indicates how speech such as the *Ethics* contributes to the trust (*pistis*) (often translated as "cause of trust") that is the beginning of knowledge. The grounds of trust are threefold: first, the character (*ēthos*) of the speaker as it is revealed in his speech; second, the passion (*pathos*) of its addressee that responds to the speech and its speaker; and third, the speech itself (*logos*) that mediates between speaker and addressee (1356a2–21). The speech, whether its argument or the character of the speaker indicated by his argument, or both, is trusted when it "affects" or "moves" the addressee, when in other words it resonates with his soul, even as it calls forth that resonance.

When Aristotle says in the *Posterior Analytics* that the one possessing science has "knowledge to begin with" (*proüparchousē gnōsis*) (71a1), he uses the same word he uses to describe the munificent person, who has resources "to begin with" (*proüparchei*) (1122b30). The problem of what we are given, which allows us to begin, belongs to the intellectual virtues as much as it does to the ethical ones. Like the munificent person, we have what we need to begin, and so our beginning is not simply a beginning, that is, we have a "longing mind" or an "intellectual longing" that Aristotle calls the "beginning" or "principle" (*archē*) of the human (1139b5–6). But even this is not all that we are "given" at the beginning. Longing is stirred by the objects we long for; knowledge depends on the objects we know. At the outset of book 6, we saw Aristotle divide the rational part of the soul on the basis of its affinity or kinship with the objects in the cosmos—a division that presupposes that knowledge is possible. It is as if we know that we are at home in the world and our confidence that this is so allows us to learn much, much more about that world and about ourselves, and even ways in which we do not fit perfectly in that world. When Aristotle says in the *Analytics* that the one who is to possess science must "know and trust the beginnings more than what is demonstrated" (72a35–b1), he reminds us of what is given to us, which has priority over what we accomplish (in this case, the proofs or demonstrations that belong to science) because what is given makes these possible. Our perceptions of particulars, our experience of those with comprehension, and our "being better off" (*beltion diakeimenos*) from the knowing that comes from trusting are among the ways in which what is given to us appear in Aristotle's discussion in the *Posterior Analytics* (71a1–7, 72a32–35).[12]

We might expect that after discussing science Aristotle would turn to mind and wisdom, since they too involve what is eternal and unchanging and therefore might shed further light on the conundrums left by his treatment of science. Aristotle nevertheless leaves these issues suspended, to examine art and prudence. This ordering, as Kass points out, has the result that "the human is surrounded by the more-than-human."[13] Those things that admit of being otherwise, about which art and prudence can attain truth, are closer to home. Their causes or beginnings lie in human beings, as makers and as deliberators who choose. Aristotle turns to what art and prudence are able to accomplish in spite of or perhaps precisely because of the changing and variable objects with which they deal. As it

---

12. Following Aristotle's suggestion in the *Ethics*, Bruell, "Aristotle on Theory and Practice," esp. 6–11, examines the *Analytics* for further elaboration of his view of science. Aristotle admits there, he notes, that the inability of science to demonstrate the starting points on which it is based has led some to despair of the possibility of science (72b5–6), but that Aristotle "gives the impression of thinking" that science is nevertheless possible. Inquiring where the "beginnings" required for science can be found, Bruell looks at Aristotle's treatment of the question at the end of the *Posterior Analytics*, in the *Metaphysics*, and in the *De Anima*. He finds in each case, "Aristotle's reserve as to his view of theory or philosophic science." Bruell therefore concludes that "Aristotle thinks that . . . the very possibility of genuine science as he understands it is problematic," but this does not mean that he "abandoned the cause of science," especially given "the immense effort he made on its behalf." He does not mention trust.

13. Kass, "Professor or Friend?," 17.

turns out, Aristotle's first observation in dealing with art and prudence also involves trust.

ART (*TECHNĒ*) AND PRUDENCE (*PHRONĒSIS*)

With regard to art and prudence, which concern what "admits of being otherwise," Aristotle "trusts in the exoteric arguments," the sorts of arguments that circulate *outside* the academies of learning. Aristotle appealed to such arguments earlier for the distinction between the rational and nonrational parts of the soul, but showed their exoteric view neglected the struggle within the soul and hence a part that could share in reason by following its lead or that might fail to do so (1102b13–36). Now, in book 6, Aristotle trusts the exoteric arguments for their distinction between making and acting: "In making, the end is something other than the making itself, whereas in action there would be no other end" (1140a1–6, b6–8). This distinction that he claims to trust appears at odds with the perspective of the architectonic art that Aristotle described in book 1, for which "it makes no difference whether the ends of actions are the activities themselves or something else apart from them" (1094a16–17). All fit into the ordered whole. Rather than take their bearing entirely from any ordered hierarchy of arts and their ends, the exoteric arguments Aristotle mentions here insist that actions at least have ends of their own, which of course may or may not serve the ordered whole.[14] They point to what is "outside" the city's hierarchy and purpose, since for them it does make a difference if "the ends of the actions are the activities themselves." Aristotle says that they can be trusted.

Aristotle elaborates the exoteric argument about art by observing that "every art involves a coming into being, that is, making and contemplating how something that admits of existing or not existing comes to be." Thus "the beginning of a thing made lies in the maker rather than in the thing

---

14. In explaining the exoteric distinction between making and acting, Aristotle says "the one is not contained in the other, for action is not making, and making is not action" (1140a5–6). He uses the same word for "contain" (*periechein*) as he did in justifying the architectonic character of politics: because it makes use of the other arts and sciences in ordering the political community, its end "contains" those of the others (1094b4–7).

made." So too "there is no art of what exists or comes into being of necessity, or according to nature" (1140a13–16). Aristotle quotes a poet: "Art is fond of chance, and chance of art" (1140a20). Chance or fortune (*tuchē*), which appeared earlier as a source of uncertainty and suffering because it might deprive the prosperous of happiness, has a benign side. Whatever its sway over human life, chance leaves room for art, or for human beings who can bring order. Art determines what is otherwise left to chance. Chance, for its part, is fond of what it makes possible. At least one poet says so. Aristotle has found a poet who supports human activity rather than crushes it with tales of divine jealousy (*Metaphysics* 982b2–4) or the overwhelming subjection of human life to chance. The poet's name, which Aristotle mentions, is Agathon (1140a19).[15]

Aristotle proceeds even further in the direction of human freedom in his discussion of prudence, which he describes as "a characteristic involving action, accompanied by reason, and concerned with things good and bad for human beings." Prudence guides our deliberations, choices, and actions about what is good or bad (1140b5–7). Unlike art, which has its end in the thing made rather than in the making, the end of the action guided by prudence lies in itself. "Acting well is itself an end," Aristotle says, in terms similar to those he used of the beautiful or noble actions undertaken for their own sake (1140b8, 1105a33, 1115b22–24). That action has its end within itself rather than in something external frees human actions from a determinate place in a whole, as belongs to the art of the

---

15. In the *Symposium*, there is a play on Agathon's name. On the way to a drinking party at Agathon's home, Socrates meets Aristodemus and urges him to come along, even though he is "uninvited." Socrates quotes Homer, "the good go of their own accord [*automatatoi*] to the feast of the good." Of course, Aristodemus is not going "of his own accord," but at Socrates's bidding (174b). Later, Agathon claims that Love is beautiful and good (rather than a desire or longing for it), and, consistently, traces the arts to the gods, who inspire or work through human beings (196e–197b). Agathon seems to deify himself—as a poet through whom divine love flows—and also to erase himself, since he is nothing without divine inspiration. Aristotle—and presumably Socrates—would question his piety. In any case, Agathon should look to himself, someone who is hosting his own party and who has issued invitations. He needs Socrates's insistence that love desires rather than possesses the beautiful and the good, just as Aristodemus needs Socrates's invitation to go to Agathon's party. The Agathon whom Aristotle quotes seems to stand corrected.

general, for example, which is determined by its work for the political community.[16] Aristotle now finds what has an end in itself manifest in actions in relation to others in a political community. Prudence belongs to the statesman, and Aristotle refers to Pericles as someone known for his prudence. But household managers are also prudent, Aristotle tells us, as are individuals who "deliberate beautifully [or nobly] about things good and advantageous" for themselves and other human beings (1140a26–26, b7–10).

By including art and prudence among the intellectual virtues, Aristotle gives in effect a gentler or more sympathetic treatment of those whom Socrates examines for their wisdom as he recounts in the *Apology* (21b–23b). Aristotle associates not only the activity of the scientists with a rational part of the soul, but also that of makers (artisans and poets) and politicians, whose works and activities proceed from one or another of the "truth-attaining" capacities Aristotle includes in book 6. All these groups manifest in their own ways, not the pretensions to wisdom Socrates encountered in his inquiries, but rather the activity of reason that distinguishes a human life.

The *Republic* also lies in the background of Aristotle's treatment of the intellectual virtues in the *Ethics*. Like Aristotle, Socrates distinguishes the eternal from the changing, "what is always the same in all respects" from the many appearances that "wander about" between being and nonbeing. The first are grasped by the faculty of science or knowledge (*epistēmē*) in Socrates's account, and the latter belong merely to opinion (*Republic* 478b, 479a–480a). But, unlike Aristotle, Socrates includes beauty itself and justice itself among "what is always the same in all respects," and therefore the objects of science. His distinction supports the rule of those who know, the philosopher-kings, over those who opine. Socrates thus seems to leave the world of changing and "wandering" objects to opinion, which he says "knows nothing of what [it] opines" (479e), like many whom Socrates encounters in his conversations with others. Aristotle, in response, introduces the intellectual virtue prudence into that world of change. Indeed, he directs his own inquiry in the *Ethics* to what "wanders" and "admits of variation," the beautiful and the just, whose wandering does

---

16. This is not to say that a general cannot look at his political community from the outside, and so disrupt its ordering, and even seek to provide a new ordering.

not mean that we can "know" nothing about them, but that we should expect less precision in their study than in such disciplines as mathematics (1094b15–17). Aristotle even uses the word that Socrates applies to the highest part of the soul, the reasoning, *to logisitkon* (439d, 440e), to describe the part concerned with the changing things to which prudence belongs. He also refers to this part as "the part involved in the formation of opinions" (*doxastikon*) (1139a15, 1140b27). Reasoning and opining are not as far apart as Socrates suggests in the *Republic*. In effect, the Socrates of the *Republic* expects more of wisdom than it can provide (a science of rule), and less of politics than Aristotle does (an intellectual virtue called prudence that can deliberate about those things that admit of being otherwise and are subject to choice). As Aristotle says at the beginning of the *Politics*, his predecessors (who would include Socrates) fail to distinguish politics from other forms of rule, such as despotism, and understand ruling to be a "science" (1252a7–16).[17]

Aristotle's discovery of prudence not only elevates political life by associating it with reason (see *Politics* 1253a8–10), it also attacks any pretension that wisdom or science may make to rule. Those who theorize only about the eternal and unchanging, those with wisdom and science, Aristotle proceeds to show, do not investigate what is good for human beings. They do not appear to understand Aristotle's starting point in book 6—the *human* kinship to what is eternal and unchanging.

MIND (*NOUS*) AND WISDOM (*SOPHIA*)

After examining the virtue of the politicians, Aristotle examines those who are reputed wise, such as Thales and Anaxagoras, when he turns to the two remaining ways of the five he designated in which we attain

---

17. Although these passages in the *Republic* are useful in highlighting what Aristotle is doing by way of contrast, Socrates qualifies or refines this separation between knowledge and opinion as the dialogue proceeds. For example, Socrates later describes a "divided line" that connects as well as divides the various objects of cognition. Moreover, in Socrates's dialogues with others, as Plato depicts them, Socrates searches for truth about the beautiful and the just in the opinions his interlocutors express. See Nichols, "Plato's Democratic Moment," 79–84. In other words, Aristotle has learned much from Plato's Socrates.

truth—mind and wisdom. He reiterates the conclusion of his discussion of science: there is no demonstration of the principles or beginning points of science. Having discussed art and prudence, he can dismiss them as candidates for help with science, since art and prudence are concerned with what admits of being otherwise. Since wisdom, he says, can demonstrate some things, it cannot be merely what attains the principles or beginning points. For this capacity there "remains" mind, for it is the only other way of attaining truth in his original list. *Nous* is often translated as "intuition" or "intellectual intuition," inasmuch as Aristotle describes it as an immediate grasping rather than demonstration or reasoning.[18] As a result of his identification of *nous*, Aristotle is able to identify wisdom as consisting of science (*epistēmē*), which proceeds from first principles, and mind (*nous*), which grasps them (1141a19).

Aristotle left his discussion of science with reference to the contribution of trust to knowing the first principles on which science is based. He now explains why "trust" is possible: a truth-attaining faculty, mind, grasps principles that cannot be derived *from an argument* that verifies them. When Aristotle says that wisdom not only grasps the first principles but also "attains the truth *about* them" (1141a19), presumably it understands the truth that grasping the first principles involves trust. Of course, it is only because Aristotle includes mind (*nous*) at the outset as one of the ways in which we attain truth does it "remain" (*leipein*) (1141a8) to do this work that Aristotle now assigns to it.[19] In other words, his very procedure

---

18. Bartlett and Collins, *Aristotle's "Nicomachean Ethics,"* 123, capture the meaning of *nous* when they translate it as "intellectual grasp" at 1141b3.

19. See also the end of the *Posterior Analytics*, where Aristotle reiterates what is almost his first word in that work, that there is no science of the starting points (*archai*) of science, no demonstration of the starting points of demonstration. There too he infers that mind must grasp the starting points since there is no other faculty available to do so (100b5–17). Aristotle's way of proceeding in both works only superficially resembles that of Anaxagoras, whom he criticizes in the *Metaphysics*. Although Aristotle praises him as the first who proposed that mind (*nous*) is "the cause of the cosmos and all order [in nature]," he also reproaches him for the way in which he put mind to work in his thought: whenever Anaxagoras encountered a perplexity about why something is the way it is, he dragged in (*parelkei*) mind as an explanation (984b17–18, 985a18–22). Aristotle's recourse to mind as a cause of wisdom is one of trust, not force. Aristotle refers to Anaxagoras, but never to himself, as "a cosmos-maker" (985a19). It is no accident that

manifests a trust in the world and our knowledge of it, or in the kinship between the world and our souls. Without access to first principles, and hence trust, wisdom is not possible—nor science (see *Posterior Analytics* 72b5–6).[20]

Aristotle's laying down five ways in which the mind attains truth, and then finding the one that grasps the principles of science by a process of eliminating the others, imitates an approach that Socrates uses in searching for the virtue of justice in the *Republic* (427e; see also *NE* 1105b18–1106a13). There Socrates proposes that a perfectly good city would be wise, courageous, moderate, and just, and that after locating the first three, justice will be manifest as "the left over" (*to hupoleiphthen*) (427e, 433c), or "the remainder" (*to loipon*) (432b). Had Socrates added a fifth virtue, for example, piety (*hosiotēs*), to his list of what constitutes a good city, a virtue that is included along with these other four in the *Protagoras* (e.g., 330b), justice alone would not be the remainder once the other three are subtracted.[21] What Socrates does to find justice, Aristotle in effect does to find wisdom, or, more specifically, to find mind as a faculty that grasps the first principles of science and hence makes science and wisdom possible. For Aristotle, wisdom cannot so easily be spotted as it can in Socrates's "city in speech," where it is found in the city's ruling class (*Republic* 428a–429a). Although Aristotle's procedure might read like a mere spoof of Socrates's in the *Republic*, it contains an important lesson. By designat-

---

Anaxagoras was known as a mentor of Pericles, one of the proponents of Athenian imperialism. See *Phaedrus* 270a, where Socrates says that Anaxagoras filled Pericles with "star-gazing discourse" (*meteorōlogia*), who when he came to "mind and mindlessness" dragged (*elkein*) what was useful to his art of speaking. Aristotle's use of the even more forceful *parelkein* in the *Metaphysics* echoes Socrates's language, but Socrates's attributing *anoia* to Anaxagoras (and Pericles) is pointed enough.

20. I would therefore take issue with Pangle's reference to the intuitions grasped by mind as merely "soothing reassurances that Aristotle's more gentlemanly readers will be inclined to trust" (Pangle, *Reason and Character*, 201).

21. Just before Socrates begins his search for the four virtues in the city, Glaucon reminds him that he "promised" he would look for justice because it would be "impious" if he did not assist justice (427e). In diverging from the *Republic*, Aristotle typically takes his cue from something in the dialogue itself. Piety is left out of the virtues in the city in speech, but it is not left out of the dialogue's deeds.

ing the ways in which we attain truth to be "five in number" (1139b16),[22] Aristotle does not leave out piety. Wisdom is dependent on what cannot be demonstrated or what cannot become an object of science, a kind of intuition that he associates with trust. It is a trust that our ways of attaining truth are not limited to what we can demonstrate (science), make (art), or choose (prudence), but reach to an intuition and trust in the world's intelligibility that extends to its very foundations of what we can know. The appropriate response to Aristotle's presentation of the intellectual virtues is a gratitude for what we are given and for what we can accomplish, rather than a despair about the limits of what we can know or a sense of empowerment that those limits open up.

Aristotle begins his treatment of wisdom with "what we believe" to be the case (1141a9–13). First, we ascribe wisdom to those who are "most precise in the arts," such as Pheidias, "a wise sculptor" in marble, and Polycleitus in bronze, "signifying by wisdom nothing other than the virtue belonging to art." Second, we also believe that some are wise "with respect to the whole, and not in any one particular thing," as Homer says in the *Margites* about someone whom "the gods made neither a digger nor a ploughman nor wise in any other way" (1141a9–16). From this comic epic attributed to Homer, Aristotle derives a universality that transcends any particular thing and then combines this supposition with the precision characteristic of the arts. He thereby finds support for his claim that wisdom is "the most precise science ... of the most honorable things" (1141a16–20). Aristotle thus moves to wisdom via the arts, which he has already distinguished from wisdom given their belonging to the world of change, and a line from a comic epic that seems to blame the gods for leaving a human being without endowments or gifts. In the *Poetics* in reference to the *Margites*, Aristotle claims that Homer introduced comedy "not for blame, but for laughter" (1448b28–37). His turn to common opinions about the arts and from a line in a comic epic to describe what wisdom is should give us pause, or perhaps even evoke laughter. Wisdom in effect disappears, manifest only in a particular product such as a sculpture,

---

22. Aristotle's initial list places mind in the fifth place. He changes the order of presentation between wisdom and mind presumably because wisdom cannot be understood without a trusting grasp of the first principles of science. His change of order highlights this dependence. See also *Politics* 1328b13.

or in something we cannot see at all because it involves nothing in particular.

Indeed, these two opinions Aristotle offers about wisdom might just as plausibly support the conclusion that the only wisdom available to human beings lies in particular things, rather than in the whole, and that one claiming wisdom with respect to the latter is wise in nothing. Such a conclusion echoes Socrates's discovery that among those he questions, only the artisans "know many beautiful things," even though on account of their wisdom they think that they are also wise with respect to "the greatest things" (*Apology* 22d–e). But Socrates shows that they do not know the greatest things and hence they do not know themselves—that is, he shows what they know and do not know. In his own—more gentle way—Aristotle follows Socrates in questioning those who suppose they are wise.

Aristotle continues to report what people say about wisdom when they contrast it with prudence. The two cannot be the same, they say, for the prudent are concerned with what is advantageous to themselves, and this differs from species to species. The good for fish, for example, differs from the good for human beings, but wisdom does not differ from species to species. Hence it is said that some beasts are prudent, those "that have forethought [*pronoiētikē*] about their own lives" (1141a23–28; see Plato, *Statesman* 263d). So too "people say that Anaxagoras, Thales, and the wise of that sort are wise, but not prudent, when they see them ignorant of what is advantageous to themselves." It is also said that the wise like Thales and Anaxagoras "know what is odd, wondrous, difficult, and daimonic, but useless, for they do not search for human goods" (1141b3–8).[23] If this were correct, the wise would lack forethought about

---

23. Aristotle's inclusion of Thales as one spoken about as wise recalls the common story of the laughter Thales incurred from a slave girl when he fell into a well while stargazing, an activity that so distracted him from his own good that he could not see what was at his feet (*Theaetetus* 174a). In the *Politics*, Aristotle recounts a story that shows a different view of Thales. When he was reproached for his poverty on the ground that his philosophy was of no benefit to him, he observed from his study of the stars that there would be a good harvest of olives. He rented all the olive presses at low cost, and then hired them out at a high price when they came to be in demand. Thales was able to make a great deal of money, Aristotle observes (1259a7–19). Perhaps Thales learned from stumbling what

their own lives. And if there were a competition in providing for oneself, prudent beasts would have the advantage over them. Aristotle is poking fun at a wisdom that lacks self-knowledge and that demotes prudence to what could belong to beasts. A beast, whose soul lacks a rational part, could not possess prudence or deliberate about its own good. Those who contrast wisdom and prudence in this way do not know what Aristotle shows about the human soul, not even what he lays out at the end of book 1 for use by the statesman in his own work.

Aristotle's presentation of the wise, such as Anaxagoras and Thales, is indebted to Socrates's criticism of Anaxagoras in the *Phaedo*. Although Anaxagoras taught that "mind orders and is the cause of all things," his explanations, even of human actions, turned on material causation rather than on what is best for each thing to be or on how it is best for it to act. Anaxagoras would say, Socrates conjectures, that Socrates is sitting in jail awaiting execution because of the arrangement of his bones and sinews rather than because the Athenians thought it best to condemn him and because he thought it best to abide by their decision (*Phaedo* 98b–e). Socrates refuses to separate mind from the good, as his examples of the Athenians and himself attest. Aristotle's definition of choice as the principle of the human at the outset of book 6, we see now, responds in part to Anaxagoras: "mind," at least in the case of human beings, is "longing mind." It must be understood as directed toward the good.

Whereas Socrates refuted those he cross-examined in his search for wisdom and aroused the anger that eventually led to his trial and execution, Aristotle, in contrast, allies himself with Homer for a comic treatment of pretension. Perhaps this difference turns on Aristotle's finding what others know rather than revealing what they do not, while offering to both philosophy and politics something more than a knowledge of ignorance—the many ways in which human beings can attain truth. Of course, Socrates's human wisdom is more than mere ignorance, but Aristotle draws out his own contribution in a more positive way than Socrates did by insisting time after time that the end of investigating virtue is not only to know what virtue is but to act virtuously—for that is what

---

Aristotle knows. His story of Thales shows that the wise man's studies were good not in spite of their uselessness but because they were useful after all. As we shall see, Aristotle himself raises the question of the utility of both wisdom and prudence near the end of book 6.

constitutes happiness for human beings. Aristotle even criticizes those who take refuge in words and who suppose that by doing so they are philosophizing (1095a7, 1103b28–30, 1179b1–2, 1105b12–23). Aristotle's philosophizing does not take refuge in words rather than in deeds; nor is his way that of Anaxagoras, Thales, and "the wise *of that sort*" (1141b6–8).

By claiming that the human being is not the best thing in the cosmos, Aristotle makes a judgment about the relative goodness of the different beings in the cosmos, specifically about human beings compared to those "whose natures are more divine than [theirs]" (1141a22–24, a36–b2). He makes a judgment that could be made neither by the wise whose gaze is only on the most honorable things in the cosmos, nor by the prudent who look only to their own advantage or that of those like themselves. Those who judge that a human being is not the best thing in the cosmos, in contrast, can draw this conclusion only from understanding the place of the human being in the cosmos, specifically, from understanding that the human species is only part of a whole. They are aware that there is something higher than themselves, different from themselves, whatever their affinity with it or their belonging to it. They are aware of both difference and likeness, and it is certainly not "a difference that makes no difference" (see 1094a16–17). The self-knowledge that we can attain comes not only by way of kinship and likeness but also by way of difference.

Book 6 is Aristotle's book about self-knowledge, for we know ourselves by exercising our capacities to know, as Aristotle presents them in his account of the ways in which we attain truth. But we also know ourselves through our errors. We have seen that Aristotle distinguished the five ways of attaining truth from supposition and opinion, for these "admit of error [or falsehood] [*diapseudesthai*]" (1139b15–18). We are liable to error. However helpful Aristotle's list, we still have to distinguish whether in any particular instance we know or only suppose that we do, and therefore we must distinguish truth from error. Error remains a constant threat in book 6. Science does not demonstrate its beginnings, but unless it knows its beginnings to an even greater degree than its conclusions, it is science "only accidently" (1139b33–35). In the case of art, Aristotle says, it is more choiceworthy "to err" voluntarily than in the case of prudence (1140b23–24). Prudence concerns universals and particulars, and "errors in deliberation" can involve both (1141b15–16, 1142a22). Our errors cause us to stumble, like Thales who fell into a hole while looking up the heavens.

When we see our errors, we know ourselves, for we do not possess the truth we tried to grasp. We come home, not with empty hands—for the attempt has been made and we have gained experience in the search—but with hands less full than we hoped. We know ourselves as beings who long to know. Aristotle has not erred in omitting self-knowledge from the ways of attaining truth he discusses in book 6, for self-knowledge is not one way of knowing among others, for it is implicated in the human longing to know.

For similar reasons, Aristotle did not count piety as one of the virtues among others. Our divination that the good belongs to us grounds our striving for virtue while leading us to see that we do not perfectly possess the good. We find self-knowledge along with piety, for the "two go together" (see 1155a15). Wise men such as Thales and Anaxagoras, who look up to the heavens, must also look to themselves, if only to better understand the highest, for it is that to which human longing is directed. If Anaxagoras, for example, had understood mind as "longing mind," to use Aristotle's phrase, he would have known that he could not consider mind's rule of the cosmos in abstraction from the good. Aristotle is no "cosmos-maker," as he calls Anaxagoras (985a19).[24] His science cannot promise to make us masters and possessors of nature, for it begins with trust, in contrast not only to Anaxagoras but also to Descartes, who begins with doubt instead of trust.[25] So beginning, he can trust only himself and what proceeds from his own mind. The certainty of knowledge based on a certainty of self leaves human beings alienated from any world that is not of their own making. Aristotle might have called Descartes too a "cosmos-maker."

On the other hand, those who possess a prudence that does not look beyond the political community for the human good will find nothing

---

24. The word Aristotle uses for "cosmos-maker" (*kosmopoiia*) may be another of his coined words. Its construction follows the pattern for the "coining words" (*onomatopoiein*), literally, "name-making," that Aristotle found necessary when language did not have a name for the virtue he was describing (110818–19). Aristotle "makes names" for virtues. He does not "make" the virtues themselves.

25. For a similar contrast between Aristotle and Descartes, see Roochnik, *Retrieving Aristotle*, 11–13, 97, who also contrasts Aristotle with Bacon, Spinoza, and Locke. See also Clark, *Aristotle's Man*, 81.

higher than themselves there. Without a vision of the full range of the virtues of the human soul that Aristotle presents in the *Ethics*, including a wisdom that recognizes what is more divine than human beings, their prudence will tend to collapse into a cleverness at attaining their goals (1144a23–24) and their understanding of human beings, including themselves, into one of prudential beasts. Aristotle's word to the wise is at the same time one to the prudent, for he urges both to self-knowledge, the former by understanding the higher in light of their longing for the good, the latter by understanding that securing and preserving the good for a political community is more beautiful and even more divine than securing only their own (see 1094b10–11). We might understand Aristotle's thought as a pious mean that avoids the excesses of modern approaches that elevate human beings to gods (cosmos-makers) or reduce them to beasts. The former is impious in collapsing human and the divine, the latter in severing them.

Aristotle gives the last word in his discussion of wisdom to prudence, referring to it as "architectonic" (1141b23). This is his first use of "architectonic" since his discussion of politics at the beginning of the *Ethics*. Wisdom is not "architectonic," and the exalted work of politics requires prudence, exalted not by its authority over everything in the city to which it gives order, but by the good at which it aims in doing so. In the last sections of book 6, Aristotle expands prudence, or at least lets us see how far prudence is shared, with other members of the community and ultimately with Aristotle himself in his philosophizing about human affairs.

PRUDENCE AND POLITICS

Following his reference to the architectonic character of prudence, Aristotle turns specifically to politics. He designates several forms of the prudence directed to political life. He assigns an "architectonic prudence" to the work of the lawgiver, and a political prudence concerned with particular cases to the tasks of deliberation and judging. The work of the lawgiver may be architectonic, but he shares rule with those who occupy other offices in the city, such as those who serve in the assemblies that deliberate about what to do and courts that judge (see *Rhetoric* 1345b1, 6, 22). Moreover, political prudence (whether manifest in the legislator, assemblyman, or judge) is not the only form of prudence, since there is a prudence exercised in family life. Prudence is also exercised, Aristotle says, when one is concerned with one's own affairs (1141b24–1142a11).

The statesman's virtuous activity that involves the good of the city does not replace the prudence of the head of a household, or even that of individuals about their own affairs. The capacity that first appeared as architectonic because it "contained" or "encompassed" the ends of all other activities (1094b6) now shares its activity with others. We saw something like this at the outset, when after announcing that the architectonic art of politics ordered all learning in the city, Aristotle announced his own inquiry into politics. Immediately after assigning to the statesman the most prominent place in the city, Aristotle reminds the statesman, as it were, that it is Aristotle's own work of political inquiry that establishes that prominence. As Aristotle yields an authority to the statesman, the statesman must yield to others, not only to Aristotle, and not only to the many artisans on whom the city depends, but also to its families.

Aristotle's lessons for the statesman once again extend to the wise. His reminder that people "seek their own good" and his focus on family and politics, which received no mention in his discussion of wisdom, underscore the self-forgetting character of any wisdom that seeks only useless things, however wondrous and beautiful they may be. His wry observation in response to those who locate prudence only in the individual's deliberation about his own good—"perhaps one cannot do well for oneself in the absence of household management and a regime" (1142a9–10)—applies also to the wise who do not deliberate about their own good.

Prudence in one way or another should be possessed by those engaged in politics, by those who make decisions in families, and by individuals as they seek their own good, Aristotle says, but prudence does not belong to the young. A youth may speak of those things about which prudence is exercised, Aristotle points out, but he has no trust in them. Trust comes only over the "long period of time" that experience requires. That is why the young can excel in mathematical disciplines, which involve abstraction from experience. But experience alone is not sufficient, just as prudence does not necessarily come with old age. Prudence involves both universals and particulars, and errors in deliberation could involve either (1142a11–22, 1141b15–17). Although we induce universals from the "clarity" of particulars, as Aristotle says in the *Posterior Analytics*, he does not say there that the universals are as clear as the particulars. Rather, he proceeds to acknowledge the difficulty when he observes there that universals can be acknowledged by "those with comprehension" (*sunientes*) (71a6–9). Not everyone comprehends the universals that arise from experience of particulars. Very soon in book 6, Aristotle will associate comprehension with prudence, associating it with good judgment about what another says (1143a13–15). How, then, does prudence obtain the universals that guide its deliberation about particulars?

Aristotle states near the end of book 6 that ethical virtue makes the target correct, while prudence deliberates about what is conducive to the target (1144a6–7, 20). It is easy to suppose that Aristotle has reasoned in a circle, in that the ethical virtues require prudence as their guide, while prudence requires ethical virtue as its guide.[26] Such a view, however, takes too restrictive a view of the work of deliberation. When discussing deliberation in book 3, Aristotle says that "we deliberate not about the ends, but about what is conducive to the ends." Among his examples are "the rhetorician who does not deliberate about whether he is to persuade and the statesman who does not deliberate about whether he should produce good order [*eunomia*]" but rather "how and by what means" they will come to be (1112b12–17). His examples are instructive. The rhetorician's end, persuasion, does not tell him either how to persuade or of what he should persuade his listener. His deliberation about how to persuade requires deliberation about the end of his persuasion. That is, persuasion becomes a means to a further end. Similarly, the statesman's end, good order, though it itself is not up for deliberation, requires deliberation about what constitutes good order, and what is best under the circumstances, including who should participate in ruling and what ends the regime should serve. Through deliberating about how to achieve one's ends, one must reflect on them. In other words, the ends given by their arts require further de-

---

26. See, for example, Tessitore, *Reading Aristotle's Ethics*, 47; Bruell, "Aristotle on Theory and Practice," 26–28. Bartlett and Collins, "Interpretive Essay," 283, argue that since prudence is limited to the selection of means to ends supplied by the moral character that comes "at the hands of the community," the prudent person "cannot be said strictly speaking to know why he acts." They are therefore able to conclude that prudence is "less an intellectual virtue than the completion or necessary accompaniment of the moral virtues."

liberation, deliberation of the sort that Aristotle undertakes throughout the *Ethics*—and the *Rhetoric* and the *Politics*.[27]

When Aristotle says that the ethical virtues provide the ends of deliberation, he therefore does not mean simply that the one well brought up in his habits will be able to discern the end that he must seek (see 1095b5–7). To be sure, good habits facilitate our performing good deeds, but one requires the sort of reflection on experience exemplified by Aristotle's inquiry in the *Ethics* to understand the virtues that guide prudence.[28] Along with identifying the virtues, as we proceed through this inquiry with Aristotle, we also identify the perplexities they involve, as we have seen time after time. In his treatment of courage, for example, Aristotle revealed the virtue's ambiguous relation to the beautiful and the good, to say nothing of its relation to pleasure. His examination of moderation opened up a range of pleasures beyond those that are the concern of moderation as he defined it and that therefore are not subject to the standard of the mean. How, then, do we fit them into a good life? Liberal giving runs the risk of the ruin to which the prodigal comes, and veers toward the prodigal's failure to look out for himself (1120b), and the self-dependence of greatness of soul needed to be qualified by the virtues of living together. Justice comes from habituation, or the performance of just deeds mandated by law, but justice is spoken of—especially by Aristotle—"in more ways than one" (1129a24–26).[29] That prudence takes

---

27. See the helpful discussion of Aristotle's understanding of deliberation in Bickford, *The Dissonance of Democracy*, 27–30. Sherman, *The Fabric of Character*, 88–89, argues that "to deliberate about what contributes to an end includes specification and qualification of the end." By deliberating and choosing, one "comes to qualify and refine ends as they find their place besides other ends in a life."

28. See Roochnik, *Retrieving Aristotle*, 162: "habit is the origin of excellent character," but it is not "the pinnacle, for that requires thinking and acting knowledgeably."

29. Pangle, *Reason and Character*, 85, recognizes that Aristotle's own deliberations in the *Ethics* involve both means and ends, giving the example of his discussions of pleasure, honor, virtue, money, and knowledge as potential ends of human life in book 1. As she points out, "deliberations about what to do can also lead us into the kind of investigation about who we are and what we want that the whole of the *Ethics* seems to foster." Such an investigation, she claims, "is not itself an act of deliberation but a philosophical inquiry." She thus draws a line between

its end from the ethical virtues means less that it is guided by preformed habits than that it derives insight from reflection on the ethical virtues for which Aristotle offers a model. Prudence guides the ethical virtues as much as it is guided by them, toward living well and achieving happiness in their practice. Thus those who are prudent "are able to theorize about [or discern] the good things for themselves and other human beings" (1140b9–10).

The prudent person, we might say, listens to one who speaks well when Aristotle gives his account of the virtues, and learns to judge what another says about such matters (1095b12–13; see also 1143a15). The guidance Aristotle offers makes possible and indeed demands further deepening of our experience through our own virtuous actions. It also demands our reflection on that experience in light of the difficulties and perplexities that we experience with Aristotle. With Aristotle we have begun, and it is a substantial beginning, for his many observations about the good, the beautiful, the just, and the pleasant can guide our deliberations. But it is only a beginning for us. We must do our part.[30] And Aristotle continues to offer guidance, for there are other capacities related to prudence left to discuss and a perplexity yet to be raised, and other books of the *Ethics* to come.

---

the deliberations required for ethical virtue and those belonging to philosophic inquiry, attributing the first to gentleman, the second to the philosopher exemplified by Aristotle. But if "the whole" of the *Ethics* fosters such deliberations, would it not do so for all its readers, whatever differences Aristotle recognizes among them? Sorabji, "Aristotle on the Role of Intellect in Virtue," 206, argues that "the man of practical wisdom deliberates with a view not merely to particular goals but to the good life in general." His interpretation does not require distinguishing two forms of prudence, the one belonging to ethical virtue, the other to a philosopher. What appear as inconsistences in Aristotle's account that lead Pangle to her theory of two forms of prudence lead Sorabji to a fuller account of Aristotle's view of prudence (ibid., 216–17).

30. Zuckert, "Aristotle's Practical Political Science," 147, understands Aristotle's political work to serve as a guide to the considerations that deliberation should take into account, including "attempts to maintain or improve existing regimes." That is, Aristotle is offering many considerations that should be taken into account when we deliberate. He is not deliberating for us, or choosing for us. See also Salkever, "Aristotle and the Ethics of Natural Questions," 7; and Smith, *Revaluing Ethics*, 217.

SEARCHING, EXPERIENCING PERPLEXITY, AND PARDONING

Aristotle continues to provide models and considerations that bear on action when he turns to three more capacities: good deliberation (*euboulia*), comprehension (*sunesis*), and consideration (*gnōmē*). Aristotle offers no explanation or introduction to this section that follows his discussion of the five-truth attaining qualities, but in the course of his treatment of them he connects each with prudence. It is not clear, however, what they add to the discussion of prudence. Aristotle has already said that prudence involves deliberating well (*eu bouleuesthai*) (e.g., 1141b8–11; see also 1140a26, b1). "Comprehension" is so general a term that it could apply to any of the intellectual virtues without adding anything specific to their meaning (see 1103a5). The word that I translate as "consideration" is related to the common verb "to know" (*gignōskein*), and literally means "anything known," "anything one is acquainted with or considers." Had Aristotle left out the discussion of these three capacities, readers might not have noticed anything missing. By including them, however, Aristotle gives us the occasion to reflect on his own activity in the *Ethics* (and therefore ours along with his), and on the ways in which it is similar or akin to prudence.[31]

The first, "good deliberation" is "a sort of searching" (*zetein*), but the two differ, he begins (1142a32–33; see also 1112b23). He says no more here about the larger class to which good deliberation belongs (searching), but focuses on "good deliberation," "which belongs to prudence" and "guides

---

31. We have seen this self-reflective character of the *Ethics* also near the end of book 4, when Aristotle brought up the three so-called social virtues possessed by the one who is friendly, truthful, and witty. Similarly, in book 5, after completing his discussion of justice in the universal sense, as the lawful, and of the particular forms of justice, distributive and corrective, which fulfills the plan he lays out at the outset (1129b1–2, 1130b19–20, 1130a30–31a3), he proceeds to discuss three more ways in which we might speak of justice. Justice as reciprocity begins with acts of graciousness that prompts others in turn, political justice incorporates natural justice, and equity includes demanding less for oneself than is strictly due—all of which play a role in Aristotle's relation with his addressees. On each of these occasions, he serves as a model and guide for others and for political life itself.

us toward an end" (1142b30–33). But what other activities belong along with good deliberation to the class of "searching," a word in Greek that can also be translated as "seeking" or "investigating"? Aristotle has often used "searching" to refer to his own work. In book 1, for example, he refers to the good that is the object of his inquiry as "the good being sought" (*to zētoumennon*) (1097a15), in contrast to the wise such as Thales and Anaxagoras who may know extraordinary and wondrous things but do not "search for" or "seek out" (*zetein*) the human goods (1141b8).[32] If prudence is the good deliberation that guides us toward an end, Aristotle's political inquiry in the *Ethics* does the same by searching out the human goods at which prudence aims, for example, by examining what virtues constitute a good human life.

Aristotle next turns to "comprehension" (*sunesis*) or "good comprehension" (*eusunesia*), which is concerned with "those things about which one might *be perplexed* and deliberate. Hence it is concerned with the same things as prudence" (1132a7). Indeed, it seems to simply add perplexity to prudence. Aristotle throughout raises numerous "perplexities," as when he even presented the question of where to begin his inquiry as a perplexity, only to tell us we must begin with what we know, and thus leaving the perplexity of how we come to know what we need to begin (1095a33–b4). The deliberations of prudence, we now learn, not only the inquiries of Aristotle, involve perplexities.

Whereas prudence issues commands, Aristotle continues, comprehension is characterized by judgment (*kritikē*). Aristotle associates it with "learning" (1143a8–12). He refers to the activity of comprehension as "using opinion to judge *what another says*" in matters with which prudence is concerned (1143a13–15). Throughout the *Ethics*, Aristotle brings up a host of opinions that he examines, such as the opinions about happiness (1095a17–31, 1098b9–1099b8), and, most recently, opinions about the wise (1141a9–16). Some he refines, others he refutes, and he at times brings them to bear on other opinions. Very soon, in the next book of the *Ethics*, he explains his procedure: posit how things appear, raise perplexities about

---

32. After introducing deliberation as a sort of searching, Aristotle says that what deliberation is "must be searched out [*zētētea*]" (1142b17–18). That is, he quite clearly points to his own search as a kind of searching, and therefore belonging to the class in which prudence belongs.

them, bring to light all the received opinions, or at least the greatest number or most authoritative, with the expectation that "some of the difficulties will be resolved and some opinions left standing" (1145b2–8).

So too, in following along with Aristotle, we use opinions, our own and those Aristotle puts before us, to judge what Aristotle says (notice that he speaks in the singular in his statement about the one who should be judged, almost as if he had himself in mind). Judging Aristotle's work falls under our capacity for comprehension. Aristotle has found a word that can signal our judging what he says to us. By doing so, he alerts us to our need to do so. Comprehension judges "beautifully [or nobly]" (1143a16), Aristotle says, expanding once again the scope of the beautiful. It is, as the word for judgment (*kritikē*) suggests, critical, in the sense of discerning. Aristotle's addressees are not simply like Hesiod's type who "is persuaded by one who speaks well" (1095b11), in that they also judge. Or, rather, judgment is involved in being persuaded.[33] When Aristotle refers to the reasoning (*logistikon*) part of the soul as the *doxastikon*, "the opining part" (1140b27), he does not necessarily refer to the soul's capacity to receive opinions but its capacity to judge them, especially to judge what "another says."

The capacity to judge others, in even a broader sense, also comes into play in the next addendum to prudence that Aristotle examines, "consideration" (*gnōmē*), which he defines as "correct judgment concerning the equitable." He finds support in the fact that the equitable person is especially characterized by forgiveness or pardon (*suggnōmē*), literally, the "knowing with" another, or recognizing matters as another does when he acts, which allows us to pardon or forgive (1143a19–24). As he nears the end of book 6, Aristotle thus returns to the equitable, which he introduced near the end of book 5 as the correction of the law when it speaks in universal terms that do not apply to the case at hand. He makes even more explicit now than he did there (1137b33–36) that equity inclines to pardon. Equity corrects not merely the universality of the law but its severity. The two issues are related: applying the universal without considering particulars would be harsh. Aristotle also makes explicit one way in which equity itself is universal: "equitable matters are common to *all* good human beings in their relations with one another" (1143a33).

---

33. Frank, "On Logos and Politics," 26.

Aristotle spoke of forgiving or pardoning before, in the context of voluntary and involuntary actions (1109b30–34), but now his emphasis is on the cognitive element in forgiving, although it is implicit all along in the Greek word. The English "pardon" or "forgive" does not entirely capture the Greek "knowing with." The one who pardons is someone who judges another, whereas the one who "knows with" another understands another as like himself, as someone with a capacity to know, especially when he fails to know, or comes to know only when it is too late. That is why forgiveness is appropriate. Necessary to our experience of forgiving as Aristotle presents it is our own capacity to know another. Aristotle's inclusion of *gnōmē* and especially *suggnōmē* among the soul's intellectual capacities is the last of the many he describes in book 6, putting "a head" or "bringing to completion" that discussion (cf. 1141a20). But it influences our deeds just as much as any ethical virtue he discusses, even if it is a deed that consists in holding back from punishing.

Aristotle's discussion of pardon flows into remarks about those things that exist of necessity in contrast to those that admit of being otherwise, and about "the ultimate things" that we grasp for understanding both. Mind, it turns out, which gave us access to the first principles of science that could not be demonstrated, does something similar in matters of action, bringing us into touch with the ultimate particular thing, as Aristotle refers to it, the principles or beginnings, which guide our deliberations. In both cases, those principles are "first" or "beginnings," not merely because so much else follows from them, but also because there is no *logos* that can arrive at them or that can demonstrate them (1143b1, 1142a26). Aristotle stretches the word for sense perception (*aisthesis*) to refer to this grasping of beginnings (1143a36–b6, 1142a26–29). It belongs to prudence as much as it belongs to wisdom. It is what makes equity possible.

Just as Aristotle introduced trust in our attaining truth about the beginnings of science, he advises that "it is necessary to pay attention to the undemonstrated assertions and opinions of experienced and older people, *or of the prudent*, no less than to demonstrations, for they have an experienced eye" (1143b12–14). Aristotle is not identifying the old with the prudent. His language allows us to see both as models for guidance. Moreover, to pay attention to opinions is not necessarily to follow them. We have Aristotle himself as a model, who has throughout the *Ethics*, we could say, been "calling attention" or "directing our mind," as the Greek idiom involving *nous* indicates, to opinions without ever failing to examine them. Undemonstrated assertions or opinions need not be unexamined ones.

Aristotle's three addenda to his discussion of prudence—good deliberation (as a kind of searching), comprehension, and consideration (and pardon), all of which he links to prudence (1142b33; 1143a16, 29–30)—also serve as addenda to his discussion of wisdom. The three together suggest another sort of wisdom, which differs from that of the wise who contemplate the things in the heavens (1141b1–2). The first overlaps with "searching," the second deals with "perplexities" yet comes to a judgment about them without issuing commands, and the third insofar as it pardons by "knowing with" others directs our capacity to know to other human beings, whom we know not as objects of our knowing but as knowers themselves. Just as the three "social" virtues Aristotle examines at the end of book 4 bring the great of soul down from their height "to share in speeches and deeds in living together," so too these capacities Aristotle associates with prudence turn the wise from gazing at the heavens to searching for the good for themselves and others, a search that issues in "knowing with" others and therefore knowing them as knowers too. Such a wisdom is more appropriate for one who knows he is not "the best thing in the cosmos," and who can therefore be perplexed about and proceed to investigate the relation of the eternal and unchanging things to the one who investigates them. This is true of an inquiry such as the *Ethics*, which begins by declaring that all things aim at the good and goes on to examine the human soul and its capacity to know. It is also true of an inquiry such as the *Metaphysics*, which begins by declaring that all human beings long to know and proceeds to move from the question of being to that of the good.

ENDING WITH PERPLEXITY

Aristotle himself proceeds to bring up a perplexity that prolongs his investigation of the intellectual virtues: someone "might be perplexed as to why wisdom and prudence are useful [*chrēsimoi*]" (1143b15–18). One also might be perplexed that Aristotle brings up this question at all, since if wisdom and prudence are the virtues of the rational part of the soul, as he argued, they would like all virtues be sought for their own sake. Although

Aristotle soon offers this response (1144a5–6, 1145a3–4), he nevertheless raises the question of their utility. Once again, Aristotle reminds us by his deeds that he differs from the great of soul, who possess beautiful things that have no profit or result, and from the wise, whose objects may be extraordinary and wondrous but useless (1125a11–12 and 1141b3–8). To raise the question of the utility of the virtues—even though they are also sought for their own sake—reminds us that something chosen for its own sake may also contribute to another good, whether a good for others or for ourselves (e.g., 1097a32). It is to remind us of the perplexity of being human—which is to be free rather than a slave who lives for the sake of another and at the same time a political being living in relation to others.

Although Aristotle continues to maintain that prudence is good deliberation that accompanies ethical virtue (e.g., 1144a6–10, 21–23; 1145a4–7), his discussion expands our understanding of its utility. There is a sense in which each of the ethical virtues is present in us by nature, he observes, for we are inclined to being just, moderate, courageous, and the rest straightway from birth. But such "natural virtue" is not sufficient. Virtue in the sovereign or authoritative sense requires mind (*nous*), and does not arise without prudence, for natural virtue is like a strong body without sight that could stumble or fall (1144b13–18). Aristotle's reference at the end of book 6 to "natural virtue" affirms the support our natures lend to virtue, and though he does not deny that virtue in the authoritative sense proceeds by habituation, he makes clear that what we accomplish through reason makes no small difference, but a very great difference. Presumably performing virtuous deeds merely by habit would be as liable to stumbling as the natural virtue Aristotle describes. In contrast to natural virtue, "virtue in the sovereign sense does not arise in the absence of prudence." Socrates was therefore on the right track, Aristotle observes, when he connected the virtues with prudence (1148b18–22, 29–30).

By bringing his investigation around to Socrates, Aristotle calls attention to the fact that he has examined the intellectual virtues without mentioning Socrates, even if he followed his footsteps in examining the wisdom of others. Of course, Socrates never claimed to be wise, but only a philosopher, a lover of wisdom (see *Apology* 28e, 29c, 29d; *Phaedrus* 278d). And now Aristotle brings him into book 6 as a philosopher who like Aristotle himself "investigates" (*zetein*) virtue and vice rather than like those who contemplate the things in the heavens (*NE* 1102a8; see

Apology 18b–c, 30e–31b).³⁴ Socrates's wisdom is of another sort from that of Anaxagoras and Thales, who did not investigate what is good for human beings (see 1141b5). This investigation Socrates shares with Aristotle.

It was not only Socrates who connected prudence with virtue, but "everyone seems to divine that the disposition that accords with prudence is virtue" (1144b25–26). The divination requires "only one small change": instead of saying that virtue is in accord with (*kata*) prudence or correct reason, we should add that virtue "is accompanied by [*meta*] correct reason" (1144b21–27). If virtuous action merely conformed to reason, it might be imposed from outside, whether by the laws of a political community or by the ruler or by parents. Aristotle adamantly denies, however, that "it makes no difference whether human beings themselves have prudence or obey others who have it." In this regard virtue is not like health: "Although we wish to be healthy, nonetheless we do not learn the art of medicine." Merely obeying the commands of a prudent person, Aristotle says, "would [not] be enough for us" (1143b32–33). In such a case, our virtuous actions would not be our own. What applies in matters of health does not apply when it comes to happiness. The "small addition" that Aristotle adds to our divination that virtue accords with prudence is thus the divination that has been with us since the first book of the *Ethics*, namely, that the good "is our own and not easily taken away" (1095b26–27).³⁵ The utility of prudence, then, is not simply that it guides us toward our ends, but that in acquiring prudence *we can guide ourselves* toward our ends.

The utility of wisdom, however, seems even more perplexing than that of prudence, especially if, as Aristotle says, wisdom is not concerned with anything that comes into being but only with what is eternal and

---

34. According to Burger, *Aristotle's Dialogue with Socrates*, 111–12, in book 6 Aristotle highlights the separation of wisdom and prudence "by treating each as the perfection of a different way of life," the one exemplified by Thales and Anaxagoras, the other by Pericles. The competition in rank "is settled in favor of the cosmological thinkers before Socrates finally appears on the scene." Of course Aristotle is on the scene throughout, or at least directing the scene as the work's author. See also Tessitore, *Reading Aristotle's "Ethics,"* 50.

35. These are the only two times that Aristotle uses the verb "to divine" (*manteuesthai*) in the *Ethics*.

ungenerated. It therefore "contemplates nothing on account of which a human being becomes happy" (1143b19–21). Aristotle responds with an analogy to medicine: wisdom produces happiness not in the way that medicine produces health, but rather as health produces health: "Wisdom, *being a part of the whole virtue*, makes one happy by being possessed and by being active" (1144a3–6). Apart from the fact that wisdom alone is insufficient for happiness, since it is only a part of virtue, Aristotle's explanation leaves standing the fact that the wise are not concerned with anything that comes into being. They therefore know nothing of the genesis of wisdom, either in themselves or in others. If they know nothing about coming into being, they could not convey their virtue to another by teaching.[36] But Aristotle has told us that the intellectual virtues owe their genesis primarily to teaching (1103a14) (see also *Metaphysics* 982a14–15, 28–30). But if not the wise, who teaches wisdom? Aristotle later mentions those who claim to be teachers, such as the Sophists, and though he speaks of the Sophists disparagingly, he does include among those to whom we owe so much that there cannot be just recompense (gods and parents) "those with whom we share in philosophy" (1164a31–32, b3; see also 1163b20–22). Presumably, those who share in philosophy teach and learn in turn, experiencing a sort of reciprocity that Aristotle develops in his discussion of friendship.

Not only does Aristotle leave unresolved the perplexity of how wisdom comes to be, but he raises even more perplexities about the relation between prudence and wisdom. Assuming that prudence "makes" (*poiein*), "rules" (*archein*), and "gives order to" (*epitattein*) everything in the political community, and therefore to wisdom, how could it have greater authority or sovereignty (*kuriōtera*) than wisdom, since it is inferior to it (1143b33–36)? The perplexity could be resolved simply by denying that anything rules wisdom or makes arrangements for it, even if the genesis of wisdom is then left without explanation or even up to chance. Aristotle does not take this route, which would leave our happiness up to chance and indicate that all things were not arranged for the best (see 1099b20–24). Instead of denying prudence's authority over wisdom, he argues that its relation to wisdom is like that of medicine to health: "The art of medicine is not sovereign over health, for it does not make use of health but

---

36. Schaeffer, "Wisdom and Wonder," 651–52.

sees how it comes into being. It is for the sake of health that medicine issues commands, but it does not issue them to health" (1145a7–9). Prudence, in pursuing the good for itself and others, at least if guided by Aristotle, comes to see that there is a good beyond prudence and beyond the political community, that is, that prudence too is only part of virtue. Such a discovery would make sense of Aristotle's analogy between prudence and medicine: just as medicine issues commands not to health but for the sake of health, so prudence gives orders not to wisdom but for the sake of wisdom. Of course, exactly how prudence might accomplish this work would depend on the circumstances and the deliberations of the one exercising prudence.

Aristotle's final word in book 6 illustrates the relation between prudence and wisdom with an analogy not to health, but to politics, using language he had used at the beginning of book 1: politics gives orders (*epitattei*) about everything in the community, including, we presume, matters of worship (e.g., 1134b22–24), but it does not rule the gods (1145a8–10, 1094b1). Aristotle's analogy between wisdom and the gods does not suggest that wisdom takes the place of the gods as the end of human life to which politics is subordinate. Rather, the analogy between the divine and the wisdom for which we strive and on which our good depends suggests that wisdom like the divine remains "beyond us" (see 1145a20). It is the good at which we aim. That politics gives orders about everything in the community does not mean that it should rule the gods, just as it should not issue orders to the wise, especially to those like Socrates who are wise in human wisdom and who, like the political community, defer to the divine (*Apology* 28e–29a, 42a; *Phaedrus* 278d). The political community both rules and does not rule. It rules only in part.

Although Aristotle has filled in the outline of the ethical and intellectual virtues that he laid down earlier (1103a3–10, 1107a33–b1), he continues on to other books of the *Ethics*, even calling for another beginning in book 7 that expands his account beyond the virtues and vices, especially to "lack of rule" (*akrasia*) and the question of reason's authority over the desires and the passions. In this way, he moves from the authority of politics in the community (a question bookended by the authoritative art at the beginning of book 1 and its limited authority over the gods at the end of book 6) to the authority of reason in the soul, considering even further the utility of knowledge to the deeds of life. Aristotle then explores the perplexities of self-rule and self-knowledge in the context of friendship (books 8 and 9), which form the center of the last four books of the *Ethics*. Finally, in book 10, Aristotle returns to the question of the best way of life, specifically whether the theoretical and practical lives are alternatives or "go together" in any fully human life. He appears to continue his reflections on that very question when at the end of book 10 he gives an outline of his *Politics*, emphasizing that the work he will undertake next involves both theorizing and practice.

CHAPTER 6

Human Strength versus Divine Perfection

Deepening Our View of Virtue (Book 7)

With no explanation, Aristotle declares at the beginning of book 7 that "another beginning must be made." There are three things pertaining to character that should be avoided, he says: vice, lack of rule (*akrasia*), and bestiality (*thēriotēs*). He has discussed the first as the extremes between which the ethical virtues lie; the latter two remain (1145a15–17).[1] Aristotle will now investigate them—and their contraries, self-rule and divine virtue.

In light of Aristotle's beginning anew, commentators have argued that Aristotle adopts a new perspective in the last part of the *Ethics*. Kass even refers to books 7–10 "as a second whole booklet within the *Ethics*." According to Kass, book 6 "points to a transcendent, or at least transpolitical, end or activity of mind"—"something beyond the realm of the human understood as the composite 'rational animal.'" Thus Aristotle prepares us for what he does in the last books of the *Ethics*, in which he

---

1. Although Aristotle does occasionally mention self-rule and its lack, and even says that he will discuss it later (1102b13–28, 1128b34), he does not include it in the outline he gives in book 2 (1107a33); nor does he prepare us for his placing lack of self-rule and bestiality alongside vice as three things that must be avoided—and hence discussed.

"leaves behind the strictly political perspective, the perspective co-incident with the paramount attention to virtue and vice" to teach about "human prospects both lower than vice and higher than virtue."[2] So too Tessitore understands "the unifying theme" of the last four books as an excellence "that transcends the horizon of moral virtue." There "emerges most clearly" in book 7, he argues, "the radical dissimilarity between the life of the philosopher and that of the *kalos k'agathos*," the "gentleman" whose horizon remains bound by the political community. At the same time Aristotle transcends the moral horizon in the direction of philosophy, Tessitore argues, he offers "a standard of moral seriousness [for the non-philosopher] that is lower and more accessible than the lofty target by which he initially set the sights of his readers," that is, a more accessible ruling of one's desires that resist the habituation (and harmony) manifest in the lovers of the noble who act virtuously for its own sake.[3]

Along similar lines, Burger observes that with this "new beginning" in book 7 Aristotle "seems to have left behind the gentleman as a member of [his] audience, along with the attempt to capture ethical virtue as the virtuous person understands it." It looks as if the *Ethics* has been "freed . . . from seeing things through the lens of morality," so that it can turn to "a preoccupation with nature," especially "our natural attraction to pleasure and repulsion from pain." Leaving behind the perspective of the gentleman, of course, does not mean leaving behind an attention to politics. A transpolitical perspective, Burger suggests, may be one that best sees politics for what it is. Burger argues that the statesman as legislator, with the task of molding character through reproach and exhortation, is replaced in book 7 by the statesman as healer, or "doctor of the soul," who must address "psychic illness" stemming from our susceptibility to pleasure and pain.[4]

I agree that in book 7 Aristotle takes a more comprehensive look at human beings and politics by pointing to what is below and what is above humanity. I also agree that what is higher than political life in the ordi-

---

2. Kass, "Professor or Friend?," 19–21.

3. Tessitore, *Reading Aristotle's "Ethics,"* 51–52, 72.

4. Burger, *Aristotle's Dialogue with Socrates*, 132–33. For other thoughtful accounts of the ways in which the last books of the *Ethics* constitute another beginning, see Cropsey, "Justice and Friendship," 254–55; and Block and Cain, "Socrates's Spirited Defense of Knowledge," 3–29, esp. 11.

nary sense comes into greater prominence in the last books of the *Ethics*, such as friendship and Aristotle's own way of philosophizing. For example, book 7 is Aristotle's book of perplexities, in which he engages most directly with both the Sophists and Socrates, the former making knowledge impossible by stifling thinking, the latter making virtue unnecessary by replacing it with knowledge. Against both, Aristotle defends the *Ethics*. It is in book 7, moreover, that Aristotle refers to himself as "one who philosophizes about politics" (1152b1–2). The books on friendship culminate in friends who share in philosophy (1172a5–8), and in the last book Aristotle refers to "the wondrous pleasures" of philosophy (1177a26). At the end of the book he proposes another inquiry, one about politics, which will complete "the philosophy about human affairs" (1181b15). He has been philosophizing about human affairs and will continue to do so.

I argue, however, that these books do not transcend the moral-political sphere, but rather elevate it by showing ways in which it both supports and reflects philosophic activity. When Aristotle reminds us in book 10 that happiness lies in the activity of the most excellent virtue, that which belongs to what is most excellent in us, he refers to "mind, or something else that seems by nature to rule, to lead, and to have thought of [*ennoian echein*] [or have in mind] the noble and the divine things" (1177a12–18). Here he couples the noble or beautiful, with which he earlier defined the end of ethical virtue, with the divine things he had identified with the best in the cosmos. Human beings are not the best things in the cosmos, but they can live their lives (*diagōgē*; e.g., 1177a11, 27) with them "in mind." And when he says that the activity of mind is "contemplative" or "theoretical" (1177a19), he does not restrict this activity of mind to any one of the myriad ways in which human beings "theorize," from the statesman's "contemplation" of the soul, as facilitated by Aristotle's *Ethics*, to Aristotle's own inquiries, such as his *Metaphysics* and even the *Politics*, in which he will "theorize" about regimes (1181b18–21). However we rank such theoretical activities, and whatever criteria we use in doing so, they illustrate the activity of mind, of what is most divine in human beings. Aristotle's work involves connections and similarities as well as differences. We shall see this not only in his discussion of theoretical activity in book 10, but also in the books on friendship in which he highlights the similarities between friendships within families and those between ruler and ruled within political communities and between these and the friendships of those who share in philosophy. So too, I argue, his discussion of self-rule in book 7, far from lowering the horizon for the many who cannot attain even ethical virtue, explores and even praises the human strength that virtue demands.

"Self-rule" (*enkrateia*) means literally "in control" or "strong over oneself," whereas its lack (*akrasia*) is the absence of rule, in which one is without strength or rule over oneself. Joseph Cropsey's translation of *enkrateia* as "moral resoluteness" or "moral dominion" and his observation that "the term should convey the sense of mastery [*kratein*]" capture the elevated sense that Aristotle gives it.[5] *Enkrateia* demonstrates our capacity to rule ourselves. I therefore prefer "self-rule" as its translation rather than "self-restraint," since the latter suggests holding back from something.[6] The self-ruling restrain their passions so that they can act virtuously. They do not only avoid vicious deeds; they also perform virtuous ones. Aristotle even distinguishes self-rule from "endurance" (*karteria*), in that the latter "holds out against" something, the former gains strength over it (1150a34–35).

Self-rule, which contends against and controls desires contrary to reason in order to perform virtuous deeds, more clearly reveals an individual's rule of himself that is implied in virtue but that may be less apparent because of its reliance on habituation and the pleasure derived from virtuous deeds. Those who rule themselves, as Aristotle describes them, cannot rely on habit. And whatever pleasure they find in their virtuous deeds, it does not eliminate their painful resistance to the pleasures they desire. The *correct* reasoning of those who rule themselves about what they should do involves what is good for a human being to do. This they have in common

---

5. Cropsey, "Justice and Friendship," 253, 257.

6. Another possible translation of *enkrateia* is "self-mastery," which also captures the positive sense of the word, but reminds us of mastery over a slave, which Aristotle distinguishes from political rule. In the *Politics*, Aristotle claims that mind's rule of the soul's longings is not despotic but kingly or political (1252a8–15, 1254b4–10). Other traditional translations of *akrasia* and *enkrateia* are "incontinence" and "continence." These words work well in reference to the desires for food and sex, which Aristotle says is the primary use of the word, but not as well in reference to other forms of self-rule and its lack that Aristotle mentions, such as those involving wealth, honor, or spiritedness. The translation of *enkrateia* as "self-rule" (as does the translation of "self-restraint") indicates the act's reflexiveness, which is not literally in the Greek word. It is nevertheless implied.

with the prudent, as Aristotle describes them, but the struggle is more pronounced for those who rule themselves and therefore more apparent to themselves. Choice is the beginning of the deeds of ethical virtue, which are therefore "up to us," and we act with awareness (1105a31–32). To an even greater degree, however, those who rule themselves know that they are the source or beginning of their actions because they experience its difficulties and because they might have acted otherwise. This is implicit in the deeds that proceed from virtue. No act of virtue comes to be of necessity, for virtuous actions "admit of being otherwise," to use Aristotle's phrase (e.g., 1139a9, 1141a1). Even while maintaining that the deeds of ethical virtue are pleasant for the virtuous, Aristotle never says that that they are easy. Even in the earlier books of the *Ethics*, he warns that it is difficult "to combat against pleasure," and "like art, virtue always arises in connection with that which is more difficult: doing something well is better when it is more difficult" (1105a8–11). "Self-rule" is not so much "a lower target" than ethical virtue, but a description of how ethical virtue comes to be, how it is preserved, and what is involved in its practice. Although book 7 is another beginning, it does not thereby adopt a radically new perspective, different from that of the preceding books. Rather, it elaborates and builds on the earlier books. In this, it is not unique. Aristotle's *Ethics* throughout can be understood as a book of beginnings, or a book of choices, which are the beginnings that human beings make and that make them human (1139b4–6, 1113b18, 1102a13).

In book 7 our task of self-rule therefore becomes clear, but this too has been implied from the beginning. Aristotle taught that we must acquire the ethical virtues, proper dispositions toward our passions, which without virtue are insufficient guides to our good (1105b25–29). And at the end of book 6, he insisted that virtue is not only in accord with prudence but is also accompanied by prudence (1144b25–28). To the extent that the human condition requires healing, human beings must heal themselves. Their doing so is neither "by nature" nor "contrary to nature," as Aristotle says of ethical virtue. Nature leaves it to us. It is through self-rule that we come to know ourselves, both what we can accomplish and that we might have done otherwise. In the self-awareness and the virtuous deeds that come from ruling ourselves we find the happiness possible "for human beings" (see 1101a21). Such happiness belongs neither to beasts, who have no awareness of their happiness as their own, nor to a divinity, whose pleasure Aristotle tells us at the end of book 7 is simple and hence unmixed with pain.

The contrary of failing to rule oneself is succeeding in doing so, and the contrary of vice is virtue, but the contrary of bestiality, apparently, is not as clear. Aristotle nevertheless gives it a name, or at least a description: for the contrary of bestiality, "it would be most fitting to speak of a virtue that is beyond [*huper*] us, a certain heroic or divine virtue" (1145a15–16). In the first section of this chapter, I look at Aristotle's brief references to heroic or divine virtue that introduce book 7. By calling such "divine virtue" an "excess" (*huperbolē*) and referring to Priam's boastful praise of his son, Aristotle reminds us that virtue is a mean (1106a29–31). His warning sets the stage for book 7 as a whole, and for avoiding the excesses that lead to a denial of our humanity, whether in the direction of god or beast. Aristotle attempts to secure and protect human life from these dangers, by encouraging self-rule, and teaching us the resources we have not simply to resist these pulls but to experience the pleasures available to us as human beings.

In the second section of this chapter, I examine the perplexities Aristotle reports concerning self-rule. Prominent among them is one that Aristotle traces to Socrates's insistence that knowledge is virtue, or that the one who knows the good does it (1145b22–28). The one with knowledge would therefore be self-sufficient, needing no assistance from habit, or from the law, or even from self-rule, to act virtuously. Such an understanding of knowledge turns it into another version of divine virtue, not the heroic version Priam saw in his son, but one that lies in the autonomy of mind or wisdom.[7] Such an understanding, paradoxically, diminishes

---

7. Block and Cain, "Socrates's Spirited Defense of Knowledge," 3–7, 28–29, argue that in book 7 Aristotle's treatment of self-rule serves as a warning against the attempt "to divinize the soul and transcend the limitations of mere human virtue." Aristotle must address Socrates's view that knowledge (or science) is virtue, they argue, because such "a science of action" would leave no "place for prudence, and therefore moral virtues in the best *human* life." Their groundbreaking essay connects Aristotle's account of self-rule with the problem of the relation between the human and the divine with which Aristotle begins and ends book 7, and with his often neglected treatment of spiritedness in that book—the passion, they argue, that underlies Socrates's position on knowledge. I have benefited from their many insights. I agree with their formulation of Aristotle's purpose in book 7, but

human achievement, challenging Aristotle's account not only of self-rule but of ethical virtue. Neither would be needed by those who know, nor would they be of use to the ignorant, who need to be taught to know what is good for themselves (see *Apology* 25c–26a).

In the third section of this chapter, I examine how Aristotle addresses the perplexities he raises, resolving some and letting others remain, especially his exploration of how we can know and not know at the same time, for example, how we might possess knowledge but not use it, or how we might use one thing we know but not another. In the end, he accepts Socrates's position on knowledge in one way but not in others, while preserving his own teaching about virtue and self-rule in a way that distinguishes him from Socrates and furthers our understanding of how necessary self-rule and virtue are for human life.

In the fourth section of this chapter, I follow Aristotle's account of different ways in which we might fail to rule ourselves—not merely with respect to the necessary desires for food and sex but also in regard to spiritedness, a passion that Aristotle associates with freedom and ruling (e.g., *Politics* 1327b28–29). Although Aristotle acknowledges the excesses that spiritedness can generate (he mentions father-beating), he recognizes that spiritedness must play a vital role in protecting the human against the most degrading forms of bestiality to which human beings can sink. At the same time, spiritedness's quick defense of its own reinforces the goodness of human life even when or because it remains limited to goods that are not "beyond us." Spiritedness, so understood, is not simply a passion that must be ruled or restrained, but one that itself rules. It is therefore central to book 7, the book about self-rule and its failure, in which Aristotle continues his inquiry into "the activity of the soul, in accordance with virtue."

That human pleasures are to a large extent mixed with pains, as the need for self-rule indicates, leads Aristotle to contrast the mixed and ephemeral pleasures of human life with the simple and eternal pleasure of the god, as I discuss in the last section of this chapter. Aristotle's treatment of self-rule and its lack is thus framed by the question of "heroic or divine virtue," an "excess" that is "beyond us" (1145a29 and 34) and by the pleasure

---

I hold back from their interpretation of self-rule as requiring a universal science or knowledge over action and hence as another manifestation of what Aristotle would regard as the problematic attempt to divinize the soul.

of the god, which is also "beyond us."⁸ Human life is more variable—and perplexing—than the life of other animate beings that do not have intellect and hence do not face its possible corruption (1150a1–6), and it also differs from that of the god that Aristotle presents here that is as unchanging as its pleasure. In further driving home the distinction between human and divine, Aristotle examines the boundaries of human life, while indicating ways in which the human desire for pleasure elevates human beings above the beasts—in the ways in which they pursue pleasure, in the pleasures they pursue, and in their reflections about them (cf. 1095b20). At the same time, he prepares us for the next books of the *Ethics*, the books on friendship, where he shows us the happiness that those boundaries make possible and that therefore constitute their best defense. We have good reason for ruling ourselves, not only because self-governance is good for a human being, but because it makes possible another good, friendship itself, a relationship that requires us to be both "strong over ourselves" and dependent on "another self."

HEROIC OR DIVINE VIRTUE

To illustrate divine or heroic virtue, Aristotle quotes Priam's claim in the *Iliad* about his son Hector, that he was so exceedingly good that "he seemed not to be a child of a mortal man, but of a god" (1145a22–23; *Iliad* 24.258). "If, as *they* say, human beings become gods on account of an ex-

---

8. Tessitore, "Political Reading of Aristotle's Treatment of Pleasure," 254–62, also connects Aristotle's account of divine perfection at the end of book 7 with his reference to Hector's divine virtue at the beginning of that book. He argues that "Homer's poetic myth of godlike virtue, with which Aristotle began Book VII, is now replaced with a philosophically refined image of divine nature." That image, he argues, implies the harsh truth that happiness is unattainable for most human beings, for it is "the preserve of a very few, those [godlike individuals] whose lives are given over to the activity of contemplation." That is why he finds the image "philosophically refined" rather than tragic. My argument, in contrast, emphasizes the fundamental similarity between the images of the divine that Aristotle gives at the beginning and end of book 7, rather than the philosophic refinement of the latter. Both images of the divine imply that the good lies "beyond us" rather than in the ethical and intellectual virtues of the *Ethics*. If true, it would be a harsh truth indeed, one that I argue Aristotle denies.

cess of virtue, such a disposition would clearly be the one antithetical to bestiality" (1145a23–26). But Aristotle does not himself say this, and it is a father, Priam, who boasts of his son's virtue.[9] He does so, moreover, after Hector is dead, and when he is on his way to retrieve his body for burial. His very mission should have led him to doubt his comparison of his son to immortal gods. In his own name, Aristotle earlier denied that an excess of virtue is possible: inasmuch as virtue is a mean, "an excess" is a vice (1107a20–27). Aristotle thus begins book 7 by calling into question any "divine" virtue for human beings. As in book 1, we are trying to "grasp a boundary" for the sake of happiness (1097b12).

On the other hand, if Hector seems to Priam to be like the son of a god, he does not seem to him to be *his* son. How could mortals give birth to something divine? Since, in such a case, the greater would have to come from the lesser, and the effect exceed its cause, Hector's origin (or beginning) could not fully explain him. Priam sees in his son what is "beyond" himself. His boast may express awe rather than pride. In dividing the rational soul in order to discuss the intellectual virtues in book 6, Aristotle states the principle that "knowing is possible through similarity and kinship" (1139a6–12). Like is known by like, but Priam observes that his kin, even his offspring, differs from himself. Even though Hector is not immortal, he is at least sufficiently different from and even superior to his father that Priam can sense something that could not have come from himself. Priam's observation that Hector seems to be the child of a god is more like an expression of wonder than a boast. He knows that what is his own is not entirely his own.

When it comes to things "beyond us," we, like Priam, cannot know *what* they are (and thus Priam calls his son divine), but we can know *that* they are, just as Priam knows that he cannot be completely responsible for what his son has become. Similarly, Socrates claims that "the soul divines *that* [the good] is something, but . . . is unable to get a sufficient grasp of *what* it is" (*Republic* 505d–e), and Aristotle argues that there must be a

---

9. Aristotle's second example is as problematic: the Spartans "are accustomed [*eiōthasi*] to addressing someone of whom they are exceedingly fond as a divine man [*anēr*]" (1145a28–29). The Spartans, whom Aristotle elsewhere criticizes for understanding one virtue, courage (*andreia*) as the whole of virtue (e.g., *Politics* 1271b1–2), cannot be Aristotle's authority on divine virtue, especially regarding what they do as a matter of custom.

highest good, since otherwise our longings will go to infinity and be pointless and vain (1094a18–23). Aristotle knows that the highest good is something, but whether he can grasp, even in outline, "to which of the knowledges or capacities it belongs" remains an open question, even if politics is the obvious candidate (1094a25–b1). Politics may arrange everything in the city, as Aristotle tells us at the end of book 6, but it does not rule the gods (1145a10–11).

If human beings can in these different ways know and not know what is "above" or "beyond" themselves, perplexities might pervade their lives. Book 7 could be called Aristotle's book of perplexities in the *Ethics* (as is Beta in the *Metaphysics*, in which Aristotle lays out one perplexity after another; 995a24–1003a20). In book 7 Aristotle presents numerous perplexities about knowing and acting. He acknowledges that though some of the perplexities he raises allow release or resolution (*lusis*), others "remain," observing that "the release from perplexity is a discovery" (1146b6–7). Aristotle's Greek could also be translated as "the discovery of perplexity is a release"—perhaps a release from the authoritative opinions that one holds. In any case, a discovery could both answer one problem and reveal another one. Aristotle associates perplexity with wonder in the *Metaphysics*: we wonder "first about things near at hand, then going forward little by little come to perplexities about greater things" (982b12–15; see also 1072b25–27). Aristotle's perplexities in book 7 prepare us for perplexities about greater things in the books on friendship, in which a friend becomes aware of another who is also his own. Aristotle preserves a parent's wonder at his offspring in his account of friends.

MANY PERPLEXITIES

The reasoning (*logismos*) and the desires (or passions) of both the person who rules himself and the one who fails to do so pull in opposite directions (1145b8–14). Both manifest divided souls (1102b13–19), or, as Aristotle calls self-rule, "mixed" (1128b35). The one who rules himself resists his desires; the one who fails to do so resists what he thinks reasonable (see *Republic* 430e–431a). Neither the self-ruling nor the unruly is simply good or simply bad, but a mix of good and bad. We praise their reasoning, Aristotle says, when he introduces them in book 1, which "summons toward the best," at the same time that another part of their soul resists and battles against reason (1102b13–19). The soul of both is a battleground. By implication, we might blame that part of their souls that resists reason. The same individual might deserve both praise and blame. Only when he comes to book 7 does Aristotle speak of praising self-rule and blaming its contrary, rather than the different parts of the souls that are responsible (1145b9). Not only is the soul's reasoning praiseworthy, but also its success in battle. Aristotle likens the difference between enduring and self-ruling to the difference between not being defeated and winning (1150a36).

If the success of the self-ruled merits praise, however, and the one failing to rule himself deserves blame, how can we know of such success and failure? Only their deeds, not the struggle from which they emerged, are visible. Their deeds do not necessarily reveal the state of their souls, the struggle they have undergone, or their success or failure in that struggle. Indeed, the self-ruled, whose deeds look the same as those of the virtuous, would appear to be virtuous, while the unruly are better than they appear. They do not choose to do vicious deeds; rather, they struggle against them, even if they finally succumb. We see neither the reasoning that calls the latter to the good, nor the base desires of the former, to say nothing of the one's defeat or the other's victory. By the same token, the difficulty we have of seeing within the soul of the person who acts applies to both virtue and vice, if the deeds of the self-ruled appear the same as those of the virtuous, and the ones of those who fail to rule themselves appear the same as those of the vicious.

The difficulty in judging others from their deeds is implied in Aristotle's account of how virtue comes to be. Virtue comes from performing virtuous acts, the same acts that the virtuous person who has acquired virtue performs (e.g., 1103b1–3). Whether virtuous deeds come "from" virtue or are on the way to virtue cannot be seen simply from the deeds themselves. Indeed, we might suppose from Aristotle's account that human beings, at best, are always on the way to virtue, however much support their habits provide. If choice is necessary for virtue, the one who acts virtuously might choose to act otherwise. If his virtuous deed simply followed from his nature, or from his habits, which are "like" nature,[10] would

---

10. However much habit seems *like* nature, and is therefore difficult to change, "habit is easier to change than nature." Aristotle therefore has reservations

his praise be merited? When Aristotle distinguishes the virtuous person from the self-ruled in explaining the division of the soul in book 1, he claims that the former, lacking the strong and base desires of the latter, heeds the commands of reason "more readily" (1102b27–28). Even then the distinction seems to be a matter of degree.

Although we cannot see the soul of those who do virtuous deeds or of those who do vicious ones, as can Rhadamanthus, who judges souls after death, our praising the one and blaming the other are always appropriate. Even when they do not entirely deserve the praise or blame they receive, praise and blame serve as support for virtuous deeds. Judgments of others may be imperfect, but we must judge as best we can. Equity, which is "common to all good [human beings]" (1143a30–33), considers not only the deed but the "choice" from which it comes and the sort of person the one judged has been "always or for the most part" (*Rhetoric* 1374b14–16). "For the most part" is not "always." Like the law itself when it speaks in universal terms, when equity judges, it is aware that it may be in error. That is why equity inclines to pardon (1143a22–24).

No such complexities—or difficulties—come into the position that Aristotle attributes to the Sophists, who argue that "folly, when accompanied by failure of self-rule, is virtue," since those failing to rule themselves would act contrary to the foolish deed their faulty reason tells them to do. The conjunction of two defects would produce a virtuous deed. Unlike Aristotle, who asks us to consider the character of the person acting, even if we cannot know it with certainty, the sophistical argument simply focuses on the action. It cares nothing for the choice made. The Sophists propose this "paradox," Aristotle tells us, in order to refute others and to appear clever. But the outcome "fetters thinking," or ties it up in a knot, for our thought wishes to move forward but finds no release from the argument (1146a23–32). Aristotle's response treats the argument not on its own terms but in light of the Sophists' purpose in making it (to refute others and to appear clever) and its ill effect (it brings thought to a standstill). His response may seem merely ad hominem, but by pointing to the purpose behind their argument he indicates what separates him from the Sophists, for whom the deed is sufficient, regardless of its purpose or

---

against the saying of the poet Evenus, whom he quotes: "Practice of long duration . . . is in the end nature for human beings" (1152a31).

the state of soul of the one who performed it, and regardless of the consequences that flow from it. They themselves, in making this argument, fail to rule themselves, for they are moved by their desire for victory and reputation as well as by their folly, for their thinking stifles thought. No virtuous deed, however, follows from their own coupling of lack of restraint with folly. In the *Metaphysics* Aristotle distinguishes Sophists from philosophers: although the former don the appearance (*schēma*) of the latter, the difference between the two lies in "the choice of [a way of] life." Philosophy seeks to know (*gnōristikē*), whereas sophistry's wisdom is only apparent (*phainomenē*) (1004b18–27; *Rhetoric* 1355b18). Aristotle distinguishes sophistry by the choice made. But the choice is not manifest from the deed. The Sophists are like the individual of their paradox—we cannot see their choice from their deeds—but Aristotle exposes them. They only pretend to be philosophers. They are boasters, as their name, literally, "wise ones," or "wise guys," as we might say, suggests.

Whereas the Sophists propose that failure in self-rule is good, if conjoined with folly, Socrates proposes that failing to rule oneself is not possible, for "no one acts contrary to what is best, while supposing it to be so, but only through ignorance." Aristotle even quotes Socrates's words in Plato's *Protagoras* when Socrates objects to the view that "science [*epistēmē*] [or knowledge] could be dragged around like a slave" (*NE* 1145b23–28; *Protagoras* 352b–c). Just as would the Sophists' "paradox," the position that knowledge is virtue removes any need to look beyond the deed itself to understand the person who performed it. Bad deeds come from ignorance, good ones, by implication, from knowledge. Socrates's challenge pertains not merely to self-rule and its lack, but also to virtue and vice as states of character. All virtue appears from this position to be intellectual virtue, and vice to be ignorance. The virtuous have nothing to choose, if their deeds follow solely from their knowledge or lack of it. In the *Protagoras*, the alternative Socrates formulates to the slavery of knowledge by the passions is its mastery: "Knowledge is able to rule when someone who comes to know good and bad will be ruled [*kratēthēnai*] only by his knowledge, and so does only what knowledge orders" (352c). There is, by implication, no self-rule, no *enkrateia*, no choice. Knowledge may not be enslaved to passion, but a human being becomes enslaved to knowledge. Whereas the Sophists tie up thinking, so that there is no way to break through the perplexity they pose, Socrates has in effect tied up human beings, so they have no way to initiate action.

After bringing forward this host of perplexities (*aporiai*) about self-rule, Aristotle tells us that he will resolve some, but others remain (1146b6–7). It is as if his own work brings together resource (*euporia*) with poverty, for he has resources for some resolutions, but not for all. Consequently, he knows that his work will offer neither the perfect knowledge nor the perfect virtue that comes out of the formula that he attributes to Socrates. Of course, the mating of poverty and resource is one that Aristotle would have found in Socrates's tale of Eros in the *Symposium* and that serves Socrates's account of philosophy as a conjunction of ignorance and wisdom (203b–204b). Aristotle's recourse to perplexity, so characteristic of Socratic philosophizing (e.g., *Meno* 79e–80a), does not so much remind Socrates of what he already knows as it apologizes for attributing to him such a simple view of knowledge.

SOCRATIC PERPLEXITY AND DIFFERENT WAYS OF KNOWING

In response to the perplexity that he finds in Socrates's position, Aristotle tries to explain how someone who knows the good can fail to do it. He offers several explanations of how this might happen. He first proposes that there is a difference between "having" (*echein*) knowledge and "using" or "exercising" (*chrēmasthai*) it (1146b25–36). The one who fails in self-rule "has" knowledge but does not use it. This explanation may be plausible, but it does not account for why one person uses his knowledge when he encounters a pleasant object and another does not. Aristotle's distinction between having and using knowledge, far from establishing that one who knows the good does it, indicates the limited force of knowledge in the soul—it must be used. One does not rule oneself if one does not use one's knowledge.

Nor does Aristotle's next distinction resolve the problem. Knowing a universal, he observes, differs from knowing some particular. Desire might leave the first standing, but it defeats the second. For example, those who know that they should avoid strong drink, and also that a particular drink is strong, might be led by desire to ignore the latter. They act not against the universal that they know when they act, but only contrary to their knowledge of the particular (1146b36–1147a3). But why do some bring their knowledge of a universal to bear on the case at hand and others do not?

An action informed by knowledge might require knowing more than one universal, Aristotle next observes, and this time he offers the example of one who knows that *all* dry foods are beneficial for *all* human beings. Action then requires that one know that a particular food is dry so that the universal applies to it and also that "one is a human being" and hence someone to whom the universal applies (1147a3–9). The case of those failing to apply their knowledge of the dangers of strong drink is similar to that of those failing to apply their knowledge of the benefits of dry food. What is distinctive here is the addition of a second universal, but it is implied in the earlier examples. Those who do not rule themselves do not apply their knowledge of what is good for human beings to themselves.

When Aristotle quotes Socrates's denial that knowledge can be dragged around like a slave, it is Aristotle who includes the observation that it would be "terrible" if this were the case (1145b23–24). We might ask what "terrible" thing lies in passion's dragging around knowledge in the case of those who ignore (or deny) their humanity merely to miss a distasteful meal of beneficial but dry food. Aristotle hints at more "terrible" acts, however, when he mentions those in the grip of passions such as spiritedness or sexual desire—they pay no attention to what they think is right—and he even observes that such passions sometimes produce madness (1147a12–13).

Aristotle goes even further when he warns that the appearance of rationality does not always signal the difference between those who are drunk or mad and those who are sober or sane. The drunk or mad can state arguments that proceed from science or knowledge, as can those in the grip of sexual desire or spiritedness. They might, for example, give mathematical demonstrations or recite verses of poetry (1147a10–21, b12–13). Reason does not merely yield to passion in such cases but provides a cover for the passion in charge. Aristotle also mentions the case of those who lack self-rule who make use of reason (*logos*) to defend their passions. They might indulge their desires for sweets on the basis of a universal premise that all sweets are pleasant and should be tasted, while ignoring another universal premise that forbids tasting sweet things (1147a29–b1). The lack of self-rule now comes from a passion appealing to reason, indeed, to a universal principle that should be obeyed. Not all examples may be so saccharine. The defeat of reason that is so terrible, perhaps, is not that which follows from desire's ruling in its place, but desire's appearance as reasonable (1147b1). The Greek word for "terrible" also means "clever" (see 1144a23–24). It is not merely a case of having reason and not using it, but using reason to justify desires. Here we might think of masters giving reasons for the justice of slavery out of a desire to enslave other human beings and even persuading themselves of its justice, or at least its necessity for the support of higher human activities (see *Politics* 1255b38). Earlier Aristotle pointed out that "unwavering opinion that believes it knows precisely" is no less a ruling force in the soul than knowledge (1146b24–26).

When Aristotle says that failing to rule oneself cannot apply to beasts, since beasts have only memory and imagination, but no ability to conceive universals (1147b4–6), he indicates not only that they have no universals or reasons that check them, but also that they have no reason that can be perverted into service of strong and base desires. When Aristotle soon turns to bestiality, he states clearly that the bestiality of human beings is far worse than anything we find in beasts themselves, for humans have what beasts do not—"a better part that can be corrupted." Beasts may be destructive, and frightening, but because human beings have "mind" or "intellect" (*nous*), "a bad human being can produce ten thousand times greater evil than can a beast" (1150a1–9).

As he draws his discussion of knowledge or science and self-rule to a close, Aristotle makes a concession to Socrates. "What Socrates was seeking turns out to be the case," for it is not knowledge or science in the sovereign sense, which involves universals, that is dragged around by the passions, but rather knowledge that "is bound up with perception" (1147b14–18). We perceive particulars, and do not connect them with what we know about the class to which they belong, and action involves particulars (1142a27–29, 1110b8, 1107a29–33). Aristotle has expressed reservation throughout the *Ethics* about knowledge that is not put to use, as when in book 1 he criticized ideas that were "separate" and "unrelated to action" (*ouk...praktikon*) and in book 2 those who "take refuge in speech" about virtue rather than in performing virtuous deeds (1096b33, 1105b10–16). To seek a knowledge that cannot be dragged around by passion removes knowledge from any effect on action. One who knows *only* that dry foods are beneficial, to return to Aristotle's example, would not know what to eat. One who knows only that he should act as prudence determines would not know what to do. One who knows only that he is made happy through the activities of virtue, but who does not know what those activities are, could not engage in those activities and thereby attain happiness. And the craftsman who knows only "the universal good" will not become more proficient in his art (1097a5–13).

Whether or not knowledge in the sovereign sense can be dragged around by the passions, the pull of passion remains to drag around human beings. Aristotle agrees with Socrates's position as Aristotle himself formulates it—it would be "a terrible thing" if our knowledge is slave to our passions—but he shows in just how many ways this very thing occurs. We do not use our knowledge; we have knowledge of universals, but particulars govern action; we apply a universal that favors our desires; and we exempt ourselves from what holds for human beings. We may be drunk or mad or in the grip of sexual desire or spiritedness. In all these cases self-rule is necessary for our acting well. We must own our knowledge by using it and applying it to particular cases, especially to our own case. Only then do our actions become our own. And only when we put our knowledge to use does our knowledge become our own. But why do we do so?

When he first introduced Socrates's position that no one acts contrary to what he knows to be best, Aristotle observed that Socrates "always did battle" against the argument that anything could drag knowledge around like a slave (1145b23–25). Although Socrates did not describe himself as doing battle for this argument, Aristotle sees his fighting spirit in his actions. He presents Socrates as a warrior for his position. He is not only a knower (at least one who claims to know the source of wrongdoing is ignorance), but also a fighter.[11] Of course, Socrates himself knows that reason is in need of spiritedness to rule desire, for he has recourse to a spirited part of the soul in the *Republic* to do this very thing (440e; see also 536c). Does Socrates not use what he knows when he ignores the battle in the soul to argue against Protagoras that knowledge is virtue? Or does he have reasons apart from the argument itself, perhaps discrediting the admired Sophist to a young man desiring to study with him, or teaching indirectly by bringing everyone into a state of perplexity—the very thing for which Socrates is famous (see *Meno* 79e–80a)? This is in fact what Socrates says

---

11. For a fuller discussion of Aristotle's reference to Socrates's "doing battle" against the degradation of knowledge, see Block and Cain, "Socrates's Spirited Defense of Knowledge," 14–16.

at the end of the dialogue has happened: since his position that knowledge is virtue is at odds with his earlier argument that virtue cannot be taught, and since they have not reached a conclusion about the questions at issue, further discussion is necessary (*Protagoras* 360e–361d). By the end of the *Protagoras*, we see the Socrates who knows he does not know, not an unwavering defender of the position that knowledge is virtue. Aristotle might justify his quoting Socrates out of context by appealing to the consequence of an argument that questions human responsibility. It is one that Aristotle himself fights against.

Aristotle brings his treatment of Socrates's view of knowledge to a close with the following entreaty: "About the knower [*eidota*] and the non-knower, and *how a knower can lack self-rule*, let this much be said" (1147b19). On the assumption that failing in self-rule is possible, Aristotle proceeds to discuss different passions from which lack of rule proceeds and the perplexities they raise.[12] Self-rule and its lack involve not only the desires for food and sex. Aristotle gives several examples, but he devotes most attention to spiritedness. Aristotle's spotting Socrates's fighting in defense of knowledge prepares for this turn. So too does Aristotle's discussion of self-rule and its lack more generally, for their possibility is a sign of human freedom and rule, which arise from and are protected by spiritedness (*Politics* 1328a6–8). If the difference between self-rule and its lack turns on whether one uses one's knowledge and another not, or on which knowledge one puts to use in a given case, the difference turns on what is "up to us." This may be why Aristotle does not explain why some use their knowledge and others do not, or why some use their knowledge of something but not of something else—for human beings are the causes of their actions. After all, those who lack self-rule show regret, and are curable (1150b30–33). They know that they are responsible, that they might have acted otherwise.

RULING SPIRITEDNESS

In addition to lack of rule in regard to food and sex, which Aristotle claims is the primary meaning of the term *akrasia*, there are other sorts that involve our desires for things that are not necessary but are never-

---

12. Ibid., 23.

theless choiceworthy. These include honor, victory, and wealth, and other good and pleasant things of this sort (1147b24–35). As regarding the ethical virtues he discussed earlier, he is examining the pull of the necessities we share with beasts, and our potential to rise above them in the pursuit of other things, "what is by nature beautiful and serious" (1148a23). And yet it is the desires for what transcends the necessities, Aristotle soon suggests, that seem to lead to worse excesses (see *Politics* 1267a3–9).

Among the choiceworthy things that admit of excess, Aristotle includes the affection between parents and offspring (1148a28–32). His examples involve human beings who claim divinity for those they love, such as Niobe, whose excessive love of her children led her "to fight even against the gods" (1148a35). Spiritedness is therefore involved in Aristotle's example of excessive affection between parents and offspring. Although Aristotle says no more than this, stories of Niobe report her boasts that her children were superior to even Apollo and Artemis, the divine offspring of Leto. Niobe had Priam's pride in his offspring, but she lacked his awe, his deference to the divine. Apollo and Artemis, as the tale is told, inflicted a terrible punishment on Niobe for her pride.

From the spiritedness—and hubris—involved in Niobe's excessive love for her offspring (to say nothing of the spiritedness involved in Apollo and Artemis's brutal response), Aristotle turns to the dangers of spiritedness, but delays his discussion for a brief survey of bestiality (1148b13–20). There is nothing beautiful or good about Aristotle's "beastlike" (*thēriōdeis*) examples, many of which he has heard by report and for whose authenticity he does not vouch. They include a woman who rips open pregnant women to devour their infants, a man who sacrificed his mother and ate her, a slave who ate the liver of a fellow slave, a tyrant whose tortures of his victims were so egregious that they may explain why Aristotle merely names the man rather than his deeds (1148b19–27). He later hints at them when he mentions this man's desire to eat children (1149a15). These are not merely an excess of a natural desire for pleasure; nor are their objects pleasant by nature, but rather come from deformities, habits, or corruptions of nature (1148a23–29, b16–18). Aristotle's description is filled with references to disease and madness.

Among the causes for such abominations, Aristotle mentions the habits that arise in someone who was "wantonly abused" or "violated" from childhood (1148b30–31). He uses the word from which hubris is derived, *hubrizein*, which means not only "to insult," but also "to violate."

The one who violates in this case seems to be the most monstrous of all, for he not only violates others but causes "habits" in them that lead them to violate others in turn. In contrast to those encouraged by the Graces who initiate a chain of goods, they initiate a chain of evils. Their perversion is even more shocking when we consider that such outrage might come from parents, whose proper task includes inculcating habits in their children that lead them to virtue. Regardless, in these cases of outrage, parents did not protect their children, who were abused "from childhood."

Spiritedness, to which Aristotle immediately returns after his treatment of bestiality, is aroused at insult (*hubris*) or slight (1149a33). Spiritedness, then, would resist the hubristic (and beast-like) violations he has just described. Whatever excess comes from spiritedness, it also comes to the defense of the human. Although Aristotle earlier associated spiritedness with beasts when he denied that spiritedness is courage, he did say then that if joined with choice and a noble end, it would become courage (1117a4–9). And now Aristotle in effect appeals to spiritedness to resist violations of humanity (see *Republic* 439e–440a). He even speaks of spiritedness as "going to war" against perceived wrongdoing (1149a34).

Spiritedness, to be sure, admits of excess and error. Moreover, like those who appeal to the universal that all sweets should be tasted, spiritedness misuses reason. Spiritedness infers that when one is insulted or harmed, one should wage war against the act, as if it were drawing the conclusions from a syllogism—a universal about fighting an outrage, a perception that an outrage has occurred, and the command to act that follows. Therefore spiritedness "seems to hear reason in some way, but to mishear it, like swift servants who run off before they hear everything that is said and then err in carrying out the order, or as dogs bark at a knock on the door, without examining [*skepsasthai*] whether [the one knocking] is a friend" (1149a26–30). Reason only appears to support the spirited act, as Aristotle's reference to error indicates. A spirited person would think his acts reasonable even when they are not so. He does not examine what his reason orders him to do.

If Aristotle could teach spiritedness—which after all reacts against being ruled (*Politics* 1328a6–8)[13]—to be skeptical of reason's "command,"

---

13. In the *Politics*, Aristotle observes that "freedom and ruling come from spiritedness, which is commanding and indomitable." He raises the question of what sort of people are best suited for politics. Because the peoples living in the

specifically, to examine whether what seems like an insult comes not from an enemy but from a benefactor, or even a friend, a spirited individual might heed reason as if it were a father or a friend (see 1102b32–34). By implication, Aristotle would object to the spirted dogs of the *Republic*, who obey the commands of their wise rulers without examining them (375e–376c). Rather, Aristotle implies, these spirited guardians should stop to "examine" who is a friend, as Socrates himself does with his interlocutor earlier in the *Republic* (334c–335b). However much spirited human beings act like dogs in "barking" at any knock at the door, they are not dogs but human beings, who are able to examine whether their universal rule that enemies should be attacked applies to the case at hand.

Aristotle's examples of the spiritedness "common to all" indicate that it is a passion that asserts human freedom, but at the same time its unruly tendencies are in need of a check. His first example is that of a son who beats his father and who gives a defense of father-beating. The spirited son defends father-beating by reminding his father that he too struck his own father, and by acknowledging that his own son will strike him in turn "when he becomes a man," for "it belongs to our kind [*suggenes*]" (1149b4–11). This son who beats his father, and thereby asserts his independence from his authority, also recognizes that his father exercised such freedom and that his own son will do so too. His spirited defense of his freedom from his father both looks to his own father as his model and acknowledges that his own authority over his son is limited, just as his father's is over him. He asserts his freedom, while aware that such freedom will also belong to his son. His defense of father-beating differs strikingly from that of Pheidippides in Aristophanes's *Clouds*, who both claims that he is "born free" and appeals to what animals do as his model (*Clouds* 1414, 1427–30). Aristotle's example, in contrast, appeals to what human beings do, those "of their kind," and to the freedom that he shares with his father and that he will share with his son.[14] He knows that human beings are not "born free."

---

regions of Asia "have souls endowed with art and thought" but lack spiritedness, they remain ruled and enslaved. In contrast, those nations "filled with spiritedness" but lacking in art and thought have greater freedom but are incapable of governing, either themselves or their neighbors (1327b23–28, 1328a6–8).

14. Pheidippides even imagines that he might not have a son (1435–36), and so might escape the fate of fathers.

Aristotle's second example is also of a son asserting himself against his father. As he is dragging his father out of the house, his father asks him to stop at the door, for he himself dragged his own father only that far (1149b11–12). This father understands his son's desire for independence or freedom, for he himself also possessed it. He provides a precedent for his son. A father who understands his son's desire for freedom, moreover, need not be thrown out of the house. In such a case, a son might do well to heed his father, just as "desire, and longing in general" (and therefore spiritedness, which is an expression of longing) (see *De Anima* 414b2–3) might listen to reason, as Aristotle says in book 1.

Aristotle's treatment of spiritedness leads him to further reflections on lack of self-rule, especially in contrast to vice. However shameful it is to be conquered by one's passions, the one lacking self-rule is superior to the vicious (1150a31). Aristotle extends the forgiveness we give to the person with unruled spiritedness because he follows "natural longings" to those who "are overcome by strong and excessive pleasures and pains." Unlike the vicious person, they do not choose to do what they do, and it is fitting that they receive forgiveness or pardon, especially when they struggle against their passions (1150b7–9). Unlike the vicious person, who "abides" by his choice, those failing to rule themselves are characterized by regret. After all, they have struggled against their deed, and they have some knowledge, however incomplete and however inactive at the moment they act, that they should not do what they do. Moreover, because a failure in self-rule is like an intermittent disease, whereas vice is continuous, the former cannot escape notice. In contrast, "vice escapes the notice of those who have it," for their choice is in accord with their desires (1150b34–a1).

For all these reasons—their knowledge, their struggle, their regret—those who yield to their passions are curable (1150a22 and b30–33; cf. 1146a32–36). Because they know in some way, when they act contrary to their knowledge, they can be "released" from ignorance, "and become knowers again" (1147b6–7), that is, they might put their knowledge to use. The verb Aristotle uses for "release" is not only the one he uses for the fetters of the sophistic paradox, but also the one he uses for the "unraveling" or "resolution" of a tragedy (*Poetics*, e.g., 1454a35). But unlike the tragic protagonist, the "learning" of the one failing in self-rule need not be too late to act on in the future (see *Antigone* 1270).

In book 7, Aristotle refers to Neoptolemus's deed in Sophocles's *Philoctetes* as a possible example of lack of self-rule: after being persuaded by Odysseus to deceive the wounded Philoctetes into returning to Troy with his famous bow to help the Achaeans, he could not endure the pain of telling a lie (1146a17–22). He tells the truth even though he had accepted Odysseus's reasons to deceive Philoctetes. Has he failed to rule himself and is he therefore worthy of blame? Aristotle's answer is clear: it was not from "lacking self-rule" that Neoptolemus did not abide by the reasons for deceiving Philoctetes, but on account of "a beautiful pleasure." For him, "telling the truth was beautiful," Aristotle says (1151b17–22). Lying to Philoctetes would not have been beautiful (or noble), even for the sake of his fellow soldiers. And, once more, Aristotle offers an example of the beautiful or noble that differs from the beautiful death of Neoptolemus's father Achilles (see *Rhetoric* 1359a1–7).

In the *Philoctetes*, Neoptolemus expresses not only shame at deceiving Philoctetes, but also pity (*oiktos*) for his suffering and a friendship (*philia*) that bids him take Philoctetes home rather than to Troy (903–9, 1228–34, 965–66, 1074, 1375, 1385). The gods in Sophocles's play, however, take little notice of Neoptolemus's struggle, his pity, his intended act of friendship, or his beautiful truth-telling. At least at the end of the play, the deified Heracles comes "from his seat in the heavens" as a sort of deus ex machina to announce "the plan of Zeus," which is that Neoptolemus take Philoctetes back to Troy in a way that offers something advantageous for everyone (1408–44). Divine fiat resolves the situation, so the Achaeans need not suffer from Neoptolemus's telling Philoctetes the truth. But there is a price. With Heracles's announcing Philoctetes's return to Troy, Neoptolemus's beautiful deed has no effect on the action. Moreover, their fiat deprives Neoptolemus of the opportunity to act as a friend in taking Philoctetes home.[15] Philoctetes's words of reproach to Odysseus resound

---

15. For a thoughtful account of Sophocles's play, see Badger, *Sophocles and the Politics of Tragedy*, 114–18. Badger offers a more positive reading of Heracles's dictum that determines events at the end of the play, arguing that Heracles envisions the integration of Philoctetes and Neoptolemus into the community of the Achaeans fighting at Troy through their friendship with each other, each "guarding" the other in battle (*Philoctetes* 1433–37) It is a reading that I believe has much affinity with Aristotle's view of friendship and community. Even if Heracles

in the background: "Are we slaves and not free?" (995). Aristotle offers a partial answer to the question that Odysseus does not answer, when he discusses self-rule and its failure. Freedom is possible because self-rule is possible. And in the next books of the *Ethics*, there are some friendships in which advantage is not at odds with the beautiful (as it was for Achilles, and as it was for Neoptolemus). Once again, Aristotle brings up a case from tragedy, while connecting the beautiful with the truth, and implicitly criticizing the resolution of the Zeus who intervenes at the end of the play.

Aristotle's implicit response to Philoctetes's question in favor of freedom turns on the self-awareness that comes from the struggle in the soul, both of those who rule themselves and those who fail to do so. Such a struggle, Aristotle says, could not escape notice. And just as those lacking self-rule learn that they might have acted otherwise, so too do those who succeed in ruling themselves. To the extent that the activity of virtue is perfect or complete, it might escape the notice of the one who has it. On the ground of self-awareness, self-rule trumps virtue, at least perfect virtue, if that were possible for a human being. Self-rule may therefore have an edge over virtue on the ground of self-awareness and its pleasures and even of the pleasure of self-possession that an act of ruling oneself entails. Aristotle turns toward self-rule in book 7 as a support of virtue, for even a virtuous individual is susceptible to a loss of control. Aristotle turns to it also as a condition for self-knowledge. Unlike the case of those who possess a divine or heroic virtue that is "beyond us," it cannot escape the notice of either those who rule themselves or those who fail to do so that they fall short of divine perfection. Nor can this escape the notice of human beings when they experience pleasures mixed with pains, as Aristotle discusses in the last section of book 7. His examination of pleasure and pain culminates in a simple and eternal pleasure that he attributes to the divine, and from which the changing nature of human beings precludes them. His defense of Neoptolemus's choice, even when the gods of

---

pronounces that "two go together," however, the two are going to war. I suspect that Aristotle would find the prospect of these friends guarding each other—the aged and disease-worn bowman and the young warrior—as problematic as the friendship between Achilles and Patroclus, famous friends who did not "go together" in battle. Neoptolemus and Philoctetes refer to Neoptolemus's taking Philoctetes home as an act of friendship, never in the context of their joining the army at Troy.

tragedy negate its effect on the action, prepares us for this exposition of divine pleasure, his final comment on the pursuit of divinity in book 7.

PLEASURE AND PAIN

It belongs to one who philosophizes about politics (*politikē*) to theorize about pleasure and pain, for he is the "architect of the end in relation to which we speak of things as simply bad or good" (1152b1-3). Aristotle reminds us that he is a philosopher concerned with the good and the bad, unlike the wise who do not investigate human goods (1141b8). He identifies such a philosopher as one who philosophizes about politics, hence a political philosopher. His way of philosophizing involves theorizing and acting, at least as the architect does, who presents the design or framework in which parts have a place and in which good and bad can therefore be distinguished. By comparing himself to an architect, Aristotle reminds us that his philosophizing is an architectonic ordering that aims at the highest good, and that he therefore remains like the statesman, to whom this task also belongs. Aristotle continues to seek the good, as he turns to the relation between the good and the pleasant.

Aristotle also reminds us, explicitly, that pleasure and pain have been a concern of his discussion throughout, not merely in his exploration of self-rule and its lack but also in his treatment of ethical virtue, for "both ethical virtue and vice are concerned with pains and pleasures," and "most say that happiness is accompanied by pleasure" (1152b5-6). Although he earlier attributed to the many and most vulgar the supposition that pleasure *is* happiness (1095b14-16), he now attributes to most people the more elevated view that happiness is "accompanied" by pleasure. He does not refer to them as the vulgar. If this is common opinion, it has taken a step up. Aristotle observes that in support of this view people derived the "name" of the "blessed" (*makarios*) from "experiencing joy" (*chairein*) (1152b4-6). It may be a fanciful etymology, but one that elevates common parlance about pleasure. Most people are looking not for the pleasures of a Sardanapalus, the legendary king known for his sensual indulgences (see 1095b22), but for joy, blessedness. The verb "to experience joy" is related to grace (*charis*) and to the Graces (*Charites*).

The various opinions about pleasure that Aristotle brings forward for examination, moreover, distinguish pleasure from the good. At one extreme is the position that denies that any pleasure is good. Others say that some pleasures are good, but most are base. Others who admit that pleasures may be good still deny that pleasure is the best thing or the highest good (1152b9–13). People are not simply pleasure-seekers; they desire the good and reject pleasures that are not good. None of these common opinions about pleasure could support the life Aristotle dismissed in book 1 as worthy of cattle (1095b13–22). Common opinion seeks something more than pleasure, or at least it distinguishes pleasures that are worth pursuing from those that are not. Opinion holds that there are shameful pleasures that are subject to reproach (1152b22). It too, like Aristotle, reflects on pleasure and pain, and makes judgments about them; it does not simply pursue the one, and avoid the other.

Aristotle also mentions the concern that critics of pleasure voice that pleasure is "an impediment to thinking," and that "the more enjoyment pleasures provide the greater the impediment they are" (1152b18). Human beings understand themselves to be thinking beings, and their good to consist in using their minds. So too they observe that the prudent person does not pursue pleasure but rather avoids pain (1152b17). Whether or not they are correct about the prudent person, they appeal to him as a standard. In arguing against pleasure, they also point out that everything good is the work of art and that there is no art of pleasure, and that children and beasts pursue pleasure (1152b19–21). All these positions are skeptical of pleasure because of their respect for human reason. The ones who hold these opinions demand too much of human life in the name of reason, Aristotle in effect responds when he defends pleasure, almost as if their spiritedness has heard that pleasures corrupt and follows a command of reason to struggle against them, without stopping to examine which pleasures benefit and which harm. Aristotle calls these critics of pleasure to an examination of pleasure, to which they should be open. After all, they already show an inclination toward reason.

By arguing that not all pleasure or enjoyment is at odds with living a rational life, Aristotle defends our capacity for joy or delight. In the first place, even though some seek pleasures in excess (which, Aristotle concedes, they should not), everyone delights (*charousi*) in food, wine, and sex (1154a18–19). If they did not, as Aristotle made clear in his description of moderation, they would diverge from the mean toward the deficiency (1107b8, 1119a8), to say nothing of dying of starvation, or failing to provide for generation of the species. In that discussion of moderation, he also contrasted pleasures of the soul with those of the body, including learning among the former (1117b28–31). Now, in book 7, in answer to the charge that pleasure is an impediment to thinking, he explains that activities are not impeded by pleasures arising from them, but only by pleasures foreign to them, and even that pleasures accompanying an activity can enhance and prolong that activity. Even if the pain of ignorance moves us to philosophizing (see *Metaphysics* 982b18–22), the pleasures of theorizing (or contemplating) and learning "make us theorize and learn the more" (1153a21–23).

Aristotle also objects to those who criticize pleasure as a movement (*kinesis*) or "coming-into-being" (*genesis*) rather than an end (*telos*). Since the end is a higher good than the movement toward it, their argument holds, pleasure cannot be the highest good (1152b13–15, b23; see *Philebus* 54b–d). Once again, Aristotle is quick to defend pleasure. Those who give this argument against pleasure assume that all pleasure is involved in movements toward an end. This is true of bodily pleasures, such as food and drink, when our natures undergo replenishment or restoration. Because they depend on our nature being "in need," they are mixed with pain (1152b36–1153a6). We take pleasure in eating, for example, only when we are hungry. Pleasure in this case entails relief from pain. But not all pleasures involve motions or processes of coming-into-being, Aristotle responds. We experience pleasures not only when moving toward an end but in the activity (*energeia*) or completed state (1153a1–15).

In the course of this argument, Aristotle gives an example of a pleasure "without pain and desire"—of theorizing or contemplating (*theōrein*), but he qualifies it by adding "when one's nature is not in need" (1153a1). But is *human* nature ever "without need"? Aristotle never says so. Nor does he suggest that our theorizing comes to a halt, or that our longing to know, which is his starting point in the *Metaphysics*, reaches an end, for in exploring perplexities we come to perplexities about even greater things (980a21, 982b12–15). If learning is a motion toward knowledge, that end does not preclude further learning and theorizing, since, as Aristotle says, the pleasures of learning and theorizing make one learn and theorize the more. Among examples of pleasant things in the *Rhetoric*, Aristotle includes learning and wondering, "for in wondering, there is a desire to learn." And in wisdom, "there is knowledge of many wondrous things"

(1371a31–33, b28). Wisdom, at least for human beings, entails wonder. And it is wonder that keeps philosophy alive.[16]

Whereas Aristotle attributes pleasures to needy human beings, there are "those who study nature" (*hoi phusiologoi*), literally, "the physiologists," who say that "a living being is always in a state of labor or strain." They "bear witness" (*marturein*) that even sight and hearing are painful, but we do not experience pains because we are accustomed (*sunētheis*) to them (1154b8–10). Life itself would be painful if habituation did not desensitize us to its pain. We must become habituated not to feel pain at the ordinary sensations of life; should we uncover nature, we would uncover pain. These physiologists nevertheless do not go so far as the chorus in Sophocles's *Oedipus at Colonus* when it says that the best thing is not to be born and the second best is to return whence one came (*OC* 1225–29), for the physiologists understand that custom or habituation offers relief. Relief comes, however, at the price of truth.

Aristotle says that the physiologists "bear witness" to what they say. But what could their "testimony" prove? If they themselves are habituated against experiencing pain in the ordinary sensations of life, they would hardly make reliable witnesses to what their habits prevent them from experiencing. If they lack the habituation that in their view makes life bearable, on the other hand, and nevertheless remain alive to bear witness, they must have some experience that makes them want to continue to live. Their deeds would bear witness that life is choiceworthy despite its pain. Their deeds would contradict their words. They could not serve as sound witnesses for their argument. Of course, if they "bear witness," Aristotle's judicial metaphor suggests, they should be cross-examined, as Aristotle in effect does, for by claiming that they "bear witness" Aristotle shows that they contradict themselves.

Having distinguished the pleasures mixed with pain that belong to "coming into being" or "motion" and pleasures that belong to the "activity" of a completed state, Aristotle concludes by describing the "single and simple" pleasure that "the god enjoys always." He claims that "there is an activity [*energeia*] not only of motion but also without motion [*akinesia*], and pleasure resides more in rest than in motion" (1154b23–28). For human

---

16. As Aristotle says in the *Metaphysics*, through wondering, human beings begin to philosophize, *both* at first and *now* (982b10–15; see also 1072b25–27). See also Schaeffer, "Wisdom and Wonder," 654.

beings, in contrast to the god, "the same thing is not always pleasant because our nature is not simple, and when one part of us experiences pleasure, the other might be pained, and whenever both are in equilibrium there is neither pleasure nor pain (1154b21–23). From this perspective, pleasures for human beings are always mixed with pain. For them, unlike for the god, "all change is sweet," Aristotle says, quoting Electra's words to her brother, Orestes, in one of Euripides's tragedies (*Orestes* 234). Change is sweet because life is painful, and, Aristotle observes, "the nature in need of change is in a sorry state [*poneros*]" (1154b25–32).[17]

Although the tragedians present *human* life in their dramas, they seem at one with the physiologists who study all living things rather than focusing on human beings. Perhaps they are influenced by the physiologists: when in discussing friendship Aristotle dismisses accounts that appeal to nonhuman nature, rather than to what is "distinctively human," he mentions not only Heraclitus and Empedocles, but also Euripides by name (1155b1–10). At any rate, Aristotle insists, contrary to both Sophocles's tragic chorus and the physiologists he mentions, that "perceiving that one lives belongs among those things pleasant in themselves, for life is by nature a good thing" (1170b1–2).[18] In the *Politics*, Aristotle mentions "the natural sweetness of life," which leads human beings to cling to life despite its hardships (1278b28–29). So too his treatment of the ethical virtues offers a different understanding of nature from that of the physiologists, for habituation in the virtues completes nature rather than suppresses it (1103a24–26). It is not only change that is sweet for human beings, for virtue is firm and steadfast (*ametakinētōs*) (literally, "unchanging") (1105a35), and it involves "enjoying [*charein*] as well as being pained by what one ought" (1104b13–14, 1107a1, 1144b27).

---

17. My translation of *poneros* attempts to capture the ambiguity of the word, which ranges from "wicked" to "wretched" or "defective."

18. See also the *Generation of Animals*, where Aristotle says that "being is better than non-being and living than non-living" (731b30–31), and the *Metaphysics*, where, contrary to the physiologists he mentions in the *Ethics*, he observes that we are fond of our senses even for their own sakes, apart from any use (980a22–23). It is in his discussions of friendship that Aristotle is most insistent about the goodness of life, and where he makes the remark that I quote above that life is good by nature (*NE* 1170b1–2; also 1168a5–5; 1170a7, 19–20, 27–29).

Just as we can question what experience makes the testimony of the physiologists about pleasure and pain credible, we can question what experience makes credible Aristotle's contrasting the simple, unmixed, and eternal pleasure of the god with the "sorry state" of human nature. He of course makes no claim to have experienced anything like the divine pleasure he attributes to one whose nature is simple and unchanging, but we have seen him refer in his own name to the wondrous pleasures in learning and theorizing that lead one to learn and theorize the more. When Aristotle objects to those who demote pleasure as "a perceptible coming into a natural state," and proposes instead that pleasure can also be an "unimpeded activity of a natural state" (1153a13–15), "unimpeded" activity takes the place of "perceptible" motion. Inasmuch as his use of "perception" ranges from the activity of the senses, such as seeing and hearing, to awareness more generally, Rackham can translate the definition Aristotle rejects as "a conscious process toward a natural state."[19] This definition requires awareness of pleasure.[20] After replacing "perceptible" with "unimpeded," Aristotle proceeds to arrive at the simple and eternal pleasure enjoyed by the god.

Burnet notes that "unimpeded" is a rare word for Aristotle.[21] Since "no impeded activity is complete" (1153b17), Aristotle's word choice may turn on the awareness that impediments provoke. When Aristotle referred to the shrines to the Graces that were set "in the roadway" (*empodōn*) (1133a3), he used a word more literally translated "as an impediment." Unimpeded activity does not necessarily produce awareness, as would be present in a "perceptible coming into one's nature."[22] Awareness that one is coming into one's nature is pleasant, even if mixed with the pain from awareness of one's lack or need (see *Philebus* 51b and 60d–e). Focusing on the perfect pleasure enjoyed by the god, simple and eternal, in con-

---

19. Rackham, *Aristotle: "Nicomachean Ethics,"* 431, also 435. So too does Tessitore, "Political Reading of Aristotle's Treatment of Pleasure," 252. See also Burnet, *Ethics of Aristotle,* 330.

20. See *Problems*, where Aristotle writes, "the natural road is pleasant, *if it is perceived*" (878b11).

21. Burnet, *The Ethics of Aristotle,* 334.

22. Aristotle calls attention to his making the substitution: "one must speak of" (*lekteon*) "unimpeded" instead of "perceptible" (1153a15). The word he uses, "instead of," *anti,* suggests their opposition.

trast, which after all not even Aristotle can know by experience, tends to obscure the pleasures that human beings experience. Those pleasures are not imperfect experiences of the pleasure enjoyed by the god, for they are possible only for beings who face impediments, as they learn and act along the way to "becoming [*ginesthai*] good" (1105b12). As Aristotle observes in the *Rhetoric*, "accomplishing [*epitelein*] [or "completing"] what is lacking is pleasant for human beings because it becomes their own work [*ergon*]" (1321b26–27). The god whose pleasure is eternal and unchanging, whom Aristotle describes at the end of book 7, suffers no impediments. The pleasure of the god is not mixed with pain. Nor would the god experience the struggle in the soul undergone by those who rule themselves or fail to do so, to say nothing of the pleasure from succeeding in the struggle. An unchanging god would be without talk or speech to others, and so could not experience "the beautiful pleasure" that Aristotle attributed to Neoptolemus—"the pleasure of telling the truth"—as opposed to the pain of lying. Without experience of pain, the god would not, like Aristotle, "theorize about pleasure and pain." Aristotle's discussion of pleasure in book 7 ends with the unchanging god but it begins with Aristotle's self-presentation as one who theorizes about pleasure and pain because he "philosophizes about politics."

Considering how all living beings pursue pleasure of some sort, Aristotle speculates that "perhaps all things by nature possess something divine" (1153b33). Here he responds to those who disparage human life, and nature more generally, in light of a divine perfection, such as those who seek a heroic or "divine" virtue that Aristotle claims is "beyond us," and those who contrast the "sorry" lot of human beings with the simple and eternal pleasure of the god.[23] Aristotle substantiates his observation that if everyone pursues pleasure there must be something correct about it by quoting a line from Hesiod about "talk" (*phēmē*): for when there is much talk, there must be something to it (1153b27; Hesiod, *Works and Days* 763). Readers of Hesiod would know that his poem continues, "Talk too is a goddess," and might reflect on an activity that better deserves being called divine *for human beings* than the motionless—and hence speechless—activity of the god of which Aristotle speaks.

---

23. Cf. Tessitore, "Political Reading of Aristotle's Treatment of Pleasure," 254–62.

When Aristotle speculates about a divinity belonging to "all things," or at least to all living things, he specifically mentions "beasts as well as human beings" (1153b26). He suggests that there is something divine not only about mind, but about life itself, just as he claimed in the *Politics* that it was impious to destroy life.[24] That there is something divine that we share with all life is hardly a cause to boast of our lot, but it may be a cause of awe or wonder, as is our capacity for thought, which is not possessed so universally.

Aristotle sums up book 7: "It has [now] been said what concerns self-rule and its lack, and pleasure and pain, what each is and how some are good and others bad" (1154b33–34). Although Aristotle has made mention of bestiality and divine virtue or activity in book 7, he leaves them out his summary. They are either beneath or beyond the human. But we are still in need of more: "In what remains we will speak about friendship" (1155b35). The focus on self-rule may offer the pleasure of self-possession and self-awareness, as I have argued, but it still places the emphasis on holding the desires for pleasure in check. It remains to speak about friendship to more clearly meet the challenge represented by tragedy and those who study nature, at least by those poets and the philosophers who leave human life in a sorry state. And it now becomes possible to speak about friendship, for the self-possession and self-awareness that emerge in self-rule make friendship possible, and they are fostered by it in turn. As Aristotle's analysis of friendship will show, those who are able to love themselves are capable of loving another (see. e.g., 1166a1–6, b14–18).

Aristotle does not bring in friendship as a deus ex machina in order to save human life from this bleak view of the human condition. Nothing descends from the heavens that is not kin to human life to save it from itself, as do gods in Greek tragedy. Like ethical virtue itself, friendship is "neither by nature nor contrary to nature, but comes to be for us, whose nature is such as to receive it" (1103a24–26). Aristotle's discussion of

---

24. Consider the story Aristotle recounts in *Parts of Animals* about the visitors to Heraclitus, who hesitated when they saw him warming his hands by the stove: "He bid them to come in, for there are gods even here." Aristotle tells the story in support of his exhortation to his readers to study all of nature, even those things that provide no delight to the senses, for there are "immeasurable pleasures that nature fashions for those philosophers by nature who are able to discern causes." Indeed, "there is something wonderful in all natural things" (645a6–23).

friendship in books 8 and 9 points to an even further increase in human pleasure and further reveals the pleasures that are available to human beings, pleasures that do not require suppressing pain through habituation, as the physiologists theorized about the ordinary perceptions of life. Like pleasure, friendship has been present in the *Ethics* all along as a subtext—as when Aristotle referred to those who introduced the ideas as his friends. His discussion has reached a point that friendship must be discussed directly.[25] If Aristotle has been successful in his inquiry, his reader would be prepared to take this next step. If not all learning is sweet, some is. And if not all sweet things should be tasted, some should.

---

25. For an exploration of the many ways that friendship serves as a subtext leading up to the books of the *Ethics* explicitly on friendship, see Block and Cain, "Good, Truth, and Friendship," 13–34.

CHAPTER 7

Friendship

Family, Political Community, and Philosophy (Books 8–9)

Aristotle devotes two books of the *Ethics* to friendship. He spends more time on the goods it provides than on any virtue he has previously discussed. He makes the startling pronouncement at the outset that "without friends no one would choose to live, even if he possessed all other goods" (1155a5–6). Along with the blessings of friendship, however, he presents the dilemmas of friendship, and those dilemmas at times have tragic overtones. In the best of friendships, those who are "most of all" (*malista*) friends "wish the good things for their friends for their friends' sake" (1156b10–12). Yet Aristotle also observes that "one wishes the good most of all [*malista*] for oneself" (1159a13). How, then, is friendship between the good, the complete friendship that Aristotle describes, possible?

Aristotle asks in the course of discussing the perplexities that arise from friendship: Would friends wish their friends to become gods? Since a certain degree of equality is necessary for friendship, we could no longer be friends with someone who becomes a god (1159a3–8). We would lose our friend. Must our love for our friend lead us to sacrifice our own good for the sake of our friend's good, and therewith lose the very friendship that calls forth such love? Whether we make our own good decisive or generously prefer the good of our friend over our own, we would dissolve our friendship. But, if friendship is a good, and even a good "without which no one would choose to live," the dilemma would be tragic: our pursuit of our friend's good, as demanded by our love, would lead to the end of our friendship.[1] Pierre Aubenque formulates the difficulty in similar terms: perfect friendship requires that one wishes one's friend the greatest goods, but the greater the goods one's friend obtains, the greater one's friend becomes than the well-wishing friend, destroying the equality essential to friendship. He calls this "the tragic destiny of friendship" and concludes that "perfect friendship destroys itself."[2] In contrast to tragic readings of Aristotle's treatment of friendship, I argue that throughout his discussion Aristotle attempts to save friendship from such tragic consequences.

In the first section of this chapter, I explore Aristotle's definition of friendship in the opening sections of book 8, including its various components and forms. His discussion serves as an introduction to both books 8 and 9, the two books of the *Ethics* on friendship. Friendships require awareness of reciprocal good will, and are distinguished by their ends: the advantageous, the pleasant, and the good. Do mutually advantageous associations, and even fleeting but pleasant companionships, deserve the name of friendship, or does only the mutual love of those attracted to each other's virtue or goodness deserve the name? Aristotle refuses to rule out associations of advantage or pleasure, perhaps because of what they share with the highest form of friendship, and because of their potential for preparing us to experience it.

Aristotle traces the development of friendship to families, which were hitherto the scenes of the greatest conflicts dramatized on the tragic stage, such as the tales involving the families of Agamemnon and of Oedipus. Aristotle offers a different story: "It is in the family [*oikia*] that

---

1. Bartlett and Collins, "Interpretive Essay," 291, find Aristotle's denial that one could wish one's friend to become a god, which implies one wishes the good for oneself "most of all," a "striking" example of "the crucial difficulty bound up in, or precisely in, complete friendship." They escape the tragic consequences by recourse to Aristotle's view of happiness in book 10, which transcends friendship and its dilemmas. Aristotle escapes tragedy through philosophy, not through friendship. See also Pangle, *Aristotle and the Philosophy of Friendship*, 194–99.

2. Aubenque, *La prudence chez Aristotle*, 179–80. See also the response of Ward, *Contemplating Friendship*, 13–14.

we first see the beginnings [*archai*] and springs [*pēgai*] of friendship, regime, and justice" (*Eudemian Ethics* 1242b1). In book 8 of the *Ethics*, Aristotle shows us how the relations that develop within families—between parents and children, between husband and wife, and between siblings—are reflected in different kinds of political communities, or regimes, as I discuss in the second section of this chapter. Political communities both further relationships that have their beginnings in families and depend on families for their own beginnings.

By the end of book 8, however, Aristotle indicates the tensions within families that require addressing and the resources that families offer for doing so, as I discuss in the third section of this chapter. Conflict arises, for example, because children have received from their parents gifts so great that they can never repay them—their education, their nurture, and their very existence (1162a3–8). That Aristotle traces such gifts to the mother as well as to the father, and to the gods as well as to parents, moderates the claims of authority that families, especially fathers, can make. Thus Aristotle can claim at the end of book 8 that a father might claim less than he is owed, both because of the extent of human indebtedness, including his own, and because of the soul's capacity for giving, especially through loving (1163b23).

In book 9, Aristotle turns to friendships that extend beyond those within the family. We learn that political life does not merely reflect friendships within families but also offers opportunities for other kinds of friendships, including a like-mindedness or concord among citizens. Tragedy originating in families does not flow out into political life (as in the plague inflicting Thebes at the beginning of *Oedipus Tyrannus* or the war into which the conflict between Oedipus's sons led their city). Rather, political life offers ways to moderate potential conflict (for example, sons become citizens and share in rule). In discussing what we owe to our fathers, near the beginning of book 9, Aristotle observes that we should not give back all things to our fathers, just as "one does not make all one's sacrifices even to Zeus" (1165a15–16). Zeus, it is recounted, divided his rule with his brothers, Poseidon, the god of the sea, and Hades, the god of the underworld (*Politics* 1284b31). Just as Zeus divides his rule with others, his example teaches, parents should share theirs over their children, not only with each other, but with political communities, with those with a variety of skills useful for life, and ultimately with teachers, especially those who "share in philosophy" (1164b22–28). Such an imitation of the god does not manifest self-sufficiency, simplicity, or absolute rule, but rather insufficiency and sharing of rule and authority. In this depiction, Zeus can become a model for authority not only in the family but also in political communities.

The last three sections of my chapter cover book 9. In the first, I trace Aristotle's discussion of a variety of friendships that go beyond family life, especially the "political friendship" or "like-mindedness" that exists for fellow citizens who come to agreement about "the advantageous and just and aim at them in common" (1167a28–33, b9). Here Aristotle builds on his discussion in book 5 of justice, with its reciprocity of goods that holds a city together, and his exploration of the natural justice that demands shared rule. Here too he suggests an alternative to tragedy, explicitly contrasting such like-minded citizens with the tragic "like-mindedness" of Oedipus's sons, who sought to rule their city. His books on friendship thus expand his treatment of justice. When first referring to the "like-mindedness" of citizens, he claimed that "friendship holds a city together" and that "lawgivers are more serious about it than about justice" (1155a23–26).

Aristotle goes beyond both families and political communities, however, in order to understand the full potential of friendship. In the last half of book 9, he examines how friendships arise as an extension of self-love, as I discuss in the next section of this chapter, especially his account of the love of the benefactor for his beneficiary, whose love of his activity expresses his love of life (1167b16–1168a19). This applies to the love of parents for their children, of the poet and craftsman for their work, and by implication statesmen and public benefactors who leave enduring benefits for their communities.

The benefactor's love for his beneficiary demonstrates how self-love expands into love of another, but it does not in Aristotle's view offer an adequate model for the reciprocity of friendship, or even for sharing in rule in political life, as I argue in the last section of this chapter. Friends give and receive from each other through imitation and correction, each making the other his own not only by loving him but also by contributing to his goodness. Aristotle's treatment of friendship culminates in a showing that through loving and being loved friends grow in self-awareness, "sharing in speeches and thought," which is what "living together" means for human beings (1170b12–13). Their memories and hopes give them objects for their contemplating or thinking (1166a24–26). Their sharing speaking and thinking therefore belongs to beings who live in time, and it extends to their sharing their joys and sufferings (1171a8). Such sharing involves both giving and receiving love (1171a35–b13). Just as political relations reflect and expand the friendships that begin in families, so too does the love between friends in which book 9 culminates. Aristotle shows the limits of families and the need for political life to address those limits, and his description of the giving and receiving in friendship, at least in its highest form, demonstrates what is at best only intimated in the likemindedness of fellow citizens.

INTRODUCING FRIENDSHIP

Aristotle begins his discussion of friendship by observing that friendship "is a virtue or it is accompanied by [*meta*] virtue" (1155a3). Without being more precise, Aristotle indicates that virtue is inseparable from friendship, almost like friends, who "go together," as Aristotle proceeds to say (1155a16). That virtue accompanies friendship does not imply that friendship accompanies virtue, but both could be said to be dear, as Aristotle does of truth and friends (1096a16). Aristotle, however, suggests a closer connection between virtue and friendship when he observes that no one would choose to live without friends, even if one possessed all the other goods. His observation implies that the virtues, ethical and intellectual, even their activities, are inadequate for happiness, unless conjoined with friendship. If the human work constitutes the happiness of human beings, as Aristotle indicated in book 1 (1098a12–18), it must include friendship.[3]

In this way and others, Aristotle begins book 8 with an encomium to friendship and its contribution to a good human life. He observes that friends are good to have at times of both good fortune and bad. Good fortune is sweeter when one has someone with whom to share it. So too can friends alleviate misfortune, if only by providing comfort (1155a3–13). Like greatness of soul, which is "neither overjoyed by good fortune nor overly grieved by bad fortune" (1124a14–17), friendship offers a buffer

---

3. Heyking, *Form of Politics*, 40, argues that "Aristotle's discussion of virtue friendship is the apex of his teaching on virtue" and that this form of friendship presupposes the presence of the virtues he has previously discussed. See also Sokolowski, "Phenomenology of Friendship," 460–61.

against the vicissitudes of chance or fortune. It is a buffer that—far from tending toward self-sufficiency—highlights dependence on friends.

So too are friends of help to the young in avoiding error and to the old in their weakness (1155a13–14). Need, and the good that friendship offers in response, pervades all ages of human life. Aristotle singles out the importance of friendship to those "in their prime," inasmuch as two together are "better able to think and to act" (1155a15–16). One is therefore better able to engage in the activities of the intellectual and ethical virtues with friends than without them. This point, which Aristotle introduces here by quoting Homer's statement that "two go together" (*Iliad* 10.224), foreshadows the need underlying even the best sorts of friendships.[4] It also foreshadows the differences between friends, even in friendships based on virtue. The two who "go together" in Homer, Diomedes and Odysseus, do so because they are able to make different contributions to their mission.[5] As Diomedes recognizes when he explains his choice of Odysseus to accompany him, "his mind is best at devices" (*Iliad* 10.247). The pair go together under the cover of darkness into the enemy camp and kill their foes while they sleep. Aristotle thus reminds us of war and deeds that may be necessary but not beautiful or noble at the outset of his discussion of friendship, in which he offers us different ways of thinking and acting that are desirable for friends.[6]

---

4. See Burger's (*Aristotle's Dialogue with Socrates*, 182–89) pathbreaking argument that Aristotle understood the highest friendship as existing not between two self-sufficient friends, joined by their perfect goodness and wisdom, but between two who "philosophize together," and thus help each other pursue what they lack. In this way, Aristotle is able to incorporate *eros* into *philia*, and what Burger calls "the dialogic self" that emerges in friendship becomes "the joint realization of our rational nature and our political nature."

5. Consider also Salkever's ("Taking Friendship Seriously," 55) comment that although Aristotle refers to the sayings that "what belongs to friends are common" and that "friends have one soul in two bodies" (1168b7–9), he "disputes and revises" both of them, "particularly by noting that true friends must be separate as well as other selves." Also Heyking, *Form of Politics*, 42.

6. According to Salkever, "Taking Friendship Seriously," 55, Aristotle's account of friendship challenges the typical Greek understanding of "great friendships" as "pairs of great male warriors or political heroes—Achilles and Patroclus, Hercules and Iolaus, Harmodious and Aristogeiton," which Aristotle associates

Parents and offspring, Aristotle observes further, have friendship or affection (*philia*) for each other by nature, as do birds and most animals, and those alike in kind (*homoethneis*), especially human beings. Thus we praise "those who love humanity" (*philanthropoi*), and we learn in our travels that every human being is kin (*oikeios*) and a friend (1155a17–22). We make friends when we travel and understand others as "kin." Aristotle's word for "kin" also means "our own," a word derived from home, or family. Our "love of humanity" is manifest in coming to see human beings whom we meet as kin, that is, in extending our "home" to them. Aristotle's "philanthropy" is less an abstract love of humanity than a sort of hospitality, even if we come to express it on our travels, when we are away from home.

In turning to friendship found in cities, Aristotle observes that friendship "holds cities together," using a similar expression to the one he used when he observed that the reciprocal exchange of goods "holds cities together" (1155a22–24, 1132b32–1133a5, 1133a26–28). Aristotle now extends the work of the Graces, to whom he attributed encouraging such exchange, to friendship.

To be sure, "not a few things about [friendship] are in dispute," such as whether it is those who are like each other who are friends, a view held by Empedocles. The old saying "jackdaw to jackdaw" supports this; others say that "potter quarrels with potter." That those unlike each other make the better friends is proposed by Heraclitus, who says that "the most beautiful harmony comes from differences," and by Euripides, who says that the parched earth loves rain, and the "august heaven" when filled with rain loves to fall to earth. Natural scientists and poets thus dispute about nature when they try to find in nature a model for human friendship (see Plato, *Lysis* 213e–214b, 215c–d, 216b–c). Once again, as with the physiologists and poets Aristotle mentioned in book 7, their views are insufficient for understanding human life. In this case, tracing human attraction to either similarity or difference alone fails to capture the complexity of friendship, for friends are both like and unlike each other, and even change in the course of friendship.

Human friendships differ in both kind and degree, Aristotle explains, depending on the extent to which they are based on the utility, pleasure,

---

"with spiritedness, anger, and revenge." Aristotle's allusion to the exploit of Odysseus and Diomedes is another dimension of this challenge.

or goodness that one finds in one's friend, or various combinations thereof. It is even possible that one becomes a friend to another primarily for pleasure, and the other for the sake of advantage (1155b13–21, 1157a3–7). Friendships are like and unlike one another, as are friends. Nature cannot be as simple as the natural scientists and poets think, if human life is taken into account. When Aristotle mentions nature again, after he has laid out the characteristics of friendship, he claims that the "longing" of nature is for the middle (*to meson*) rather than its opposite, since nature longs for the good. Thus the dry longs not to become wet, nor the wet to become dry, but both long for the middle (1159b19–24), he says, almost as if his own examination of human things might give insight into nature itself.

Friends wish the good for the other, and thus "have good will" (*eunous*) for the other (literally, are "well-minded" toward the other). Good will, however, is only the "beginning" of friendship (1167a3). Good will must be reciprocal for there to be friendship, but even mutual good will is not sufficient. Two individuals with good will toward each other but unaware of it would not be friends (1155b27–1156a5).[7] Friends know that they are friends, for they know that their good will is reciprocated. They know that they are loved by another, whether because of benefits or pleasures they give, or simply because of their own goodness. Those who seek honor from those who are prudent and from those who know them so that they can trust their own goodness seek judgment from those they trust as good judges (1095b28–29; cf. 1124a9–11). It seems to have escaped the notice of those who seek honor that they might find satisfaction in friendship. By accepting the judgment of friends, they would confirm in turn the goodness of those who render judgment. Like friendship itself, such trust would be reciprocal.

Only in the case of the perfect or complete (*teleia*) friendship, in which friends love what is good and not merely useful or pleasant in the other, moreover, do friends love each other for themselves, or on account of each other's goodness as well as for the goods they derive from their

---

7. Aristotle underlines the importance of *awareness* of another's good will as a requirement for friendship, by pointing out that "people say" that mutual good will is necessary to friendship, but awareness of that good will "must be set down in addition." There can be no friendship if mutual good will "escapes notice" (1155b31–1156a6). The requirement of awareness appears to have escaped notice. It is Aristotle's addition to what "people say."

friendship (1155b18–1156a5, 1156a15). Only such a friendship is stable or lasting, not only because it combines all three causes of friendship, but because it is based on virtue, and "virtue is a lasting thing" (1156b12–13). What is useful, in contrast, "does not remain constant, but differs from time to time," and friendships based on pleasure, so characteristic of the young, "change together with what they find pleasant," and "so the young swiftly become friends and cease being so" (1156a33–b1). Aristotle's exposition of the "complete" or "perfect" friendship offers not the unchanging pleasure of the god, with which Aristotle concluded book 7, but a pleasure—and good—that lasts over time, to human beings who themselves live in time. The friendship that Aristotle calls complete or perfect is lasting, without lasting forever. Time is not necessarily hostile to friendship, and in fact is necessary to at least the best kind of friendship, which "requires time [*chronos*] and the forming habits together [*sunētheia*]." It is only over time and by living together, Aristotle says, that people can come "to know each other," and can "appear to each other as worthy of love and become trusted" (1156b25–30). Once again, time is a "co-worker" (1098a24). To his treatment of the habits (*etheis*) of virtue that form character (*ēthos*), Aristotle now adds the habits that arise "with" another.

Although Aristotle classifies relationships based on only utility or pleasure as forms of friendship, he also claims that they are only "like" friendship (1156a16–18 and 1157b1–4). Friendships of utility and pleasure are both like and unlike friendship: like because those involved share some good, either benefit or pleasure or both, and unlike because they are not based on the character of the other and are therefore not as lasting (1158b4–11, 1164a11–13). Aristotle nevertheless includes such relationships in his discussion of friendship. He locates all these relationships in the same class, even at the cost of a clear answer to the question of who should be called friends.[8]

As his discussion proceeds, however, we see that a clear distinction between perfect and imperfect friendships is difficult to make. After all, one's benefiting and giving pleasure to another does to a degree proceed

---

8. Burger, *Aristotle's Dialogue with Socrates*, 164–65. Aristotle insists in the *Eudemian Ethics* that we must have it both ways. There he maintains that all of the elements of friendship are found only in the "primary" friendship, "that of the good." Yet to refuse to call other sorts of friendship by the name "does violence to the appearances" (1236a14–36, b20–23).

from one's character, and one's doing so over time might contribute to the formation and development of character. Some imperfect friendships end, others grow and deepen.[9] Aristotle mentions that many relationships of utility or pleasure have a potential of becoming more than that, even lover and beloved, for example, who seek different goods from their relationship, such as pleasure and advantage, might remain friends, when as a result of spending time together they become fond of each other's characters (1157a11–12).

Moreover, although friendships between the good are lasting, they last only as long as the friends remain good. Aristotle refers to "perfect" friendship, but never to perfect friends. Because a degree of equality is necessary for friendship, change in one of the friends threatens friendship, even change for the better. Friends are no longer friends when a great disparity arises between them regarding virtue, resources, or some other thing, but "there is no precise definition regarding the point up to which the friends remain friends" (1158b33, 1159a4). But when the disparity between friends becomes as great as that between human beings and gods Aristotle can say for sure that there cannot be friendship (1158b36–38). In whatever way Aristotle understands the proper relation between human and divine—and he does not presume to give a name for it here—it cannot be classified as one kind of friendship among others. Friendship involves need on the part of both friends, even in the case of the best friendships, if only a need to trust their own goodness. Friendship therefore belongs to imperfect beings. In the *Eudemian Ethics*, Aristotle argues that because "the god has no need of a friend" does not mean that a good

---

9. Salkever, "Taking Friendship Seriously," 65, 66, argues that all friendships emerge from self-interest. But "once formed, they are no longer reducible to the self-interested motives from which they indispensably spring." For a good discussion of how even friendship aiming at mutual advantage depends on the exercise of virtue, see Frank, *Democracy of Distinction*, 152–56. Approaching the issue from the other but equally weighty direction, Heyking, *Form of Politics*, 36–37, argues that our experience of virtue-friendship informs our other "friendships": our experience and memory of our friendships based on virtue reminds us that the way in which we engage with persons for mutual advantage is not simply utilitarian.

human being does not need one, for "our well-being is in relation to another, whereas [the god] himself is his own well-being" (1245b9–19).

In arguing in the *Nicomachean Ethics* that friendship cannot apply to the relation between human and divine, Aristotle raises the question of whether we could wish our friends to become gods. He responds that since friendship is a good for human beings, we could not wish that our friend lose his friends, as his becoming a god would entail (1159a3–8). Our friend confirms our own goodness by loving us, but if we did not love ourselves, we would not suppose that our friendship were good for our friend. As Aristotle further explains, the good for someone cannot mean his becoming other, for then the good would not be his but someone else's. A friend will wish the greatest good for his friend, not for someone else who he might become. One wishes for his friend's greatest good "as a human being" (1159a3–13). We wish *his* good, and we wish *him* to become good, but his becoming good must be compatible with his being who and what he is. Aristotle's insistence that we could not wish our friend to become a god thus turns on our wishing the good for our friend, rather than for ourselves, even if our own good would also be served as a result. By the same token, although we wish the good for ourselves, we would not wish to become gods, for then we would lose our friend, who is good for us. Besides, we wish the good for ourselves, as we do for our friend, insofar as we are "the sort we are," that is, insofar as we are human beings (see 1166a21–23).

In friendship, then, we love *someone*, not humanity, not a universal. Even the love of humanity that Aristotle mentioned comes into play when we travel and meet human beings whom we can regard as kin, or as our own. That love is for *someone* sheds light on a question that Aristotle left implicit in his discussion of equity. Equity corrects the universality of the law by considering situations that arise in time (1137b25–1138a3). But why would a judge not simply see the particular in light of the universal, applying the law as his calling seems to require? What leads him to see that some particulars do not fall under a universal rule? And how does the lawgiver who frames the universal rules that legislation demands know that he "errs" when he does so (1137b16)? In loving another, we learn from experience that human life cannot without loss be reduced to a universal good or a universal law. The experience of friendship in various degrees, including friendships that arise in families, undergirds equity, as it does the virtue resembling friendship that Aristotle describes in book 4. One acts "like" a friend because one is the sort of person one is, Aristotle said there, but one is that sort of person in part because of one's experiences and these include one's friendships. It therefore makes sense that the just need friends in addition to justice and that "lawgivers are more serious about friendship than justice" (1155a28, b26–29).

FRIENDSHIP IN FAMILIES AND REGIMES

Just before Aristotle explains how different forms of rule within cities reflect friendships that develop within families, he points out that justice and friendship exist between the same persons and are coextensive. Both extend through all communities of human beings, which "resemble parts of the political community" (1160a9). But communities that only "resemble" parts of a political community are not simply identical with them.[10] Communities differ in kind from one another. The same rules do not apply to all alike. It is "more terrible" "to strike a father than to strike anyone else," for example. It is also more terrible "to steal money from a comrade than from a fellow citizen" (1160a2–10).

Aristotle's examples of communities in which different measures inhere include not only armies, which serve cities, but also sailors, who seek advantage "through seafaring" and therefore outside the bounds of the city. They also include, Aristotle observes, "Bacchic revelers" (*thiasōtai*) and those who come together for feasts or festivals to offer sacrifices and honor the gods (1160a14–17, 19–26). Aristotle leaves the relationship of Bacchic revelers to the city undefined. Do their revels occur within the city, or outside of it, as Euripides portrayed them in the *Bacchae*?[11] In ei-

---

10. See Smith's (*Revaluing Ethics*, 206–11, 213, 221) discussion of Aristotle's view of the family and city as "analogical communities" rather than "identical" ones. As he points out, "analogical terms are employed for realities that are both like *and different*."

11. See Euripides, *Bacchae* 548, for a reference to the god Dionysus as a *thiasōtēs*. In that play, Euripides dramatizes an unhappy outcome of the god's entering the city. There, however, the god comes to replace the political ruler who failed to give him due recognition and drives him out of the city to his death. That ruler, Pentheus, lacks the political art that gives order to the city without ruling the gods (see 1145a14).

ther case, their revels would be more moderate than those in that play, if Aristotle can refer to them along with dinner clubs, whose purposes include "getting together with others" as well as honoring the gods. Although the destructive religious fanaticism Euripides depicted may lurk in the background, Aristotle alludes only to a more benign role for Bacchus (or Dionysus) in fostering human community rather than tearing it apart. At the same time, he suggests a range of human activities from commerce to worship that are not entirely encompassed by the city's walls. As Burger observes, "it is only from the perspective of the city and its end, as Book I has already suggested, that every human association is a subordinate part of the political whole." She asks, "Of what political community is the relation between Plato and Aristotle a proper part?"[12]

Aristotle's observation that striking one's father is more "terrible" than striking anyone else implies that it is more terrible than striking a ruler. By alluding to the sanctity of the relation between parent and offspring, Aristotle indicates the unique status of families within the city. Families are parts of a city (*Politics* 1253b1–3), but they are not only parts. They are the associations from which cities develop, and their ends—for example, educating the young and fostering the virtues of their members more generally (1161a18, 1162a8; *Politics* 1259b19–21, 1260b13–17)—can be more fully realized in the city. Cities depend on families for their coming into being and serve ends that originate in them. Aristotle finds in the relations within families—between parents and offspring, husband and wife, and siblings—models (*paradeigmata*) of the different political structures, or "regimes," which give structure to rule in cities. Families are reflections of all regimes. A regime realizes what families only begin, and yet insofar as it is only one regime among many regimes of which families provide models, families intimate also what might have been. They point beyond any given regime to other possibilities, and to other kinds of friendship that the laws of a city can support but not encompass. With this introduction to regimes, their potentials and limits, Aristotle turns to the different regimes, which are reflections of relations within families. Some illustrate more benign possibilities than others.

By reserving his discussion of regimes for his books on friendship, Aristotle both elevates regimes (since they reflect relations based on affection) and limits them (since they depend on these prepolitical associations

---

12. Burger, *Aristotle's Dialogue with Socrates*, 169.

for their development and serve their ends). Aristotle also suggests that families need political communities not merely to further their purposes, such as the education of the young, but also to check their potential injustice. Families in Aristotle's analysis provide models not only of good forms of regimes, but also of deviant ones, of injustice as well as justice. Aristotle finds a model for kingship in the father who cares for his children, who considers their good and not his own. Fathers who use their sons as slaves serve as Aristotle's model for tyranny rather than kingship. Aristotle models aristocracy on the community between husband and wife, when rule is divided according to merit, in contrast to an oligarchic relation between them when the husband rules over everything because of his power and wealth. Finally, the community among brothers resembles the rule of the many, when ruled is shared, whereas a corruption of the rule of the many occurs when equality and freedom lead to anarchy (1160a33–1161a9).

In Aristotle's classification of regimes in the *Politics*, the king rules for the sake of "the common advantage" (1279a34–35). There is something common to ruler and ruled, in which they share. The king he describes in the *Ethics*, in contrast, looks to what is beneficial for the ruled rather than for himself. Here too he rules for the sake of the community, but he is not a part of it. The king considers the good of the ruled, Aristotle explains here, because he is self-sufficient, superior in every good, and lacks nothing (1160b1–6). He confers benefits, like the great of soul (1160b6, 1124b9), and cares for the ruled so that they fare well (1160b25 and 1161a14).

Aristotle's inclusion of this king among regimes modeled on friendships within the family is puzzling, if only because he insists that too great a disparity between parties makes friendship impossible. Indeed, when he referred to the disparity between human beings and gods that renders friendship impossible, he also mentioned kings, almost in passing, who could not be friends with those they rule, *if they too* "exceed [human beings] in all goods to the greatest degree" (1158b33–1159a6). Aristotle reminds us of this disparity between a king and his subjects when he mentions Homer's reference to Agamemnon as "shepherd of the people." The king, Aristotle says, cares for the ruled "as a shepherd for his sheep" (1161a13–15; *Iliad* 2.243).

Aristotle's analogy between the father and this self-sufficient and benefactor king becomes even more perplexing when he remarks that the benefits conferred by a father on his children are "of greater magnitude" than those given by a king to his subjects.[13] One's father is "the cause of one's very being," and of one's "rearing [or sustenance] and education" (1161a16–18). The benefactions of the king fall short of those of the father. Aristotle even proceeds to qualify the father's claims when he remarks of the benefits the father bestows on his children that "ancestors too are credited with these things" (1161a16–18). A father's begetting his son is dependent on his own father's having begotten him, as are rearing and education. Like that of the spirited son in Aristotle's story of father-beating, the rule of fathers must acknowledge their dependence on their own fathers and by implication their eventual dependence on their own children (1149b8–11). Aristotle reminds them of this, just as he reminded the elderly at the very beginning of his discussion of friendship that in their weakness they require others to care for them (1155a14).

By including rearing and education among the benefits the father confers, Aristotle indicates that the father's care includes preparing his children to become adults. Earlier Aristotle found justice proper in the relation between a father and his children only when they reach a certain age and become independent, for *until then* children are like a part of their father (1134b9–11). Children become independent of their parents when they grow up, but when do subjects become independent of a king? However much the king serves the advantage of the ruled, those ruled by a king need never look to their own good. Their ruler does it for them, and therefore treats his subjects as children, as Aristotle's reference to Agamemnon as shepherd suggests (at best). Aristotle's comparing Agamemnon's rule of his army to a father's, moreover, reminds us that he sacrificed his daughter so that his army could proceed on its mission against Troy. When Aristotle observes that there is little or no friendship between a tyrant and his subjects, just as there would not be between a human being and a horse or an ox, nor between a master and a slave insofar as he is a slave (1161a30–b6), his observations might also apply to the self-sufficient king in his care for his sheep. Aristotle's attempt to find a model for kingship within the family is therefore, by and large, a failed attempt. At least, it blurs the line between kingship and tyranny. Building on his analysis in the *Ethics*,

---

13. For penetrating discussion of the problems that arise in Aristotle's comparison of fathers and kings, see Cain, "Friendship, Rights, and Community," 122–28.

Aristotle reins in kingship in the *Politics* by including it among the regimes that rule for the *common* advantage and distinguishing it from "absolute" kingship, whose unlimited power reduces the city to a household (1284b29–33).[14]

Aristotle proceeds to speak about the friendship between husband and wife, and then the friendship between brothers, which provide better models for rule within cities than does kingship.[15] In the *Politics*, Aristotle explicitly designates the rule between husband and wife as political, distinguishing it from that between father over children (paternal rule), king over his subjects (kingly rule), and a master over slaves (despotic rule) (1259a36–41). So too in the *Ethics* Aristotle gives the relation between husband and wife a central place in his examination of the family for models of regimes, finding in their friendship a model for aristocracy, which could mean both "rule by the best" and "best [form of] rule."[16]

---

14. See Nichols, *Citizens and Statesmen*, 72–81; and Burger, *Aristotle's Dialogue with Socrates*, 170.

15. Cropsey, "Justice and Friendship," 268–69, observes that it is difficult to reconcile Aristotle's description of the king as "absolutely independent of his subjects with respect to all 'goods,'" with his statement that "an excess of inequality between parties [destroys] friendship and justice between them." Considering the greater equality in democratic regimes, he suggests that "friendship between ruler and ruled is not at a peak in the best regime but in the least bad one," or rather "this will be true if the best regime is the simply best one ruled by the philosopher whose superiority in excellence and power is absolute." See also Ward, *Contemplating Friendship*, 118, who argues that kingship is the best regime with regard to justice, whereas timocracy is most conducive to friendship. My own reading questions whether kingship is Aristotle's best regime, at least the "overall" or absolute king he describes in the *Politics*, and with which he contrasts more limited kingships, qualified by law, by time, or by sharing rule (1284a35–1285a33). In such regimes, justice and friendship may not be as far apart as their analyses suggest.

16. Nichols, "Both Friends and Truth," 79–81. In the *Politics*, when Aristotle gives a similar classification of regimes, he singles out aristocracy as one whose name can have different meanings, "either that the best rule, or that the rulers rule with a view to what is best for the city and those who participate in it" (1279a35–38). Aristocracy is an anomaly in Aristotle's classification. Not only does its name have more than one meaning, but its definition (especially in its latter meaning) might apply to any of the correct forms of regime, whether rule is by

In the family, Aristotle says, "the man rules in accord with merit (or worth) those things over which a man should rule, whereas all things suited to a woman, he gives over [or yields] to her" (1160b33–34). If a man rules in accord with merit only those things over which he should rule, so too does the woman rule in accord *with her merit* those things over which a woman should rule.[17] When Aristotle says that the man yields to the woman what is suited to her, he does not suggest that it is up to him to determine what is suited to her but rather to recognize it and to act on it. So too, Aristotle leaves implicit, must the woman yield to her husband the tasks that are suited to him. That the relation between men and women is based on superiority therefore means not that one is superior to the other, but that each rules the tasks or works that are suited to each, and therefore in which each is superior to the other. As Aristotle says, a husband and wife "have different virtues and tasks, and so love each other for different things" (1158b18–19; see *Politics* 1277b25). Although their tasks are different, they help each other by bringing what is their own (*ta idia*) to their common lives (*to koinon*) (1162a23–24; see *Politics* 1263a38–40). Their friendship is therefore both useful and pleasant, and might also be based on virtue, if they are good (*epieikeis*), for "there is a virtue for each, in which they delight [*charein*]" (1162a27–28).[18] Their relation is "aristocratic," then, not because the better, the man, rules but because the "best" rule involves each doing the work that he or she does best.[19] Aristotle

---

the one, the few, or the many, insofar as they too rule with a view to what is best for the city.

17. Aristotle later reiterates that the works of husband and wife are immediately divided, without saying either the basis of the division or who makes it (1162a21).

18. Equity, which came into prominence in book 5 as a correction to the law's universality, and then recognized by Aristotle as extending to everyone in book 6 (1143a31–35), is also at work in the family.

19. Although Ward, *Contemplating Friendship*, 125–26, 129, understands Aristotle to imply the superiority of the male when he uses the relation between husband and wife as a model for aristocracy, she points out that Aristotle also suggests a "more natural" rather than "politicized" relation "that allows for a greater equality." Thus husband and wife share a common purpose in begetting children and sharing in things that contribute to life. Since she understands the highest friendship for Aristotle to be based on likeness rather than complementarity,

describes a division of labor, not a hierarchy of talents. Husband and wife share in ruling, with each contributing what is his or her own to the family.[20] If the best friendships that Aristotle discusses, friendships based on the goodness of the friends, involve different virtues and contributions, the friendship between husband and wife at its best provides a model.

In the friendship between brothers, in contrast, Aristotle emphasizes equality in similarity rather than in difference. If brothers differ too greatly in age, the friendship characteristic of brothers cannot exist (1161a5–6), just as a certain degree of equality is necessary for all friendships. Aristotle calls the regime that reflects their friendship "timocracy," defining it as the participation of those who meet a certain property assessment (*timēma*) (1160b19–20). Aristotle's "timocrats" are not defined as lovers of honor (*timē*), as they are in Plato's *Republic* (545a–b), but as men of property. Indeed, far from encouraging its leading men to strive for preeminence over others, as might lovers of honor, the regime that reflects the friendship between brothers is the correct form of the rule of the many, and "all those who meet the property assessment are considered equal" (1160b17–21).[21] The regime grounded on property rather than on honors would resemble the middle-class regime that Aristotle discusses in the *Politics* (1295a25–b34). Aristotle's formulation does not preclude bestowing honors that confirm worth, as honor lovers seek. However, honors would be more widely spread, based as the regime is on the equality between brothers. Aristotle describes "the citizens" in a timocracy as wishing "to rule in turn, and therefore on an equal basis," using language that he

---

however, she concludes that true friendship for Aristotle cannot exist between men and women. However, she finds in a mother's love for her child "an altruism that points toward [women's] participation in a perfect form of friendship."

20. In describing the friendship between husband and wife, at 1161a23–25, Aristotle says that "to the better person goes more of the good and to each what is suited to each." He does not say which is the better person, or what goods are appropriate. Presumably, both vary from situation to situation.

21. Aristotle says that "timocracy," the good form of the rule of the many, is commonly referred to as "polity" (1160a35–36). This latter term is the only one he uses in the *Politics* for the good form of the rule of the many (*Politics* 1279a38), and he does not use the word "timocracy" anywhere in that work. Honor—and the competition that it involves—recedes even further in the background of Aristotle's discussion of regimes there.

uses in the *Politics* to describe political rule, where in contrast to both despotism and kingly rule, rulers and ruled share in rule, or rule "in part" or "in turn" (*en merei*) (1161a29, 1134b14–18; also *Politics* 1252a16, 1261b4; 1279a10; 1317b1, 15, 20; 1318b24; 1325b8).

In the *Politics*, Aristotle uses the same Homeric phrase he uses of friendship, "two go together," as part of an argument against kingship as the best regime (1287b7–15). Rule is more effective when it is shared. There too he builds on his discussion in the *Ethics* when he says that political (or shared) rule is appropriate not only to political communities but also in families, with regard to the relation between husband and wife (*Politics* 1259a42). Regimes that reflect friendships within families are therefore those in which rule is shared, as the differences between husband and wife warrant and as the similarities between brothers demand. Justice requires recognition of both difference and similarity, while the community benefits from the different contributions of its members (see *Politics* 1280a9–15,1281a43–b9).

FAMILY FEUDS

In discussing the relations between husband and wife, and their delight in each other's virtue, Aristotle observes that children are a bond, "hence childless couples break up more readily, since children are a good common to both parents, and what is common holds things together" (1162a27–29). There is also a difficulty common to both parents—a difference between their love for their children and their children's love for them. Parents love their children as extensions of themselves, whereas children love their parents as the source of their being. But parents, especially the mother, Aristotle points out, know their children to be their own to a greater degree than children know their parents to be their source, and as a result parents may feel greater affection for their children than their children feel for them. Moreover, "a begetter feels greater kinship with its offspring, than its offspring with its maker, for what comes from the begetter is its own [*oikeion*]." "The begetter is not the offspring's own, or it is [its own] to a lesser degree" (1161b17–25).

Aristotle's observations about the lack of reciprocity between parents and offspring prepare for his discussion in the last part of book 8 about the accusations and complaints that occur in friendships (1162b5–63b27). After all, the more equal relations in families—those between husband and wife and between siblings—offer the more promising models for politics. One source of complaint in families that Aristotle mentions involves the relation between fathers and sons. It seems impossible for a son to repay his father, who is the cause of his birth, rearing, and education (1162a8). Although a son must repay his debt to his father, "nothing he can do is worthy of what was done for him, with the result that he is always in debt" (1163b22–23). The immensity of the son's debt is no doubt related to the instance of father-beating Aristotle mentions in book 7 (1149b8–11), the result of a son's longing to break free.

Consistent with his stories of father-beating there, Aristotle now claims that the father has the capacity to release his son from such an immense debt (1163b23). The father who does so resembles the individual who possesses equity, who does not "demand strict justice," and is able to take less than his due (1137b34–37). The spirit of equity hovers over Aristotle's argument that "friendship seeks what is possible, not what accords with the worth [of the giver or the gift]" (1163b15–16). When Aristotle now mentions the father as cause of his son's birth, rearing, and education, who can "never be repaid for what he has given," he speaks not of the father but of parents, and he speaks not only of parents but also of the gods (1163b15–18, 1162a3–8; cf. 1161a18 and 21). That the father is not the sole benefactor moderates his claim on his son. Although Aristotle argued earlier that the discrepancy between human and divine is too great for there to be friendship between them, he now says, "The friendship of children with parents, and of human beings with gods, is friendship with the good and superior" (1162a5–6). Aristotle thus connects our friendship for the gods to the affection we experience for our parents, who begot, reared, and educated us. Of course, our friendship with the gods cannot include the reciprocity that Aristotle holds exists between friends, for it is "friendship with the superior," and even greater superiors than our parents. Perhaps it could be called piety. At any rate, the father is not the only superior, his superiority to his offspring is an honor he shares with his wife, and they both share it with their superiors, the gods. The father is not the only one who must accept less than his due, and he himself has given less than his due, to his own parents and to the gods, since such debts cannot be repaid.

Although such debts are too great to return what is merited, Aristotle observes, "the equitable person gives back whatever he can" (1163b17–18). Equity, which demands less than its due, must also accept returning less than is due. Family life requires parents (as benefactors) to demand less than their due, and their offspring (as recipients) to accept returning less than they owe. But so too must all human beings, who have parents and who may have children, and who also form friendships in which to various degrees they are both benefactors and beneficiaries.

In explaining that love consists more in loving than in being loved, Aristotle singles out mothers who give up their own children to be raised by others to see them prosper, even when it means that their children cannot render them what is fitting to mothers since they do not know them (1159a26–33). The generosity of such a mother may be directed to her children because they are her own, and Aristotle makes clear that if circumstances permitted, the mother would prefer to receive the return, even the recognition, that mothers ordinarily receive from their children (1159a31). She gives this up for the good of her children, not because she seeks to be the sole giver or the benefactor from whom all goods flow to her children, but because she loves them. She offers proof not only that "friendship consists more in loving than in being loved," but also that out of love one can release another from returning everything that is owed.[22] In this, she serves as a model for fathers, who must come to do just this. If the virtues of women are manifest in "serving," as Aristotle says, while those of men are manifest in "ruling" (*Politics* 1260a24), the mother's expression of her virtues toward their offspring complements her husband's, and each has something to contribute, not merely to each other but to the way in which they express their love for their children. If her love of their offspring can inform his, she shares in her husband's "ruling" virtue by serving, and thereby learns to *rule* in turn. As her husband learns from his wife, his "ruling" comes to partake in sharing, or in ruling *in turn*. Their release of their children from the unpayable debts incurred from birth and

---

22. Cain, "Friendship, Rights, and Community," 142–44, finds in the mother's affection and willingness to release her child from what he owes her "a model for friendship." Ward, *Contemplating Friendship*, 126–29, also offers a subtle discussion of the way in which Aristotle "uses motherhood as the model of what it means to be a friend."

nurturing allows their children's lives to expand beyond their families without having to resort to "father-beating," metaphorically speaking.

One becomes like what one loves, Aristotle says (e.g., 1165b13–17). The virtues of husband and wife who delight in the virtues of the other take on the stamp, so to speak, of what pleases them (1172a13–14). In this and other ways, they prevent each other from erring, as Aristotle says is true of good friends (1159b6–7). Aristotle's account of the friendship between husband and wife offers a model for a correct regime based on a justice proportionate to capacity and worth. It also prepares us for his further discussion of friendship in book 9, where both difference and similarity are necessary for friendship. Aristotle calls a friend "another self." In the family, the manifest difference between husband and wife illustrates that a friend is not just another "self" but "an-other" self (1166a32, 1170b6).[23] Because we love another "self," our self-love extends or overflows into friendship; because we love "an-other" self, our love is not simply a manifestation of self-love. We do not love only ourselves in our friend. He is "other" or "different" from us.

Only with a release from the family can human beings come to develop their potential as political animals. Early in book 9, Aristotle considers debts that are acquired to others outside the family. Multiple debts may be a source of conflict. That we acquire debts outside the family complicates our lives, but such debts are also proof that human life is not exhausted by debts to our family. We also have a debt to our teachers, whom Aristotle brings up in this context (e.g., 1163b25–33). Not our father alone, and not even our father and mother together are the only causes of our education. It is in book 9 that Aristotle discusses "political friendship," the "like-mindedness" (*homonoia*) that exists among fellow citizens (1167a25–30 and 1167b3). He also discusses those who share in the activities they love, including those who "philosophize together" (1172a5). In finding models for regimes within the family in book 8, Aristotle demonstrates what politics owes to the family. Aristotle demonstrates in book 9 how through friendship human life transcends families to include politics and philosophy.

---

23. Frank, *Democracy of Distinction*, 159; Burger, *Aristotle's Dialogue with Socrates*, 182.

GIVING IN RETURN

Debts too great for repayment remain at issue in book 9, but Aristotle adds to the weight of human indebtedness by highlighting friendships we form outside our families. Aristotle begins with "heterogenous" friendships, in which the friends seek different things from the friendship, such as the lover who seeks pleasure, while the beloved seeks profit from their affair, such as gifts and assistance the lover provides (1164a3–6). Such a relationship would fall apart when one or both do not receive what they expect. He gives the examples of a beloved who complains that although his lover promised everything, he does not fulfill his promise, and that of a lover who complains that although he loves beyond measure (*huperphilein*), he is not loved in return (*antiphileisthai*) (1164a3–6).[24] The latter sounds like a father who expects an impossible repayment in kind for what he has given. Aristotle's use of *antiphileisthai* for the love in return that the lover desires, rather than *anteran* (see *Phaedrus* 255d–e), helps us to understand what the lover may not—that the lover is looking for friendship. Aristotle appears to be attempting to turn the attention of lover and beloved, or those who seek advantage or pleasure from the other, to friendship (see Plato, *Lysis* 306b–c, 222b). In friendship, the lover who desires to be loved in return by his beloved would share in the reciprocal loving and being loved characteristic of friends, and the beloved would gain a friend, instead of ending up with nothing of what his lover promised. He too must release (his lover) from debt—accepting that he will not provide everything his love moves him to promise—but both take on debts of a different sort, the reciprocal debts of friends.

Aristotle's next example of disappointed expectations from a relationship also bears on what we can expect of friendship. He gives the example of a musician who is promised pay according to how well he plays, but when he demands payment he is told that he has received pleasure in return for pleasure (1164a20). Because of his need, Aristotle observes, he is intent on receiving pay of the usual sort, and matters are not well executed

---

24. The lover "over-promises," just as he "over-loves." And the beloved tries to hold him to his word. His desires are also excessive. He wants everything from his lover while it escapes his notice that if his lover gave him everything, he himself would have nothing that came from himself, nothing in effect of his own.

when only one of the participants receives his wish (1164a20–21). Aristotle quotes the words of a poet, "a wage for a man" (1164a27). In the work from which he quotes, Hesiod's *Works and Days*, the poet speaks of friends, and even brothers, and recommends not only agreeing to a wage but having a witness for transactions, for "trust and distrust alike destroy men" (Hesiod, *Works and Days* 370–72). Ruin comes from trusting and leads to distrust. The only remedy is fixing a wage and securing a witness.

Aristotle may agree with the poet in the case at hand, and more generally in assigning values to goods that are exchanged in commercial transactions (1133b14–16), but when it comes to friendship he rejects the poet's view, especially on the role of trust. He explains, for example, that as friends come to "know each other," they "appear to the other as worthy of love and become trusted" (1156b25–30). In the passage from *Works and Days*, from which Aristotle quotes, Hesiod also recommends "to become friends with those who are friends, to go to those who come to you, and to give to those who give but not to those who do not (*Works and Days* 353–54). He in effect recommends giving in return, without acknowledging that this cannot take place unless someone gives first. The Graces whom Aristotle describes in book 5 know better. They remind us not only to do good in return but to initiate or begin (*archein*) good deeds (1133a3–6). In the *Theogony*, another work credited to Hesiod, its author mentions the Graces as the daughters of Zeus, but he says nothing about their calling on human beings to initiate giving (*Theogony* 907–11). He does not know as much about them as Aristotle does. Although the musician was offered "pleasure in exchange for pleasure" instead of the wage he desired, and the offer shows (at best) a misunderstanding of the relationship or (at worst) an attempt to avoid paying what one owes, the example points to higher possibilities. In addition to the wage he expected, and indeed might need to meet life's necessities, the musician might derive pleasure in sharing his music, for example, with another who seeks it out.

The disappointed expectations in Aristotle's examples of lover and musician not only warn us against a naïve trust but also hold out hope for friends who have good reasons for trusting. Aristotle moves gradually from caution to hope as his inquiry into friendship proceeds, just as trust itself requires time to develop between friends. In the case of friends, it is difficult to know whether knowing or trusting comes first. Perhaps we should say as Aristotle does of friends that "two go together."

Aristotle next turns to the teacher in his discussion of what the recipient of a benefit owes to the one who conferred it. He notes that the Sophists not only fix their wages for their teaching, but also require that they be paid in advance. Perhaps they must do so, Aristotle playfully remarks, in order to be paid at all, since no one would pay them for what they know (once they were taught it). At another pole is the Sophist Protagoras, who allowed his students to judge the worth of what he taught them, and to pay him accordingly (1164a23–33). In one way, his practice is consistent with his famous teaching: if "man is the measure," each individual is the judge of what is good, and Protagoras should allow his students to judge the worth of his teaching. But, if so, by what expertise could he claim to teach others (see *Theaetetus* 161c–e)? The Sophists who demand payment in advance have a poor judgment of their teaching, and Protagoras's teaching renders him unable to judge it. Protagoras is its measure, but only for himself—and hence not of his worth as a teacher.

Aristotle, in contrast, proceeds to offer his judgment that teachers are among those, like parents and gods, to whom one's debts are so large that no return seems possible, at least he says this is true for "those who share in philosophy" (1164b2–5). Aristotle does not go so far as to claim that the latter are "teachers." Teachers have students, but those who share in philosophy teach and learn from each other, if to different degrees. In such cases, Aristotle advises, the one who benefits must simply make return in whatever way he can (1164b3–6). Whatever the measure, it cannot exceed the possible.

Such receiving beyond measure from so many of course puts a burden on the recipient, one that Aristotle proceeds to highlight by bringing up "the perplexity whether one should render everything to one's father and to obey him in everything." He begins with a case that a father might find difficult to deny, namely, that when someone is sick he should trust a doctor, or when one elects a general he should rely on someone with military skill (1164b22–25). More difficult is the question of whether one should do a service for a friend or for a good person, and should one return a good deed to a benefactor or give something to one's comrade, when both are not possible? Acknowledging the difficulty of general rules in such cases, Aristotle advises merely that "one should not make return of the same things to all people, nor all things even to one's father" (1164b21–29, 1165a3–16).

Indeed, the honors we owe to our father differ from those we owe to our mother, Aristotle observes, and those we owe to our parents differ from those we owe to a general or to a wise person. With the elderly, our comrades, our relatives, those of our clan, and fellow citizens, all of whom Aristotle mentions, our relations become extensive. We "must make the attempt to compare [or, to judge them side by side (*sugkrinein*)], and to give them what is their own or is fitting." If people have similar relations to us, it is easier to compare what we owe them than when their relationships to us differ. In the latter case it is "a greater work" (*ergōdesteron*) (1165a30–33). It is "a greater work" than Aristotle can do for us, for it involves our own relationships, including but beyond those with our family members. Aristotle's observation about this "greater work" we face echoes his definition in book 1 of the human work (*ergon*), which is the activity of our soul, in accordance with virtue. When Aristotle indicates how much our work is bound up with our lives with others, to whom we owe a variety of debts, he also reminds us that it is our work.

Although Aristotle cannot "judge" or "compare" for us, there is one thing Aristotle can say: we should provide sustenance (*trophē*) especially to our parents, and it is "more beautiful [or nobler] to provide for those who are the causes of our being than to provide for ourselves" (1165a22–36). Aristotle earlier mentioned parents as causes not only of our being but of rearing or sustenance (*trophē*) and education (1161a16–17, 1162a6–8). He now advises that we should provide sustenance to our parents. We should provide for them in turn as they advance in years. Moreover, if we provide for our parents before ourselves, we are choosing what Aristotle judges the more beautiful thing, and in this sense becoming a cause of our actions, even though we act in turn, and in return, for all our parents have done for us. Such choices, coming from ourselves, make us co-causes of who we are. That our giving in turn is grounded in our debts to our parents renders our return less an assertion of freedom than an expression of gratitude. Aristotle's proposal that we can do only the possible when we owe so much releases us from the paralysis that might come from overwhelming debts without releasing us from the debts themselves. Rather, his advice asks us to judge and to act.

With our care of our parents, the family has taken its rightful place in the larger context of human life. Moreover, teachers and other caretakers (such as doctors and generals) to whom we may be indebted have appeared in the discussion. We belong not only to our families, but to broader communities of which our families are also parts. Indeed, it is the multiple influences on who we are that allows and even requires our own activity. Our parents are only "joint causes" of our being, just as we ourselves are (Aristotle says) of our own characters (1114b23–25). In other words, when Zeus does not have all the sacrifices, our work becomes the greater at the same time it becomes our own.

It is clear that Aristotle has moved his discussion beyond the family when he turns to what he calls "political friendship." There is a "likemindedness" (*homonoia*) that belongs to fellow citizens who are "of the same mind" about what is advantageous, choose the same things, and do what is resolved in common (1167a27–29). Political communities do not merely reflect friendships. They also expand the scope of friendship. The political friendship of citizens aims at mutual advantage, but it also requires a concern with justice. It exists, Aristotle elaborates, among the equitable (1167b3–9).[25] In the *Politics*, which builds on the *Ethics*, Aristotle objects to those who understand the political community merely as a compact for purposes of commerce or defense. Although the members of such an association should not act unjustly toward one another, they would have no care for citizens becoming good and just (1280a31–b12). The members of a political community would have such care and participate in political friendship at its best.

Aristotle is well aware of the difficulties of maintaining political friendship among citizens. He mentions two cases that exemplify political friendship: "agreeing to conclude an alliance with the Spartans," and "having Pittacus rule when he was willing to do so" (1167a31–32). Athenian history itself, as recounted by Thucydides, shows both conflict and agreement over whether to conclude an alliance with Sparta, and even the need for a Pericles to keep the Athenians on track (e.g., *PW* 1.139, 2.59, 4.21.1–2, 5.43.1–2, 8.70.2–71.1). Pittacus was unwilling to continue to rule

---

25. For helpful accounts of Aristotle's conception of political friendship, see Frank, *Democracy of Distinction*, 16, 149–56; Yack, "Community and Conflict, 92–112, esp. 104–106; Yack, *Problems of a Political Animal*, esp. 125; and Bickford, *The Dissonance of Democracy*, esp. 39–41. See also Ludwig's magisterial work on political friendship and its role in liberal polities, Ludwig, *Rediscovering Political Friendship*.

beyond ten years, even though the Mytilineans wished him to do so,[26] a problem to which Aristotle alludes when he mentions the need for the ruler and the citizens to agree.

Most ominous of all is Aristotle's distinction between the like-mindedness of political friendship and that of two rivals who each has in mind that he himself should rule. They are of like mind and cause civil strife. Aristotle gives the example of Euripides's *Phoenician Women* (1167a21–33). The "like-minded" in this case were the sons of Oedipus, Polyneices and Eteocles, who were of like mind in desiring to rule Thebes, and they fought to their deaths to do so. Their "like-mindedness" makes political friendship impossible. Nor could the relation between these brothers be reflected in the good form of the rule of the many. A good regime must address such conflicts that arise in family life, for example, by structuring shared rule under law to offer opportunities to potential rivals for rule. Aristotle illustrates political friendship with citizens who agree to make political offices elective, for example, and who agree about who should rule (1167a32–33). Families require political communities to minimize potential family quarrels and to offer their members satisfaction through sharing in rule. In the *Politics*, Aristotle alludes to other grave problems that political communities alleviate, patricide and incest, when he points out that they make possible marriages in a larger community, in which new families can be formed (*Politics* 1280b35–36).

Aristotle's hopeful discussion of political friendship suggests a conjunction of self-love and friendship, despite his cautious warnings, including his observation that like-mindedness is impossible for the base, except to a small degree, because they are unable to be friends (1167b9–13). Self-love as an obstacle to friendship remains to be discussed. By the end of book 9, Aristotle offers his profoundest response to this tension, which emerges in families and exists among fellow citizens. He describes friends who know themselves by seeing themselves in each other as they share in the activities they love, and who share their speeches and thoughts. Aristotle moves toward this account of friendship through his examination of self-love, as I proceed to discuss in the next section, and through his exploration of the giving and receiving involved in friendship, as I discuss in the last section of this chapter.

---

26. Burnet, *Ethics of Aristotle*, 417n.

SELF-LOVE

What one owes to oneself as well as to one's friend, Aristotle argues, factors into whether one should remain friends with those who do not remain the same. In cases in which the friends are friends because of utility or pleasure, if either friend no longer serves these ends, the answer is obvious (1165a46–b13). But when a friendship is based on character, and one's friend "becomes corrupt, should one still love him?" One can only love what is lovable, Aristotle observes. Moreover, if one remains friends with someone who has become base, one becomes like him, for one becomes like the one whom one loves. Aristotle refers to the expression "like is friend to like" (1165b13–17). Earlier when Aristotle refers to this saying, the question at issue was the cause of friendship: Do we befriend those like or unlike ourselves? There he dismissed poets and students of nature who fell on one or the other side of this issue looking only at nature rather than at what is distinctively human (1155a33–b9). By doing the latter, Aristotle gives a more complex answer to this question, using the phrase to refer to the effect that friends have on each other. Friends are never simply alike, if they can become so, or more so, through loving. Changing on account of loving a friend could be for the better or the worse. Although there is a danger in remaining friends with one who has become corrupted, one might also help one's friend to become better. Friends "set [a friend] right" (or "correct") (1165b18–19). Although Aristotle recognizes a limit to "setting right," since one's friend might be incurable (1165b22–23), how would one know this before one has attempted to help one's friend?

This question about the dissolution of a friendship also arises, Aristotle explains, in the reverse case, when one friend comes to differ greatly from the other in virtue. Should the one who grows in virtue continue to treat the other as a friend? Aristotle gives the example of a friend who develops into an excellent human being, whereas his childhood friend remains a child in his understanding. In such a case, Aristotle admits, friendship would be difficult, since they would no longer be delighted and pained by the same things. And yet one should remember the friendship, and "render something to those who were once friends, unless the dissolution [of the friendship] occurs through an excess of wickedness" (1165b23–37). We even might suppose that the more one comes to surpass one's friend in virtue, the more would one become able to help one's friend, and obligated to render what one can, even if one can no longer "live together" as friends (1165b31). Our obligations to our friends in all these cases, great though they may be, find limits in what is good for ourselves.

Our love of our friend, Aristotle explains, is an extension of our love for ourselves. The marks by which friendships are defined "seem to have arisen from what pertains to oneself" (1166a1–2). Just as one wishes good for oneself, for example, one wishes good for one's friend; one is of the same mind with oneself, as one is with one's friend; and one (at least who is good) wishes to spend time with himself, as he does with his friend (1166a11–17, 24). A friend "stands in relation to his friend as he does to himself, for a friend is another self" (1166a31–32). Aristotle uses an expression similar to the one we have seen him apply to the relation between parents and children: one's offspring are like "other selves" (1161b28). But if parents extend their love of themselves to their children (since their children come from themselves), why would one extend one's love of oneself to a friend? Why would one love "another" self? If one's friend is "of the same mind" as oneself, what would one's friend have to contribute (1169b3–7; also *Lysis* 214e–215c)? What could our friend give us that we do not already have? If we wish to spend time with ourselves, because we are good, why would we wish to spend time with anyone else? Some say that we should love most the one who is most our friend, Aristotle observes, but the one most our friend is the one who most wishes our good, and this is found most in one's relation to oneself. One seems therefore to be one's own best friend, and so one should love oneself most (1168a28–b11).

Aristotle sheds light on this difficulty when he turns to benefactors, whose self-love leads them to love another. Some benefactors love those whom they benefit even more than their recipients love their benefactors. Some say that a person loves to be benefited, and when one benefits another, one expects one's beneficiary to render benefit in turn. Aristotle points out, however, that some benefactors love those whom they benefit even when there is no expectation of return. They are similar, he says, to craftsmen who love what they make, to poets who are fond of their own (*oikeia*) poems, and to parents who love their children as extensions of themselves. In all such cases, they love life, and life is activity (*energeia*). It is not only that they love what they make, but through their activity they become the one they have the potential of becoming. Just as poets live in their work, benefactors live in their good deeds. Aristotle's reflections on benefactors shed light on why friendship consists more in loving than in being loved (1167b28–1168a21). We live or exist in our activity, and loving is more active than being loved.

Aristotle does not rest his account here, however, for he points out that artisans would love their work more than their work would love them if it were to come to life, literally, if it were to become "ensouled" (1167b34–1168a1). But if it became "ensouled," could it simply be the work of another? If "ensouled," it would have the potential to act itself, to become what it is potentially through its own activity. Children, in any case, are alive, and Aristotle pointed out in his discussion of the family the lack of reciprocity between parents and offspring. So too a benefactor's recipients are alive. Self-love in the case of benefactors may account for love of their beneficiaries, insofar as their beneficiaries are extensions of themselves, manifestations of their own activity. Human beings who love another as an extension of themselves have a problem that artisans do not—the other whom they love is not merely another "self" but an "other" self. To love an "other" self requires something more than self-love. To state the obvious—which is not to explain it—friendship requires loving another, unlike the craftsman and poet to whom Aristotle appeals. This may be why Aristotle used a verb that indicates excess when describing poets' fondness (*huperagapan*) for his poems, for such self-love may give them a sense of self-sufficiency that thwarts their loving another.

The problem that self-love poses for friendship becomes even clearer in Aristotle's description of the "true self-lovers who love the beautiful [or noble]" and "assign the greater part of the beautiful to themselves," and by implication a part greater than they assign to their friends. When noble self-lovers give up money, offices, and honors so that their friends will have more of such goods, they secure the greater nobility for themselves. Finally, they stand back so that their friends can act, for "it is more beautiful to be the cause of their friends' deeds than to do them themselves" (1169a18–35). Even if their self-love were truly noble—and they did not simply delude themselves about their nobility by allowing their friends to risk their lives while they stay out of the fighting[27]—Aristotle's description

---

27. Aristotle alludes to Achilles, who sends Patroclus to fight in his place. When Patroclus dies in battle, however, does Achilles achieve greater nobility

reveals the difficulty in their friendship. On the one hand, noble self-lovers rise above self-interest in any narrow sense, in giving so much to their friends. On the other, they take for themselves the greater good, the greater nobility. But suppose their friends also want to do beautiful deeds, to secure for themselves the most beautiful or noblest things, and hence to be the cause of their friend's action more than to act themselves. "After you," they say to each other, as they stand before the beautiful deed, and each deferring to the other and both remaining at a standstill. Whereas the like-minded sons of Oedipus, who want to rule, do act, and they kill each other, the like-minded lovers of beauty yield to each other, and there is no action at all. But human happiness, as Aristotle defines it, lies in the *activity* of virtue (1097b29–31). Aristotle prepares us for this difficulty by his earlier description of friendships based on virtue: virtuous friends "compete" in benefiting the other, and they "retaliate" a good deed by doing one in turn, for "one who surpasses in doing good obtains his aim" (1162b6–12, 1169a8).[28] Does friendship remain anything more than a useful convenience for human beings who "most of all" love themselves?

GIVING AND RECEIVING FRIENDSHIP

Aristotle begins his explanation of why the good need friends for happiness by reminding us that happiness is an activity (not a possession), and that the activity of a good person is itself good and pleasant. However, we are better able to see those near us than ourselves and to see their actions

---

because he is the cause of Patroclus's noble deed? In any case, Achilles and Patroclus do not "go together" into battle. Once again, the Homeric heroes are not Aristotle's models for friends. When Aristotle describes the noble self-lover who "chooses to live nobly for one year over living haphazardly for many years" (1169a23–24), he reminds of Achilles's choice of a short but noble life over a long life without glory.

28. Cropsey, "Justice and Friendship," 271–72, infers from this apparent conflict between two noble friends that "nobility goes far but does not succeed in perfecting the paradigm of friendship" and that philosophic friends replace them in Aristotle's reflections on the best friendships. Pangle, *Aristotle and the Philosophy of Friendship*, 183–97, goes even further insofar as she suggests that the conflict faced by the noble self-lovers infects friendship more generally for Aristotle, who therefore "refuses to put friendship at the very center of the best life."

better than our own. "The person who is blessed" will therefore need friends who are good, "if he chooses to contemplate actions that are good and his own" (1169b28–1170a3). Once again, Aristotle suggests that activities alone are not sufficient for happiness, but one must also be aware of them. But now he directs that awareness to the activities of a friend that Aristotle claims are "one's own."

Why, however, does seeing one's friend's good actions not yield awareness of another's happiness rather than of one's own?[29] Moreover, if one who is blessed needs another "to contemplate actions that are good and his own," why must that other be his friend? That is, if another's actions are one's own insofar as they are good, why would they be one's own any more than the actions of any good person? But Aristotle is not speaking simply of good actions, but those of friends.

Aristotle helps with this difficulty when he observes that "it is not easy to be active continuously by oneself, whereas it is easier to do so with others and in relation to others" (1170a5–7). Activities can be performed more continuously with another than when engaging in them alone. If sharing activity can prolong it, we become the cause of our friend's acting over time, just as he is the cause of our doing so. To cause our friend's activity, we cannot hold back from acting. It is acting together that prolongs activity. We must act together. Unlike the case of parents and children, in which the former are the cause and the latter the effect, friends are at the

---

29. Questioning whether the actions of one's friend can ever be one's own "except in a weak and derivative sense," Pangle, *Aristotle and the Philosophy of Friendship*, 187–89, argues that Aristotle's account of friendship applies to the young and immature, for "people are often more inclined to claim others as their own, or rest upon the laurels of others, or try to live through others, than is reasonably justified." Her interpretation assumes that "the most blessed, being wisest," have a "more sensible recognition of their own separateness." When Aristotle "includes such factors [as contemplating oneself in the activities of one's friend] even in his final statement on the goodness of friendship, she understands this as "evidence" that friendship has more to do with the ascent to the best life than with the best life itself. Aristotle's inclusion of just such factors as contemplating oneself in the activities of a friend, however, strikes me as evidence that Aristotle understands friendship to belong to the best life and not merely to the ascent toward it, at least if self-knowledge belongs to the best life. The difference in our readings turns on whether we consider the best life for human beings to be a self-sufficient one.

same time cause and effect. They are benefactor and beneficiary, each assisting the other in acting. They both give and receive. They see themselves in their friends' activity—and therefore in their lives—not merely because they are like their own, but also because they are in part the cause of their activity and life. By the same token, they can also see their friends in their own lives and activities, because their friends are in part their cause.

Aristotle says more specifically what friends give and receive from each other when he turns to a "more natural" (*phusikōteron*) account of human beings. He refers not to the theories of students of nature and poets who look to the heavens and the earth for a natural explanation of friendship (cf. 1170a14 with 1155b1–8), nor to the physiologists who say that life is toil—and hence painful—even ordinary perceptions like seeing and hearing until one becomes accustomed to them (1154b8–10). Aristotle refers instead to those whose natural account distinguishes humans from other animals. They "define living in the case of animals as a capacity for perception, whereas they define living for human beings as a capacity for perception or thought" (1170a16–17). Aristotle is among those who do so (*Eudemian Ethics* 1244b23–26; *De Anima* 413b1–2, 414b18–19; *On Sleep and Waking* 455b22–24). He then adds that we perceive that we see when we see, we perceive that we hear when we hear, and we perceive that we walk when we walk. Since we exist in our activity, as Aristotle told us when discussing benefactors (1168a7), to perceive our activity is to perceive our own existence: "Perceiving that one lives belongs among those things pleasant in themselves, for life is by nature a good thing" (1170b1–2). "There is something [in us] that perceives that we are active," Aristotle says (1170a33). But it does not necessarily do so. Thales, at least, was reputed to be so eager to see the things in the heavens that he did not perceive that he was walking right into a pit in the way of his feet (Plato, *Theaetetus* 174a).

What is this something that perceives that we are acting, and what activates our using it? Why does perceiving sights or sounds give us a perception of ourselves as seeing and hearing? How do we become an object for ourselves?[30] Do we perceive that we are walking—or that we are per-

---

30. Aristotle speaks in *De Anima* of our perceiving that we perceive. He asks there whether it is by sight or by another sense that we perceive that we see. He presents perplexities with both answers, such as the difficulty of an infinite

ceiving and thinking—or do we only suppose that we are? How do we know that we aren't deceiving ourselves? We would have greater assurance if we had a walking companion who affected the direction or other circumstances of our walk, or a friend whose perceptions and thoughts affected our own. We may not feel the need to rest from our walk, for example, but we rest—or speed up or slow down—when our companion asks to do so. We become aware that we are thinking when we think thoughts that do not originate with us but come from another who shares them with us. We know ourselves as acting when we know that our doing so involves another who affects on our activity. The god's command on the temple at Delphi to know oneself leads Aristotle in the *Ethics* to discuss not only the virtues but also friendship. To know oneself, even or especially as someone who thinks, requires knowing another like oneself, someone who also thinks, who affects one's own thinking and whose thoughts one affects in turn.

That friendship provides the opportunity for self-awareness, that is, of oneself as a being who perceives and thinks, is borne out by Aristotle's describing friends as "perceiving together" (*sunaisthanesthai*) (1170b5). He

---

regress if a sense other than sight were required to see that we are seeing (418a8–20, 425b11–25). He says more in *On Sleep and Waking* about what perceives perceiving when he describes the work of what he calls there "some part common [*koinon*] to all the senses," "one sense that is sovereign over all the sense [organs]." The tasks that he attributes to this "common-sense" include perceiving sensibles, such as motion and rest that are common to more than one sense, distinguishing the sensibles peculiar to a specific sense organ from one another, such as white from sweet, and forming images of what we perceive that we store in memory. It is to this common sense that Aristotle attributes the task of perceiving that we are perceiving (454b13–27). This versatile part of our soul appears to connect our knowing with the objects we know (since it allows us to store them in memory), and our sensing with our thinking. As Roochnik, *Retrieving Aristotle*, 129, observes with some understatement, this "common-sense has a variety of responsibilities." Aristotle's account of the "common-sense" reflects his understanding of the bounty of nature that is not so stingy when it comes to human beings that it restricts one of their capacities to only one thing (*Parts of Animals* 687a2–b25; see *Politics* 1252b2–5). In any case, *On Sleeping and Waking* hardly resolves the perplexity of what moves us to perceive that we perceive, even if it locates our capacity to do so.

apparently coined this word for the purpose of describing friends.[31] The preposition *sun* (syn) added to a verb often indicates acting "with" another, as in "hunting together" (*sugkunēgein*), "exercising together" (*suggumnazein*), and "playing games together" (*sugkubeuein*), all shared activities Aristotle soon mentions (1172a4–6). The "perceiving together" that belongs to friends, then, means perceiving something together with one's friend, who is also perceiving it. But how does this give us any perception of ourselves? Moreover, Aristotle's coinage cannot mean merely that one perceives something at the same time as one's friend does. We might perceive a sunset at the same time as another, for example, or think that two and two equals four at the same time that another does so. If knowing or perceiving at the same time were all that is required for "the living together" characteristic of friendship, Aristotle could not proceed to argue that this requirement of friendship limits the number of friends whom we should seek (1171a1–2). Indeed, in the *Eudemian Ethics*, he argues that the activity of perceiving together itself limits the number of friends (1245b22–24). But there is no limit to the number of people who can perceive the sunset at the same time, or who know that two plus two equals four. However, there is a limit on the number who can go on a walk together and affect its circumstances. Why is perceiving together more like going on a walk together than perceiving a sunset at the same time as others?

"Perceiving together" can refer not only to perceiving something together with another but perceiving two things together, as when Aristotle uses *sugkrinein* to mean "to judge two things together" or "side by side," or "to compare" (e.g., 1165a30–33). Following this pattern, "to perceive together" could also mean to perceive two things together or at the same time. That Aristotle uses "perceiving together" to do double duty appears from his observing that one "perceives together with one's friend that [one's friend] exists" (1170a10–11). That is, one perceives one's friend *and*

---

31. The word is rare in extant Greek literature, found primarily in Aristotle's texts, and primarily in the context of his describing friends. Aristotle uses it in his treatment of friendship in the *Eudemian Ethics*, for example, where he also uses "knowing together" (*suggnorizein*) and "theorizing together" (*suntheōrein*) to describe what friends do together (1244b25, 1245b5). For helpful discussions of Aristotle's understanding of "sunaisthetic friendship," see Kosman, "Aristotle on the Desirability of Friends," 135–54; Flakne, "Embodied and Embedded," 37–63; and especially Heyking, *Form of Politics*, 35–56.

that he is one's friend. So does one's friend, since friendship is reciprocal. Together friends perceive themselves together, as friends.³² Aristotle makes clear how this self-awareness comes about: Whereas Aristotle says that "living" for a human being means perceiving and thinking, he says that "living *together*" (*suzēn*) for human beings means "sharing in a community of *speeches* and thought" (1170b12–13, 1171a1–3).³³ He includes speeches as well as thoughts. Friends share perceptions and thoughts by *speaking* to each other, and hence perceive another who both gives and receives in the "living together" characteristic of friendship.³⁴

In sharing their perceptions and thoughts through their conversing, friends become aware of what they give to and receive from each other, and hence that they are cause and effect, as their own perceptions and thoughts become reflected in those of their friend, and their friend's perceptions and thoughts become reflected in their own. Insofar as we give to our friend, we become aware of our friend's need and incompleteness. Insofar as we receive from our friend, we become aware of our own need and incompleteness (see *Eudemian Ethics* 1245a16–17). We saw earlier in Aristotle's discussion of the virtues that we also come to know ourselves as incomplete when our attempts to know fall short and when we fail to rule ourselves. However, to be aware of one's incompleteness and limits is not sufficient for self-knowledge. Perceiving that we give—and seeing

---

32. Kahn, "Aristotle on Altruism," 35, 37–39, argues that because for Aristotle one's true self is one's mind, which when active "must be one and the same for all human beings," to know oneself is necessarily the same as knowing one's friend. But Aristotle suggests not that knowing oneself entails knowing another, but that knowing another (one's friend) entails knowing oneself. Moreover, Kahn's explanation would mean that knowing oneself entails knowing any other human beings who use their minds. When Aristotle says that a friend is "another self," however, his use of *heteros* for "other" connotes difference. The friends whom Kahn describes, finally, would be of no use to each other (1169b7–8). For further discussion of Kahn's argument, see Flakne, "Embodied and Embedded," 41–42, 44.

33. Consider Aristotle's question in discussing friendship in the *Eudemian Ethics*: "What differences does it make if eating together and drinking together take place when we are near or apart, if one takes away speech?" (1245a13–15).

34. When in the *De Anima* Aristotle leaves open how we perceive that we perceive, he does not mention "perceiving *together*," as he does in the *Ethics*. Aristotle appears in this case to work out in the *Ethics* a problem he left hanging in *De Anima*. See Flakne, "Embodied and Embedded," 37.

through our conversations that our friend receives what we give—makes us aware of ourselves as cause, while our friend's doing so for us makes us aware that he too is a cause. We know that we exist because we see our activity in our friend whom we have affected, much as do benefactors in their beneficiary, and we know that our friend exists when we see his effect on us, much as do beneficiaries who see what they have received from their benefactor. Friends are both benefactor and beneficiary.[35]

As Aristotle says near the end of his discussion of friendship, "the perception a person has about himself—that he exists—is choiceworthy" and "arises [for friends] from their living together." Indeed, friends strive for this (1171b34–1172a1). And, as Aristotle also says, "existence is choiceworthy because of a person's perception that he is good" (1170b10). That is why self-knowledge comes from sharing perceptions and thoughts not with just any human being but with a friend, someone who loves one for one's goodness and whose goodness one loves. As Kass summarizes, "Aristotle brings us to understand that virtue is essential to friendship, friendship as essential to self-consciousness, and self-consciousness as essential to happiness."[36]

When Aristotle says that we are most of all our thinking, the thinking he has in mind belongs to someone who lives in time, for it includes "memories of what has been done" and "good hopes for the future," and thus we are well supplied with objects for thought (1166a23–26). Living with friends especially provides us with such memories and hopes. Friendships have "beginnings" in time, Aristotle indicates, when he says that

---

35. Burger, *Aristotle's Dialogue with Socrates*, 182, also emphasizes Aristotle's reference to sharing in speeches as well as thoughts, which suggests the dialogic relation between friends. She argues that "sharing speeches and thoughts is motivated by and at the same time produces an awareness of one's partial perspective or incompleteness; it introduces into friendship the possibility of some kind of longing, which the friendship of those simply good as originally conceived seemed to preclude." Flakne, who also emphasizes the importance of speaking for shared awareness, captures the other side of my argument (that by sharing in speeches and thoughts friends become aware of their giving as well as of their receiving) when she argues that in Aristotle's account the sense of self that emerges from friendship supports human agency and choice. See Flakne, "Embodied and Embedded," 40, 43–45, 46–47, 49, and 56.

36. Kass, "Professor or Friend?," 26.

"good will" is the "beginning" of friendship. Friendship develops from "forming habits together" (*sunētheia*) (1166b33–35). Friendships take time. When we see our friend, we remember the past in which our friendship has begun and developed and the future in which we hope our friendship continues to exist and flourish. The thoughts and speeches even of friends who "philosophize together" include memories and hopes, memories of shared conversations, problems solved, impasses reached, and hopes for future progress. Friendship reminds those who love wisdom that their pursuit of the timeless and eternal itself occurs in time.

Those who live in time will be subject to the joys and sorrows that come with changes in fortune. Friends share not only memories and hopes, but also joys and sorrows that belong to human life. This sharing, too, Aristotle notes, indicates a limit on the number of one's friends, for it would be difficult to rejoice with one and at the same time sorrow with another (1171a7–9). Aristotle further underscores the temporal character of human life when he asks whether one needs friends more in good fortune or bad. The problem of the friend who prefers to do good deeds rather than to receive benefits surfaces for one more consideration now in the context of good and bad fortune (1117b17, 25–26; see also 1124b10–13). It is beautiful or noble to benefit another but not to seek benefits, Aristotle observes again (1171b17, 25). Someone who desired to benefit his friend would be eager to share his own good fortune with him, but he would hesitate to share his suffering with him, since he would derive comfort while causing his friend pain. His friend, on the other hand, hesitates to receive his friend's bounty, especially if he is unable to reciprocate, while he wants to comfort his suffering friend even though he will be pained for his friend's sake (1171a34–b28). They both want to give and not to receive. In good times and bad, noble friends run away from the friend running toward him. And when are times neither good nor bad? The difficulty of two "going together" remains.

Aristotle suggests a way through the impasse when he distinguishes "manly types" from "women and men who are like them." Whereas manly types do not want others to grieve with them, women and those like them, in contrast, take comfort or even derive joy when they share their grief with others, and they love as friends those with whom they share their grief (1171b4–13). They allow their friends to do the beautiful thing—to come to their relief and to share their suffering (1171b5–6). Friendship is receiving as much as it is giving. Able to share their own suffering with their friends, they are presumably able to share the good fortunes of their friends. In this too, they receive from their friend. That the giving of the manly lovers of the beautiful should be imitated, and that its giving is essential to friendship is easy to see. It is less easy to see that receiving is an equally necessary expression of loving.

Drawing to a close his discussion of manly types and of women and men like them, Aristotle says merely that "one must imitate the better in all things" (1171b12). Unlike Socrates in the *Republic*, who relegates lamentations to "women—and not to serious ones among them—and to all bad men" (387e–388a), Aristotle does not say explicitly which is better. He does conclude, however, that "being with friends is to be chosen in every case" (1171b29).[37]

One cannot choose to be with friends in their good fortunes and in one's own misfortunes unless one is willing to receive benefits from one's friend. After saying that one must imitate the better, Aristotle offers advice that if followed would moderate a manly desire to give pleasure without causing pain, namely, to "to summon friends when they will be put to little trouble and yet will greatly benefit oneself," for one who "refuses aid" from another could be thought "unpleasant." Conversely, "it is fitting to cooperate eagerly in a friend's good fortunes, for even in these there is need for friends" (1171b18–26). Even the one who prospers is in need. The giver needs a recipient in order to give, and therefore the latter gives too. That is why it is "more beautiful and more pleasant *for both parties*" (1171b24) when one benefits a friend in need without waiting to be summoned. This is Aristotle's last word on the beautiful in his discussion of friendship, and he links it with pleasure rather than with pain. If manly types could learn from women and men like them, friends would go to each other in times of both good fortune and bad. They would remain

---

37. Assuming it from the context, Rackham, *Aristotle's Nicomachean Ethics*, 571, translates "one must imitate the better in all things" as "we must copy the example of the man of nobler nature." The man of nobler nature, however, would not choose to be with his friends in every case, for example, when his own pain would cause them pain. Aristotle does give an answer, even if he leaves it implicit (see also 1161a23–25 and *Politics* 1278a28–30). Nor does Rackham's translation of Aristotle's "women and such men [i.e., who are like them]" as "weak women and womanish men" help us to follow Aristotle's point (ibid.).

subject to chance, but they would enrich its good turns and lessen the sufferings of its bad ones. Once again, the work of time gives opportunities for the work of friendship.[38]

Aristotle thus brings his discussion back around to a way that "like to like" works in friendship, if friends learn from each other to share in giving and receiving. He concludes that the friendship of the good (*epieikeis*) grows through their association, and they themselves become better, "by engaging in activity together and correcting each other" and they "take an impress from the other of what pleases them" (1172a14). Aristotle is not describing two human beings who are perfectly alike, since they can grow more alike through loving, nor two perfectly good human beings, since they benefit from correction by the other. But they can become more like what they love, and they are able to become better.[39] This is the last point that Aristotle makes in his discussion of friendship. Friends see themselves in each other, then, not only because they share in the same activities, but because they themselves play a part in their friend's becoming good. We see our deeds in those of our friend, not merely because they are like ours, but because we are in part their cause, as they are of ours. The goodness of friends cannot therefore be measured merely by a good that is the same in each of them, but rather by the ways in which they contribute to their friend's goodness, and the ways in which they respond to their friend, both in accepting correction and changing in the course of loving and being loved.[40]

---

38. Without the experiences of women and men like them, the difficulties in friendship carry the day. Aristotle's account of friendship suggests ways to minimize those difficulties. Pangle, *Aristotle and the Philosophy of Friendship*, 194–95, in contrast, emphasizes them, describing "the fissures that lie beneath the surface of ordinary friendship," pointing out that though the noble friend feels pain from a friend's misfortune, the noble friend also "welcomes" it, since it is the occasion for acting as a benefactor. It is therefore "not in the sharing either of fortune's blows or fortune's smiles that friendship is in fact at its best." Rather, Aristotle advocates a life of Socratic wisdom, in which there is "little mourning of misfortune, whether one's own or another's, and indeed little rejoicing at good fortune, since so little is required of fortune." See also Cropsey, "Justice and Friendship," 273.

39. See the account in Heyking, *Form of Politics*, 53.

40. Kosman, "Aristotle on the Desirability of Friends," 148, is surely correct when he observes: "That my friend enjoys a similarity of kinship with me is true

Such a friendship of "two [who] go together," as Aristotle has brought it to light, is one that the whole range of friendships is able to reflect, however much and in whatever ways they seek mutual advantage, pleasure, and the good, as all human beings do. These include the friendships within families in which human lives and friendships begin, and in political communities, where like-mindedness might (or might not) keep in check the likes of Polyneices and Eteocles. Such would-be rulers must always be kept in check. Rule remains. The loving and being loved that friendship makes possible, on the other hand, cannot be adequately understood in the political terms of ruling and being ruled. As Aristotle says at the beginning of his discussion of friendship, friends have no need of justice (1155a27).

Aristotle concludes, "Let this much be said about friendship. It follows to discuss pleasure" (1172a15–16). This will be his first topic of book 10. Aristotle has already discussed pleasure (in book 7) in the context of his examination of lack of self-rule, and suggested that the pleasures of a human being, his condition being defective, would always be mixed with pain, in contrast with the unmixed and enduring pleasure of the god (1154b21–32). But then he had not yet spoken of friendship. His treatment of friendship is replete with references to its pleasures and with explanations of human life as good and pleasant (e.g., 1170a7, 19–20, 27–29; 1170b1–2). It therefore "follows" that Aristotle should provide another examination of pleasure and allow us to see in it an expansion of his earlier one, an expansion that presents a more positive view of the pleasures available to human beings.

In book 10, Aristotle also returns to the question of human happiness, and the activity in which it consists, contrasting theoretical activity with political activity. The gods also return as models for human beings in book 10, not only in their theoretical activity but also as benefactors for those most like themselves. Aristotle's final statement in the *Ethics* of the human work most conducive to happiness is an imitation of such gods that in-

---

and of interest in so far as he enables the enlargement of my being, not in so far as he replicates and objectifies it." Aristotle makes the point that friends give and receive correction in the *Rhetoric*, their give-and-take perhaps lightened by their friendship: those with whom we wish to be friends "are dexterous in teasing and enduring it," and "able to makes jests and to accept them agreeably" (1381a33–35).

volves "theorizing and judging" regimes and laws, which are beautiful or noble and which are not, what preserves and what destroys cities, and why some regimes are governed beautifully and others not (1181b8–21). In book 10, therefore, Aristotle's teaching about the gods goes hand in hand with his political teaching: In heightening our awareness of the gods and how and to what extent we can imitate them, he unites the models of friendship that he has developed in books 8 and 9 with the vision of citizenship and statesmanship that he will articulate in the work to follow on politics. Even so, the limits of human friendship, to say nothing of the limits of political life, teach us how far our approximations to divinity are from the divine itself. Our piety is manifest in both our attempts at those approximations that elevate human life and in our acceptance of our distance from the divine that protects it.

CHAPTER 8

Divine Thoughts and Political Reform

Summing Up and Moving Forward (Book 10)

In this chapter, I examine Aristotle's final word on happiness in the *Ethics*, emphasizing throughout the range of activities that he incorporates into his understanding of human happiness and the interconnections among them. In book 10, Aristotle recapitulates some of his main points about happiness. He gives the greatest attention to pleasure, theory, and politics, discussing each in turn, and thus revisits the three ways of life that he brought up in book 1 (the life of pleasure, the political life, and the theoretical life) as contenders for the best (1095b15–19). Drawing together previous discussions, book 10 seems designed to help us to assess what different aspects of human life contribute to our happiness. We expect that Aristotle will provide a conclusive answer to the governing question of the *Ethics* as a whole: What is human happiness and what is the best way of life to achieve it?

Aristotle's culminating discussion, however, does not provide a definitive answer to that question as originally posed as a choice between three contenders. Building on his argument throughout the *Ethics*, he now speaks less of different ways of life (*bioi*) than of different activities that are good, and suggests that pleasure, theorizing, and politics *all* belong in different ways to every human life. Human lives partake of many goods, including ethical and intellectual virtues, and the pleasures that accompany them. They are the pleasures of a composite being (*suntheton*), whose virtues are characteristically human (1178a9–23).

In the first part of book 10, on pleasure, Aristotle criticizes understandings of pleasure that neglect what is distinctly human in our experience of pleasure. He mentions a range of activities belonging to a composite and temporal being that provide pleasure without pain, including some related to sense perception and also learning, memories, and hopes (1173b16–19). Far from contrasting human life and its fleeting pleasures with the simple everlasting pleasure of the god, as he does in book 7, he attributes to pleasure itself an experience of wholeness, even timelessness, even as pleasure is experienced by human beings whose lives are measured by time (1174a15–b13, 1177b24–26). Pleasure emerges as a good belonging to a full human life, and, indeed, a blessing or grace that accompanies a life lived well. I discuss Aristotle's treatment of pleasure in the first section of this chapter.

We evaluate pleasures by their contribution to happiness. But, again, what constitutes happiness? In the second part of book 10, Aristotle offers a "recapitulation" of his argument about happiness. Among "those activities chosen for their own sake" are those "in accord with virtue," he summarizes, using words that describe the ethical virtues that have played a prominent role in his *Ethics*. Instead of proceeding to his discussion of theoretical activity or contemplation, however, he brings up play, since its pleasures are also chosen for their own sake (1176b9). He thus interrupts his summary with a brief discourse on play, which therefore serves as an interlude between his reference to the ethical virtues, "beautiful and serious" activities, which are chosen for their own sake, and the "activity of the intellect," which because it is contemplative "is held to be superior in seriousness" (1176b7–10, 1177b21). Play is the opposite of seriousness.

Since Aristotle had not previously discussed play in relation to happiness, it cannot be part of his "recapitulation" (literally, his "taking up again what has been said previously") (1176a33). Aristotle has moved outside his work, or rather brought something new into it. His path from the ethical activities to theory has been brought to a standstill with play, much like the chorus of a classical Greek comedy, who in the play's "parabasis" (literally, "going to the side of" or "going outside of") interrupts the action of the play to speak to the audience directly. The parabasis seems independent of the action, while it typically speaks about the drama as a whole and the playwright's intention (e.g., Aristophanes, *Clouds* 518–62). Even though it moves outside, the parabasis is a part of the comedy. So too play, I argue, may seem separate from the serious work of life, but it belongs essentially to human life, sustaining and even elevating it. Although play is an activity undertaken for relaxation so that we can return to our serious work (1176a34), it is also a manifestation—and celebration—of the freedom without which neither the ethical nor the intellectual virtues would be possible. Neither would philosophy. Aristotle's inclusion of a discussion of play and seriousness in this section on happiness, I also argue, points to the place of both in the activity of philosophy. In the second section of this chapter, I discuss Aristotle's unexpected treatment of play.

Moving from play to theoretical activity, Aristotle seems about to offer the thematical discussion of the theoretical life, which in book 1 he deferred until later (1096a5). Only after using "theorize" to refer to myriad human activities throughout the *Ethics* does Aristotle focus his discussion on theorizing. Again, he identifies us "most of all" with our minds, which are "something divine present in us" (1177b8, 1178a9, 1166a23–24). Contrary to many readings, which understand Aristotle to elevate the life of the mind over the active life of politics and ethical virtue (see 1178a9), I argue that Aristotle finds the theoretical activity that belongs to humans at their best, who are "composite beings" (1178a22), in a range of activities. His references to "theorizing" throughout the *Ethics*, both in his own activities and those of others, suggest that the *Ethics* is as much a theoretical work as it is a practical one, or rather that thinking (*noiein*) and acting (*prattein*) "go together."

So much does the *Ethics* culminate in a conjunction of theory and practice in a good life that Aristotle even attributes both to the activity of the gods, when he imagines them doing good deeds in turn (*antieupoiein*) for those most kin to themselves. These are the ones whose lives show that they cherish and honor what is most divine in themselves, their minds, and thereby act "correctly and beautifully." Consequently, they are most loved by the gods (*theophilestatoi*) (1179a23–30). The gods too are subject to the benign influence of the Graces. In Aristotle's formulation here, human beings initiate their good deeds in return not by benefiting them directly, but by living up to the highest of which they are capable, by imitating the gods as they are able. It is almost as if Aristotle has imagined human beings who by honoring what is divine in themselves, their minds, and by acting correctly and beautifully in accordance with it, move others, the gods no less, by being loved (cf. *Metaphysics* 1072b4–5). Since he does not offer evidence of such divine beneficence, or even give an example of what he might mean by it, he leaves that beneficence as a hope, grounded in what he has discovered about the human and therewith about a cosmos that human beings can make their home. Aristotle wishes, in other words, that what he has discovered in human life reflects the highest level of being, or that the human is truly not the best in the cosmos. If so, we have cause for confidence, for we are akin to what is greater than ourselves, and cause for deference to what is greater than ourselves. For Aristotle, caution comes along with encouragement: it is only "likely" (*eikos*) that the one "dearest to the gods" is the happiest (1179a30–32).

When Aristotle returns in the last part of book 10 to politics and its role in human life, his move might be considered a descent—from the theoretical activity that is the highest that humans can attain—to the necessities required for life itself. Such a reading finds evidence in Aristotle's contrast between those who can be persuaded by speeches about virtue and the many who live by their passions and lack experience of the beautiful and the good, and who consequently must be checked by laws with force behind them (1179b5–19). As we shall see, however, Aristotle turns to politics not simply because of the limitations of the many. In the first place, he reiterates that the statesman "wishes to make others *better* through his care, *whether many or few*" (1180b23–26). His role is not only to check, but to improve, and not only the many but the few, presumably those who are able to be persuaded by speeches such as Aristotle's. Aristotle directs the statesman's care to both the many and the few.

Moreover, only by theorizing about politics "might the philosophy concerning human affairs be completed," if only "as far as it is possible" (1181b13–15). What pertains to lawgiving and politics has not yet been discovered, Aristotle points out, either by the statesmen who are active in politics without being able to give an account of it or to teach it, or by the Sophists, who claim to teach but lack the requisite political experience. Neither experience nor arguments alone are sufficient for understanding politics or guiding it toward the good. Nevertheless, Aristotle says once again that we must "make the attempt" or "acquire the experience" (1180b24), presumably an experience that can culminate in teaching, unlike that of the statesmen Aristotle mentions, who have experience but who cannot teach.

Aristotle teaches how to construct such edifices or regimes in which human beings can live and flourish. The proof that this is possible will come from the attempt, the experience. The pursuit of knowledge about politics requires the philosopher to act politically, in his urging human beings to rule themselves. Only then can he come to know what human beings can accomplish, by ruling themselves especially in politics, with its far-reaching consequences, and in his own case by his encouraging them to do so by his teachings about virtue, friendship, and pleasure. Of course, only time can tell, and Aristotle must therefore leave his work in outline, for others to fill in. Unlike an unmoved mover, Aristotle moves by loving, with a love that demands that those who are benefited then benefit others in turn. This is why beneficence belongs to philosophy, not as a virtue "in addition," but essential to its pursuit of the truth. Aristotle concludes by announcing a further work that will contribute to political reform by showing, for example, "why some regimes are beautifully governed and others not" and "what sort of regime is best" (1181b20). As he also said at the outset, to secure and preserve the good for cities or nations is more complete than doing so for one alone. As much as we should cherish the latter good, the former is "more beautiful and more divine" (1094b8–11). It is a task that Aristotle himself undertakes.

PLEASURE

At the end of his discussion of friendship, Aristotle says that it remains to speak about pleasure. Although he has discussed pleasure at the end of book 7,[1] he revisits pleasure after his discussion of friendship. Time and

---

1. That Aristotle discusses pleasure again in book 10, after discussing it at the end of book 7, has led scholars to suspect that one or other of the treatments of pleasure was part of an earlier work or development and that it does not belong in the *Nicomachean Ethics*. For discussion of the scholarship, see Tessitore, "Political Reading of Aristotle's Treatment of Pleasure," 247–48. Tessitore argues that book 7's account of pleasure, and book 7 more generally, constitutes a theoretical peak of the *Ethics*, addressed to potential philosophers, and that Aristotle reintroduces the topic of pleasure in book 10 "because of its importance for moral education" (ibid., 249, 259). Burger, *Aristotle's Dialogue with Socrates*, 191, also contrasts Aristotle's treatment of pleasure in book 10 with his earlier one, in that the

change are signs of our imperfection, in comparison to the unchanging nature of the god, as appeared at the end of book 7, but Aristotle has shown especially in his books (8 and 9) on friendship that they also make good things possible for us. The poet who says that change is sweet for human beings suggested that nothing abides for us, but Aristotle points to the enduring (*monimos*) character of friendships based on virtue (1156b18). For human beings some things abide, and they too can be sweet, as can the changes that might arise through friendship. Aristotle too, but for different reasons, could say that change is sweet. Friendships, for example, are strengthened over time, as when friends develop habits in the course of living together and take an impress of the good they admire in the other (1156b26–30, 1172a11–14). Near the end of his discussion of friendship Aristotle is able to say that perceiving that one exists belongs among things pleasant in themselves, for life is by nature a good thing (1170a33–b4). These words, as he draws book 9 to a conclusion, prepare us for Aristotle's reopening the discussion of pleasure, and therewith of the good at which we aim.

In book 10 (as in book 7), Aristotle answers the critics of pleasure, this time engaging the extreme position that says that pleasure is *altogether* base. Among those who make this claim, he distinguishes those who are persuaded that this is so from those who believe that "it is better for our lives to say [that all pleasure is base], even if it is not." They suppose that because "most human beings incline to pleasure and are slaves to it, they must be led in the contrary direction to reach the middle [*meson*, or the mean]" (1172a27–33). Their position cannot but remind us of Aristotle's, since he also argues that most human beings incline toward pleasure, and advises them to aim away from pleasure, so as to approach the virtuous mean (1109a14–19, a32–b13). Aristotle, however, unlike those who try to *deceive* others into hitting a mean, asks his addressees to examine themselves, in order to learn to which extreme they incline, so that by aiming in the contrary direction they might hit the mean. We must become aware of ourselves, if our actions are to be up to us. Ethical virtue involves choice (1105a32–33); it does not come from deception. Consistent with his own

---

one in book 10 asks "whether there is a distinctively human pleasure or pleasures." In her analysis, however, this does not necessarily indicate a lowering of the horizon. My reading overlaps with hers in understanding book 10's return to pleasure in light of what has emerged in the books on friendship.

deeds, Aristotle is quick to dismiss someone who lies to others for the sake of their own good. Because we desire pleasure (and, by implication, experience it as good), we will never believe that it is altogether bad. A salutary lie will not be trusted. Those who tell such lies are not credible. Nor do they "speak beautifully [or nobly] [*kalōs*]" (1172a34–35). Theirs is not a "noble" or "beautiful" lie. Their misguided attempt at beneficence cannot even be pleasant, at least if we trust Aristotle, who judges Neoptolemus's telling the truth to be a "beautiful pleasure" (1151b20).

Moreover, if not all pleasures are base, would it not be "better" to choose the good ones among them rather than to suppose that none are good in order to hit the mean? In censuring all pleasure, those who aim at salutary lies do not distinguish between pleasures that should be chosen, and those that should be avoided. If one were to advise human beings to choose only those pleasures that are good or accompany what is good, such advice would require the difficult task of sorting out which pleasures should be pursued and which not. Then they would not choose pleasure as such, they would choose the good. In a way, this is the task that Aristotle undertakes in the *Ethics*, as he suggests when he says that "theorizing about pleasure and pain belongs to the one philosophizing about politics" (1152b1–2).

The second view that Aristotle criticizes is that pleasure is *the* good, which he attributes not to common opinion but to Eudoxus, who saw that all things, rational and nonrational alike (*kai elloga kai aloga*), seek pleasure. "That all things are carried toward the same thing reveals, he thought, that this is the highest good [*ariston*] for all," inasmuch as "what is good for all and what all things aim at is the good" (1172b9–14). Once again, Aristotle could be thought to be describing himself, inasmuch as he attributes to Eudoxus a sort of teleological view of nature that is directed toward the good and that echoes the words with which he himself began the *Ethics*: "Every art and inquiry, action and choice" seem to aim at some good, and thus "the good is that at which all things aim" (1094a1–3).

Whereas Eudoxus speaks of rational and nonrational beings who all aim at pleasure to support his view that pleasure is the good, Aristotle speaks of art and inquiry, actions and choice, which belong only to rational beings, when he argues that all things aim at the good. Even if all things aim at the good, there is something distinctive about the way or ways in which human beings aim at the good. When Eudoxus refers to both rational and nonrational beings—to illustrate that all things aim at pleasure—he infers nothing from the difference between them in making his argument.[2] Yet it is a difference on which his making these arguments itself depends, as Aristotle indicates by referring specifically to Eudoxus's "arguments" (*logoi*) (1172b16). In presenting an account of the world, Eudoxus neglects his own act in accounting for it, just as the position of the physiologists on pleasure whom Aristotle discussed in book 7 would not have been able to account for their bearing witness to it, or the determinist who engages Aristotle in dialogue in book 3 would be unable to explain why he is attempting to persuade anyone of his position.

In the *Politics*, Aristotle denies that all things aim at their good when they seek pleasure, when he traces political life to the distinctive human capacity for speech or reason (*logos*). We share "voice" with the other animals, which signals a perception of pleasure and pain, but speech reveals the advantageous and harmful, and hence the just and the unjust (1243a9–19). If we simply followed our desires for pleasure, our good might elude us, just as it would if we merely followed Eudoxus's teaching.

Aristotle points out that Eudoxus himself does not follow his teaching, explaining that because he seemed to be "exceptionally moderate," and therefore "no friend to pleasure," his arguments "seemed to be true." They "were trusted more because of the virtue of his character than on their own account" (1172b15–18). Those who trust Eudoxus's arguments because of his character, however, are misled because they do not examine the implications of their trust. Not only do human beings experience pleasure as good, and so would not trust an argument that it is altogether base

---

2. Aristotle also claimed in book 7 the fact that "all things, both beasts and human beings, pursue pleasure is a sign that it is somehow the best thing." There too his statement seems to resemble the position he attributes to Eudoxus in book 10. However, Aristotle continues in book 7 to observe that those who pursue pleasure "suppose and say" what pleasures they pursue (1153b26–31). That is, he implicitly rules out the evidence of beasts, who do not "suppose and say" anything. In suggesting that we give weight to what all things pursue, he finds support in Hesiod's words: "Talk never dies down entirely, if it is uttered by many" (*Works and Days* 763). It is "talk" to which we must listen, not the pursuits of beasts. The position he attributes to Eudoxus, in contrast, does not depend on talk, but on the assumption that all things, rational and irrational, "are carried" (*pheresthai*) to pleasure (1172b13). In stating Eudoxus's position, Aristotle seems to collapse the middle voice—with the implication that one might carry oneself—into the passive.

(1172a33), but they also experience moderation as good—that is why they trust Eudoxus. Like Eudoxus himself, those who accept his arguments for pleasure are better human beings than those arguments give them credit for being. Just as Eudoxus fails to appreciate his own moderation when he maintains that pleasure is the good, those who trust Eudoxus's argument fail to see why they do. Aristotle lets us see what has escaped their notice. Indeed, what has escaped notice of those who give a teleology that assimilates human beings to the rest of nature is human rationality itself and the freedom it implies. So too has it escaped the notice of those who lie for the good of their addressees, for they do not know how to speak to rational beings since they tell them what they suppose are noble lies.

To support his position that pleasure is the good, Aristotle recounts, Eudoxus argues that if something can be added to a good to make it more desirable, then what is added must be good. He then points out that this is true of pleasure: just or moderate actions will be more choiceworthy if they are pleasant (1172b23–26). He, too, it seems, understands moderation—and justice—as goods. But whereas Eudoxus makes this observation to support his argument that pleasure is *the* good because it increases the good of any good thing, Aristotle concedes only that it shows that pleasure is *a* good: "Every good thing, when accompanied by another good, is more choiceworthy than when taken alone." On this ground, Aristotle points out, Plato argues that pleasure is not *the* good because a pleasant life is more choiceworthy with prudence than without it (1172b24–31; *Philebus* 60c-e). As Aristotle recounts Plato's argument: if "the mixture [*to mikton*] of prudence and pleasure is superior to pleasure, pleasure cannot be the good, for the good does not become more choiceworthy by the addition of anything to it" (1172b31). By the same token, prudence (or wisdom) is not *the* good but *a* good among others. There are many goods.

If pleasure is a good, however, what is pleasure, and how is it related to other goods? Aristotle returns to one of the arguments about pleasure he discussed in book 7, which defines pleasure as a motion or process of coming into being. He again associates this view of pleasure with those who identify pleasure with the replenishment of a natural condition, or a restoration of a deficient condition to a healthy one, such as the pleasures of eating when hungry or drinking when thirsty. Such pleasures are mixed with pain, and they led Aristotle in book 7 to distinguish between the imperfect pleasures of a human being and the simple and unchanging pleasure of the god. Now, in book 10, Aristotle emphasizes that there are many pleasures that human beings experience that cannot be understood as the replenishment of a bodily condition, and hence mixed with pain. These include "learning" and sense perceptions, such as that of smell, "in addition to many sounds, sights, memories, and hopes" (1173b16–21). These pleasures pertain to beings who live in time (such as memories and hopes) and who undergo change (such as learning). In book 7, in contrast, Aristotle gave only the example of "theorizing" or "contemplation" as a pleasure unmixed with pain, "at least when one's nature is not in need" (1153a1), an example more conducive to his contrasting human pleasure with that of the god, whose nature is not in need. Since learning implies need or deficiency (*Eudemian Ethics* 1245a16–17), it is not a pleasure experienced by the god, to say nothing of the pleasures of sense perceptions, memories, and hopes, which belong to corporeal beings who live in time. These numerous examples of pleasures unmixed with pains in book 10 offer a more positive view of the sweetness of human life than does the poet he quotes in book 7. Even "needy" beings such as ourselves can experience pleasures without pain.

Aristotle returns to one of the objections to pleasure he discussed in book 7—that pleasure is as a movement (*kinesis*) or "coming-into-being" (*genesis*) rather than an end (*telos*). He again denies that all pleasures involve motions (1152b13, b23). Pleasures, he repeats, involve not only motions or processes, but also activities or actualized states (*energeiai*) (1173a28–b3). He contrasts constructing a temple, in which the finished product differs from the steps in its construction, with the act of seeing (1174b20–25). The end of constructing a temple lies in the completed temple. The act of seeing, in contrast, is complete at any given moment; its end lies in its activity. Like seeing, pleasure is "something whole" that resides in "the now" (1174a15–28, b3–13). It is almost as if time might pause for us, if only for a moment. That is how, at any rate, Aristotle says we experience pleasure.[3] Since "pleasure is something that is both a whole and complete" (1174b8), our experience of pleasure gives us a wholeness or completeness. It allows us to touch eternity, even *within our lives in time.*

Although there is a wholeness in the act of seeing, in contrast to any act that goes into constructing a temple, our vision of the finished temple

---

3. Roochnik, *Retrieving Aristotle*, 103, clarifies: "This does not mean that the temporal duration of a pleasurable experience cannot be measured," but "as usual, Aristotle is keenly fixed on what takes place inside the experience."

suggests something incomplete about sight itself, precisely because of the wholeness of its vision. The many different actions that bring the temple into being serve an end outside themselves, the finished temple, but so does the finished temple itself. Human beings construct the temple to worship the divine. Through worship, we revere a wholeness or perfection that we lack but recognize by building a temple in its honor. To see only the finished temple, to experience it in "the now," reveals only the temple's form, its beautiful structure, but not its origin or end, its past or future, or those who constructed the temple and their purpose in doing so. In terms of Aristotle's four causes, we "see" the temple's material and formal causes, but not its efficient or final ones, even though they belong as much to the temple as its matter and form. In other words, the wholeness of our experience of the present, which Aristotle exemplifies by the act of seeing and by pleasure, conceals how much the present is incomplete without the past and the future. That very concealment, however, makes available to us the truth about the whole, or the god, which qua eternal cannot be understood in terms of past and future, origin or final cause.

Our experience of wholeness (as Aristotle attributes to the act of seeing and to experience of pleasure) not only reflects and gives us access to the divine, but also differentiates us from it. Aristotle soon points out that we do not feel pleasure continuously, but rather we grow weary, just as in the case of sight, as when we stare or look at something (1175a4–11). Time diminishes our experience of wholeness, yet that experience both of wholeness and of its fading opens us to a greater wholeness of which we can partake, but only partake. Aristotle has been suggesting this throughout the *Ethics*, as when he located the beauty of courage in the one who by his death lost the greatest goods, as when he quoted a father's praise of his son's divine-like virtue only after his son has died and his prowess failed, and as when he indicated that the great of soul could find greater completeness in friendship. Even the law, which speaks "universally" (*katholou*), or "for the whole," speaks "for the most part," for some cases fall "outside" (*para*) of it. Then equity must fill in "what has been left out" (1137b13–23). What happens over time makes the complete incomplete and begs for ongoing correction. Aristotle will end the *Ethics* by announcing the need for another inquiry "to complete the philosophy of human affairs," but only "insofar as it is possible" (1181b14–15). That inquiry, also a political one, will involve regimes, or the forms that political communities can take that make them wholes and what causes their dissolution. It will investigate why some regimes are governed beautifully while others not, and what regime is best (1181b19–22). That is, on the basis of the *Ethics* ("having made this beginning"), he expects the beautiful to appear in more than one form, but not everywhere, and he does not expect the beautiful to converge with the good.

Aristotle argues that pleasure fades because it "accompanies activity," and because "engaging in continuous activity is not possible" for human beings. Thus we cannot maintain our intensity when we stare at an object. "Novel things [nevertheless] give delight," for "they summon our thinking and stretch its activity to the utmost," but they "do not do so as much over time [when they are no longer novel]" (1175a3–12). Seeing and thinking, of course, would have more novelty if they involve learning, which involves seeing something new or in a new way. Moreover, there could be more opportunity for novelty if we learned from another as well as from ourselves. Once again, our temporal lives offer us pleasures—*human* pleasures—unavailable to an unchanging and perfect being. The possibility of such pleasures, like that of friendship itself, tempers any desire to become a god. As Aristotle said in his discussion of friendship, we desire the good for ourselves and our friends only on the condition that we remain beings such as we are (1159a3–8, 1166a22–23).

Aristotle explains further how pleasure "comes in addition" to an activity rather than as something inherent in it, just as "the bloom of well-being comes to those in their prime" (1174b24–35). One's prime does not last forever. Aristotle nevertheless recognizes that, as Burger says of his account here, "pleasure graces an activity," or is "an added grace that accompanies the activity of a living being when it is at its best."[4] Having associated pleasure with activity, for it "follows" the latter, and indeed "completes" it, Aristotle can provide a conclusion to his discussion of pleasure: just as activities can be judged or ranked, so too can their accompanying pleasures. Pleasure is not the good, but good is a measure by which we can judge and even rank pleasures: "As the activities are diverse, so are the pleasures."[5]

---

4. Burger, *Aristotle's Dialogue with Socrates*, 190, 195, and 197.

5. Tessitore, "Political Reading of Aristotle's Treatment of Pleasure," 260, argues that whereas in book 7 "Aristotle had defined pleasure as an activity of a certain kind," thus offering a definition of pleasure, in book 10 he describes rather than defines pleasure. Because pleasure comes to be in addition to an activity,

Of course, human beings experience pleasure in different things, for what delights one causes another pain, even though what appears pleasant to the good person is pleasant, and "the pleasant things would be those in which he delights" (1176a18–20). Aristotle proceeds with his characteristic tentativeness, for this is so, he claims, whether the activities that belong to someone "complete and blessed" are "one or more than one" (1176a27). Aristotle returns here to a version of the question of happiness from book 1, where he defined the human good as activity in accord with virtue, and if the virtues are more than one, then "in accord with the best and most complete" (1098a16–17). If there is more than one activity belonging to someone complete and blessed, however, and if one cannot engage in them at the same time, how does one choose between them? Once again, Aristotle questions whether any human activity can be "complete," and reminds us that human beings can be "blessed" but only "as human beings."

Having spoken of virtues, friendships, and pleasures—Aristotle speaks of them in the plural as he looks back over his work—he will revisit the question with which he began the *Ethics*, the question of happiness (1176a30–31). He will give greatest attention to theoretical activity and its relation to happiness, but he first brings play into his discussion of happiness.

A PLAYFUL INTERLUDE

When Aristotle announces that he is going to speak of happiness, taking up in outline what was said previously in order to "cut short the argument" (1176a30–33), he seems to signal the conclusion of his work. He proceeds to remind us of familiar points: happiness resides in an activity in accord with virtue, an activity choiceworthy for itself rather than for the sake of anything else, and it is subject to the vicissitudes of fortune. The

---

Aristotle is able to propose "a standard by which to rank and judge pleasure," and "to support the commonsense opinion that pleasure is a good but not the only or the supreme good." I agree with Tessitore's analysis of the difference between Aristotle's two treatments of pleasure, but I think that the commonsense opinion he presents is his own. Moreover, I have tried to show that the *Ethics* becomes more comprehensive as it progresses. As Aristotle has indicated, outlines come first and must be filled in later (1098a20–2).

activities of the virtues, "beautiful and serious actions" fall into this class, "for nothing beyond the activity itself is sought," presumably even when these activities are graced with happiness. So too, Aristotle continues, are "the pleasures of play" chosen for themselves and not as means (1176a33–b9). Aristotle's discussion of the activities of the virtues fills more or less the whole of the *Ethics*—even self-rule is understood in relation to virtue, and friendship is "a virtue, or with virtue" (1151b33–1152a7, 1154b35). Play, however, has received so little explicit attention in the *Ethics*—only as an occasion for the exercise of wit, the mean in giving others pleasure in times of verbal play (1128a3–9)—that it almost seems as if Aristotle has introduced something new in his recapitulation. Instead of cutting short the argument, he has added to it. He has not previously mentioned the pleasures of play among those chosen for themselves, although wit, like the other means, would presumably fall into this class. At any rate, his attention to play now delays his consideration of theoretical activity as an activity chosen for its own sake, the activity of what is most divine in us, our minds, which when it is in accord with the virtue proper to it would be "complete happiness" (1177a13–18). He may be approaching the end, but he is not hastening toward it.

Aristotle no sooner refers to the pleasures of play as chosen for their own sake, however, than he dismisses them, as if he were offering something only to immediately withdraw it.[6] The negatives are many. The pleasures of play are harmful, he points out, when people neglect their bodies and property in pursuit of them. Indeed, Aristotle offers this as evidence that such pleasures are chosen for themselves, insofar as they are sought even though no further benefits ensue and even harms result (1176b9–11). His argument against play cannot be entirely serious, however, since his observation applies to the beautiful and serious deeds of virtue chosen for their own sakes even though they might result in harm to one's body (courage) or run the risk of depleting one's property (liberality). Nor is a life of philosophy exempt from this difficulty, since it too could lead to neglecting the material conditions of life, as evidenced by Socrates's poverty (*Apology* 23b–c). Aristotle's argument against play—

---

6. Roochnik, *Retrieving Aristotle*, 176, too, is struck by Aristotle's quick and seemingly unqualified dismissal of play, which "makes it all the more striking that Aristotle bothers to discuss play at all."

that it might cause harm—indicates the mixed character of the goods we seek, whether in play or in virtue itself. His argument cannot rule out play without also ruling out the activity of virtue. This cannot be Aristotle's last word on play, and Aristotle proceeds to further considerations.

It is "the many" and "tyrants" who "seek refuge" in play, he claims as a further strike against play, for they know only "bodily pleasures" rather than any "pure and liberal pleasure" (1176b20–21). His reference to pure and liberal pleasure raises the question of whether there is a more liberal side to play. The existence of liberal pleasures belonging to play, in fact, are at work in wit, which involves what is fitting to say to others and to hear from them in times of play. As he discusses in book 4, wit is manifest in the "turns" or "movements" of "character" or soul rather than those of the body (1128a19–21). When Aristotle distinguishes there the playfulness of an educated person from that of an uneducated one, and that of a free person from that of a slave (1128a20–23), he indicates that the play he has in mind belongs neither to an uneducated "many" or to "tyrants," who seek bodily pleasures. There he proposes that the liberal or free person—who experiences pleasures beyond any sought by tyrants and the many—is the appropriate judge of what is fitting in times of play (1128a21, 26, 33).

Aristotle in fact reminds us of wit in the course of his arguments against play: the witty are highly regarded by tyrants, for they "make themselves pleasant in the very things that tyrants are after, and hence are the sort of people tyrants need" (1176b13–16). How could tyrants, however, if they have no experience of liberal and pure pleasures, appreciate the witty? Because Aristotle does not explain, he leaves open the possibility that far from gratifying the low tastes of tyrants, the witty are most needed by them as an introduction to higher forms of pleasure. Only, then, could the witty be highly regarded by tyrants. They would have exposed tyrants to elevating forms of pleasure, involving speech that brings delight and having more to do with the soul than the body. The pure or purposeless delight of wit in such a case would serve a higher, even political, purpose.

Raising even more perplexities about play, Aristotle quotes the saying of Anacharsis, one of the traditional "Seven Wise Men" of Greece: "We play in order to be serious" (1176b34–1177a3). As Aristotle explains Anacharsis's position, play serves as a relaxation or rest (*anapausis*) so that we can return to work, useful because we are unable to labor continuously (see also *Politics* 1137b36–1138a2). Of course, if we play so that once refreshed we can return to work, play is among those activities that we choose for the sake of something else, and those who play for its own sake are in error. To play for its own sake is "excessively childish" (*lian paidikon*), Aristotle says, alluding to the etymological connection between play (*paidia*) and child (*pais*) (1176b22–23 and 33). It is children who play. When one plays in order to be serious, in contrast, one's play has a serious purpose. One's play is not child's play. Relaxing (*anapausis*), "ceasing [from work]," would also be necessary for work, at least for doing one's work well.

If one undertakes play with such seriousness, however, could it serve the purpose that Aristotle, or at least Anacharsis, assigns to it? Anacharsis is known for his wisdom, but Aristotle does not say he is wise. We can assume at least that he is a serious person, since he places seriousness above play. But since play is the antithesis of seriousness, could the serious person serve as a good judge of play? Aristotle nevertheless appeals to the serious person as a standard for doing so when he observes that "what is honorable and pleasant to the serious person is in fact such." That the serious person is a standard for others "has been said many times," Aristotle reminds us (1176b25), but repetitions, insofar as they are opposed to novelty, are fatiguing (1175a4–10). Is Aristotle trying to tire us out with such appeals to the serious person, or is he in fact playing, rescuing us from the seriousness that dismisses play? Aristotle introduced a novelty in his recapitulation about happiness, namely, play itself, almost in the way play enters life, unplanned and without apparent purpose, for his turn to play appears to be unnecessary to any argument made previously, nor does it bear in any obvious way on a future one. Aristotle's exposition would not have appeared to lack anything if he had left out play, just as Aristotle's panoply of ethical virtues would not have seemed lacking if he had left out wit.

Moreover, even if Aristotle has brought the serious person to the fore as a standard "many times," he has not done so in every case. When Aristotle discusses wit, he refers to the liberal or free person as a standard for what is fitting in play. A free person is a better guide to play, for he "exists for his own sake, and not for the sake of another" as does a slave (*Metaphysics* 982b27–28; *Politics* 1054a10). Freedom too characterizes play insofar as play is chosen for itself, and not for the sake of anything else. The free person would therefore be more attuned than a serious one to which pleasures of play are proper and which not, or which belong to freedom and which characterize slavishness. To call forth the serious person as a standard or judge, if it has been done many times, is not novel, but allowing him to judge play is. Aristotle's doing so seems playful.

What, then, does play add to human life, if it is not merely instrumental to work, much as the restorative pleasures of food and drink might serve health? Recognizing that Aristotle's inclusion of play in his summary of happiness begs for an explanation, Roochnik suggests that since "the player plays without an eye to an external reward," his activity is "isomorphic with genuine happiness." In its absorption in the present, play is like pleasure as Aristotle described it, he argues, for it "takes us out of the flow of time." It therefore "affords a taste of eternity, and so a touch of the divine."[7] His suggestion lets us connect Aristotle's inclusion of play in the *Ethics* with his account of the virtues: in its likeness to "genuine happiness," play gives us reason to trust that we are able to choose things for themselves rather than for their consequences, simply because they are worthy of choice, such as the deeds of ethical virtue that we choose for the sake of the noble and the activity of thinking and its wondrous pleasures to which Aristotle will soon turn. That is, we can paraphrase what Aristotle says of his inclusion of wit and the other "social" virtues among the means he discusses: the experience of play demonstrates that we can engage in activity for its own sake and thereby gives us cause to trust that this is possible in other cases too, namely, in the activity of the ethical and intellectual virtues (see 1127a17–18). Play could be said to celebrate that this freedom and happiness are possible.[8]

Roochnik makes a persuasive case about why play belongs in Aristotle's discussion of happiness, but why does Aristotle offer arguments against play and associate those who play with tyrants and the many, or (at best) with children? Why does he propose that the serious person rather than the liberal one be its judge? Is he merely warning us that play, though

---

7. Roochnik, *Retrieving Aristotle*, 176–77 and 103.

8. Heyking, *Form of Politics*, 39, makes a similar argument about the festivity belonging to civic friendship for Plato and Aristotle. "Festivity," he writes, "takes place in special time, the time when the regime comes together with and before itself, ... over and above its factions.... [Festivity] takes place with a higher degree of freedom because it is a form of play and as such transcends (however momentarily) the realm of necessity in which politics is normally so deeply embedded."

it is isomorphic with genuine happiness, is not genuine happiness and should not distract us from it? Or does he have reservations about this understanding of genuine happiness for human beings and thus about play as its analogue? To play for its own sake, after all, is especially childish. Is there something incomplete, in other words, in activity that is supposedly the most complete, activity chosen for its own sake and for nothing beyond itself?

Throughout his treatment of play, Aristotle considers the *purposes* that play is able to serve precisely because it has no purpose outside itself, whether elevating the pleasures sought by tyrants and most human beings, refreshing us for the activity of the human work, or giving us an experience of what characterizes our higher activities. Aristotle has an eye to both its purposelessness and purpose, which he weaves together in his discussion. We must play for the sake of play if we are to play for the sake of our serious work. Aristotle takes a break from his discussion for play not because play is without purpose nor because it is instrumental to the serious deeds of life, but because it is both. It is in the inseparability—which we might find even in Anacharsis's paradoxical statement—of being for itself and of being for something other than itself that play is isomorphic with genuine happiness. Aristotle includes play in book 10 alongside the deeds of ethical virtue and the activity of what is most divine in us, our minds (1177b27, 1178a8). The deeds of the former aim at the beautiful, at nothing external to their own beauty, and yet Aristotle also indicates their service to a larger whole, such as the political community that requires the courage of its defenders or that benefits by deeds of munificence. He concludes his discussion of the intellectual virtues with the question of their use. When he turns to theoretical activity, as I discuss in the next section of this chapter, he attests to the "wondrous pleasures" of philosophy, the pursuit of wisdom, and only infers the pleasures of wisdom from those belonging to the pursuit. If philosophy holds wondrous pleasures (such as the pleasures of learning), it is worthy of choice on its own account, but only because one has a further end in mind, wisdom itself, does one engage in the pursuit.

In discussing play, Burger asks whether the philosopher "belongs, or solely belongs, on the side of the serious."[9] If he does not, play would not

---

9. Burger, *Aristotle's Dialogue with Socrates*, 198. Consider also that one of Aristotle's last words in the *Politics* that has come down to us recommends a harmony that "involves simultaneously both order and play" (1342b32).

merely be *like* the highest, but it would *belong* to it. How, then, does philosophy weave together play and seriousness? With this question in mind, we will follow Aristotle's move from his perplexing excursus on play to his discussion of "theorizing" or "contemplation." If Aristotle does offer a way to understand the conjunction of seriousness and play in philosophy, his brief inclusion of play in book 10 arises out of his search for happiness and serves the argument to come. Aristotle's celebration of our freedom through play may have more than one purpose. It is playful without being simply playful, like philosophy itself. If this is so, we can expect that Aristotle's play occurs not merely during his discussion of play, even though that discussion alerts us to it, but it will continue, just as it has been present all along. It belongs to his philosophizing, to his way of life. Thus we should not be surprised when he summarizes his previous discussion concerning happiness, he mentions philosophy and its pleasures, almost in passing, on his way to his discussion of theorizing and wisdom.

THEORIZING

Happiness is an activity in accord with virtue, Aristotle says, the virtue that belongs to our mind, the best and most divine thing in us. The activity of the mind is theorizing or contemplation, and its virtue is wisdom. It is agreed, he continues, that this activity is the most pleasant of the activities in accordance with virtue (1177a13–25).[10] Who agrees, and why do they think so? Aristotle does not say. Rather, he turns from wisdom to the love of wisdom, or philosophy, observing that "philosophy seems to hold wondrous pleasures in purity and firmness." Hence there is good reason (*eulogon*) that "those who know [*eidosi*] pass their time with greater pleasure than those who are seeking [*zētoutōn*] [to know]" (1177a22–28). Aristotle does not confirm the pleasures of wisdom with any experience of his own or of others to whom he appeals, but only infers them from the "wondrous pleasures of philosophy," that is, from the pleasures of those who are still seeking to become wise. Aristotle has given no thematic discussion of philosophy in the *Ethics*, mentioning it merely in passing when he examined

---

10. For an insightful study of Aristotle's arguments in favor of contemplation in book 10, see Walsh, "Problematic Relation between Intellectual and Practical Virtue," 71–81.

the opinions of philosophers along with those of others (1098b18), when he referred to his own activity (e.g., 1096a15; 1096b32; 1105b14 and 18; 1152b1; 1181b15), and when he included those with whom we share in philosophy among those to whom we owe the most (1164b3, 1172a5). The word "philosophy" or its derivatives does not occur in any form in his treatment of wisdom among the intellectual virtues in book 6, or in fact anywhere in book 6. We know of philosophy from the *Ethics* primarily from Aristotle's own deeds, his composing the *Ethics*, and their result, the *Ethics* itself.

Aristotle's reference to the pleasures of philosophy indicates that pleasures, even wondrous ones, attach to the pursuit, or to the way toward wisdom and not only to the end, wisdom itself.[11] What, however, are the pleasures that belong to philosophy? We experience perplexities, and we attempt to make our way through them. As Aristotle says in the *Metaphysics*, "being has been, is now, and will always be perplexing" (1028b3–6). If the perplexities will always be with us, why would we search? And, if we did, what sustains us in our search when we encounter limits? If we are serious about completing our search, we might become weary or tire from the roadblocks or impasses that keep us from our goal. The serious (*spoudaioi*), literally those who hasten (*spoudazein*), might turn away from an activity if there is no end in sight. Or they might in their haste push forward despite difficulties. They would want to resolve perplexities because they long to know. Their eagerness, however, might lead them to suppose they know when they do not. If they are also playful, however, they might relax or even suspend their focus on their end and delight in the search itself, the novelties that "summon thinking, and stretch its activity to the utmost," and thereby hold off weariness (1175a4–12). Such playfulness protects philosophy from both weariness and self-deception, weariness if the search seems endless and self-deception if it seems complete. Instead of either tiring of the search or hastening toward perfect wisdom, or doing the latter because of the former, philosophers whose serious search is at the same time playful could enjoy the wondrous pleasures of philosophy, for example, pleasures arising from the novelty of the perplexities encountered, from reflections on them, and from sharing both with others. Such

---

11. In the *Rhetoric*, Aristotle says that "it is pleasant to learn and to wonder" (1371b5–6).

pleasures, at the same time, protect philosophy from the playfulness of those who, like the Sophists, tie reasoning up in knots, confounding others as they themselves are confounded (1136a23–28; *Euthydemus* 278b–d). No more than the serious, whose end leaves no room for play, are the playful proper judges of play, for they have no end outside of their play to guide their judgment. A philosopher, in contrast, whose activity endures because it holds together play and seriousness, exemplifies the free or liberal person whom Aristotle identified as the proper judge of the pleasures of play.

If we understand the activity of our mind, theoretical activity, in terms of philosophy rather than wisdom, moreover, there may be less self-sufficiency in theoretical activity than we might suppose. Even when Aristotle says that the wise can theorize by themselves, and that the wiser they are the more capable they are of doing so, he does not say that they are self-sufficient, but only that they are "the *most* self-sufficient" (see also 1124b18). In any case, he admits, "it may be better to have co-workers [*sunergoi*]" (1177a28–b1). Even the most self-sufficient of activities is facilitated by "working together" with others.

Aristotle advises us to make ourselves immortal "as much as possible" and to live in accord with what is best in ourselves, what each of us is most of all, for this would be complete happiness for a human being. Once again, he adds a qualification: "provided that it goes together with a complete span of life" (1177b23–1178a8; see 1098a17–19). Aristotle reminds us of our mortality. Aristotle's advice is both serious and playful, for even as it urges us to achieve the highest possible for us, when we do so we hit upon our distance from the divine. His playfulness, in other words, lets us learn from our experience, in effect leaving our learning "up to us."

Aristotle observes in the *Metaphysics* that the life of the god is like the best that is ours only "for a short time," but the activity of the god is always the same, which is impossible for us. That the god is always "in the good condition that we are at times is to be wondered at" (1072b16–17, 24). We wonder at the god and his eternity, which is beyond our experience. Aristotle's god does not wonder. It is human beings who can become full of wonder, or "wonderful," especially when they think of divinity in contrast to their own mortality. Even if their lives in some way continue, they are beings who unlike the gods will suffer death. Aristotle observed earlier in the *Metaphysics* that divine knowledge could refer either to the knowledge a god has or to knowledge about the divine (983a7–10). That is, thoughts can be considered divine either because a god thinks them or because they are about the god. Both hold in the case of a god who thinks about himself. When in the *Ethics* Aristotle advises human beings to think immortal thoughts, even though they are mortal, only the latter could apply. Their immortal thoughts are about immortality, not the thoughts belonging an immortal being. Far from thinking of themselves when they think divine thoughts, their thinking about themselves would entail the difference between themselves and the divine or immortal being they think about. Consequently, neither their thoughts of the divine nor their thoughts of themselves would be as perfect as the god's. Someone who must be advised to think immortal thoughts is not immortal. Aristotle's advice to think "immortal thoughts" in the *Ethics* cannot but remind us of this, and therefore that the divine is "beyond us."[12]

It is a beautiful move on Aristotle's part that no sooner than he reminds us of our mortality, and then of our lives in time that make our pleasures ephemeral, he also reminds us of our friends. After advising us to live in accord with our minds, what is most divine in ourselves, he observes that "it would be strange if someone would choose not the life that is his own but rather that of something [or someone] else" (1178a3–5). His language here is almost identical to that which he uses in his observations about friendship, when he shows that friendship teaches us not to wish either ourselves or our friends to become gods, since such a wish if realized would destroy friendship (1159a3–8, 1166a22–23).

Soon after this reminder of friendship and its teaching, Aristotle turns to the virtues that belong to our "composite" nature, which are characteristically human (*anthropikai*). They occur in our relations to one another, for it is there that we act justly and courageously and do what is

---

12. In discussing Aristotle's rejection of the saying that human beings "ought to think only mortal thoughts," Mara, "Interrogating the Identities of Excellence," 319–20, observes that following Aristotle's advice entails "a paradoxical, yet essential, sense of self-limitation." The condition for "thinking more than mortal thoughts is the cosmological truth that 'the human species is not the best thing in the universe.'" Sherman, *The Fabric of Character*, 101, points out that Aristotle's advice to make ourselves immortal "as far as possible" implies that we must pursue contemplative activity "not as a god would, but as a human would, within the boundaries defined by our social and moral lives" or "as far as the circumstances of practical reason allow."

fitting with respect to all manner of passions and actions. The life in accord with these virtues is happy "in a second way."[13] This second way is the human way, in contrast to what belongs to the mind alone, which is "separate" from the human (1178a9–23). These ethical virtues as Aristotle understands them are also in accordance with the best thing in us, our minds, for virtuous deeds are accompanied by reason, or prudence, as Aristotle soon reminds us (1178a17–18). So too is friendship in accord with what is best in us, our minds, since friends share in speeches and thoughts (1170b18). Moreover, there are many human ways of theorizing Aristotle mentioned throughout the *Ethics*, in passages of some prominence, such as his reference to the statesman's theorizing about the soul as necessary for his making citizens good. More recently, in his account of friendship, he says that we are better able to theorize about or contemplate the actions of those near us than our own (1169b33–44). So too the good human being is well-provided (*euporein*) with memories and hopes as objects of contemplation or theory (*theoremata*) (1166a26). Thus Aristotle has provided us with resources for thinking about theoretical activity for human beings and the range of activities in which it occurs. Just as "divine thought" has two meanings—thought about the divine and thought that a god can think—so human thinking or theorizing can mean theorizing about human beings and theorizing in the way that human beings can. For Aristotle the two meanings of human theorizing are inseparable, just as the two ways of divine theorizing are inseparable, but only for a god.

In the *Metaphysics*, Aristotle asks us to think of theorizing as a perfect or complete activity, a realization of our natures, when he compares theorizing to the act of seeing. Human beings are able to theorize and therefore theorize, just as they have sight and therefore see. Theorizing

---

13. *Deuteros* is the word that Aristotle used earlier in the phrase "second sailing" (1109a30). In this expression it refers to a way to sail (or take to the oars) when the first approach is not possible. It is the only, but more difficult, way to reach one's goal. Mara's ("*Logos* of the Wise," 841) argument about Aristotle's discussion of the political and philosophical lives in book 7 of the *Politics* supports my reading of the *Ethics*. He finds that "Aristotle not only refrains from designating one of these ways of life (which are 'the ones chosen by those who are most ambitious toward virtue' [*Politics* 1324a29–32]) as superior but also raises the possibility that these two choice-worthy practices could have multiple specifications (*Politics* 1 324a35–b3)."

and seeing are part of their natural endowment. Aristotle nevertheless adds a qualification: "They do not theorize to acquire the ability to theorize, unless they are practicing [*melatan*] theorizing" (1050a10–15). Practicing here does not mean doing what one knows how to do, as a workman might practice his trade, but preparing for something beforehand, as we might train or practice for a competition or activity (*NE* 1114a5). As Aristotle observes, those who "practice" theorizing theorize only in a qualified sense. If they were able to theorize, they "would have no need to practice doing so" (*Metaphysics* 1050a16). Humans who practice theorizing may engage in divine activity, cultivating as Aristotle recommends what is best in themselves, but they are unlike gods, who have no need to practice. Aristotle does not mention how, or even whether, we can distinguish practicing theorizing from theorizing itself, thus reminding us of the deeds of ethical virtues, which can indicate either that we have acquired the virtues or that we are on the way to acquiring them (e.g., 1103b1–3). In any case, we could say of the intellectual virtues what Aristotle says of the ethical ones, they are not present in us by nature, but nature allows us to receive them. Our very distance from the divine—we must practice our virtues—gives us space to be part causes of our virtues, "to complete ourselves through habit"—and through practicing (*NE* 1103a23–26). It is also a space in which friendship can develop. Among the words that Aristotle used to describe the activities of friends are not only "perceiving together" but "theorizing together" (*suntheōrein*) (*Eudemian Ethics* 1245b5). That, too, is the human way of theorizing.

Aristotle illustrates the human way of theorizing not only in the *Ethics* and the *Politics*, but also in works such as the *Metaphysics*, which he begins not with being, which he presents as the concern of that work, but with the longing or desire to know (1003a4–5, 980a22). So too he moves from his investigation of being to the question of the good (esp. 1075a12–1076a6).[14] He even concludes book Lambda with the observation that the

---

14. Sachs, *Aristotle's "Metaphysics,"* 52n2, points out two ways in which Aristotle describes the concern of first philosophy, as "what pertains to being as being" and as what pertains to "the highest kind of being." According to Sachs, the former suggests that the work is an ontology, the latter a theology. Roochnik, *Retrieving Aristotle*, 84, cf. 108–9, finds a tension in Aristotle's formulations of the subject matter of the *Metaphysics*: as the study of being as being and as theology. He suggests that metaphysics must proceed on "the dual tracks" of both ontology

beings (*ta onta*) in the cosmos wish (*bouletai*) not to be "governed badly" (*politeuesthai kakōs*) (1076a4), a word that connotes living as a citizen (*politēs*) or participating in a regime (*politeia*). Aristotle speaks as if the beings that his *Metaphysics* studies must be understood in terms provided by a political inquiry.[15] Like the ending of the *Ethics*, the ending of Lambda in the *Metaphysics* points to the *Politics*, especially when Aristotle quotes Homer in the *Metaphysics* for an example of governance—or misgovernance.[16] Good governance remains a matter of wish—one that leads from the *Metaphysics* to the *Politics*, which explores "good governance," the very thing Aristotle says is wished for by the beings in the cosmos. It may be that Aristotle's *Politics* completes not merely Aristotle's philosophy about human affairs (1181b15), but his philosophy simply, in that what human beings might accomplish in their political communities has an indispensable bearing on the goodness of the whole.[17] Just as the *Ethics*

---

and theology. I would add that Aristotle's move from ontology to theology in that work (and his keeping them close) illustrates the human way of theorizing. Human beings long for the good, just as they long to know. This does not mean that Aristotle thought that they could arrive at a theology.

15. This conclusion about the beings is reminiscent of his move at the beginning of the *Ethics*, from all human actions aiming at the good to "all things" (*panta*) doing so (1094a1–3).

16. Burger, "Eros and Mind," 365–80, discusses the Homeric line Aristotle quotes: "The rule of many is not good. Let there be one ruler" (*Iliad* 2.204). The one ruler in question, however, is Agamemnon, who at the point when these words are said has failed miserably to bring order to the Achaeans whom he commands at Troy. As Burger so well expresses it, "if one wanted to pick one line from all of Greek poetry to support the claim that the universe is an ordered whole under the rule of one highest being, the one Aristotle quotes might be the absolutely worst choice possible!" On the basis of the line Aristotle quotes from Homer, we could not say that there is any satisfaction for the wish to be well governed, but then Homer is not the last word for Aristotle on politics. Neither is the *Metaphysics*. Even Homer himself questions whether the rule of one is best, at least if the one happens to be Agamemnon. The line Aristotle quotes is uttered by Odysseus, who in fact rules with Athena's help when Agamemnon fails. It is Odysseus, not Agamemnon, who rules. But he is not simply the "one ruler," for he follows the direction of the goddess (*Iliad* 2.166–81).

17. The abrupt ending of *De Anima* also points to the *Politics*. Aristotle observes there that even though animals require the sense of touch for the sake of

requires the *Politics* for its completion of its philosophizing about human affairs, so too does the *Metaphysics* require the *Politics* for its understanding of the beings and their place in the whole. Philosophy that remains in the pursuit of wisdom must turn to politics.

In elaborating "the second way," the "human way," Aristotle contrasts theorizing, which is cherished for its own sake and not for anything that it produces, first with military actions, which are undertaken for the sake of peace, and then with politics, which is also, he says, without leisure, and which aims at something outside itself, whether it be offices or honors, or the happiness of the statesman himself and of his fellow citizens.[18] The ruler he describes now differs from that of the self-sufficient king he described earlier, who aims only at the good of the ruled and not at his own (1260b1–5). Indeed, Aristotle says now even that the ruler "engages as a fellow citizen in political life" (*politeuesthai*) (1177b3–17). He too, like "all the beings," does not wish "to be governed badly," but for him this requires his own participation in politics. This statesman is more "mixed" than that of the self-sufficient king, for his political activity aims at both his own happiness and that of his fellow citizens.

---

living, other senses serve "living well," such as sight so that an animal may see, taste so that it may perceive qualities such as sweet and bitter, hearing so that signals may be given to it, and the tongue so that it can signal to another (435b17–26). His distinction between living and living well, which he applies here to living beings, echoes the dual purpose of the political community—living and living well—and of the sharing of speech, for which the tongue serves along with tasting (*Politics* 1252b30, 1253a9–18). Aristotle's political works complete the *De Anima*'s inquiry concerning the soul.

18. Aristotle fudges as to whether politics can be considered a leisure activity under certain circumstances. At least he distinguishes political activities from those of war, which are "altogether" (*pantelōs*) without leisure (1177b9). In the *Politics*, moreover, he associates political participation with leisure, insofar as such participation requires a certain freedom from a life of necessity (e.g., 1292b32, 36–37; 1293a6). At 1329a1–2, he states that "there is need for leisure both with a view to the birth of virtue and with a view to political activities" (see also *Metaphysics* 982b23–27). The issue remains how one should live one's life, and therewith what activity is appropriate for leisure. For a more detailed discussion of the passages in the *Politics* and their relation to the issues in the *Ethics*, see Walsh, "The Problematic Relation between Intellectual and Practical Virtue," 77–78.

For his last argument concerning theoretical activity Aristotle proceeds by appealing to the activity of the gods as models for us, as he has done on other occasions, such as the Graces, whose shrines encourage us to initiate good deeds and to return those that have been done for us, and such as Zeus, whose division of rule with his brothers illustrates sharing in rule rather than the rule of one alone. In his final series of observations about the activities of the gods, he does not mention any by name, as he had in these and other earlier cases, perhaps further distancing his understanding of the divine from any that the poets of his time presented. To be sure, there is no source in extant literature for the specific tasks of the Graces that Aristotle assigns to them, nor do Zeus and his brothers serve as promising examples of divided rule (e.g., *Iliad* 15.157–99). The Olympians have little in common with "the god" whom Aristotle mentioned in book 7, who enjoys one simple and unchanging pleasure forever (1154b26). But neither do "the gods" whom Aristotle speaks of now, whose activities are not simple and unchanging pleasures, but mixed, in that they include both theoretical activity for its own sake and good deeds for others akin to themselves. His series of observations themselves seem mixtures of play and seriousness.

Aristotle finds support for the view that "complete happiness lies in a certain theoretical activity" in the opinion that the gods are especially blessed and happy. But what activity other than theorizing can we attribute to the gods? he asks. We surely cannot attribute just actions to them, for they would appear laughable making contracts and returning deposits. What fears or terrors would gods face, so that courage would be fitting? To whom would the gods show themselves liberal? As to moderation, would it not be crude to praise the gods for not having base desires? Surely everything concerning action would be small and unworthy of gods (1178b7–23). Aristotle's series of observations, indeed primarily what we call rhetorical questions, indicate how incomprehensible the gods are in terms of virtues for which we are praised and blamed. But for living beings, as everyone supposes the gods to be, if action (*to prattein*) is stripped from them, along with making (*to poiein*), nothing is left except theorizing, which must be "the activity of the god," Aristotle concludes, slipping from the plural to the singular.[19] The human activity most akin

---

19. Just as Aristotle asks in the *Ethics* (1178b12) Would the gods not appear laughable if they made contracts, return deposits, or other things we call just

to the activity of the god, he continues, would bring the greatest happiness (1178b23–24). Happiness for human beings is therefore "a sort of theorizing" (*tis theōria*) (1178b32). Aristotle's formulation raises the question of what "sort of theorizing" is possible or fitting for human beings, whose lives are *not* "stripped of actions" and of "making"? Theorizing for human beings may be akin to divine activity, but in what sort of theorizing is our divine-like activity manifest?

Aristotle has illustrated throughout the *Ethics* the theorizing that belongs to human beings who act and make, in his own inquiry into what is good for such beings, including himself, and in his composing the *Ethics*, the product of that inquiry. His deeds in the *Ethics*, in other words, provide resources for thinking about acting and making. Both prudence, which involves acting, and art, which involves making, are among the ways in which human beings attain truth, as Aristotle argued in his examination of the intellectual virtues (1139b15–16). And his *Ethics*, as we shall see, closes with our need to theorize about cities and regimes (1181b18–21). Like our end in studying virtue, the purpose is not simply to know but to

---

actions?, he asks in the *Metaphysics*. Would it not be absurd (*atopon*) if the (divine) mind thought about some things? (1074b25). If this were so, "something else would be more honorable than mind," namely, what it thinks. From this he concludes that the divine mind thinks itself (1074b30–36). In the *Ethics*, there is nothing left for the activity of gods once we strip acting and making from them except theorizing. In the *Metaphysics* there is nothing left for the divine mind to think but itself once we strip away other objects on which its thinking would depend. The argument's parallel to that of the *Ethics* is striking, even though Aristotle offers other explanations of thought thinking itself. On the one hand, Aristotle holds back from saying that the god thinks himself by becoming identical with the objects of his thought (because then the latter would be more honorable than the god who has no independence from them). On the other hand, if the god thinks himself in abstraction from any other objects of thought, he would be separate from the world, or, in the words that Aristotle quotes from Homer's comic poem, "neither a digger nor a ploughman, nor wise in any other respect" (1141a15–16). Aristotle's god appears to reproduce the problems with the ideas that Aristotle lays out in book 1 of the *Ethics*: the ideas are either identical with the other goods and therefore cannot serve to account for them or too independent of them to be of any use in doing so. Could the *Metaphysics* come around to honoring Plato, in spite of its criticisms of him?

reform, or at least to improve (1179b1–2, 17–19). Before turning to this concluding section on politics, Aristotle further prepares us for this task and the human way of theorizing in three ways: by reminding us of our dependence on external resources, by his discovering support for his own work of education in Solon and Anaxagoras, and by revisiting the divine activity that is a fitting model for human beings.

Aristotle warns us that "for human beings, nature is not self-sufficient for theorizing," for the body must be healthy, and nourishment and other care must be available. He reminds us not only of our composite nature but also of our temporal being when he refers to "the external prosperity" we need as *euēmeria*, which means literally experiencing "good days" (1178b33–1179a9). Our theoretical activity must find a place in a life subject to chance, as Aristotle reminds us by again mentioning Solon, who was the source for Aristotle's question in book 1 of whether we can call anyone happy who is alive, given human susceptibility to misfortune (1100a10–18). Now Aristotle relies on Solon's support for his argument that the happy person needs only a measured amount of external goods to do beautiful or noble deeds and live moderately. He has become Aristotle's authority for diminishing the power of chance and for moderate living, to say nothing of questioning the good fortune of the rich and the powerful (see Herodotus, *Histories* 1.30–33). Anaxagoras too agrees with Solon, Aristotle says, when he observes that a happy person without great wealth or power would appear strange to the many (1179a10–17). One of those thought to be wise but useless because they do not investigate human goods (1141b5–8) has now become useful to Aristotle for what he says about the requirements for human happiness and about the opinions of the many. Anaxagoras is aware of the opinions of the many about happiness, which he implies are incorrect, and hence concerned about what is good for human beings. Aristotle brings up these "opinions of the wise," as he now calls Solon and Anaxagoras, to affirm not that happiness resides in theoretical activity, but in moderation.

Aristotle proceeds to remind us that "in practical matters," arguments or speeches should be trusted only to a certain extent, for "in practical matters the truth must be judged on the basis of the deeds of life," which are "authoritative" (*to kurion*) (1179a17–23; see also 1168a35–b1; *Politics* 1254a20–21). He presumably is referring to his most recent arguments that theoretical activity is the only activity that belongs to gods and to his appeals to the wise about happiness. The question of happiness, of course, is a practical matter, for it is a question of how we ought to live. By what deeds should we judge Aristotle's words or arguments? Although we might consider Aristotle's own deeds in the *Ethics* to be "authoritative," the deeds to which he now has recourse in support of his argument are those of the gods. If the gods care for human beings, as it seems they do, Aristotle observes, they would "delight in" (*charein*) and "do good deeds in turn" for those who are most akin to themselves, and these are the ones who cherish and honor mind above all (1179a25–32).

Aristotle's appeal to the deeds of the gods for confirmation of his arguments is a surprising turn, especially since he has just argued that only theorizing could be attributed to the gods, since it would be "laughable" to attribute to them anything like just or liberal actions. After all, he asked then, to whom would the gods give (1178b8–15)? Now, it seems, Aristotle himself has embraced the "laughable," in finding those whom the gods benefit no other than those like himself who cherish mind above all. But do the "deeds" confirm Aristotle's words? Was Socrates, for example, who cherished mind above all by constantly examining his life and those of others, honored by the gods with a place in the prytaneum rather than executed by Athens (see *Apology* 37a)? Socrates, of course, was joking when he imagined that he deserved to be hosted by the city like the Olympic victors, and he knew that he had already received a divine gift, the oracle that set him on his life of philosophy and taught him human wisdom is knowledge of ignorance. The comic aspect of Aristotle's presentation of beneficent gods works in a similar way, for it laughs at the pretensions of wisdom assumed by those who honor their minds most of all and their pretensions of divine favor bestowed on them because they do so.

Aristotle's laugher therefore has a serious purpose, capturing the point that we do not really know enough about the gods to rule out their beneficence, or to know what form their beneficence might take. Do we dare strip the gods of acting and making, leaving to ourselves the life that can include such activities *and* theorizing? Should we claim for ourselves an exclusive capacity for beneficence?[20] What Aristotle will soon reiter-

---

20. In discussing the great-souled individual, Pangle, *Reason and Character*, 140–41, argues that he is "impaled on the inner contradiction" between his vision of himself "as sublimely self-sufficient" and "his desire to be a benefactor." She

ate as he turns to politics at the end of the *Ethics* is that the purpose of his work is not only to contemplate virtue but to act virtuously (1179b1–4). Aristotle can state his own purpose, even if he does not know the extent to which the highest is akin to him. And yet he knows enough from the perplexities that have engaged him in the *Ethics*, and the goodness of life that he has been able to affirm as a result, that he can attribute to the gods what his deeds have let him experience as good—such as his deeds as a benefactor who lives in his activity. Nor does he hesitate to allow the Graces to do their work, both on his own doings and on the gods themselves. Far from the jealous gods of the poets (*Metaphysics* 982b31–983a5), the gods of whom Aristotle speaks, who benefit those most akin, have been reminded of the Graces, for they do good deeds in turn to those who delight and honor them by their own activities.

The gods' beneficent deeds for those who, like themselves, engage in theoretical activity serve as the last explicit example of divine activity in the *Ethics*. When Aristotle soon announces that he must undertake another inquiry, one about politics, because the legislative and political art remains as yet undiscovered by his predecessors, he presents himself too as a benefactor. This political art is a gift the gods have not bestowed and so allow us to discover it. Aristotle's beneficence extends not to those who deserve it because of their divine-like activity and hence least need it, but to those who need help in improving their common lives. His beneficence will be manifest in the political inquiry that he announces at the end of the *Ethics*.

In the last part of book 10, he describes the need for this new work, and he ends with an outline of it, which to some extent he follows in his *Politics*. Having remembered the past by recapitulating what he said about

---

points out that this contradiction is one "that the church has always acknowledged in speaking of the impenetrable mystery of divine charity." It is a contradiction she argues further that does not plague Aristotle since it is "the popular model of the divine and not Aristotle's that in fact captivates the great-souled man and inspires his desire to be a benefactor." See also Charney, "Spiritedness and Piety," 73 and 77; and Howland, "Aristotle's Great-Souled Man," 41–42. And yet it is just such a "contradiction" in the divine that arises in Aristotle's final depiction of the gods in the *Ethics* and in one of his final words about happiness in that book (cf. Pangle, *Reason and Character*, 275). To some extent, the "popular model of the divine" captivates and inspires Aristotle himself.

happiness, he now presents his hopes for the future. Those hopes would be unfounded, however, if our memories of the past did not include choices we made and actions that were up to us, and of the consequences of the choices that we made, and therewith of our freedom to choose when circumstances admit of being otherwise. Only then would we have cause to make choices for the future. Only then, in other words, would politics be possible.

POLITICS

If Aristotle has given an "outline" of perfect (or complete) (*teleia*) happiness, his inquiry has not reached an end (*telos*), for the end "in practical matters is action rather than contemplating (or theorizing) and knowing" (1179a33–b4). Although Aristotle has made similar statements earlier in the *Ethics*, this time—immediately after discussing theorizing—he points out the insufficiency of "theorizing" along with "knowing," as if theorizing were not only an end but a beginning. With this observation, Aristotle introduces his plan to undertake another work about politics, for even though speeches can incite to virtue "those youths who are free [*eleutherioi*]" and "lovers of the beautiful," they fail with most human beings, who live by their passions, "governed by compulsion more than by speech" (1179b10–16 and 1180a5). Aristotle returns to the question of the appropriate addressees of his work, and instead of disqualifying the young because they live by their passions and lack experience, he appears to expect that those youth who are free and love the beautiful will heed his speeches, but presumably they could be young in years or in character (1295a8). Aristotle now attributes the deficiencies he earlier associated with the young to most human beings, who both live by their passions and lack the requisite experience, for "they do not have in mind the beautiful and truly pleasant, having never tasted it" (1169b15–16). Indeed, they are not naturally inclined to shame or reverence (*aidōs*), Aristotle points out; rather, they are moved by fear of punishment (1179b11; cf. 1116a27–35). Rhadamanthus must back up the Graces.

If most human beings cannot be "persuaded by the speeches of another who speaks well," they resemble Hesiod's third type, who "neither thinks for himself, nor takes to heart what he hears from another" (1095b10–14). But Aristotle does not, like Hesiod, dismiss such human beings as "useless" (1095b14). It is their condition he seeks to ameliorate by writing another work, the *Politics*, as he announces at the end of the *Ethics*. In fact, there is good reason that the majority have not tasted what is beautiful and truly pleasant, Aristotle soon tells us, for they lack a good education. They even have had a bad education: it is "not possible, or not easy" to alter by means of speech what has long been engrained by habits (1179b11–18). Acquiring habits and the character they form, a goal of ethical education, can also be an impediment to its taking place. Moreover, "it is difficult to chance upon [*tuchein*] a correct education [*agōgē*] in virtue from childhood unless one is reared under laws of the requisite sort" (1179b32–33). It is not the need for force as much as it is the need for education that explains Aristotle's turn to politics, for the lack of education increases the need for force.

But can laws of the requisite sort be found anywhere? One finds "in most cities" not the attempt to inculcate proper habits in the citizens, but "utter lack of care" (*examelein*), and "each lives as he wishes, laying down sacred law [*themisteuōn*] in Cyclops fashion for his wife and children" (1180a27–29). In this passage from Homer that Aristotle quotes, Odysseus refers to the Cyclops as overweening and lawless (*athemistoi*) (*Odyssey* 9.106, 115). They recognize no gods or any restraints whatever on their rule (see also *Politics* 1252b22–24). Among cities that have come into existence, only in Sparta (or Sparta "together with a few others"—in the *Politics* Aristotle mentions Crete [1324b8]) is the legislator held "to have taken care for the rearing and practices of the citizens" (1179b25–27). But the laws of Sparta are hardly the "requisite sort" for inculcating virtue, for its legislator aimed at only part of virtue, military virtue or courage, and not at the whole of virtue, as he says in the *Politics* (1271b1–2). Aristotle even denies that the Spartans attain the virtue of courage by their severe training, for they turn out resembling savage beasts (*Politics* 1338b12–32). No more than those living under laws that neglect education do Spartans "taste what is beautiful or truly pleasant." No more than the many are they able to heed speeches rather than force. Aristotle suggests that political reform is required for the completion of his project, indeed, for his "philosophy concerning human affairs" (1181b15). Good political life, like ethical virtue itself, may be neither by nature nor contrary to nature, but experience has yet to demonstrate that we are such by nature that we can receive it.

Aristotle further indicates that a reformed political life will rest more on persuasion than force and on the law's cultivations of habits only to the extent that they facilitate our ability to deliberate and choose. In elaborating the position that "the many obey the governance [*peitharchousi*] of necessity more than of speech," Aristotle claims at least four times that this is what some suppose or say (1180a5–19). Once again, he plays on the dual meaning of *peithein* as "obedience" and "persuasion" (see 102b30–1103a1, where he refers to "admonition," "blame," and "exhortation" in connection with persuasion by, or obedience to, one's father or friends). One *must* "obey" necessity, but one *can* be "persuaded" by speech. Those who "suppose" or "say" that politics requires more force than persuasion neglect the ambiguity in the word; these also say the "incurable" should be banished, that legislators should seek revenge in their penalties, inflicting pain as on beasts of burden (1180a8–13). Aristotle's advice differs from that of these advisors of legislators. The latter refer not only to those who require the use of force but also to those "who are guided beforehand by habits [*tois ethesi proēgmenōn*] [who] will be obedient" (1180a8). The language that Aristotle attributes to them echoes the language he uses for those who will be proper addressees of the *Ethics*, those beautifully "guided by habits" (*tois ethesin ēchthai*). However, those to whom he refers in book 10 look to proper upbringing to produce obedience, whereas Aristotle is looking for those who will be able to hear and be persuaded by his arguments about the beautiful and the just (1095b3–8). To these he has been speaking throughout the *Ethics*. Aristotle's turn to politics will address those who suppose that inculcating habits is merely for the sake of obedience, not because they are correct that the many require force or compulsion, but because they have much to learn from Aristotle's new political science that distinguishes politics from despotism (*Politics* 1152a7–9). They are not incurable.

For the legislators of the future and for fathers seeking to educate their children, Aristotle emphasizes that families and political communities must work together in educating human beings. He points out that the speeches and customs of the father hold sway to a greater degree than do laws because of the kinship of family members, the care of fathers for their children, and the affection that arises between them (1180b4–8). Moreover, a private education may surpass a common one because of the care or attention paid to the individual. One education does not fit all (11808–13). Homeschooling is nevertheless not enough, as underscored by Aristotle's reference to the Cyclops. Moreover, a human being who opposes the desires of another becomes hated, whereas the commands of the law are not invidious, at least when law "orders [*tattein*] the equitable." Paternal rule does not have such a ready buffer for conflict. In this regard, "common care" is preferable to that of families, and common care comes by way of laws (1180a19–31). The very universality of the law recommends it, for its equal treatment of everyone it commands does not cause resentment, and at the same time its attempt to "order the equitable" acknowledges the limits of its universality regarding future events. "Order," as Aristotle uses it here, does not mean primarily "to give orders" (i.e., commands) but "to give order," or "to arrange in an orderly way" (*taxis*). The law "orders the equitable" by "making arrangements" that allow for its correction when that is warranted, or, as Aristotle said earlier, by acknowledging that "it errs knowingly" (1137b16–17).

Moreover, the best care even in the individual case comes from someone who knows the universal. By knowing the universal, one can judge when one's particular care might be improved by becoming better aligned with it—and when not. One would better understand what belongs to the human being for whom one cares. Care for particular human beings leads one to the universal, at the same time that it prevents one from using the universal as a refuge from the deeds of life. Those who wish their own children to become good must therefore study politics and legislation. In the context of criticizing "the universal [good]" and those who introduced the ideas, Aristotle emphasized individual case: the doctor inquires not into health, but "into the health of a human being, and even more, perhaps, into that of the human being [whom he treats]. For he treats patients individually" (1097a11–13). But the doctor does study health in general, at least for human beings. So too when equity is needed to modify the law and its universality to take circumstances into account, equity is not possible without the law, to which equity looks even when the law fails in particular cases (1137b20–24). Only in considering the universal can one see what is unique about the particular, and therefore treat it in the best way possible. And that is why the experience of mothers and fathers helps to educate legislators: love of their children—and also of their parents—provides an experience that helps spot the error of the law. When such experience can be brought to bear on political life, the law errs "knowingly" (1137b16–17).

How, then, does one become a skilled legislator or statesman? Aristotle asks. Where do we find a teacher? Are teachers easier to find than good laws? In the case of "the other sciences and capacities," he points out, those who teach them also practice them, as in medicine and painting. Regarding politics, in contrast, the Sophists profess to teach it, but do not practice it, whereas those who engage in politics do so from experience (*empeiria*) rather than from thought (*dianoia*) (1180b20–1181a12). The former lack the experience that would teach them to take particulars into account. They identify politics with rhetoric, Aristotle says, or understand politics to be inferior to rhetoric (1181a15–16). They assume that speech can move everyone alike. So too, Aristotle continues, the Sophists merely collect well-regarded laws as if those laws could fit everyone and as if judgment were not necessary (1181a16–b2). They could not be models for fathers seeking to teach their children to be good. Those who practice politics, in contrast, have the experience of politics without knowledge, and are therefore unable to teach it. Aristotle points out that they have taught it neither to their sons nor to their friends, but there would have been nothing better to leave to their cities had they been able to do so (1181a5–13). They cannot serve as models for fathers who seek to know what is needed for educating their sons, nor for friends for improving each other.

We therefore can look neither to those who profess to teach politics, Aristotle concludes, nor to those who practice it to obtain what we are seeking. Because our predecessors "have left what pertains to legislation undiscovered," it is left to us "to investigate it ourselves," Aristotle says (1181b13–14; see also *Politics* 1260b34, 1264a4). Aristotle does so in the *Politics*. The many appearances of the statesman (or lawgiver) in the *Ethics* have prepared us for what practicing politics might entail, if guided by Aristotle. The statesman has appeared, for example, as one who seeks honor in order to trust his own goodness, or to know his goodness through the recognition of others whose judgments he trusts (1095b27–29) (book 1); as a lawgiver who wishes to make citizens good (1103b3) (book 2); as a lawgiver who must distinguish voluntary and involuntary actions, in order to render praise and blame, and to bestow honors and to punish (1109b30–35) (book 3); as a legislator who forbids slander in some matters and by implication protects deference and awe (1128a30–32) (book 4); as a legislator and judge who is involved in distributive and corrective justice and who errs knowingly in framing laws in universal terms and so allows equity (1137b14–20) (book 5); as the individual with prudence who plays a pivotal role in Aristotle's account of the intellectual virtues (e.g., 1145a4–

11) (book 6); and even as the one who "is more serious about friendship than justice" because friendship holds cities together (1155a23–25) (book 8). In book 10, he "engages as a fellow citizen in political life" (1177b13–15). And now, also in book 10, he "wishes to make others better through his care, whether many or few" (1180b23). The statesman is both a standard and guide to others, upon whom he nevertheless depends and with whom he participates in political life.

In outlining his *Politics* at the end of the *Ethics*, Aristotle says that we will first attempt to investigate whatever has been beautifully said by our predecessors about politics (1260b28–36). The need for his *Politics*, it turns out, arises from the deficiencies not only of those who do not think for themselves—to use Hesiod's language of human types—but also of those who do, as Aristotle makes explicit in the *Politics* when he criticizes his predecessors who have made proposals about politics, including proposals for the regime that is best for human beings.[21] There Aristotle includes among those who put forward regimes in speech Plato's Socrates, who in this way as well takes refuge in words (*Politics* 1261a5–1264b26). Speaking about the regime is not sufficient, Aristotle implies, when he observes that the problems with Socrates's city would become clear if one could see it instituted "in deed" (*Politics* 1264a5–6). But Socrates does not suppose that such experience is necessary for understanding; at least he says in the *Republic* that the city he has described in speech would not be any less good if it were impossible for it ever to come into being (472d–e). Aristotle, in contrast, when he calls the best regime he describes in the *Politics* "a regime according to prayer" means that it is one that is possible (e.g., 1295a29, 1260b31–32, 1325b33). In designating the arrangements of the best regime, we must lay down "what we would pray for, yet nothing should be impossible" (1265a18).

After we examine what has been left imperfect by our predecessors, Aristotle says in outlining the *Politics*, we will theorize about what sorts of things preserve and destroy cities, including what sorts of things do so for each of the regimes, and why some are governed beautifully and others not. Finally, these matters "having been theorized," we might perhaps better see together what sort of regime is best, and how each is given order by different laws and customs (1181b17–24). Aristotle is not turning away

---

21. Nichols, *Citizens and Statesmen*, 35–48.

from theoretical activity in inquiring into politics, as he involves his addressees in their common inquiry. He exhorts them "to make the attempt" in the first-person plural. In this way, there will be "a completion of the philosophy of human affairs, as far as it is possible" (1181b15–16).[22]

What is incomplete is Aristotle's outline of the *Politics*, which leaves out the first book of that work, with its account of the growth of the political community out of the family and the village. Aristotle spends more time in book 1 of that work speaking of the relations between masters and slaves in the household or family than those of its free members, husband and wife, parents and children (1259a37–41). For Aristotle to leave book 1 out of his outline is to leave out slavery. When Aristotle spoke of the family in book 8 of the *Ethics*, he emphasized the affection between parent and child, between husband and wife, and between siblings as models for regimes. As we have seen, to find a family model for tyranny, Aristotle had recourse to Persia, for there "fathers use their sons as slaves," and "they err in doing so" (1161b28–31). Slavery has little place in the *Ethics*.[23]

Slavery, however, comes almost first in the *Politics*. Aristotle's omission of it from the outline in the *Ethics* only intensifies its appearance in the subsequent work, highlighting the difficulty of dealing with it, and even questioning whether it has any proper place in political life. Aristotle begins his *Politics* with slavery not simply because it is an institution of his society that must be addressed, but because he develops his own concept

---

22. Although Aristotle refers to "completing" his philosophy of human affairs in his political work, the *Politics* we have is incomplete, seeming to break off in the middle of a sentence. We of course have no way of knowing whether its unfinished character is due to the destruction caused by time and chance, or to Aristotle's playful attempt to remind us of the power of chance over his own work, and thus to indicate once again that although matters are "up to us," they also require the assistance of time as a co-worker (1098a24). Of course, if it is more likely that chance is responsible for the unfinished character of the *Politics*, time itself proves to be Aristotle's co-worker.

23. For example, Aristotle denies in the *Ethics* that there can be friendship between a master and a slave, but he does claim that there might be friendship between them insofar as a slave is a human being (1161a36–b8). To the extent that friendship between master and slave is possible, however, the inequality that defines natural (and hence just) slavery could not exist between them.

of political rule in contrast to the despotic rule of masters over slaves.[24] At the beginning of the *Politics*, he objects to those who fail to distinguish different kinds of rule, such as political rule from mastery or despotism (1252a7–13, 1253b18–20). Political rule is shared rule among those for whom there is some degree of equality, as we saw in Aristotle's discussion of natural justice in book 5 of the *Ethics* (1134a26–28, b14–16; 1161a27–29; *Politics* 1261b31–35, 1325b7–10). The emergence of political life requires not only development beyond the prepolitical family, with its potentially unchecked brutality, but also the emergence of political rule as an alternative to despotism and its recognition as a standard for politics. Given that "most cities" neglect any common care for making citizens good, and the ones like Sparta that do look to virtue misunderstand it, it is politics itself that remains yet to be "discovered." Aristotle has prepared us for such reform throughout by his statements that in practical matters the end is acting no less than knowing (e.g., 1179b1–2).

An element of that reform is Aristotle's *Rhetoric*, in which he explores the relation between speech and politics in a way the Sophists failed to do. There he speaks about different kinds of rhetoric, distinguishing its objects, the advantageous, the beautiful, and the just, and also the different causes of persuasion that make rhetoric successful, the character of the speaker, the passions of the listeners, and the argument itself (1355b10–11, 1356a1–20). Aristotle's understanding of rhetoric is central to his work on politics, inasmuch as persuasion bridges the gap between force and speech

---

24. The question of the need for force or compulsion in political communities is the explicit issue as Aristotle turns from the *Ethics* to the *Politics*. At the beginning of the *Politics*, he raises the question whether there are slaves by nature so that "it is better and just for anyone to be a slave," or whether "all slavery is against nature" but exists only by law and rests on force (*Politics* 1253b20, 1254a18–20). That is, he begins the *Politics* with an implicit criticism of compulsion by associating it with injustice. Aristotle brought up the question of nature versus convention or law at the beginning of the *Ethics* in regard to the just (and the beautiful) (1094b15–17), as he does at the beginning of the *Politics* in regard to slavery. In the *Politics*, which is the sequel to the *Ethics*, he no longer questions whether there is anything just by nature, only whether slavery could be an example of it. For my discussion of slavery in the *Politics*, see Nichols, *Citizens and Statesmen*, 18–24, 145.

by giving a certain force to speech through a rhetoric that persuades by means of character and passion as well as by argument.

Aristotle can therefore present political life in the *Politics* as involving both speech and compulsion, even speech more than compulsion. There he explains that human beings are political by nature, because they have speech or reason (*logos*), through which they can reveal the beneficial and the harmful, and therefore the just and the unjust (1253a8–19). Aristotle's work attempts to help us understand our potentials, both individual and communal, and thereby nurture a politics characterized more by speech about the beneficial and just than by force or compulsion.

A politics in which we deliberate about the beneficial and the just fosters the activity of our minds, and therefore what is most divine in us, without collapsing politics into religion. The divine is "beyond us," to use Aristotle's words (1145a19), and beyond what we can either control or instantiate in our politics. Politics "does not rule the gods, even if it gives order to everything in the city" (1145a10–12). Politics, not the gods, originates laws, even when laws or conventions are guided by what is just by nature. Nor would it be simply good for us if the gods did so. Our practice of politics is our own, for we govern ourselves, elevated by the models of divine activity of thought and beneficence that Aristotle reflects in his own work. That our lives are "up to us" may be a sign of divine care. Aristotle's *Ethics* leaves this open as he demonstrates his care that we play our part.

In book 10, in summary, Aristotle deepens his presentation of our proper stance toward the divine. It is there that Aristotle objects to those who advise us "to think about only human things because we are human beings, or mortal things because we are mortal." Rather we must strive to live "in accordance with what is most excellent in ourselves," our minds. Aristotle even suggests that this may be "something divine present in us," and he soon refers to our minds as what is "most akin to the gods" (1177b27–1178a8, 1179a27). Far from being weighed down by "mortal thoughts," such as those of death, we have cause to celebrate our mortal lives, by putting to work what is best in ourselves, our minds, by aligning our activities in accord with virtue and reason. Book 10 is Aristotle's celebration of a cosmos in which this is possible, as when he revisits pleasure, even finding in the experience of pleasure a sort of timelessness or wholeness that can belong to beings who live in time, or when he illustrates in discussing play his own playfulness, not as an illusory freedom from work that in fact is in its service, but as a stepping back from the task at hand, demonstrating a capacity to transcend the necessities of human life, a capacity that also makes possible action and thought, and hence ethical and intellectual virtue. He associates pleasures "wondrous in purity and firmness" with the activity of philosophy, even though philosophers are still "seeking to know" (1177a25–28). Aristotle's turn at the end of the *Ethics* to yet another inquiry on politics does not merely indicate that his philosophizing is still incomplete, but it illustrates that it cannot be completed without a beneficence that leaves his philosophy incomplete, only "in outline" to be filled in by others in time.

The politics to which his *Ethics* leads him is therefore not possible without piety, for it requires the activity of our minds, or what is "most akin to the gods," while accepting that we are at best only akin, since we are mortal—and hence composite beings. At the end of the *Ethics* Aristotle refers to his own speech as a beginning or starting point for the work to come: "Having made a beginning," he says, "let us speak" (1181b33). He ends by exhorting himself and his addressees to share in speech.

Afterthoughts

Aristotelian Piety for a Liberal Politics

In recent decades there have been many thoughtful attempts to look beyond liberal political theory for a more satisfactory understanding of political life, and to find resources for combatting the radical individualism, moral relativism, and hedonistic self-gratification to which liberalism's theories of individual rights and human autonomy may all too easily lead. There are those who argue that liberal practice, in distinction from liberal theory, requires and fosters liberal virtues (for example, self-reliance and toleration) appropriate to free and self-governing individuals. Others appeal to participatory democracy and engaged citizenship as conducive to human and political flourishing, some even finding support in Aristotle's view of political community.[1] Paul Ludwig shows how civic friendship exists in liberal regimes, especially in widespread civic associations and even in commercial activity, and how it extends to citizen's shared assumptions about their regime. The ways in which civic friendship supports

---

1. For an excellent summary—and critique—of this literature, see Collins, *Aristotle and the Rediscovery of Citizenship*, esp. 15–41. For discussion of three prominent approaches among neo-Aristotelians (that of Martha Nussbaum, of Alasdair MacIntyre, and of Douglas Den Uyl and Douglas Rasmussen), and the problems that lie in their appropriations of Aristotle, see Zuckert, "Aristotelian Virtue Ethics," 61–91. See also Salkever, "'Lopp'd and Bound': How Liberal Theory Obscures the Goods of Liberal Practices," esp. 168–69, 175–77, 182, and 186, who attempts to strengthen liberalism by recourse to the ancients, not to their classical republicanism, or to their political theory more generally, but to their manner of theorizing, which resolves questions without closing off further reflection and critique.

liberal communities are obscured by liberal theory itself, he argues, but Aristotle's understanding of political friendship or like-mindedness provides a framework for understanding liberalism—a corrective not for its institutions, but for how we understand them. Such an understanding would nevertheless make a difference for the laws, policies, and practices that we support and reject, and even more important for what we admire in our fellow citizens and statesmen.[2]

Others reject liberalism altogether. "Integralists," for example, seek to base public life on Christian, often Catholic, principles, and thereby dissolve the separation between religion and politics. Adrian Vermeule, for example, writes that the question is not whether liberalism is desirable—for its demise is inevitable—but whether we can lessen the birth pangs of its successor. He proposes that "nonliberal actors strategically locate themselves within liberal institutions and work to undo the liberalism of the state from within."[3] Patrick Deneen, in *Why Liberalism Failed*, argues that the "accumulating catastrophe" of liberalism—its "titanic inequality," its "uniformity and homogeneity," its "material and spiritual degradation"—stem from its core understanding of human autonomy and its concomitant denial of any borders or limits, socially, morally, or politically. Unlike Ludwig, who sees the possibility of civic friendship on both the national and the local level, Deneen looks for alternatives to liberalism in local, faith-based communities, in family life, and in their transmission of culture and tradition that enriches human lives.[4] He clearly states that Vermeule's Catholic integralism is impossible "for the world's first Protestant nation,"[5] but religion is so integral to Deneen's position that at least one commentator has observed that his "desire for a viable alternative to liberalism requires that the Christian religion regain an authoritative role in public life."[6]

---

2. As illustrations of policies consistent with civic friendship, Ludwig discusses immigration reforms, a just wage, and compulsory national service. See Ludwig, *Rediscovering Political Friendship*.

3. Vermeule, "Integration from Within," 202–13.

4. Deneen, *Why Liberalism Failed*.

5. See Dreher, "Classical Liberalism Strikes Out," an interview with Deneen.

6. Smith, "Returning to Throne and Altar?"

The controversy that Deneen's book aroused suggests that it struck a nerve in the American psyche, as do the series of critiques of liberalism over the last decades attest to a liberalism dissatisfied with itself. Its weakness and self-doubt have become increasingly visible in the United States recently in the inability of its leaders to address obstacles that race presents to our political community. Too often the desire for perfect justice in defining "merit" as the principle of distributive justice or the belief that we can repair past injustices through some perfect formula of corrective justice gets in the way of generating the "like-mindedness" or "civic friendship" that might allow for a healthy diverse community.

My exploration of piety and politics in Aristotle's *Ethics* follows in the footsteps of those looking to Aristotle for a richer view of human nature and politics than found in liberal political theory. The alternative to liberal theory that I find in Aristotle provides support for liberal institutions and practices, while justifying them on the basis of higher potentials of human nature and at the same time more modest expectations. A pious understanding of what in us is akin to the divine encourages our virtuous actions and pursuit of the truth, fostered by our thinking and acting with fellow citizens and friends. Beings akin to the divine are capable of virtue, both ethical and intellectual, and beings only akin to the divine should not expect ethical or intellectual perfection, but only the "blessedness" possible for human beings, as Aristotle put it. If our kinship with the divine militates against radical secularism, our distance from the divine checks moral righteousness and impositions of religious orthodoxy. Aristotelian piety, as I have attempted to show, is based not on any divine revelation that dictates truth, or on any authoritative theology, but on inquiries such as Aristotle's in the *Ethics* that explore the affinity and distance between human and divine. On such grounds we can justify such liberal institutions and practices as deliberative assemblies, inclusive governing institutions, freedom of speech and religion, fostering a friendly environment for religious communities as well as prohibitions against an established church, and a statesmanship that guides the many components of the political order toward a common good. An Aristotelian understanding of politics can inform how we view our own liberal institutions and practices, elevate our common lives, and provide a basis for their defense against those who criticize the selfishness, hedonism, and general moral bankruptcy of contemporary liberal culture.

I therefore concur with Ludwig that we need less a reform of our institutions than a new way to understand them. To this end, I argue that Aristotle's "philosophy of human affairs," which never loses sight of the human relation to the divine, recognizes the religious or spiritual foundation of human life and community that weighs so heavily in critiques of liberalism such as Deneen's. Whereas Aristotle rejects any strict separation of religion and politics, the linking of piety and politics that he attempts to forge also recognizes the dangers to freedom from integrating the two as closely as integralists might wish. Aristotle's distinctive understanding of human beings as political and rational elevates them above the beasts and separates them from the divine. The piety growing out of this understanding supports liberal institutions and practices that foster virtue in a way that gives new meaning to a liberal way of life.

Our virtues for Aristotle are manifestations of freedom, but their exercise requires living with others and sharing in speeches and actions. They are not simply the "liberal virtues" sought as instrumental to liberal society, but the virtues that are the conditions for human happiness. They are exercised in our communities, and derive support from them, while they come in part through our own efforts. That is why our virtuous deeds are deserving of praise, and our failures are deserving of blame. Aristotle's defense of freedom therefore cannot lead to a moral relativism when it insists on the deliberation and choice essential to virtue.

The virtues for Aristotle are both ethical and intellectual. Aristotle's defense of freedom and community—and their connection—is based not only on ethical virtue but also on our desire to know the truth, especially the truth about the highest beings or being in the cosmos. We are beings who unlike beasts have "longing minds" and "intellectual longings." Our mind, Aristotle says, is something divine in us, but it is "longing" mind. Longing indicates the absence of what we long for. Aristotle never attributes longing to the divine. Our longing mind supports our trust in a good or divinity that is "beyond us" for which we long and makes us akin to the divine, even though no divine being need pursue truth or deliberate. When Aristotle says that our choices can be understood as longing mind or intellectual longing, he means that we are free beings who are moved to pursue the truth and are capable of doing so and that our longing—our desires, our spiritedness, and our wishing, indeed, our actions, including our politics—can be informed by thought.

Our freedom therefore does not make us the autonomous individuals of liberal theory. That the divine is beyond us means that we are incomplete or imperfect beings whose happiness depends on others and on what is beyond our control. Our incompleteness means that we are political by nature, that friends are goods indispensable for our lives, and that we are indebted to our families and others for our nurture and education and owe them care in turn. As Aristotle says, self-sufficiency does not mean what suffices for someone by himself, living a solitary life, but what is sufficient with respect to parents, offspring, a spouse, and friends and fellow citizens (1097b8–12). Aristotle's statement that we are "joint causes" of our dispositions and actions (1114b24) acts as a reproach to those who see themselves as sole causes of themselves, who forget what they owe to families and political communities and even to what they have been given by nature. We are like the munificent individual who has resources with which to begin, and the scientist who knows beforehand what he needs for science (1122b29–33, 1139b27). In all these ways, Aristotle's rejection of human autonomy and defense of community resonates with the concerns of many contemporary critics of liberalism. His defense of community, however, is a defense of a limited government that supports the development of the communal ties that he understands as defining a human life. These include the resources of liberalism for civic friendship that Ludwig explores.

When Aristotle says that we are "joint causes" of our dispositions and actions, he also defends individual freedom against those who emphasize the extent to which human lives are embedded in their communities. Individuals are also causes of their dispositions and actions, not only their families, political communities, or friends. Aristotle insisted that virtuous action does not simply follow the dictates of prudence but that it be accompanied by prudence (144b22–28), or that to be virtuous we must exercise our own judgment and not just follow the good judgment of another. So too our good does not depend entirely on the communities to which we belong, however much they are necessary to protect and to foster it. Our families are not the only source of our nurture and education, for political communities further the work of the family. Apart from political communities, moreover, there are those with whom we "share in philosophy" (1164b3). However much lawgivers and statesmen arrange matters in their communities, Aristotle warns that they do not command the gods (1145a10–11). That the divine is beyond us leaves us free to pursue our good; indeed, it calls us to do so. Aristotle therefore objects to those who fail to accept any responsibility for their actions but trace them to causes outside themselves, or who understand themselves as simply a part of a whole, as, for example, a father or a citizen rather than as a human being.

That the divine is beyond us suggests our incompleteness, which makes our belonging to communities necessary and desirable. The divine that is beyond us is also beyond the communities that we form with others. Piety so understood cautions us against the dangers of any identification of religion and politics. Such piety would support the separation of church and state not because both are autonomous, their integrity threatened and violated by interference from the other, but because both are incomplete, with the goods they provide necessarily tied to their incompleteness. If the divine is beyond us, religion would support moderation and tolerance, rather than seek to impose its view on others. So too legislators and statesmen who are aware of their own limits in relation to the divine would hold back from trying to dictate to religion. Just as Aristotle questions the completeness of the law, such as its need for the Graces, natural justice, and equity, and clearly insists that politics cannot replace the work of families, piety too would limit politics' reach. Both religion and politics might work together in fostering the blessings that flow from human incompleteness and in deriving support from the other in doing so. Church is separated from state, but politics and piety are entangled, in the support they need from the other.

Moreover, our incompleteness and longing that leads us to community and the achievements it makes possible also make us aware of ourselves apart from our communities. We are political by nature, but it remains for us to investigate what causes regimes to be governed beautifully or not, and what sort of regime is the best (1181b13–24). We face perplexities, while we wonder at our resources and at their source or cause. Even when we wonder with others, our wonder is our own. We act in light of our wonder, with the encouragement and moderation it gives us, in concert with others, to be sure, but also as distinct individuals who can therefore act as causes. Time after time, we have seen how Aristotle's discussions in the *Ethics* attempt to maintain this complex vision that weaves together freedom with community, private with public, and piety with politics. Consider, by way of a summary, his treatments of greatness of soul, justice, philosophy, and friendship.

Aristotle describes the great-souled individual as apparently free of the impediments that circumscribe others and limit their action, as if he could stand alone, as it were, as the best thing in the cosmos. It turns out, however, that he lacks knowledge of his own dependence on others, and that his lack of self-knowledge prevents him from undertaking the activity he craves and that alone makes him worthy of the honor he deems he deserves (e.g., 1124b18, 24–25). By appealing to his desire to perform worthy deeds, to his dependence on honor and his shame, and even to his inclination to truthfulness, and by gesturing toward friendship, Aristotle attempts to bring him into the community, in ways that sustain rather than diminish his freedom. In his treatment of greatness of soul, Aristotle shows that belonging to a community, or living with others, both frees one from the inactivity or idleness of self-sufficiency and checks any presumptions of divinity.

Although Aristotle first speaks of justice as the lawful, and of laws as commanding every virtue and forbidding every vice (1129b1, 1130b24–25), throughout his discussion of justice he shows the limits of law. In addition to the laws, the community is supported by what Aristotle calls reciprocal justice, an exchange of harms for harms and goods for goods (1132b34–35). In particular, shrines to the Graces are displayed in prominent places, hence public ones, to encourage returning benefits and even initiating them. Not all the Greek gods, to be sure, but these beneficent ones whom Aristotle calls forth, serve to illustrate the reliance of the city on the divine for fostering the beneficent deeds that hold it together and for encouraging human beings to act as causes—to initiate good deeds rather than simply to perform them in return (1133a2–6). Even more than reciprocity is needed, inasmuch as there must be a first giver for there to be giving in return. In Aristotle's example, the Graces by such encouragement are the first givers who serve as models for human beings to be so. So too there is a natural justice that belongs to political justice and that structures and informs law for those who can share ruling and being ruled in their political communities. Finally, equity, as Aristotle describes it, which corrects the universality of the law in light of individual cases, inclines to pardon (1143a19–24), thereby giving the individual case more than it is strictly or legally due. It is moved by a grace that goes beyond reciprocity.

The most significant and obvious division in the intellectual virtues that Aristotle makes is between prudence and wisdom. The division limits the scope of political life, for although prudence is concerned with only what is good for human beings, wisdom involves the highest or best things in the cosmos (1141a19–b2). At the same time, the division also protects political life against a wisdom that might claim divine-like knowledge, such as possessed by the *Republic*'s philosopher-kings, and by implication those who attempt to derive an authority to rule from religious orthodoxy, or even those whose secular orthodoxies entertain no doubt about their own wisdom. Prudence, not wisdom, is the virtue that guides politics. In a sense, however, Aristotle's own way of philosophizing bridges the gap between these intellectual virtues, for he investigates not only the human goods, but their relation to the best or highest in the cosmos. His focus therefore does not demote politics in light of the higher but rather elevates it by trying to understand its place in a whole larger than itself, and indeed the ways in which human life touches divinity.

Aristotle offers an alternative to modern liberalism's radical disjunction between public and private life also in his treatment of friendship in the *Ethics*. There he explores the ways in which families and politics remain distinct but codependent. Good family relations serve as models for good regimes and act as a reproach to deviant ones (1160a31–1161a9). Families serve politics at the same time politics serve families. Politics guards against the oppressive family relations that model deviant or unjust regimes, if only by providing a broader context for human life that limits the reach of the family over its members. More important, political communities also advance the ends of the family—the provision of life, nurturing, and education of the new generation that Aristotle identifies as the work of parents (1161a17–16, 1162a5–8). Politics depends on families to begin this work that is its highest calling.

Friendship, at least some friendships, nevertheless go beyond the scope of the law—friends who "have no need of justice" (1153a26–28), for friends receive not merely their due from each other but more than their due. Like Homer's heroes, "two [friends] go together," because they "are better able both to think and to act" (1155a15–16), but unlike Homer's heroes their thoughts and actions have less to do with war than with their own reciprocal giving and receiving and with the kind of world or cosmos in which their giving and receiving can occur. Once again, Aristotle has drawn the outlines of a limited politics, limited, on one hand, by the families out of which political communities arise and whose ends they advance, and, on the other, by friendships that transcend politics.

Those include communities that come together for the sake of worship (1160a19–25) and those that "share in philosophy" (1164b3, 1172a5). Although such friendships transcend political life, they arise with the development of political life, when human relations extend beyond family members. Paralleling the relation between piety and politics, private and public for Aristotle remain distinct but are also inseparable. Because Aristotle holds that they remain distinct, he can speak to liberals. Because he holds that they are inseparable, he has something to say.

Our Declaration of Independence speaks the language of liberal political theory, even echoing Locke when it proclaims our inalienable rights, including the right to life, liberty, and the pursuit of happiness. But it also says that we are endowed with these rights by our Creator. Our rights are a divine gift, whether from our Creator or from Nature's God, which the Declaration also mentions. Even if such phrases were included for their rhetorical appeal, that appeal recognized the beliefs of many Americans. They became inscribed in what became one of our fundamental documents that declared our political principles. "We hold these truths to be self-evident." That our inalienable rights are God-given qualifies human autonomy, even though they mean that how we choose to live, what we do with our freedom, and how we pursue happiness are "up to us," to use Aristotle's words. Indeed, such freedom means that all things are arranged "in the most beautiful way," since only if we achieve our happiness will it be truly our own. That we are free to earn our happiness is a divine gift (1099b12–24). Our happiness is not by nature, nor contrary to nature, but like the ethical virtues themselves, our natures allow us to receive it. The proper human response is gratitude. It is also an acceptance of responsibility. We have been given, and we should give in return. In this way, Aristotle fosters a reverence for life, not because we can make it what we will, but because we can make it good. A political community that recognizes this could pledge allegiance to a nation as "under God," and might print on its coins "In God We Trust." As Aristotle said, we should acknowledge what we owe and make whatever return we can, even though such debt can never be repaid.

Such moderation that emerges from Aristotle's teaching in the *Ethics* is one that is proper for those engaged in political life, since it means that politics serves something higher than itself, and proper for those concerned with what is highest, whether religion or a philosophy that is open to the divine. Their pursuit of the highest does not merely require respect and protection from political life for its flourishing. That pursuit, as Aristotle suggests by his deeds in the *Ethics*, requires investigating the relation between the highest (whether understood as the highest good, the divine, or the cosmos) and human longing, and therewith actions that aim at the just, the beautiful or the noble, and the good. That pursuit requires, in other words, attention to political life, to its highest reaches and to its limits. Learning about both requires experience, from our own attempts to contribute and from those of others. Only then should we accept limits, while never ceasing to demand the highest from ourselves and others.

BIBLIOGRAPHY

Alexander, Rachel K. "Philosophical Foundations for Political Change: Aristotle's Inquiry into Beginnings in the *Nicomachean Ethics*." PhD diss., Baylor University, 2019.

Aquinas, Thomas. *Commentary on Aristotle's "Nicomachean Ethics."* Translated by C. I. Litzinger and foreword by Ralph McInerny. Notre Dame, IN: Dumb Ox Books, 1993.

Aubenque, Pierre. *La prudence chez Aristotle*. Paris: Presses Universitaires de France, 1963.

Badger, Jonathan N. *Sophocles and the Politics of Tragedy: Cities and Transcendence*. New York: Routledge, 2013.

Bartlett, Robert C. "Aristotle's Introduction to the Problem of Happiness: On Book I of the *Nicomachean Ethics*." *American Journal of Political Science* 52, no. 3 (2008): 677–87.

———. "Aristotle's Science of the Best Regime." *American Political Science Review* 88, no. 1 (1994): 152–60.

Bartlett, Robert C., and Susan D. Collins, trans. and eds. *Aristotle's "Nicomachean Ethics,"* with an interpretive essay, notes, and glossary. Chicago: University of Chicago Press, 2011.

———. "Interpretive Essay." In *Aristotle's "Nicomachean Ethics,"* 237–302.

Basil, Christine J. "Justice Speaks: Nemesis, Nature, Common Law in Aristotle's *Rhetoric*." *Review of Politics* 83 no. 2 (2021): 174–95.

Bickford, Susan. *The Dissonance of Democracy: Listening, Conflict, and Citizenship*. Ithaca, NY: Cornell University Press, 1996.

Block, Stephen A. "Aristophanic Comedy and Aristotelian Wit in the *Nicomachean Ethics*." Paper delivered at the Midwest Political Science Association, Chicago, IL, April 2008.

———. "Aristotle on Statesmanship, Freedom, and the Spirit of Democracy." In *Democracy and the History of Political Thought*, edited by Patrick N. Cain, Stephen Patrick Sims, and Stephen A. Block, 89–106. Lanham, MD: Lexington Books, 2021.

———. "The Problem of Good Fortune in Aristotle's *Ethics*." Paper delivered at the meeting of the Northeast Political Science Association, Philadelphia, PA. November 2015.

Block, Stephen A., and Patrick N. Cain. "The Good, Truth, and Friendship in Aristotle's *Nicomachean Ethics*." In *Politics, Literature, and Film in Conversation: Essays in Honor of Mary P. Nichols*, edited by Matthew D. Dinan, Paul E. Kirkland, Denise Schaeffer, and Natalie Fuehrer Taylor, 13–34. Lanham, MD: Lexington Books, 2021.

———. "Socrates's Spirited Defense of Knowledge: Continence, Incontinence, and Human Action in Book VII of Aristotle's *Nicomachean Ethics*." *Interpretation* 42, no. 1 (2015): 3–29.

Bodeus, Richard. *Aristotle and the Theology of the Living Immortals*. Translated by Jan Edward Garrett. Albany: State University of New York Press, 2000.

Broadie, Sarah. "Aristotelian Piety." *Phronesis* 48, no. 1 (2003): 54–70.

Bruell, Christopher. "Aristotle on Theory and Practice." In *Political Philosophy Cross-Examined: Perennial Challenges to the Philosophic Life*, edited by Thomas L. Pangle and J. Harvey Lomax, 17–27. New York: Palgrave Macmillan, 2013.

———. "Aristotle on Theory and Practice: Part Two." A talk delivered at the L'École des hautes études en sciences sociales, Paris, April 2006.

Burger, Ronna. *Aristotle's Dialogue with Socrates*. Chicago: University of Chicago Press, 2008.

———. "Eros and Mind: Aristotle on Philosophic Friendship and the Cosmos of Life." *Epoché* 23, no. 2 (2019): 365–80.

———. "Ethical Reflection and Righteous Indignation: *Nemesis* in the *Nicomachean Ethics*." In *Essays in Ancient Greek Philosophy*, edited by John Anton and Anthony Preuss, 4:127–39. Albany: State University of New York Press, 1991.

———. *The "Phaedo": A Platonic Labyrinth*. New Haven, CT: Yale University Press, 1984.

Burnet, John. *The Ethics of Aristotle*. Salem, NH: Ayer Publishing, 1988.

Cain, Patrick N. "Friendship, Rights, and Community: Aristotle and John Locke on the Family and Political Life." PhD diss., Baylor University, 2010.

Cain, Patrick N., and Mary P. Nichols. "Aristotle's Nod to Homer: A Political Science of Indebtedness." In *Socrates and Dionysus: Philosophy and Art in Dialogue*, edited by Ann Ward, 54–71. Newcastle: Cambridge Scholars Publishing, 2013.

Charney, Ann P. "Spiritedness and Piety in Aristotle." In *Understanding the Political Spirit: Philosophical Investigations from Socrates to Nietzsche*, edited by Catherine H. Zuckert, 67–87. New Haven, CT: Yale University Press, 1988.

Cherry, Kevin M. *Plato, Aristotle, and the Purposes of Politics*. New York: Cambridge University Press, 2012.
Clark, Stephen R. L. *Aristotle's Man*. Oxford: Clarendon, 1975.
Collins, Susan D. *Aristotle and the Rediscovery of Citizenship*. Cambridge: Cambridge University Press, 2008.
———. "Moral Virtue and the Limits of Political Community in Aristotle's *Nicomachean Ethics*." *American Journal of Political Science* 48, no. 1 (2004): 47–61.
Colmo, Ann Charney. "The Virtues and the Audience in Aristotle's *Rhetoric*." *Interpretation* 4, no. 3 (2021): 439–56.
Craig, Catherine, and Sara MacDonald. "Wit's Justice in Aristotle's *Nicomachean Ethics*." *Political Science Reviewer* 44 (2020): 47–70.
Cropsey, Joseph. "Justice and Friendship in the *Nicomachean Ethics*." In *Political Philosophy and the Issues of Politics*, edited by Joseph Cropsey, 252–73. Chicago: University of Chicago Press, 1977.
Davis, Michael. *The Soul of the Greeks*. Chicago: University of Chicago Press, 2011.
Deneen, Patrick. *Why Liberalism Failed*. New Haven, CT: Yale University Press, 2019.
Dreher, Rod. "Classical Liberalism Strikes Out" [Interview with Patrick Deneen]. *The American Conservative*, January 9, 2018.
Flakne, April. "Embodied and Embedded: Friendship and the Sunaisthetic Self." *Epoché* 10 (2005): 37–63.
Frank, Jill. *A Democracy of Distinction: Aristotle and the World of Politics*. Chicago: University of Chicago Press, 2005.
———. "On Logos and Politics in Aristotle." In *Aristotle's Politics: A Critical Guide*, edited by T. Lockwood and T. Samaras, 9–26. New York: Cambridge University Press, 2015.
Hamburger, Max. *Morals and Law: The Growth of Aristotle's Legal Theory*. New Haven, CT: Yale University Press, 1951.
Heyking, John von. *The Form of Politics: Aristotle and Plato on Friendship*. Montreal: McGill-Queen's University Press, 2016.
Howland, Jacob. "Aristotle's Great-Souled Man." *Review of Politics* 64, no. 1 (2002): 27–56.
Kahn, Charles H. "Aristotle on Altruism." *Mind* 90, no. 357 (1981): 20–40.
Kass, Leon R. "Professor or Friend? On the Intention and Manner of Aristotle's *Nicomachean Ethics*." In *Athens, Arden, and Jerusalem: Essays in Honor of Mera Flaumenhaft*, edited by Paul T. Wilford and Kate Havard, 3–27. Lanham, MD: Lexington Books, 2017.
Kosman, Aryeh. "Aristotle on the Desirability of Friends." *Ancient Philosophy* 24, no. 1 (2004): 135–54.

Kraut, Richard. *Aristotle: Political Philosophy*. Oxford: Oxford University Press, 2002.
Ludwig, Paul. *Rediscovering Political Friendship: Aristotle's Theory and Modern Identity, Community, and Equality*. Cambridge: Cambridge University Press, 2020.
MacLachlan, Bonnie. *The Age of Grace: Charis in Early Greek Poetry*. Princeton, NJ: Princeton University Press, 1993.
Mara, Gerald M. "Interrogating the Identities of Excellence: Liberal Educations and Democratic Culture in Aristotle's *Nicomachean Ethics*." *Polity* 31, no. 2 (1998): 301–29.
―――. "The *Logos* of the Wise in the *Politeia* of the Many: Recent Books on Aristotle's Political Philosophy." *Political Theory* 28, no. 6 (2000): 835–59.
Mathie, Catherine A. "Aristotle's Liberality." PhD diss., Baylor University, 2020.
Mathie, William. "Political and Distributive Justice in the Political Science of Aristotle." *Review of Politics* 49, no. 1 (1987): 59–84.
Nichols, Mary P. "Both Friends and Truth Are Dear: Aristotle's Political Thought as a Response to Plato." In *Natural Right and Political Philosophy: Essays in Honor of Catherine Zuckert and Michael Zuckert*, edited by Ann Ward and Lee Ward, 67–98. Notre Dame, IN: University of Notre Dame Press, 2013.
―――. *Citizens and Statesmen: A Study of Aristotle's "Politics."* Lanham, MD: Rowman & Littlefield, 1992.
―――. "How Excellence Bows to Equality in Aristotle's *Politics*." In *Equality and Excellence in Ancient and Modern Political Philosophy*, edited by Steven Frankel and John Ray, 67–88. Albany: State University of New York Press, 2023.
―――. "Plato's Democratic Moment." In Block, Cain, and Sims, eds., *Democracy and the History of Political Thought*, 61–80.
―――. Review of *Aristotle: Democracy and Political Science*, by Delba Winthrop. *Interpretation* 46, no.1 (2019): 107–18.
―――. "A Shrine to the Graces: Justice and Tragedy in Book 5 of Aristotle's *Nicomachean Ethics*." In *Nature, Law, and the Sacred: Essays in Honor of Ronna Burger*, edited by Evanthia Speliotis, 121–43. Macon, GA: Mercer University Press, 2019.
Pangle, Lorraine Smith. *Aristotle and the Philosophy of Friendship*. Cambridge: Cambridge University Press, 2003.
―――. *Reason and Character: The Moral Foundations of Aristotelian Political Philosophy*. Chicago: University of Chicago Press, 2020.
Rackham, H., trans. *Aristotle: "Athenian Constitution," "Eudemian Ethics," "Virtues and Vices."* Cambridge, MA: Harvard University Press, 1935.

———, trans. *Aristotle: "Nicomachean Ethics."* Cambridge, MA: Harvard University Press, 1926.
Roochnik, David. *Retrieving Aristotle in an Age of Crisis*. Albany: State University of New York Press, 2013.
Sachs, Joseph, trans. *Aristotle: "Nicomachean Ethics."* Newburyport, MA: R. Pullins Company, 2002.
———, trans. *Aristotle's "Metaphysics."* Santa Fe, NM: Green Lion Press, 1999.
Salkever, Stephen G. "Aristotle and the Ethics of Natural Questions." In *Instilling Ethics*, edited by Norma Thompson, 3–16. Lanham, MD: Rowman & Littlefield, 2000.
———. "Democracy and Aristotle's Ethics of Natural Questions." In *Aristotle and Modern Politics*, edited by Aristide Tessitore, 342–74. Notre Dame, IN: University of Notre Dame Press, 2002.
———. *Finding the Mean: Theory and Practice in Aristotelian Political Philosophy*. Princeton, NJ: Princeton University Press, 1990.
———. "'Lopp'd and Bound': How Liberal Theory Obscures the Goods of Liberal Practices." In *Liberalism and the Good*, edited by Gerald M. Mara, Henry S. Richardson, and Bruce Douglas, 65–89. New York: Routledge, 1990.
———. "Taking Friendship Seriously." In *Friendship and Politics: Essays in Political Thought*, edited by John von Heyking and Richard Avramenko, 53–83. Notre Dame, IN: University of Notre Dame Press, 2008.
Schaeffer, Denise. "Wisdom and Wonder in *Metaphysics* A: 1–2." *Review of Metaphysics* 52, no. 3 (1999): 641–56.
Sherman, Nancy. *The Fabric of Character: Aristotle's Theory of Virtue*. Oxford: Clarendon, 1989.
Smith, Bryan A. "Returning to Throne and Altar? Integralism, Liberalism, and Toleration." *Law and Liberty*, April 2, 2018.
Smith, Thomas W. *Revaluing Ethics: Aristotle's Dialectical Pedagogy*. Albany: State University of New York Press, 2001.
Sokolon, Marlene K. *Political Emotions: Aristotle and the Symphony of Reason and Emotion*. DeKalb: Northern Illinois University Press, 2006.
Sokolowski, Robert. "Phenomenology of Friendship." *Review of Metaphysics* 55, no. 3 (2002): 451–70.
Sorabji, Richard. "Aristotle on the Role of Intellect in Virtue." In *Essays on Aristotle's Ethics*, edited by Amelie Oksenberg Rorty, 201–20. Berkeley: University of California Press, 1980.
Sparshott, Francis. *Taking Life Seriously: A Study of the Argument of the "Nicomachean Ethics."* Toronto: University of Toronto Press, 1994.
Strauss, Leo. *City and Man*. Chicago: Rand McNally, 1964.

———. *Natural Right and History.* Chicago: University of Chicago Press, 1953.
———. "What Is Liberal Education?" In *Liberalism Ancient and Modern*, 3–8. New York: Basic Books, 1968.
Tessitore, Aristide. "A Political Reading of Aristotle's Treatment of Pleasure in the *Nicomachean Ethics.*" *Political Theory* 17, no. 2 (1989): 247–65.
———. *Reading Aristotle's "Ethics": Virtue, Rhetoric, and Political Philosophy.* Albany: State University of New York Press, 1996.
Tredennick, Hugh, trans. *Aristotle: "Posterior Analytics," "Topica."* Cambridge, MA: Harvard University Press, 1960.
Vermeule, Adrian. "Integration from Within." Review Essay of *Why Liberalism Failed* by Patrick Deneen. *American Affairs* 22, no. 1 (2018): 202–13.
Walsh, Germaine Paulo. "The Problematic Relation between Intellectual and Practical Virtue in Aristotle's *Nicomachean Ethics.*" In *A Moral Enterprise: Politics, Reason, and the Human Good: Essays in Honor of Frank Canavan*, edited by Kenneth L. Brasso and Robert P. Hunt, 59–81. Wilmington: ISI Books, 2002.
Ward, Ann. *Contemplating Friendship in Aristotle's Ethics.* Albany: State University of New York Press, 2016.
Ward, Lee. "Nobility and Necessity: The Problem of Courage in Aristotle's *Nicomachean Ethics.*" *American Political Science Review* 95, no, 1 (2001): 71–83.
Winthrop, Delba. "Aristotle and Theories of Justice." *American Political Science Review* 72, no. 4 (1978): 1201–16.
———. *Aristotle: Democracy and Political Science.* Chicago: University of Chicago Press, 2018.
Yack, Bernard. "Community and Conflict in Aristotle's Political Philosophy." *Review of Politics* 47, no. 1 (1985): 92–112.
———. *The Problems of a Political Animal: Community, Conflict, and Justice in Aristotelian Political Thought.* Berkeley: University of California Press, 1993.
Zuckert, Catherine H. "Aristotelian Virtue Ethics and Modern Liberal Democracy." *Review of Metaphysics* 68, no. 1 (2014): 61–91.
———. "Aristotle's Practical Political Science." In *Politikos II: Educating the Ambitious*, edited by Leslie G. Rubin, 144–65. Pittsburgh: Duquesne University Press, 1992.
———. *Plato's Philosophers: The Coherence of the Dialogues.* Chicago: University of Chicago Press, 2009.
———. "The Socratic Turn." *History of Political Thought* 25, no. 2 (2004): 189–219.

INDEX

Achilles, 10, 89, 99n8, 104–5, 106n17, 122, 133, 144, 149, 150, 168, 219, 236n6, 261n27
action, acting (*praxis, prattein*), 15, 16, 19–20, 42; end of ethical inquiry, 3, 179, 306, 313; knowing as a result of, 29, 63, 68, 83, 279, 299, 312; versus making, 171–72; supported by friendship, 263–66; voluntary versus involuntary, 62–63, 76–80, 83, 143, 144–45, 190, 310
activity (*energeia*), 24–26; coined by Aristotle, 116; identical with life, 260–61; lasting over time, 223, 263, 286; versus motion, 13, 46–49, 223–24, 227, 284; and pleasure, 223; as virtue (human work and happiness), 46–47, 48, 56, 103, 287, 293
Adeimantus, 153
Aeacus, 134n9
Agamemnon, 133, 232, 244, 245, 299n16
Agamemnon (Aeschylus), 94n3
Agathon (poet), 172
Ajax, 99n8, 105n16, 144, 168
Ajax (Sophocles), 94n3, 104n14
akrasia. See lacking self-rule
Alcibiades, 98–99, 99n8, 105, 122; in the *Posterior Analytics*, 99, 99n8, 168
Alcibiades II (Plato), 71, 106
Alcmaeon, 78, 145

Alcmaeon (Euripides), 144
Alexander, Rachel K., 23n6, 77n9
ambition. *See* love of honor, as social virtue
Anacharsis, 289, 290, 292
Analytics (Aristotle). See *Posterior Analytics*
Anaxagoras, 11, 157–58, 178, 188; his recourse to mind, 175n19, 179; his saying about the many, 303; response from Aristotle to, 178–81, 193
anger, 93, 107–8, 150; and blame, 79, 80, 108; mean and extremes of, 71, 144
Antigone (Sophocles), 148, 151, 218
Apollo, 7n7, 142n18, 145, 215
Apology (Plato), 80, 129, 133, 134n9, 173, 178, 192–93, 203, 288, 304
Aristogeiton, 236n6
Aristophanes: in Plato's *Symposium*, 156n1. See also *Clouds*; comedy
Aristotle, his work as a model for political life, 27, 69, 87n15, 121, 159, 190, 279
art(s), 134, 157, 165, 171–73, 180, 201, 216n13; architectonic, 27; with ends in themselves, 24–26, 112, 171; hierarchy and ranking of, 23–24, 24n10, 164; and science, 159n3, 164, 175; and wisdom, 177

333

Athena, 137, 146
Aubenque, Pierre, 232
audiences of the *Ethics*, 59; the educated, 32; gentlemen, 50n38, 198, 308; philosophers versus nonphilosophers, 30n18, 198, 279n1; young, old, and middle-aged, 28–31, 306

Bacchae (Euripides), 242, 242n11
Badger, Jonathan N., 219n15
Bartlett, Robert C., 6, 27n16, 30n18, 31, 45n34, 50n38; and Susan D. Collins, 1n1, 19n1, 20, 20n2, 51n39, 65n1, 66n2, 86n14, 167n10, 175n18, 184n26, 232n1
Basil, Christine J., 153n27
beautiful, the (the noble) (*to kalon*), 4, 19, 22, 24, 33, 49, 52, 52n42, 54, 78–79, 89, 172n15, 182, 285, 199, 325; difficulty in translating from Greek, 19n1; as end of virtue, 6, 26, 47, 84–88, 94, 96, 97, 98, 104, 110, 112, 113, 142, 185, 199, 200, 215, 276, 288, 292; and friendship, 236, 256, 261–62, 269–70, 271n38; and the good, 26, 101, 101n9, 124, 149–50, 186, 192, 199, 286; and greatness of soul, 101, 102; love of, 51, 86, 87, 90, 91, 149, 150, 261, 270, 306; modifying its scope, 143, 148–50, 149n25, 189, 303; truth-telling and, 219–20, 227, 281, 283; and the young, 28–31
bestiality, 12, 197, 197n1, 202, 203, 212, 215–16; cannibalism, 88
Bickford, Susan, 185n27, 257n25
blessed, blessedness, 52, 263, 263n29; etymology of, 221; of the gods, 55; of human beings, 2, 3, 5, 21, 54, 55, 58, 153, 287, 319; over time, 48
Block, Stephen A., 24n9, 52n43, 58n46, 115n25; and Patrick N. Cain, 35n22, 37n26, 198n4, 202n7, 213n11, 229n25
Bodeus, Richard, 6n3
Brasidas, 141, 142
Broadie, Sarah, 5
Bruell, Christopher, 170n12, 184n26
Burger, Ronna, 7n8, 25, 30n18, 162, 198, 243, 286n35, 102n10, 106n18, 128n5, 129n6, 146n19, 153n28, 162n7, 193n34, 236n4, 239n8, 268n35, 279n1, 287, 292, 299n16
Burnet, John, 42n31, 226

Cain, Patrick N., 245n13, 251n22; and Mary P. Nichols, 106n17
Categories (Aristotle), 72
chance (fortune) (*tuchē*): and friendship, 235–36, 271n38, 369–72; and greatness of soul, 99n8, 103, 168; and happiness, 8–9, 41, 48, 51–55, 75, 303; and human activity, 8–9, 22, 52–53, 153, 172, 194, 312n22; and wrongdoing, 83. *See also* friendship: in good and bad fortune
change: in friendship, 237, 239, 240, 269; sweetness of, 225, 280
character, 9, 58, 66, 81, 109, 110; coming from habit, 9, 61, 116, 161; and the title of the *Ethics*, 62, 116
characteristic. *See* disposition
Charney, Ann P., 6, 88n16
Cherry, Kevin M., 69n4, 147n20
choice (*prohairesis*), 15, 19, 21, 26, 36, 44, 51n40, 53, 58, 66, 78, 79, 81, 84, 91, 100, 140, 148, 151, 157, 162, 201, 207, 208–9, 280, 281; in contrast to wish, 5, 128; in defining the human, 16, 61–62, 162n7, 179, 201, 320; meaning of term, 76–77, 77n7, 116; and prudence, 172, 174; supported by friendship, 268n35
Churchill, Winston, 87n15

citizens, 45, 111, 128, 140, 307; and deliberation, 139; in modern liberalism, 317, 318; obedient to the laws, 127, 152; self-rule by, 58, 59n48, 153, 154, 233; as soldiers, 86; in timocracy, 248. *See also* like-mindedness; statesman
Clark, Stephen R. L., 45n35, 181n25
Clouds (Aristophanes), 38, 217, 277
coining of words, 72, 77n7, 113, 116, 149n23, 161, 181n24, 266
Collins, Susan D., 7n8, 26n15, 92n1, 97n7, 103n13, 114n21, 118n27, 317n1
Colmo, Ann Charney, 69n3
comedy, 117, 118n27, 121, 177, 276–77
"common-sense," role in perception, 264–65n30
comprehension (*synesis*), 58, 165, 170, 184, 187, 188–89
consideration (*gnōmē*), 187, 189–90, 191. *See also* forgiveness
contemplation, contemplative. *See* theory, theoretical
continence. *See* self-rule
courage, 9, 28, 63, 84–88, 90, 92, 301; and the beautiful, 26, 85–86, 87, 87n15, 88, 91, 285, 288; and death, 84, 104; as a mean, 29, 62, 67, 73, 84, 86; political, 26, 85, 86; and shame, 120; Spartan, 205n9, 307
Craig, Catherine, and Sara MacDonald, 114n22
Cropsey, Joseph, 198n4, 246n15, 262n28, 271n38; on definition of self-rule (moral resoluteness), 200
Cyclops, 307, 308

Davis, Michael, 40n29
De Anima (Aristotle): on activity versus motion, 46; on knowing the soul, 161; on knowing wholes, 160n5; on longing, 20n2; on parts of the soul, 163n8; on perception 264n30, 267n34; and the *Politics*, 299n17
death: as completion of life versus end of life, 48; fear of, 9, 84; in war, 86; as limit upon human power, 5; most fearful thing, 29
Declaration of Independence, 325
deliberation, 36, 77, 79, 88, 140, 185n27, 185n29, 186; and choice, 5, 16, 77; by citizens, 3, 139; and prudence, 156, 172, 180, 182–86, 188, 195
deliberation (good) (*euboulia*), 187–88
Den Uyl, Douglas, 317n1
Deneen, Patrick, 318, 319, 320
Descartes, René, 181
despotism, 15, 308; distinguished from political rule, 15, 16, 313
dexterity, in wit, 115n24
Diomedes, 144, 236, 236n6
disposition (*hexis*), 107, 128, 137; difficulty in translating from Greek, 66n2; humans as co-causes of, 83, 321; virtues as, 66–67, 70, 79, 84, 90, 93, 100, 107–8, 201

Eleatic Stranger, 69n4, 147n20
Empedocles, 225, 237
enkrateia. *See* self-rule
equity: and forgiveness (pardon), 11, 148, 189, 208, 323; approaching wholeness, 285; and friendship, 241, 250–51, 257; and tragedy, 132, 143–50, 153; correcting the law's universality, 11, 80, 118–19, 127, 146–48, 152, 309; grasping particulars, 199; meaning of, 146–47, 146n19, 147n20; those characterized by, 128, 137–38, 148–50, 247, 251
error, tragic, in the *Poetics*, 75
Ethics (Aristotle): dialectical character of, 7; not a work of theology, 4; speech and deeds in, 7

Eudemian Ethics (Aristotle): on choice, 77; on family, 13; on friendship, 239n8, 240, 266, 267, 267n33, 298; on learning, 284; on truthful person, 113

Eudoxus, 281, 282; as like and unlike Aristotle, 282n2

Eumenides, 137

Eumenides (Aeschylus), 137, 145

Euripides, 225, 237

Euthydemus (Plato), 295

Euthyphro (Plato), 3

Evenus, 207n10

exoteric arguments, speeches, 56–57, 171

Fates, 51n40

Flakne, April, 266n31, 267n32, 267n34, 268n35

forgiveness (pardon) (*suggnōmē*), 78–80, 93, 108, 143, 144, 148, 150, 189–90, 218. *See also* beautiful, the; consideration; equity

fortune. *See* chance

Frank, Jill, 59n48, 136n12, 240n9, 257n25

friendliness (a social virtue), 72–73, 108, 114, 117

friendship, 95, 204, 206, 219, 219n15, 225n18, 228–29, 229n25, 235n3, 278; definition of, 232, 235, 237–38, 239n8; in good and bad fortune, 235–36, 269–72, 271n38; between humans and gods, impossibility of, 231, 232n1, 239–40, 250, 296; between husband and wife, 246–48, 247n17, 252; in mother's love for children, 251, 251n22; between parents and offspring, 237, 245, 249–50, 256; and political community, 130n7, 232–35, 242–44, 248–49, 324–25; shared activity and awareness, 236n4, 238, 238n7, 260–61, 262–69, 268n35, 271, 297, 298; and time, 239, 259–60, 268–69, 271, 279–80. *See also* greatness of soul; like-mindedness; physiologists; pleasure; reciprocity; regimes: modeled on friendship in families; trust

Furies, 137, 145

Generation of Animals (Aristotle), 225n18

gentleness, 71, 82, 93, 107–8, 109, 144

Gettysburg Address, 87n15

Glaucon, 153

Glaucus, 144, 149

god(s): beneficence of, 9, 51–52, 51n40, 88n16, 141n17, 172n15, 177, 194, 233, 242n11, 250, 277, 304–5, 314, 321–22; criticism of poets on, 4, 121, 150, 172, 219, 220, 228, 242n11, 254, 301, 305; deserving honor, 55, 92–93, 101,101n9, 105, 107, 142; distance between humans and, 2, 6, 13, 92, 97, 97n7, 134, 142, 158, 195, 202, 204–5, 220, 224–27, 231, 245, 297–98, 314–15; humans between beasts and, 14, 15, 21, 121, 182, 273; knowledge of, 6, 160n5, 205–6, 295–96, 304; models for humans, 6, 11, 14, 97, 135–36, 233–34, 272–73, 298, 301–2, 323; munificent acts directed to, 97, 97n6; no thematic discussion of, 3, 4; in the *Oresteia*, 137, 145–46; pleasure of, 5, 224–27, 272, 276, 308; worshipping, 70, 195, 242–43, 285. *See also Metaphysics*: on the divine, god, or highest good; reverence

good, the, 28; as enabling the ranking of pleasures, 286; as "one's own," 39, 41; relation to the cosmos, 42n32. *See also* ideas (of Plato)

Gorgias (Plato), 133–34

grace, 44, 45, 48, 53, 135, 136, 137, 144, 146, 221, 286, 288, 323
Graces, 11, 13, 135–38, 135n10, 136n12, 144, 146, 150, 216, 221, 226, 237, 254, 277, 301, 305, 306, 322, 323
gratitude, 5, 55, 135, 135n11, 137, 177, 325
greatness of soul (*megalopsuchia*), 2–3, 10, 73, 92–93, 99–106, 107, 109, 110, 115, 120, 132, 136–37, 168–69, 185, 235, 323; bodily characteristics of, 103, 115, 120, 132; and the divine, 2, 10, 92, 105, 105n15, 106, 121; and friendship, 2–3, 10, 105–6, 106nn17–18, 109, 323; in prior Greek literature, 71, 106

habit/habituation, 9, 33, 63–66; through the law, 21, 306–8; and nature, 64, 207n10, 225
Hamburger, Max, 147n20, 148n22
happiness, 21, 40n29, 43, 44, 45, 275, 295, 303; and chance, 8, 194; and death, 48, 54; as divine, 8, 55, 272, 290–92, 304n20; as final end, 2, 43–44; in friendship, 235, 262, 263; and honor and praise, 34; and modern liberalism, 16, 324–25; and play, 290; and pleasure, 221, 276; result of human effort, 8, 48, 58, 103, 304, 325; and self-awareness, 54, 201, 263, 268; and virtue, 22, 35, 46, 51, 54, 56, 61, 67, 109, 156, 180, 186, 194, 199, 287–88, 293, 320
Harmodious, 236n6
Hector, and divine virtue, 204–5, 204n8
Helen, 75, 76
Hellenica (Xenophon), 71
Heraclitus, 225, 237, 304n20
Hercules, 236n6
heroes/heroism, 105n16, 150n26, 236n6; Brasidas, 141–42; heroic or divine virtue, 12, 202–5, 220; Homeric, 86, 88n16, 120, 261n27, 324
Hesiod. See *Theogony*; *Works and Days*
Heyking, John von, 29n17, 235n3, 240n9, 266n31, 291n8
Histories (Herodotus), 140n16, 303
holy. See piety, pious
Homer, 105n15, 119, 120, 149, 172n15, 204n8, 299, 299n16. See also *Iliad*; *Odyssey*; *Margites*
honor, 45, 52, 81; as beautiful, 86; as greatest of external goods, 101; love of, 39, 107
Howland, Jacob, 34n20, 101n9, 102, 304n20
hubris, 6, 92, 121, 215–16
human nature, 9, 38, 49, 78, 91, 297–98, 319; as composite, 5, 197, 276, 277, 296, 303; as needy. 223, 224, 225, 284; as political, 8, 14, 15, 31, 45, 122, 314, 321, 322. See also nature, natural

ideas (of Plato), 39–43, 67, 109, 111, 123–25, 212, 228; in the *Metaphysics*, 40n28; in the *Parmenides*, 40
Iliad (Homer), 53, 75, 89, 105n15, 204, 244; Achilles in, 105, 133; friendship in, 106n17, 261n27; Glaucus and Diomedes in, 144, 149; Odysseus ruling with Athena's help in, 299n16; Odysseus and Diomedes in, 236. See also heroes/heroism: Homeric
impiety, impious, 88n16, 142, 182; Alcibiades as, 98; in destroying life, 38n27, 228; Oedipus as, 47, 82, 151; tyrant as, 95. See also incest; piety, pious
incest, 38, 47, 80, 88, 143, 258
incontinence. See lacking self-rule
indignation, righteous. See *nemesis*

Iolaus, 236n6
irony, 113

joy, 5, 44, 221, 222, 304, 342; and friendship, 119, 137, 235, 247, 252, 259, 269
justice, 187n31, 212, 249, 252; anomalies in Aristotle's treatment of, 126–27, 128n5; conventional or legal, 141–42; different ways of speaking about, 123–26, 129; distributive and corrective, 6n3, 110, 125, 129–32, 151, 319; and equity, 143–50; and friendship, 138, 234, 242, 246, 272; imprecise and varying, 22, 27, 87, 149n23, 159, 174; and the law, 88, 120, 122, 125–32, 323; natural, 138–41, 141n17, 314; political, 138–43, 154; and reciprocity, 132–38, 136n12, 187n31. *See also* equity; *nemesis*; *Republic*: justice in

Kahn, Charles H, 267n33
Kass, Leon R., 7, 29, 45n35, 160n6, 170, 197, 268
king/kingship, 15, 147n20, 244–46, 246n15, 249, 300, 301
knowledge, range of meanings, 159n3. *See also* science
Kosman, Aryeh, 266n31, 271n40
Kraut, Richard, 125n3, 128n5

lacking self-rule (*akrasia*), 195, 197, 206–21; distinct from vice, 218; perplexity regarding, 208–9; Socrates's position on, 202–3, 202n7, 209–14; Sophists's, 22; and spiritedness, 215–20. *See also* self-rule
law, 11, 132; and equity, 80, 118, 127, 145–48, 189, 309, 323; incompleteness of, 126, 137, 322; and justice, 88, 125–32, 141–42; against suicide, 150–53

Laws (Plato), 124n2, 142n18; the gods in, 3
legislators, 308–10, 322; architectonic art of, 65, 182–83; Cretan and Spartan, 56, 59, 142n18, 307
Libation Bearers (Aeschylus), 145
liberal, liberalism: modern, 16–17, 317–21, 317n1, 324
liberality, 10, 63, 70, 91, 94–96, 99, 114, 119, 144
life, as divine, 228
like-mindedness (political friendship) (*homonoia*), 13, 233–34, 235, 252, 257–58, 272, 318, 319. *See also* citizens
Lincoln, Abraham, 87n15
longing (*orexis*), 200n6; absent from law, 58; for a final good, 20–21, 26, 163, 206; for the good, 158, 163, 172n15, 179, 181, 182, 320; for honor 71, 92–93; to know, 4, 20n2, 21, 181, 223, 298; part of the soul, 57; pervading the soul, 158, 162–63, 162n7, 163n8, 169; translation of, 20n2; at work in politics, 163, 320, 322
love of honor, as social virtue, 71, 92–93
Ludwig, Paul, 257n25, 317, 318, 318n2, 320, 321
Lycurgus, 142n18
Lysander, 168
Lysis (Plato), 237, 253, 260

MacIntyre, Alasdair, 317n1
MacLachlan, Bonnie, 44n33, 135n11
Magna Moralia (Aristotle), 25n11, 148n22
magnanimity. *See* greatness of soul
magnificence. *See* munificence
Mara, Gerald M., 7n8, 30n18, 117n26, 296n12, 297n13
Margites (Homer?), 177, 179, 301n19
Mathie, Catherine A., 94n2, 96n5, 130n7

mean, the, 105n15, 155–56; different for each individual, 67; and justice, 127–29; overshooting the, 75; those without names, 71–72; trusting in, 109–10
Meno (Plato), 70, 210; and origin of virtue, 63–64
Merchant of Venice (Shakespeare), 149n24
Merope, 79
Messeniacus (Alcidamus), 141n17
Metaphysics (Aristotle), 32, 42, 42n31, 44n33, 46, 52n42, 103, 121, 223, 224n16; character of the work 4, 159n2, 191, 298, 298n14; criticism of Anaxagoras, 175n19; criticism of Plato's ideas, 39, 40n28, 41n30; on the divine, god, or highest good, 4, 20, 21, 40n29, 42n32, 295, 301n19; on meaning of complete, 26, 48n37; on freedom, 85n12, 91; on human longing to know, 20n2; and perplexity, 4, 21, 161, 206, 224, 294; in relation to Aristotle's political works, 42n32, 58n47, 299–300, 300n18; on self-contradiction, 83n10; on the Sophists, 209; on theorizing, 65, 297–98
mind (*nous*), 44, 202, 277, 297, 304; as attaining truth, 156, 157, 175–76, 175nn18–19, 177n22, 179, 181, 192; as a cause of human action, 82, 83, 132; in definition of human, 162–63, 162n7, 320; as divine or something divine in us, 4, 14, 228, 277, 288, 292, 314, 320; as thought thinking itself, 301n19. *See also* like-mindedness
Minos, 134n9, 142n18
moderation, 3, 88–90, 283, 322; defined, 88; as a mean, 69, 75, 89, 185
money, as product of convention, 134–35, 139

munificence, 6n3, 70–71, 92, 96–99, 102, 293
Muses, 124, 135

nature, natural, 47, 52–53, 237–38, 264, 283, 325; goodness of life by, 225, 225n18, 228n24, 264, 280; in relation to ethical virtue, 64–65, 82–83, 91; as support for human life, 2, 52, 53, 147, 192, 201, 228. *See also* justice: natural; physiologists
nemesis (righteous indignation), 73, 75–76, 126, 152–54, 153nn27–28
Nichols, Mary P., 24n7, 72n6, 140n15, 141n17, 174n17, 313n24
Nicias, 99n8
Nietzsche, Friedrich, 17
Niobe, 215
noble, the. *See* beautiful, the
Nussbaum, Martha, 317n1

Odysseus, 77, 77n9
Odyssey (Homer), 74, 89, 119, 307
Oedipus, 47, 48, 79, 80, 82,143, 150, 151, 232
Oedipus at Colonus (Sophocles), 224
Oedipus Tyrannus (Sophocles), 53, 80, 150, 233
Olympic Games, 49
On Sleep and Waking (Aristotle), 264n30
opinion, 22, 140, 173, 174n17, 206, 303; Aristotle's use of, 32, 34, 62, 71, 72, 188–89, 190–91, 206; common, 69, 107, 120, 221, 222, 281, 286n5; and science, 164
Oresteia (Aeschylus), 137, 145, 146
Orestes (Euripides), 225

Pangle, Lorraine Smith, 6, 6n3, 6n5, 19n1, 30n18, 45n34, 50n38, 53n44, 87n15, 97n6, 135n10, 153n28, 160,

Pangle, Lorraine Smith (*cont.*)
    167n11, 176n20, 185n29, 262n28,
    263n29, 271n38, 304n20
pardon. *See* forgiveness
Paris, 75
Parts of Animals (Aristotle), 228n24,
    264n30
passions (*patheis*): in relation to disposition or virtue, 66–67, 79; shame
    and *nemesis* as, 73. *See also* disposition
Patroclus, 219–20n15, 236n6, 261n27
Peloponnesian War (Thucydides), 98,
    114n23
Pericles, 114n23, 173, 175n19, 193n34, 257
perplexity (*aporia*), 158, 166, 168, 175n19,
    191–92, 194, 255, 264n30; Aristotle's, 188–89, 191, 193, 227, 294;
    Plato's, 32, 39; Socrates's, 210, 213.
    See also *Metaphysics*: and perplexity
Phaedo (Plato), 179
Phaedrus (Plato), 54, 161, 192, 253
Philebus (Plato), 223, 226, 283
Philoctetes (Sophocles), 219
philosophy, Aristotle's way of, 8, 37,
    38–39, 43, 109–13, 116, 118n27, 221,
    227, 281, 293–95; about human
    affairs, 3–4, 64, 158, 182, 199,
    278–79, 285, 299, 300, 312, 315;
    implications for politics, 319–26
Phoenician Women (Euripides), 258
Physics (Aristotle), 49
physiologists (students of nature): on
    friendship, 237, 259; on pleasure,
    224, 225, 226, 229, 264, 282
piety, pious (*hosiotēs, hosios*), 2, 3, 5–7, 12,
    14, 17, 37, 88n16, 97n6, 135n10, 142,
    172n15, 177, 250, 273, 315, 319–22;
    in honoring the truth, 37–38; not
    included among virtues in the
    Ethics, 5, 181; and politics, 273, 319,
    322, 325; in the *Politics*, 37–38; in
    the *Republic*, 7n7, 37–38, 176,
    176n21
Pindar, 114n23
Pittacus, 257
Plato, 132; as perplexed, 32; speech and
    deeds in the dialogues of, 8. *See
    also individual dialogues by name*
play/playfulness (*paidia*), 93, 276;
    activity for its own sake, 287–93;
    Aristotle's playing, 94, 115–16, 290,
    295, 301, 312n22, 315; in philosophy, 292–93, 294–95; and
    seriousness, 110, 115, 118, 276–77,
    288, 290, 294–95; and wit, 108, 109,
    114–19, 124, 289
pleasure, 221–29, 276, 279–87; Aristotle's
    different treatments of, 279–80,
    279n1, 286n5, 314; Aristotle's
    response to critics of, 221–24,
    280–83; attraction to, 73, 75, 78,
    88–90, 91; bodily versus liberal,
    44–45, 88–90, 93, 117, 204, 219,
    220–24, 289, 290; divine versus
    human, 13, 88, 202, 203, 220,
    225–27, 228, 276, 284–86, 296, 301;
    and ethical virtue, 51, 87, 185, 200;
    Eudoxus on, 281–83; experience of
    wholeness, 276, 284–85, 314; as
    gracing activity, 286; in friendship,
    36, 105, 110–11, 199, 229, 238–40,
    253–54, 259, 272; life of, 35, 37, 45,
    221, 275; and moderation, 69, 73,
    88–90; of philosophy, 199, 223–24,
    228n24, 293–95, 315; unmixed with
    pain, 223, 227, 276, 284
Poetics (Aristotle), 75, 79, 153, 169, 177,
    218
Polemarchus, 128
political science, modern versus Aristotle's, 50n38
politics (statesmanship) (*politikē*), 59,
    206, 278–79, 300, 306–10; as architectonic art, 14–15, 22–26, 23n6, 27,

56, 158, 171, 171n14, 182–83; Aristotle's predecessors on, 305, 310; difficulty of translating Greek term, 23n5; and leisure, 300, 300n18; persuasion rather than force, 15, 308, 314, 324. *See also* statesman

Politics (Aristotle), 8, 37–38, 56, 132, 160, 178n23, 185, 214, 216n13, 225, 243, 244, 248, 248n21, 258, 292, 299n17; distinguishing political rule from despotism, 15, 139, 139n13, 140n15, 313; on human beings as political, 1, 15, 88, 282, 314; outline of, 311–12; as political reform, 15, 313; as sequel to the *Ethics*, 14, 257, 305, 307, 312, 313n24; slavery in, 312–13, 313n24; as unfinished, 312n22

polity, 72n6, 248n21

Posterior Analytics (Aristotle), 165–70, 175n19, 183–84; on greatness of soul, 99, 99n8, 105n16, 168

practical wisdom. *See* prudence

precision, 27, 28, 32, 41–42, 49, 50n38, 112, 113, 149n23, 177, 212; regarding the beautiful and just, 22, 174; speaking with, 112, 113

Priam, 53, 75; on Hector's divine virtue, 202, 204–5

Prior Analytics (Aristotle), 165

Problems (Aristotle), 226n20

Protagoras, 255

Protagoras (Plato), 176, 209, 214

prudence, 35n21, 36, 58, 109n19, 117n26, 158, 170–74, 178–86, 187–91, 223; belonging to politics/statesman, 3, 67, 73, 173, 182–84, 195; and ethical virtue, 67, 155–56, 184–85, 185n29, 193, 201, 297, 321; and the law, 127; in relation to wisdom, 11, 35n21, 69, 147n20, 156, 157, 178–79, 190, 195, 323–24; utility of, 191–95

Rackham, H., 24n10, 42n31, 52n41, 86n14, 112, 226, 270n37

Rasmussen, Douglas, 317n1

reciprocity: in friendship, 106, 111, 114, 119, 137, 194, 234–35, 237, 238, 250, 252, 323; as holding the city together, 249–50; and justice, 126, 132–37, 144, 146; in play, 114, 114n22, 119; in regard to parents and offspring, 249–50, 261; in ruling and being ruled, 137, 139, 140, 152, 272

regime: best, 140, 246n15, 311; classification of, 72n6, 244, 246n16, 248n21; modeled on friendship in families, 242–49

Republic, 156n1, 248, 270, 311; justice in, 28, 68, 124, 125n3, 129, 153–54; knowledge and opinion in, 173–74, 174n17; and *nemesis*, 152; piety and impiety in, 3, 7n7, 38–39, 80; spiritedness in, 213, 216, 217; virtues in, 68–69, 70, 152

reverence (*aidōs*), 2, 17, 58, 73, 93, 120–22, 120n28, 306, 325

Rhadamanthus, 133–34, 134n9, 135n10, 136, 137, 144, 148, 208

Rhetoric (Aristotle), 135n11, 141n17, 153n27, 185, 223, 227; on equity, 148, 148n22, 208; and friendship, 271n40; as political reform, 313; on shame, 120n28, on trust, 109n19, 169; on virtues, 69n3; on young versus old, 28–31, 48, 99n8

Roochnik, David, 20n3, 36nn23–24, 45n35, 185n28, 264–65n30, 284n3, 288n6, 291, 298n14

Rousseau, Jean Jacques, 16

Sachs, Joe, 1n1, 20n2, 44n33, 86n14, 159n3 298n14

Salkever, Stephen, 1n2, 7n8, 20n2, 66n2, 77n7, 150n26, 236nn5–6, 240n9, 317n1 science (*epistēmē*), 23, 128–29, 156–57, 158, 163–70, 173–77, 180, 190, 321; and other Greek verbs of knowing, 159n3; in relation to self-rule and its lack, 209, 211–14

second sailing: as the "human" way of virtue, 297; as overshooting the mean, 74, 75

self-knowledge, 160–63; through acting virtuously, 67–68; through erring, 180–81; as fostered by Aristotle, 67–68, 94, 99, 100, 182, 226; through friendship, 262–68, 267n33, 271, 271–72n40; of the great-souled individual, 100, 323; and happiness, 35, 43, 54, 201, 263; lacked by those who study nature and the heavens, 178–79, 180; in Oedipus's answer to the Sphinx, 47–48; by seeking truth about the world, 161, 180–81, 299–300; in self-rule and its lack, 12, 200–201, 220. *See also* Socrates: his human wisdom

self-restraint. *See* self-rule

self-rule (over oneself) (*enkrateia*), 5, 11, 12, 22, 57–59, 59n48, 65, 127n4, 154, 195, 197, 197n1, 200–203, 206–21; and friendship, 228; in relation to virtue, 201, 207–8, 216–17, 220

self-sufficiency, 124, 136, 202, 236n4; divine, 12, 234; and greatness of soul, 100, 102, 103, 106n18, 115, 235–36, 295, 304n20, 323; human, 1, 44, 45, 45n34, 52–52, 52n43, 236n4, 263n29, 295, 303, 321; of the philosophic life, 5, 106n18, 202. *See also* king/kingship

separation of church and state, 16, 318, 322

serious individual, seriousness (*spoudaios, spoudē*), 277; meanings of 117–18, 117n26; in philosophy, 292–93, 294–95; as a standard, 117–18, 198, 290–93. *See also* play/playfulness

shame, 38, 58, 59, 73, 78, 93, 104, 105, 117, 119–22; as a mean, 121; as sign of responsibility, 79; and the young, 120. *See also* reverence

Sherman, Nancy, 36n23, 185n27, 296n12

slavery, 141n17, 212, 312, 312n23, 313n24

Smith, Thomas W., 29n17, 114n21, 149n25, 242n10

Socrates: example of greatness of soul, 99n8, 168; his human wisdom, 179, 195, 205, 210, 214, 304; honoring the truth, 38–39; investigating virtue, 11, 64, 192; model for Aristotle, 178–79, 192–93; myths of reward and punishment after death, 54, 133; understanding virtue as knowledge, 199, 202, 209–14. *See also individual dialogues of Plato*

Sokolon, Marlene K., 135n11

Solon, 53, 303

Sophists, 194, 209, 213; in contrast to philosophers, 209; demanding payment in advance, 255; incapable of guiding politics, 278, 310, 313; rendering virtue and thinking impossible, 199, 208–9, 295

Sorabji, Richard, 185–86n29

soul: difficulty in knowing, 160–63, 160n5; division between rational and non-rational parts, 56–59, 208; division of rational part of, 158–63, 163n8

Sparshott, Francis, 6n3

Sparta, 307, 313. *See also* courage: Spartan; legislators: Cretan and Spartan

Sphinx, 47, 48

spiritedness, 216n13; actions originating in, 79, 144, 149; and courage, 85, 86; as an expression of longing, 20n2, 132, 218; its role in self-rule and its lack, 200n6, 202n7, 211, 213–18, 222

statesman, 4, 9, 142, 278, 309–10; dependent on others, 44, 65, 154, 183, 200, 300; as lover of honor, 34–35, 41, 43, 44, 56–57, 101; making citizens good, 65, 127–28, 198, 278; and prudence, 3, 67, 173, 182–84, 195; summary of appearances in *Ethics*, 310–11; understanding the soul, 22, 56–59, 127, 179. *See also* legislators, politics

Statesman (Plato), 69n4, 47, 178

Strauss, Leo, 7, 21n4, 140

suicide, 126, 138, 150–53

Symposium (Plato), 97, 156n1, 172n15, 210

teleology, 281, 283

Tessitore, Aristide, 30n18, 184n26, 198, 204n8, 279n1, 286n5

Thales: inquiring about non-human nature, 11, 157–58, 178, 188, 264; making money, 178n23

Theaetetus (Plato), 56, 70n5, 163, 178n23, 255, 264

Theogony (Hesiod), 135, 254

theology, 4, 159n2, 298n14, 319

theory, theoretical, 42n32, 293–96; activity of the gods, 301, 301n19; activity with others, 26, 266n31, 295, 298; *Ethics* as both practical and, 3, 64, 196, 221, 277; in many activities and ways of life, 14, 36–37, 199, 221, 275, 277, 297; practicing theorizing, 298; translations of, 36n23; unmixed pleasure, 223; usages in *Ethics*, 35–36, 157, 161, 186, 227, 297; as way of life, 35, 36, 275

Thetis, 89, 90, 104; 105n15

Thucydides: on Alcibiades, 98; on worship of Brasidas, 141–42

time, as co-worker, 15, 32, 49, 239, 312n22

timocracy, 246n15; 248, 248n21

Tredennick, Hugh, 165n9

trust, 35, 36, 43, 52, 291, 320, 325; in accepting speeches, 31, 32, 109, 109n19, 111, 152, 169, 171, 282–83, 303; and friendship, 106, 167, 167n10, 238, 239, 240, 254; and knowledge, 161, 166–67, 167n11, 170n12, 175–76, 175n19, 177, 177n22, 181, 184, 190

truth, 38, 49, 116, 160, 279, 285, 325; dear to the philosopher, 37, 39, 41, 43; deeds as a test of, 303; ways of attaining, 64, 67–68, 118n27, 124, 156–57, 161, 163–83, 190, 303

truthfulness, 219–20, 281; and greatness of soul, 105, 110, 323; as social virtue, 72, 93, 108, 109–10, 111–14

tyrant, 78, 79, 95–96, 122, 138, 245, 289, 291, 292

Vermuele, Adrian, 318

versatility, 72, 114n23, 115. *See also* wit

Walsh, Germaine Paulo, 293n10; 300n18

Ward, Ann, 25, 26n15, 232n2, 246n15, 247n19, 251n22

whole, the, 4, 42n32, 97, 156, 159, 177, 178, 285, 299

Winthrop, Delba, 42–43n32, 130n7, 136n12, 140n16

wisdom, 4, 11, 12, 155–58, 164, 174–82, 183, 191, 283, 304; and mind, 174–77; and prudence, 11, 35n21, 63, 194, 323; in the *Republic*, 69; Socratic, 173, 178, 179, 192–93, 271n38,

wisdom (*cont.*)
304; utility of, 193–95. *See also* prudence

wish, 19, 20n2, 41n30, 81, 278, 299; of beings in the cosmos, 299; distinct from deliberation and choice, 5, 49, 128; in friendship, 13, 231–32, 241, 260, 296; of the statesman, 56, 127–28, 132, 278

wit (a social virtue), 72, 108–9, 114–19, 124, 289

wonder, 205, 228, 294n11; and the divine, 2, 3, 295; and greatness of soul, 103; and munificence, 97–98, 97n7; origin of philosophy, 224, 224n16; and perplexity, 206, 322

Works and Days (Hesiod): on "talk" as divine, 227, 282n2; on three sorts of human beings, 33–34, 34n20, 59, 82, 89, 306; on trust, 254

Yack, Bernard, 257n25

young, the: benefitted by friendship, 263; experience of time, 32; lacking prudence, 183; lovers of the beautiful, 85; moved toward politics by Aristotle, 153; in the *Rhetoric*, 28–32, 48; shame as appropriate to, 120; transience in friendship, 239; unable to bear slight; 99n8; unfit to study politics, 28, 306

Zeus, 104, 105, 122, 133, 135, 142n18, 144, 149, 257; as model of political rule, 233–34, 301

Zuckert, Catherine H., 186n30, 317n1

MARY P. NICHOLS is professor emerita in the Department of Political Science at Baylor University. She is the author of seven books, including *Thucydides and the Pursuit of Freedom*.

www.ingramcontent.com/pod-product-compliance
Lightning Source LLC
Chambersburg PA
CBHW021341300426
44114CB00012B/1027